PERSONALITY AND ASSESSMENT

WALTER MISCHEL
Professor of Psychology
Stanford University

John Wiley and Sons, Inc.   New York   London   Sydney

10   9   8   7   6   5   4

Library of Congress Catalog Card
Number: 67—31183   GB 471 60925X
Printed in the United States of America

For Harriet,
Judith,
Rebecca,
and Linda

PREFACE

When I started this book I intended to survey six or seven equally viable alternative theoretical approaches to personality and to examine the implications of each for personality assessment, psychotherapy, and research. In the course of this writing, the field has changed substantially and the book and my views along with it. Although a half dozen or more alternative conceptualizations each appeared to be about equally reasonable a decade ago, the list of serious contenders now seems much shorter. This change has occurred mainly because of the voluminous and vigorous empirical researches that have become available in recent years. The resulting evidence makes it possible to start choosing among approaches on the basis of empirical evidence rather than personal preference.

Research findings at this time permit one in the personality area to go much beyond the traditional chronicling of different broad views of man accompanied by the usual illustrations of studies and techniques that seem compatible with each of these perspectives. Instead, it now should be possible to evaluate basic assumptions and personality concepts not only abstractly but also in light of their specific empirical yield. The value of these ideas about personality is tested nowhere more clearly than in their contributions to the prediction and change of important psychological events in the life of the individual. This book therefore is especially attentive to evidence from the areas of personality prediction and personality change. It also should be possible now to extend principles emerging from basic research on personality and social behavior to facilitate personality assessment and therapeutic change. In this effort I am relying heavily on a synthesis of concepts about social learning and cognitive processes and have tried to show its intimate relevance for every step in the measurement and modification of personality. Studies in these latter areas of assessment and change serve, in turn, as the proving grounds for personality constructs and principles; they also have been sparking important modifications in conceptualizations of the nature of personality and of complex disturbed behavior as well as normal behavior.

It has become almost routine to urge a genuine integration of the knowledge of behavior that is emerging from basic experimental research and the findings and issues that face psychologists concerned with the measurement and modification of personality. This book tries to move in that direction. For these purposes it has been necessary to draw on a wide variety and range of studies and ideas and to trespass some of the many boundaries that usually partition the field. In discussing issues of assessment, for example, assumptions about personality that guide particular strategies are examined at least as fully as the measurement techniques themselves; likewise analyses of personality concepts and assumptions are never very far away from research findings; and explications of basic principles soon lead to their applications and specific consequences for assessing and changing personality. In trying to achieve breadth while avoiding confusion, it has also been necessary, of course, to prune and to rely on selected theoretical concepts as guides. Hopefully the biases that such selectivity may introduce are offset by the syntheses toward which this book aims.

Many people have helped me substantially in the development of this book. I am especially deeply indebted to Toni Raskoff who has been a true assistant in every phase of this work during the last year. I am also grateful to all the people who read and reacted to numerous drafts. Among the many who were especially helpful in their detailed comments are Albert Bandura, Donn Byrne, Donald Campbell, Brendan Maher, George Mandler, Joan Meisel, and Julius Wishner. I am also indebted to the students who were my research collaborators in the studies on which sections of this book draw heavily. Those investigations were supported primarily by Research Grant MH 6830 from the National Institute of Mental Health, Public Health Service. In the typing of the manuscript Darlene Lapham showed great care, patience, and secretarial skills which are sincerely appreciated.

Walter Mischel

Stanford, California
January 1968

CONTENTS

Personality and Assessment

/ 1

INTRODUCTION

Personality theory, experimental personality research, and assessment have quite different histories and their mutual implications have not been explored thoroughly. Courses on personality theory usually review the concepts advocated by different authors and offer omnibus surveys of psychological conceptions of man. Personality assessment, on the other hand, typically is relegated into the "how to do it" practical domain, and is inserted as an applied, independent course on assorted measurement techniques. Especially distressing, most approaches to personality still remain largely separated from developments in behavior theory and experimental research, in spite of many protests and some major efforts to the contrary (Bandura & Walters, 1963; Rotter, 1954).

Progress in the area of personality psychology and assessment has been hindered by the failure to apply relevant principles about the conditions that produce, maintain, and modify social behavior. The principles that emerge from basic research too often have not been seen as directly relevant to the understanding of the determinants of test responses in the clinic or the assessment project. It is as if we live in two independent worlds: the abstractions and artificial situations of the laboratory and the realities of life. In part this dualism between research and practice has resulted from the failure of basic psychological research to deal with social problems relevant to persons. Until fairly recently most experimental research offered as an aid in the understanding of human social behavior was not only nonsocial, in the sense of not dealing with interpersonal conditions, but also nonhuman, the subjects usually being rats, pigeons, or monkeys. Research with persons was confined largely to correlational studies, most frequently interrelating the checking responses of college students on different

1

paper-and-pencil inventories. More recently, however, exciting prog-ress has occurred in experimental social research with people. The resulting principles and techniques are being applied to the measure-ment and modification of the complex problems of persons—often severely disturbed persons.

Traditional separations between theory, basic research, and assess-ment practices come from historical accidents and professional biases rather than from logical necessity or convenience, and they take their toll in the training of personality and clinical psychologists. The re-sulting schisms within the field are reflected in the reactions of students who begin their practicum training and soon wonder, quite rightly, what their theoretical seminars in basic psychology have to do with their new daily activities. These frequent dissonances are being recog-nized increasingly. Anne Anastasi, for example, has called attention to the fact that the measurement of behavior is ". . . dissociated from the mainstream of contemporary psychology" (1967, p. 297) , and that ". . . testing today is not adequately assimilating developments from the science of behavior" (p. 300) . As she points out, developments in personality assessment have been largely oblivious to advances in our knowledge of the conditions that change and influence human behavior. The present state of affairs has led another critic (Kelly, 1965) to dub the contemporary graduate education of personality and clinical psychologists as "training for professional obsolescence."

This book examines developments in theory, research, and per-sonality assessment relevant to complex human behavior regardless of the usual textbook boundaries. We shall review and search these areas for their interrelationships, and examine how they do, or could, or should have critical effects on each other and on the activities of both the clinician and the researcher.

PERSONALITY CONSTRUCTS

Personality psychology seeks reliable statements either about the personality or about the directly observed behavior of one or more persons. Such statements always have to be based on observable events and behaviors, although unobservable processes underlying these mani-festations may be inferred when their link to behavior is justifiable. We say "reliable" statements to stress that they must be arrived at by reproducible steps that lead to the same descriptions when followed by different observers. This differentiates them from personal assertions that cannot be reproduced independently by others. A scientific statement has to be susceptible at some point to acceptance, modification, or rejection on the basis of evidence obtainable by other observers using replicable steps. That is what is meant by "objective" (Bass & Berg, 1959). But the human actions that the psychologist observes, and that constitute his data, can be construed in any number of alternative ways, depending on the constructs and theory through which he views them.

The psychologist's theory influences his interpretation of the problems that require assessment or study and his selection of specific procedures and criteria. His theory about the determinants of behavior and the conditions that change behavior dictates his choice of data, of specific procedures, and of criteria for evaluating them. The influence of theory becomes apparent even in efforts to assess seemingly simple bits of behavior.

To take a clinical illustration, consider the assessment of a young child brought to a clinic by his mother with the complaint that he is excessively demanding, unruly, stubborn, spoiled, and immature. Assume, also, that this boy is of average intelligence and has no gross organic problems. Even the first tentative hypotheses about the child depend on the interpreter's theoretical approach. A Freudian might be alert to the child's behavior as a sign of weak ego strength and ambivalence toward the mother related to basic problems in handling impulses, or perhaps as a reflection of the mother's own unconscious neurotic conflicts. An Adlerian would attend to rivalry between the boy and his siblings, or to his inferiority complex and compensatory strivings. The Rogerian might think about self-realization, growth crises, and problems with the ego ideal, and an Erikson disciple might entertain hypotheses about identity crises and autonomy. Enthusiasts of personal construct theory (Kelly, 1955) probably would start with an inquiry into the personal constructs of the mother to elaborate the subjective meanings and the referents she has for terms like "demanding," "unruly," and "spoiled." A behaviorist would abstain from all speculations about the psychodynamic meanings of the problem behaviors. Instead, he would define the observable behavioral referents for the described problems and seek to assess the stimulus conditions that seem to affect and maintain them in the child's current life.

For each "school" of personality there is a different orientation and focus. The hypotheses and expectations of the investigator are not merely private views: they affect not only what he looks for but also what he finds, both in research (e. g., Rosenthal, 1963) and in psychotherapy (e.g., Heine, 1953).

At present an enormous number of personality constructs exists.

3

Examples from the available collection of personality constructs include: complexes (inferiority, Oedipal, Icarus) ; needs and motivations (security, ascendance, abasement, achievement, dependency, recognition, competence) ; anxieties (sexual, social, basic, free-floating, neurotic) ; levels (psychosexual, cognitive, aspirational) ; habit hierarchies; factors (primary, surface, source, cardinal); ego strength; ego ideal; and so on. And of course "personality" itself is a construct, endowed with diverse meanings. The question that must be asked is what do particular personality constructs add to the analysis, prediction, and modification of behavior—what is their utility? This question will be posed often in later chapters.

"Personality" and "behavior" often are used interchangeably by psychologists, producing great confusion. Personality is an abstraction or hypothetical construction from or about behavior, whereas behavior itself consists of observable events. Statements that deal with *personality* describe the *inferred, hypothesized,* mediating internal states, structure, and organization of individuals. Traditionally, personality psychology has dealt with these inferences about the individual's personality, focusing on behavioral observations as signs of underlying attributes or processes within the person that serve as clues to his personality. This strategy has been the most dominant one in the field.

Until recently, the two main approaches to personality have been found in *trait* theories and in *psychodynamic* or *state* theories. Not surprisingly, therefore, most theoretical issues traditionally have hinged on controversies about the utility of specific techniques for inferring personality or, even more often, about the substantive content, structure, and organization of the psyche (e.g., Sanford, 1963).

Traditional personality theories assume an internal structural-dynamic hierarchy in which various hypothesized aspects of the person stand in superordinate-subordinate relations to each other (e. g., Sanford, 1963). This structural pyramid view is seen in such concepts as personality "levels," and in dichotomies like "deep versus superficial," "basic versus surface," or "underlying core versus symptomatic." The implication in all hierarchical personality models is that some internal entities underlie others, and that their dynamic interrelations determine or produce the behavior that the person displays. For example, impulses, motives, needs, or drives are evaluated and reacted upon by other features of the personality, as when the ego disguises or otherwise censors and modifies id impulses. In other formulations, underlying attitudinal or response predispositions are seen as the guides and monitors of behavior, and are given an instrumental role in determining the overt behavior that ensues.

4

Both trait and state theorists would interpret the excessively demanding behaviors of the previously cited boy as signs of underlying traits or psychodynamic processes that exist within the child and that predispose him to behave as he does. Assessment would concentrate on a description of these hypothesized attributes, including attempts to reconstruct their history. Any predictions about the boy's future behavior are likely to involve extrapolations from his presumed traits and dynamics as inferred from test responses or other behaviors. For example, his future achievement behavior might be predicted by clinical judgments about how a child with his personality is likely to react to the stresses, demands, and challenges of the school situation. In the same vein, one might try to predict the probability of future delinquency from inferences about his hypothesized "ego strength."

TRAITS

"Trait" has become a confusing term because it is used in several different ways. At the simplest level a trait refers to the differences between the directly observable behavior or characteristics of two or more individuals on a defined dimension. For example, "a trait is any distinguishable, relatively enduring way in which one individual varies from others" (Guilford, 1959, p. 6). In this sense a trait is merely a summary label for some observed stable individual differences in behavior.

A trait also can be a personality construct created for its explanatory convenience and power. In that meaning a trait is a construct or abstraction to account for enduring behavioral consistencies and differences; as such, it does not necessarily have any concrete real existence as a "thing," "state," or "process" within persons.

Many personality theorists, however, have conceptualized traits as underlying characteristics, qualities, or processes that do *exist in* persons (Allport, 1937, 1966). Thus, for some researchers traits are constructs, created by psychologists; for others they are real states in persons, the construct being the psychologist's inference about the underlying attribute in the person.

Generally traits have been viewed both as psychological realities that exist in some tangible form in the person and also as the *causes* of behavior (Allport, 1966; Cattell, 1950). As Gordon Allport puts it: "A trait has more than nominal existence . . . and is dynamic, or at least determinative, in behavior" (1966, p. 1). A chief aim of the trait approach is to infer the underlying personality structure of individuals

5

and to compare persons and groups on trait dimensions. Underlying traits are inferred from behavior and, in turn, are invoked to account for the observed behavioral consistencies.

Psychologists who accept the basic assumptions of trait theory believe that the personality is made up of certain definite attributes or traits. They also assume that particular traits, or "mental structures," are common to many people, vary in amount, and can be inferred by measuring their behavioral indicators (e.g., Cattell, 1957; Guilford, 1959). Most important, it is widely assumed that traits are relatively stable and enduring predispositions that exert fairly generalized effects on behavior (Sanford, 1963; Allport, 1966). These predispositions either may be acquired through learning or may be constitutionally or genetically inherent.

Much of the research on traits, especially the work of psychometricians, has been guided by a cumulative quantitative measurement model. In such a cumulative model trait indicators are related *additively* to the inferred underlying disposition (Loevinger, 1957). For example, the more submissive behavior the person displays, as by endorsing more submissive content on an inventory, the stronger the underlying trait of submissiveness. In contrast, psychodynamic theory posits highly *indirect*, nonadditive relations between behavior and hypothesized underlying states. Thus submissive behavior may be interpreted as a sign of underlying aggression, or of passivity-hostility conflicts, or of resistance disguising some other more threatening characterological problems. This inference process from indirect signs is at the core of psychodynamic theory, and its main assumptions are summarized in the following section.

PSYCHODYNAMIC ASSUMPTIONS

Psychodynamic theory, like trait theory, assumes that the underlying personality is more or less stable regardless of the situation. According to the psychodynamic view, the individual develops during childhood a basic personality core that does not change much in its essentials. In research and assessment the environmental "situation" therefore is a variable to be "controlled out" so that it does not interfere with the expression of core materials—that is, with the manifestations of the person's basic motives and defenses.

Psychodynamic theory contends that all responses from a person ultimately reveal his enduring basic problems and personality organization if the underlying meaning of the behaviors is interpreted properly. This belief is most clearly reflected in the psychodynamic interpretation of projective data (MacFarlane & Tuddenham, 1951). It is believed that in an unstructured, ambiguous, or projective situation the person's responses reveal his basic personality organization. Further, *all* aspects of his behavior are interpreted as potentially revealing this basic underlying personality configuration (MacFarlane & Tuddenham, 1951). The same assumptions guide the psychoanalytic interpretation of dream materials, free associations, memory losses. Every bit of psychological behavior, if interpreted in sufficient depth and detail, is thought to reveal the individual's underlying personality organization.

In clinical situations, the psychodynamic assessor may pay as much attention to seemingly irrelevant, trivial, and casual behavior as to evidence that the client himself says is important. For example, repeated references to current interests, strong beliefs, daily activities, or work may be construed by the clinician as "resistances" to be overcome, whereas jokes, errors, slips of the tongue, mannerisms may be deemed revealing clues worthy of further intensive exploration, since they may reflect unconscious material that partially "bypassed" the defenses. This practice is based on the psychoanalytic conviction that the individual is largely unaware of his own most important motives. It is further believed that the major determinants of human behavior are not only unconscious but also irrational, and that individuals are driven by persistent, illogical demands from within. These urgings or instinctual impulses, chiefly sexual and aggressive in origin, are believed to press for immediate discharge and satisfaction (Freud, 1953).

According to the psychodynamic view, elaborate defenses are developed to avoid anxiety and to come to terms with the vicissitudes of instinctual impulses as they conflict with the barriers of the external world and internalized inhibitions (White, 1964). These complex disguises help man to hide from himself as well as from others but may become inadequate, as in pathological conditions. Even under the usual circumstances of everyday life the defenses occasionally are penetrated and the person betrays himself. Such betrayals, according to the theory, are manifested most readily when defenses are relaxed, as in the dream life during sleep, or when situational cues are vague, as in responses to inkblots in a projective test.

The defense process involves distortion and displacement; private meanings develop as objects and events become symbols, representing things quite different from themselves, whose meanings are revealed only indirectly by behavioral signs or symptoms. Psychodynamics are inferred from indirect behavioral signs. In accord with psychoanalytic

7

theory, motives are believed to be expressed indirectly after defensive disguising and distortion. Behavior therefore is interpreted *symbolically* for its meaning as signs of underlying dynamic motives and states. A projective test story that begins with the image of "woman out of breath because she has just run up a flight of stairs," a Rorschach response in which a man is "clinging to rocks," are examples of responses considered symbol laden and for which latent meanings are sought.

Overt behavior in itself is of little interest in psychodynamic theory except insofar as it reveals something about the individual's unconscious processes and dynamics. No matter where one seeks data, however, they can be found only in the form of observable events. Talk about inner life and private events should not obscure the fact that these are known only by such observable manifestations as verbal self-reports, interview behavior, autonomic measures, and the like. The extent to which psychodynamic inferences about the meanings of these behavioral signs is justified depends entirely on the reliability and utility of the results.

TRAITS, STATES, AND INDIVIDUAL DIFFERENCES

Psychodynamic theorists often object that trait theories, because of their concern for discrete, quantifiable traits, miss the dynamic, interactive aspects of internal functioning and the configural relations among different aspects of personality. But although the names assigned to hypothesized states by dynamic theorists (id, ego, defense, internal conflicts, etc.) differ from the trait names preferred by psychometrically oriented theorists, both approaches share several key features. Both dynamic (state) and trait theories focus on responses as signs (indirect or direct) of pervasive underlying mental structures; both assume that these underlying inferred dispositions (whether called traits, states, processes, dynamics, motives, or labeled in other ways) exert generalized and enduring causal effects on behavior; and both have been devoted to a search for signs that serve as reliable indicators of these hypothesized underlying dispositions.

No one doubts that previous experience and genetic and constitutional characteristics affect behavior and result in vast individual differences among people. As has been suggested by Bergman (in Farber, 1964), psychologists who really question the import of the organism should merely substitute a sack of potatoes for their research subjects and see what happens. Indeed probably the most striking and self-evident finding in personality psychology is the fact that different persons respond differently to the same objective stimulus and that no two persons are completely alike. The existence of enormous differences among persons is recognized by all psychologists, regardless of theoretical orientation. Critical and controversial issues, however, are the consistency of particular predispositions within any individual and the utility of searching for these generalized predispositional states in the person as the determining sources of his responses to diverse situations.

If behavior is determined mainly by broad dispositions that manifest themselves stably more or less independently of stimulus conditions, then it is understandable that assessment should search for these dispositions and pay relatively little attention to other variables. Guided by the assumption that highly generalized dispositions exist, a chief purpose of personality psychology traditionally has been to identify the individual's position on one or more dimensions (e.g., anxiety, introversion) by comparing him with norms based on other persons tested under comparable standardized conditions. If one believes that an individual's position on these continua would be relatively stable across testing situations and over lengthy time periods, then the main assessment emphasis becomes the development of reliable instruments administered under standard conditions to tap accurately the presumably stable, enduring, underlying traits and states possessed by the person. That has been exactly the main concern of traditional trait theories (e.g., Guilford, 1959). In accord with this basic assumption of consistency, little attention is paid to the environmental conditions in which the dispositions presumably exert their effects. Recognizing this point in regard to the trait of anxiety, for example, Levitt (1967, p. 71) put it this way: "Because trait anxiety is theoretically a constant condition of the individual, it should not fluctuate in response to circumstances."

Similarly, psychodynamic theories posit that people develop a stable basic core personality that exerts itself pervasively, albeit indirectly and in disguised forms. If one accepts that belief it follows that great attention should be paid to clinical inferences and tests designed to reveal the individual's "underlying personality" and his dynamics from indirect behavioral signs.

The value of trait and state approaches depends on how well they facilitate the prediction and modification of individual behavior. An enormous amount of relevant evidence has been obtained in more than sixty years of prolific research. Support for the value of trait-state theories would require demonstrating, first, that people do behave consistently across many diverse situations. Such evidence (reviewed in Chapters 2, 3, and 4) would be essential to sustain the belief in the broad personality dispositions which the theories posit. It would also be necessary to show that inferences about an individual's traits and states permit important predictions about his behavior. Again a massive amount of data, reviewed in Chapters 4 and 5, is available; investigators have shown great effort and ingenuity in their attempts to reliably infer dispositions from diverse behavioral signs assessed by many different clinical and psychometric techniques.

It would be relatively simple to assess, predict, and modify behavior if it consisted mainly of stable, highly generalized response patterns that occurred regularly in relation to many diverse stimulus constellations. As later chapters illustrate, however, what people do in all situations and on all tests can be affected, often quite readily, by many stimulus conditions and can be modified substantially by numerous environmental manipulations. Thus personality theories must recognize not only the great differences among persons but also the variations within each individual's life as a result of changes in conditions. This point has been acknowledged in the abstract by most psychologists but its implications for personality have not been explored adequately.

BEHAVIOR CHANGE

While trait and state theories have searched for broad, consistent dispositions, a considerable amount of experimental research has focused, instead, on the determinants of changes in behavior and on the stimulus conditions that seem to control these alterations. The principles that emerge from studies of the variables that control behavior in turn become the bases for developing theory, not about global traits and states, but about the manner in which behavior develops and changes in response to environmental stimulus changes.

A focus on behavior change, rather than on stable dispositions, also leads to quite different emphases in assessment and in research. In behavioral analyses the emphasis is on what a person *does* in situations rather than on inferences about what attributes he *has* more globally. What people do, of course, includes much more than motor acts. Unlike rats and other lower organisms who have been psychology's favorite subjects, humans do exceedingly complex and varied things. Among many other activities, they organize and disorganize societies, create works of art, talk, think, and write theories about these phenomena as well as about each other and themselves.

Chapter 6 presents some of the principles emerging from experimental studies of the determinants of changes in social behavior. The results of correlational trait research are found to be closely congruent with these principles. In light of the empirical data reviewed, and of theoretical considerations, an approach to personality based on components from cognitive and social learning theories will be explored in detail. The last three chapters extend these principles to issues of personality measurement and change. From this perspective, Chapter 7 examines methods of personality change, Chapter 8 shows the implications for assessments designed to facilitate personality change, and the final chapter reconsiders the concept of personality and the bases of prediction.

/ 2
CONSISTENCY AND SPECIFICITY IN BEHAVIOR

For more than fifty years personality psychologists have tried to measure traits and states in order to discover personality structure and dynamics. There has been an enormous effort to investigate the reliability and, more recently, the validity of the results. This chapter examines some of the evidence for the assumption of generalized personality traits and states. Empirically, the generality of a trait is established by the associations found among trait indicators. The evidence consists of obtained correlations between behaviors measured across similar situations. Data that demonstrate strong generality in the behavior of the same person across many situations are critical for trait and state personality theories; the construct of personality itself rests on the belief that individual behavioral consistencies exist widely and account for much of the variance in behavior. Most definitions of personality hinge on the assumption that an individual's behavior is consistent across many stimulus conditions (e.g., Sanford, 1963).

Data on the generality-specificity of behavior usually fall under the rubric of "reliability" and are separated from "validity" evidence, This distinction between reliability and validity is not very sharp. Both reliability and validity are established by demonstrating relations between responses to various stimulus conditions. The stimulus conditions are the particular measures and settings used to sample responses. *Reliability* concerns the congruence among responses measured under maximally *similar* stimulus conditions (Campbell, 1960; Campbell & Fiske, 1959). *Validity*, in contradistinction to reliability, requires convergence between responses to maximally *different,* inde-

13

pendent stimulus conditions or measures. The distinction between reliability and validity research depends chiefly on judgments about the degree of similarity among the stimuli used to evoke responses with the particular eliciting techniques or tests employed. For example, correlations among two similar tests, or of two forms of one test, or of the same test administered to the same person on different occasions, all are taken as reliability evidence; correlations among more dissimilar tests, on the other hand, are interpreted as validity data. This chapter is concerned mainly with reliability evidence and evaluates the behavioral consistencies obtained under relatively similar stimulus conditions. We shall look at several kinds of data, first examining the consistency of intellectual variables and then turning to measures of personality. Throughout this chapter some of the empirical evidence for the cross-situational generality of behavior will be reviewed in order to assess more concretely the appropriateness of the trait assumptions which have had such a marked impact on the field.

INTELLECTUAL AND COGNITIVE VARIABLES

The main empirical evidence for assuming trait generality came initially from correlations among ability measures that supported the concept of *g*—a general intelligence factor supposedly found in many measures of mental functioning. Although the generality of mental ability has been the ideal model inspiring hope for the generality of personality dimensions, even the data on the consistency of intelligence are themselves controversial. For example, negligible correlations are not uncommon among tests of intellectual ability, and therefore the frequent assertion that ability measures are almost always positively related is not justified (Guilford, 1964). As Guilford showed, of more than 7000 correlation coefficients among ability measures, 17–24 percent can be considered to be zero.

Ability and Achievement

An individual's behavior across ability measures, in spite of the foregoing reservations, tends to be fairly consistent and reasonably stable (e.g., Anastasi, 1961; Bradway, Thompson, & Cravens, 1958). For example, total scores on carefully developed, standardized intelligence tests like the Stanford-Binet tend to have excellent retest and alternate form reliability. Correlations between alternate forms administered within an interval of one week or less often exceed .90 (Anastasi, 1961). Although the generality and stability of ability indices is usually impressive, even advocates of the generalized ability position acknowledge that "the notion of intelligence as a definite entity, an autonomous mental faculty, which simply matures as children grow up" needs to be abandoned (Vernon, 1965, p. 727). Moreover, it is increasingly recognized that specific stimulus conditions affect performances on ability tests and their intercorrelations (Vernon, 1965). These tests therefore are coming to be viewed more as performance samples than as indices of stable underlying generalized ability states (Anastasi, 1961).

Behaviors that are strongly correlated with intelligence often are also fairly consistent. For example, within limits achievement-related behaviors show some stability and generality, at least in comparison with other psychological domains. Rater's inferences of the degree to which children strive for achievement and recognition were found to be related positively and substantially to the children's scores on intelligence tests. Moreover, these positive relationships between achievement strivings and intelligence were maintained throughout childhood and in early adulthood (Kagan & Moss, 1962).

Even by nursery school age, children show some consistency in their achievement strivings. For example, children who seek approval from their mothers for achievement tend to behave similarly toward their nursery school teachers (Crandall, Preston, & Rabson, 1960). Likewise, children who frequently initiated achievement efforts at home displayed similar behaviors during nursery school free play. These findings are based on behavior ratings and the associations are modest but significant, with consistency in achievement strivings greatest across similar activities. Thus the intellectual strivings (inferred from behavior ratings) of elementary school children were substantially correlated with their striving on mechanical tasks, but neither was positively related to the degree of rated achievement striving in athletics (Moss & Kagan, 1961). This result is in accord with the finding that response changes generated by manipulated success or failure experiences generalize across tasks to the degree that the situations are similar or functionally related (e.g., Chance, 1952; Jessor, 1954; Mischel, 1958a; Mischel & Staub, 1965). Findings like those by Holland and Richards (1965) reported subsequently caution us, however, that the relations between actual achievements and ability indices may not be nearly as great as is often assumed.

Grades and standardized tests of academic potential often are reasonable predictors of later classroom grades (e.g., Kelly, 1966). Moreover, aptitude test scores for various content areas, like English and mathematics, tend to be substantially correlated with each other and with school grades. Recent research, however, indicates consistently small or negligible relations between such indices of academic ability and measures of real-life achievements outside the classroom (e.g., Gough, Hall, & Harris, 1963; Holland & Nichols, 1964; Holland & Richards, 1965; MacKinnon, 1960; Thorndike & Hagan, 1959).

In one carefully conducted large-scale study, for example, correlations were computed between measures of academic and nonacademic high school accomplishments for a sample of over 7000 students (Holland & Richards, 1965). The median correlation between the measures of academic and nonacademic accomplishments in such areas as science and the arts was .04, the highest correlation was only .23, and 26 percent of the correlations were negative. The investigators appropriately point out that their results cannot be attributed to restrictions in the range of academic potential sampled or to the idiosyncracies of their sample. Instead they interpret their data to imply the relative independence of academic and nonacademic artistic, scientific, and social achievements.

Cognitive Behavior and "Styles"

Simple cognitive measures like response speed and cognitive judgments have intrigued psychologists since the earliest laboratory work on "mental measurement" began at the turn of the century (Watson, 1959). Very specific measures of problem-solving behaviors, such as reaction time and weight judgments, were employed to study individual differences. As early as 1890 James McKeen Cattell devised a series of simple sensorimotor and judgment tests designed to discover the "constancy of mental processes" (Watson, 1959, p. 3). His measures included reaction time for sound, speed of color naming, reproduction of a ten-second time interval, auditory memory for letters, and many similar tasks.

The predominantly simple, specific sensorimotor and ability measures in the laboratories at the end of the nineteenth century were overshadowed and neglected when the development of practical intelligence testing commenced in the twentieth century. In 1895 Binet and Henri began to measure "intelligence" and suggested that individual differences would be reflected better in more complex tasks. They proposed a series that included measures intended to tap esthetic appreciation, attention, comprehension, imagination, memory, mental imagery, moral feelings, muscular force, force of will, motor ability, suggestibility, and visual discrimination. Between 1893 and 1911 Binet published studies that explored empirically how "bright" and "dull" children differ. Ultimately Binet's tests successfully differentiated subjects with respect to scholastic standing. His belief that complex mental tests have superior value for studying individual differences was reinforced further by the generally discouraging findings of those who tried to predict from simple sensorimotor tests to behavior in other unrelated situations.

Many specific ability tests have been developed since Binet's work. The predictions obtained from generalized intelligence tests like the Binet, however, may be as good as, and certainly they are simpler than, those from the newer factor-analyzed specific ability batteries (McNemar, 1964). For many practical purposes the concept of generalized intelligence still may be as useful as competing concepts about multiple aptitudes. At any rate it is important to compare the utility of tests purporting to measure either intellectual skill or personality traits with results from generalized intelligence tests. This requires assessing the degree to which the predictions from newer tests overlap with, add to, or detract from the predictions possible from traditional tests of generalized intelligence (e.g., Campbell, 1960).

In recent years there has been a resurgence of interest in simple variables like response time and in cognitive tasks of the kind employed in the earliest laboratories. Individual differences in problem-solving behavior or "cognitive styles" once again are being studied intensively, and often yield good evidence for consistency.

Several different research groups recently have converged on the study of cognitive "controls" or "styles" (e.g., Broverman, 1960a, b, 1964; Gardner & Long, 1960; Kagan, Moss, & Siegel, 1960, 1963; Witkin, 1965; Witkin et al., 1954, 1962). These investigators have described subjects on a dimension of active, analytical, articulated, differentiated, specific, critical cognitive functioning. Active, analytic, cognitive characteristics are contrasted with cognitive functioning that is passive, global, vague, diffuse, and uncritical. Different groups of investigators infer these cognitive styles from diverse measures.

For example, Gardner and Long (1960) used tests intended as measures of equivalence range, scanning, leveling-sharpening, and constricted-flexible control. "Equivalence range" scores were based on the number of groups formed by the subject in free sorting of seventy-three objects. "Scanning" was measured by constant error in judging the size of three small discs. "Leveling-sharpening" was inferred from accuracy scores for size judgments of a series of increasingly large squares; and "constricted-flexible control" was assessed from indices of reading time for the three parts of a Color-Word Test, including color names, color strips, and colors printed in incongruous color names. Note that these tests, if not their names, have some similarity to traditional ability measures, insofar as their scores depend on perceptual speed and accuracy. Some of the test labels, however, reflect the originators' psychodynamic orientation—for example, "constricted-flexible control"—more than the operations sampled in the test.

Witkin and his associates (e.g., 1962, 1965) have based their measures of "field dependence-independence" and "psychological differentiation" on perceptual measures like the Rod and Frame Test (RFT) and the Witkin Embedded-Figures Test (EFT). In the RFT, subjects in a completely darkened room are exposed to a luminous rod with a tilted frame and must adjust the rod to the true upright position. In the EFT, subjects must locate a simple figure concealed in a complex design, and the time required for this is scored. Kagan and his colleagues (e.g., Kagan, Moss, & Siegel, 1960, 1963) derive their cognitive style scores from the subject's verbal categorizing and sorting behavior, such as the ways in which he groups and labels the similarity among figures, and from response speed (Kagan, 1966).

The generality and stability of behaviors assessed by some of these cognitive measures often is among the best available in personality research. Nevertheless, even seemingly minor procedural differences often are sufficient to reduce response consistency dramatically. This fact is evident, for example, in Witkin's perceptual studies. In Witkin's original tilting-room/tilting-chair (TRTC) apparatus the subject is placed in a chair that can be tilted contained in a room that can be tilted independently. This measure includes four subtests that differ in the initial positions of room and chair and in whether the subject's task is to make the chair or the room upright. The scores are the sum of the deviations from the true upright on each trial. Intercorrelations among these subtests and the EFT for a sample of fifty-three male college students (fifty-two on the EFT) are summarized in Table 1 (from Linton, 1955). Most of the correlations are statistically significant, but the measures are far from equivalent. Even slight angle changes radically reduced the correlations.

Likewise, Elliott (1961) found correlations of .42 between the Witkin EFT and RFT, and the correlations between each of these and the Thurstone form of the Embedded-Figures Test were, respectively, .55 and .30 in a large sample of male college students. Similarly significant consistency among measures of field dependence also has been demonstrated at each age level from eight-year-olds to college students (Witkin, Goodenough, & Karp, 1967).

TABLE 1. INTERCORRELATIONS AMONG PERCEPTUAL MEASURES

	Tilting Room-Tilting Chair (TRTC) Subtests			Embedded Figures Test
	1b	2a	2b	
TRTC 1a	.20	.33	.27	.39
TRTC 1b		.02	.04	−.07
TRTC 2a			.31	.38
TRTC 2b				.35

(Adapted from Linton, 1955, p. 503.)

When direct performance indices like response speed are employed, strong correlations have been obtained across several tasks. Evidence for some consistency in response speed across tasks has been found since the earliest investigations of individual differences (e.g., Bridges, 1914; Johnson, 1939; Johnson, 1954, 1957). In one study, for example, correlations were computed between response speed on tasks involving angle, line, and weight judgments, brightness matching, and figure recognition (Johnson, 1957). The mean correlation among the speed measures was .48, indicating some generality.

One recent study investigated response time on a design recall test, on a visual figure-matching test, and on a task that required matching wooden forms on the basis of tactual cues exclusively (Kagan et al., 1964). The average correlations between response times across tasks were .48, .57, and .59 for boys; for girls the correlations were even stronger: .75, .79, and .82. The associations between amount of time spent exploring the wooden forms tactually and the other response time measure (time before answering) were lower: .18, .32, and .56 for boys; .22, .43, and .55 for girls.

Response time also shows some stability over time and some generality even across less similar tasks. For example, correlations between response speed on a tachistoscopic recognition task and on the visual figure-matching task taken six months later was .40 for both sexes. Correlations between the response time on the tachistoscopic task and on the tactual matching task administered one year later were .30 for boys and .32 for girls (Kagan, 1965).

19

The Generality of Categorizing Behavior

Of late there has been a growing interest in the description and correlates of categorizing behavior. Studies on the generality of categorizing behavior have dealt chiefly with consistency in the number of constructs or categories that an individual employs when he is asked to group or sort diverse stimuli. Researchers have come to call the number of categories selected by a subject an index of his "cognitive complexity-simplicity," complexity referring to many categories and simplicity to only a few. Interest in a dimension of cognitive complexity-simplicity, first initiated by Bieri (1955), has been especially keen. In part, this dimension has attracted attention because it seems relevant to the concepts of psychological differentiation and analyticity which play such a large role in theorizing about cognitive styles.

The number of categories an individual employs is different when he sorts different stimuli. For example, a person uses a different number of categories when sorting statements about objects, war, or self (Glixman, 1965). The overall results suggest some significant intra-individual consistency in categorizing behavior but also show that categorizing behavior is affected by the particular stimuli that must be discriminated (e.g., Crockett, 1965). There is also some indication that subjects use more categories to describe persons they know well than those whom they do not know well (Crockett, 1965).

A factor analysis of cognitive complexity measured on several sorting tasks did not yield any large or single factor (Vannoy, 1965). The results indicated that a person who is cognitively "simple" on one criterion might be cognitively "complex" on another and revealed no evidence for a unitary trait, or a trait cluster, of complexity-simplicity in sorting behavior. Essentially similar conclusions come from research on the complexity-simplicity of personal constructs (Crockett, 1965).

PERSONALITY VARIABLES

In sum, the previous sections indicate that performances on many cognitive and intellectual measures often turn out to have reasonable cross-situational generality and stability, especially on similar tasks. Nevertheless, even indices of intellectual performance and cognitive abilities and skills may be more situation specific than trait theorists initially assumed. Intellectual and achievement-related behaviors, like all other behaviors, are affected by the details of the particular evoking conditions in which they occur.

Just as cognitive and intellectual variables have been the objects of extensive reliability research, personality variables also have been examined thoroughly to determine individual consistencies with respect to particular dimensions or dispositions. The following personality dimensions are representative of those attracting most theoretical and research interest during the last decade, and some of the evidence for their consistency is examined. It will become apparent rapidly that the generality of these dispositions usually is far less than that found for cognitive and intellectual variables.

Attitudes toward Authority and Peers

The belief that an individual has generalized attitudes toward classes of persons pervades clinical, diagnostic, and research practice. This belief is reflected in the common assumption that problems of sibling rivalry repeat themselves in peer relations, and that attitudes toward parental figures are mirrored in reactions to diverse authority figures throughout life and toward the psychotherapist in particular. Psychologists of many theoretical orientations often agree that persons develop highly generalized attitudes toward authority. Freud, Piaget, and Rogers, among others, all posit that reactions toward authority originate in the family situation and manifest themselves as broadly generalized attitudes expressed in many contexts toward superiors in later social situations. As Piaget puts it:

> *Day to day observation and psycho-analytic experience show that the first personal schemas are afterward generalised and applied to many people. According as the first inter-individual experiences of the child who is just learning to speak are connected with a father who is understanding or dominating, loving or cruel, etc., the child will tend (even throughout life if these relationships have influenced his whole youth) to assimilate all other individuals to this father schema.*
> (Piaget, 1951, p. 207.)

These assumptions have been subjected to a rare and extensive test by Burwen and Campbell (1957). Burwen and Campbell studied a large sample of Air Force personnel by means of interviews, TAT, description of self and others, judgments of photos, and autobiographical inventories, as well as an attitude survey and sociometric questionnaire. Through each of these techniques, where possible, attitudes were scored toward own father, symbolic authority (e.g., in responses

21

to pictures of older persons on the TAT), immediate boss, immediate peers, and symbolic peers. The topics or attitude objects and the measures for scoring attitudes toward authority on each are summarized below:

Topic	*Measures*
Father	Interview; description of self and others; autobiographical inventory
Symbolic authority	Interview; TAT (scored globally); TAT (scored objectively); judgments of photos (of older persons); attitude survey
Boss	Interview; description of self and others; autobiographical inventory; sociometric questionnaire

Similar measures were used to score attitudes toward real and symbolic peers.

The interjudge reliability of all ratings on each instrument was adequately high, and scores were available on twenty variables. Their intercorrelations revealed, first of all, the major impact of stimulus similarity or "method variance": for three-quarters of all the variables the highest correlations occurred between measures of different attitudes based on the *same* instrument. When these method-produced correlations were disregarded, there was little evidence for generality of attitudes either toward authority or toward peers. Attitudes toward father, symbolic authority, and boss were no more highly correlated with each other than they were with attitudes toward real or symbolic peers, and all correlations tended to be low.

Table 2 shows the average of transformed correlations between attitude topics, eliminating those based on the same instrument. Of the correlations between different measures of attitude toward a *single* type of authority figure, only among attitudes toward father and among attitudes toward peers are there any indications that independent methods tap a specific attitude focus at least to some extent. Even these associations among different measures of attitudes toward the same type of authority were very modest, being .35 for father and .22 for peers. Attitude toward *different* types of authority figures showed no consistency at all. For example, attitude toward one's father correlated .03 with attitude toward one's boss. The authors appropriately concluded that:

Evidence for a generalized attitude toward authority which encompasses attitudes toward father, symbolic authority, and boss is totally negative, suggesting the need for reconsideration of the applicability of commonly held theory in this area. (Burwen & Campbell, 1957, p. 31.)

TABLE 2. MEAN CORRELATIONS AMONG ATTITUDES MEASURED BY DIFFERENT METHODS

Attitude toward		F	SA	B	P	SP
Father	F	.35	.12	.03	.06	.08
Symbolic authority	SA		.15	.08	.10	.06
Boss	B			.09	.13	.03
Peer	P				.22	.07
Symbolic peer	SP					.01

(Adapted from Burwen & Campbell, 1957, p. 26.)

Moral Behavior

Psychodynamic theory has emphasized the role of the "superego" as an internalized moral agency that has a critical role in the regulation of all forms of conduct and in the control of impulses. Theorizing regarding the superego has focused on the way in which authority figures and their values become "incorporated" during the course of socialization. It has been assumed that as a result of this process the child adopts parental standards and controls as his own. There is no doubt that in the course of development most children acquire the capacity to regulate, judge, and monitor their own behavior even in the absence of external constraints and authorities. An important theoretical issue, however, is the consistency of these self-regulated patterns of conduct and self-control.

In the extraordinarily extensive and sophisticated Character Education Inquiry, more than thirty years ago, thousands of children were exposed to various situations in which they could cheat, lie, and steal in diverse settings, including the home, party games, and athletic contexts (Hartshorne & May, 1928; Hartshorne, May, & Shuttleworth, 1930).

Although moral conduct was relatively inconsistent, the children

23

showed substantial consistency in their self-reported opinions and thoughts about moral issues elicited on paper-and-pencil tests administered in the classroom. High correlations also were found between various forms of these paper-and-pencil tests. However, if children took alternate equivalent forms of the same tests in diverse social settings—such as at home, in Sunday school, at club meetings, as well as in the classroom—the correlations of their scores among situations were reduced to about .40. The investigators concluded that children vary their opinions to "suit the situation" (Hartshorne, May, & Shuttleworth, 1930, p. 108) and do not have a generalized code of morals.

The specificity of responses, and their dependence on the exact particulars of the evoking situation, was keenly noted by Hartshorne and May (1928). For example:

> . . . *even such slight changes in the situation as between crossing out A's and putting dots in squares are sufficient to alter the amount of deception both in individuals and in groups.* (p. 382.)

To illustrate further from their data, copying from an answer key on one test correlated .696 with copying from a key on another test, and cheating by adding on scores from a speed test correlated .440 with adding on scores on another speed test. However, copying from a key on one test correlated only .292 with adding on scores. Moreover, the average intercorrelations among four classroom tests was only .256 (Hartshorne & May, 1928, p. 383). The more the situation changed the lower the correlations became. The average correlation between four classroom tests and two out-of-classroom tests (contests and stealing) was .167. The lying test given in the classroom averaged .234 with the other classroom tests but only .064 with the two out-of-classroom deception tests (p. 384).

Some of the Hartshorne and May data later were reanalyzed by Burton (1963) who factor analyzed the results from their most reliable tests of resistance to temptation. Hartshorne and May themselves refrained from this procedure because, as they (and Burton) noted, these different data were not always obtained from the same subjects. The original correlations for these particular tests were based on samples whose size was not reported. Burton assumed, probably quite safely, that these correlations were from large samples and therefore were good approximations to the "true population values" (p. 485). On the basis of this assumption he submitted the intercorrelations to factor-analytic procedures.

The resulting reanalysis is often cited as evidence for the consistency of moral behavior. In fact, Burton's reanalysis leads to a conclusion "not greatly different from that made by Hartshorne and May" (Burton, 1963, p. 492). Contrary to some misconceptions, Burton's reanalysis revealed no errors in the original work but only reconstrued the same correlations in a way that emphasized and highlighted the moderate consistencies that were found in the first place. The factor analysis of the many low but often positive associations in resistance to temptation across situations yielded, as expected, a weak common factor. Burton's reanalysis appropriately stressed that an individual's reactions across temptation situations were not totally random. This point was already implied by the fact that the original correlations were often statistically significant, albeit generally small. Completely in accord with Hartshorne and May's original interpretations, Burton's reanalysis noted many beyond-chance consistencies, of generally small size, that decreased as the similarities between the stituations decreased:

> *Thus as we progressively change the situation we progressively lower the correlations between the tests.* (Hartshorne & May, 1928, p. 384.)

The observations that Hartshorne and May reported for the relative specificity of moral behavior accurately foreshadowed the findings that emerged from later research on other behavioral consistencies. Response specificity of the kind emphasized by Hartshorne and May is also reflected, for example, in the finding that questionnaires dealing with attitudes and hypothetical matters may correlate with other questionnaires but are less likely to relate to non-self-report behavior (Mischel, 1962). In one study, children were asked questions about whether or not they would postpone immediate smaller rewards for the sake of larger but delayed outcomes in hypothetical situations. Their answers in these hypothetical delay of reward situations were found to relate to other questionnaires dealing with trust and a variety of verbally expressed attitudes. What they said, however, was unrelated to their actual delay of reward choices in real situations (Mischel, 1962). Likewise, measures eliciting direct nonverbal behavior may relate to other behavioral indices in the same domain but not to questionnaires. Thus real behavioral choices between smaller but immediately available gratifications, as opposed to larger but delayed rewards, correlated significantly with such behavioral indices as resistance to temptation, but not with self-reports on questionnaires (Mischel, 1962).

Moral guilt also has been studied utilizing projective test responses. For example, in a study with teenage boys (Allinsmith, 1960) moral feelings were inferred from the subjects' projective story completions in response to descriptions of various kinds of immoral actions. The findings led Allinsmith to the view that a person with a truly generalized conscience is a statistical rarity. Johnson (1962) also found that moral judgments across situations tend to be highly specific and even discrepant.

Recent research on moral behavior has concentrated on three areas: moral judgment and verbal standards of right and wrong (e.g., Kohlberg, 1963); resistance to temptation in the absence of external constraint (e.g., Aronfreed & Reber, 1965; Grinder, 1962; MacKinnon, 1938; Mischel & Gilligan, 1964); and post-transgression indices of remorse and guilt (e.g., Allinsmith, 1960; Aronfreed, 1964; Sears, Maccoby, & Levin, 1957; Whiting, 1959). These three areas of moral behavior turn out to be either completely independent or at best only minimally interrelated (Becker, 1964; Hoffman, 1963; Kohlberg, 1963). Within each area specificity also tends to be the rule. For example, an extensive survey of all types of reactions to transgression yielded no predictable relationships among specific types of reaction (Aronfreed, 1961). Similarly, Sears and his coworkers (1965, Chap. 6) did not find consistent associations among various reactions to transgression. Thus the data on moral behavior provide no support for the widespread psychodynamic belief in a unitary intrapsychic moral agency like the superego, or for a unitary trait entity of conscience or honesty. Rather than acquiring a homogeneous conscience that determines uniformly all aspects of their self-control, people seem to develop subtler discriminations that depend on many considerations, as discussed in later chapters.

Sexual Identification, Dependency, and Aggression

It is widely assumed in most dynamic and trait theories that people develop firm masculine or feminine identifications early in life. These stable identifications, in turn, are believed to exert pervasive effects on what the person does in many diverse situations (e.g., Kohlberg, 1966). There is, of course, no doubt that boys and girls rapidly learn about sex differences and soon recognize their own gender permanently. A much less obvious issue is the extent to which children develop highly consistent patterns of masculine or feminine "sex-typed" behavior. This question has received considerable research attention. The chief strategy has involved studying the associations among different indicators of masculine and feminine sex-typed behavior.

Dependency and aggression often serve conceptually as behavioral referents for sex typing, with boys expected to be more aggressive and girls more dependent. In dependency research, although Beller's (1955) correlations ranged from .48 to .83 for teacher ratings of five dependency components in nursery school children, it is likely that a "halo" effect spuriously inflated the teachers' ratings. Mann (1959) obtained ratings of fifty-five two-minute observations of forty-one nursery school children in free play on six kinds of dependency behavior. He found only one of fifteen intercorrelations among components of dependency significant. Likewise, observations of nursery school children revealed that the frequencies of "affection seeking" and "approval seeking" were unrelated (Heathers, 1953).

Sears (1963) extensively studied the intercorrelations between five categories of dependency behavior in preschool girls and boys. The five categories were: *negative attention seeking,* e.g., attention getting by disruption or aggressive activity; *positive attention seeking,* as in seeking praise; nonaggressive *touching or holding; being near,* e.g., following a child or teacher; and *seeking reassurance.* The frequency of these behaviors was carefully and reliably scored by observing the children at nursery school with an extensive time-sampling procedure. Each child was observed in free play for a total of seven to ten hours. The intercorrelations among the five dependency categories for twenty-one boys and nineteen girls are shown in Table 3. Note that only one of the twenty correlations reached statistical significance since for twenty degrees of freedom correlations of .423 and .537 would have been needed to reach significance at the .05 and .01 levels respectively.

TABLE 3.   INTERCORRELATIONS AMONG DEPENDENCY MEASURES[a]

Measures		I	II	III	IV	V
Negative attention	I		.06	.10	.15	.37
Reassurance	II	−.24		.25	.19	.26
Positive attention	III	.23	−.11		.11	−.03
Touching and holding	IV	.04	.14	−.16		.71
Being near	V	−.03	.12	−.14	.13	

(Adapted from Sears, 1963, p. 35.)
[a] Girls above diagonal, boys below.

Factor analyses also reveal multiple factors for what appears to be similar behavior. Gewirtz (1956) did a factor analysis of nine observational measures of attention seeking and showed that even this one dependency component may be at least two-dimensional. One factor seemed to involve direct, active, verbal attempts to maintain the attention of the adult; the other included nonverbal, passive actions. The interrelationships between measures of dependence and independence are also unclear (Hartup, 1963).

Some support for sex differences in the generality of particular patterns of sex-typed behaviors comes in the form of more (and stronger) intercorrelations for girls than boys on five observation measures of dependency (Sears, 1963), whereas the reverse holds for aggression, with more intercorrelations among aggression variables for boys than for girls (Lansky et al., 1961; Sears, 1961). However, individuals discriminate sharply between situations. The specificity of aggressive behavior, for example, is documented in a study of highly aggressive boys by Bandura (1960). Parents who punished aggression in the home, but who simultaneously modeled aggressive behavior and encouraged it in their sons' peer relationships, produced boys who were nonaggressive at home but markedly aggressive at school.

Rigidity and Tolerance for Ambiguity

If individuals did develop strongly consistent character structures that channelized them in stable ways, it would be important to identify these syndromes. One of the most thoroughly studied personality patterns is the "authoritarian personality." Intolerance for ambiguity attracted considerable interest as a characteristic of the authoritarian personality (Adorno et al., 1950), and a voluminous literature was devoted to elaborating its correlates.

Several behavioral signs have been used as the referents for intolerance for ambiguity. These signs include resistance to reversal of apparent fluctuating stimuli, early selection and adherence to one solution in perceptually ambiguous situations, seeking for certainty, rigid dichotomizing into fixed categories, premature closure, and the like. In one study, an extensive battery of tests to measure intolerance of ambiguity was designed and administered (Kenny & Ginsberg, 1958). Only seven of the sixty-six correlations among intolerance of ambiguity measures reached significance and the relationship for two of these was opposite to the predicted direction. Moreover, the measures in the main failed to correlate with the usual questionnaire indices of authoritarianism-submissiveness as elicited by a form of the California *F* scale.

Closely related to authoritarianism, "rigidity" is another personality dimension that has received much attention as a generalized trait (Chown, 1959; Cronbach, 1956). In one study (Applezweig, 1954), among forty-five correlations between behaviors on six measures of rigidity (including arithmetic "einstellung" problems, Rorschach, and *F* scale), twenty-two were negative, twenty-one were positive, and two were zero; only three of the forty-five correlations were significant and two of these were negative. Likewise, Pervin's (1960) data on five non-inventory performance measures of rigidity, including the water-jars problems, provide generally low associations and suggest that "individuals may be rigid in one area of personality functioning and not in another" and that "rigidity is not a general personality characteristic" (p. 394). The conclusion that rigidity is not a unitary trait is also supported by the modest intercorrelations between measures obtained by Wrightsman and Baumeister (1961) and by the specificity found earlier by Maher (1957).

For a long time it was also hoped that a tendency to yield to social norms and pressures and to comply with others might prove to be a broad attribute that characterizes an individual in many settings. Research on conforming behavior has revealed some consistency, mainly between responses in similar or strongly related eliciting conditions (e.g., Wiener, Carpenter, & Carpenter, 1956, 1957; Blake, Helson, & Mouton, 1957). Again there are numerous instances of behavioral inconsistency across different influence situations (e.g., Goldberg, 1954; Linton, 1955). When evidence for cross-situational generality is found, it is often based on post hoc comparisons between extreme subgroups after the nonlinear relationship between measures has been revealed (e.g., Vaughan, 1964). The hazards of depending on such extreme group analyses to test hypotheses have been discussed often (e.g., Feldt, 1961).

Thus investigators frequently measure and describe a purportedly general dimension of behavior only to discover later that it has dubious consistency. As a result the popular dimensions of personality research often wax and wane almost like fashions. Research on the generality of the behavioral indices of personality dimensions has generated its own truisms. Over and over again the conclusions of these investigations, regardless of the specific content area, are virtually identical and predictable. The following paragraph, from Applezweig's (1954) own summary, is essentially interchangeable with those from a plethora of later researches on the generality of many different traits:

> *The following conclusions appear to be justified:*
> *(a) There is no general factor of rigidity among a number of*

so-called measures of rigidity; the interrelationships of these measures appear to vary with the nature of the tests employed and the conditions of test administration as well as behavioral determinants within S's.

(b) Scores obtained by an individual on any so-called measure of rigidity appear to be a function not only of the individual, but also of the nature of the test and the conditions of test administration. (Applezweig, 1954, p. 228.)

Cognitive Avoidance

A key concept in most personality theories is the idea that some individuals tend to avoid anxiety-arousing and threatening thoughts and situations. There is little disagreement about the existence of this phenomenon; less clear, however, is the consistency with which particular individuals avoid threatening stimuli. How useful categorizing individuals on a dimension of degree of avoidance behavior would be depends, in part, on how consistently they tend to avoid anxiety-provoking cues.

A series of experiments by Eriksen, Lazarus, and their associates provided some evidence for consistency in cognitive avoidance of symbolic anxiety-provoking cues (e.g., Eriksen, 1952; Eriksen & Lazarus, 1952; Eriksen & Kuethe, 1956; Lazarus & Longo, 1953). Consistency evidence was found most strongly when extreme groups were preselected. Reaction time, and other indices of avoidance in the auditory recognition of poorly audible sentences with sexual and aggressive content, correlated significantly with similar avoidance indicators in response to sexual and aggressive sentence stems in a sentence completion test (Lazarus, Eriksen, & Fonda, 1951). It was found that subjects who more readily recalled stimuli associated with a painful shock tended to recall their failures, while those who forgot one were more likely to forget the other (Lazarus & Longo, 1953). People who could verbalize a pattern of electric shock experienced during a learning task were also more able to deliberately avoid giving the punished response (Eriksen & Kuethe, 1956).

On the other hand, Kurland (1954) reported a lack of generality in avoidance mechanisms. Patients were judged as using either predominantly repressive or obsessive-compulsive avoidance mechanisms for handling anxiety. These judgments were made by psychiatrists who were seeing them in intensive psychotherapy three times weekly. Rated avoidance mechanisms were unrelated to auditory recognition thresholds for emotional words.

In spite of such exceptions, however, a good deal of research (reviewed in Byrne, 1964; Eriksen, 1963, 1966) indicates some significant consistencies in approach versus avoidance responses to threatening stimuli of various kinds. Generally, however, these associations were not impressively high. Byrne summarizes the results as follows:

> . . . while significant correlations were generally reported between the various approach-avoidance indices, the magnitude of the relationships is hardly sufficient to conceptualize them as interchangeable measures of a single construct. (Byrne, 1964, p. 173.)

Perceptual recognition thresholds for threatening words have been a critical index of avoidance behavior in studies of the generality of perceptual defense. An investigation by Byrne and Holcomb (1962) provides one of the few studies focusing on the consistency or reliability of recognition thresholds for threatening versus neutral words. Twenty pairs of hostile (threatening) and neutral words were matched for length, frequency of occurrence in the language, and initial letter. Words were assigned either into the neutral (not emotionally toned) or hostile category on the basis of unanimous agreement by three independent judges.

The words were then placed on slides, arranged in random order, and projected at various speeds (from 1/100 second to one second). After each trial subjects recorded their best guess for the word content. Recognition thresholds were computed, depending on the trial in which correct recognition first occurred. A subject's mean thresholds for the twenty neutral words minus his mean threshold on the hostile words yielded the usual defense score. A positive score was taken as an index of a "sensitizing" reaction and a negative score as a sign of a "repressing" reaction. Interscorer agreement or consistency for the defense scores was excellent (.91).

The authors next took the rare step of investigating the internal consistency of the differential recognition threshold scores across the various threatening stimuli. In perceptual defense research it has been assumed widely that thresholds for threatening words provide an index of defense against anxiety-provoking stimuli and not simply individual differences in recognition of any stimuli regardless of threat. It is therefore important to demonstrate that an individual's thresholds for threatening stimuli differ from his thresholds for neutral words. To determine the internal consistency of these differential thresholds the hostile words were divided into odd and even halves or groups (in terms of sequence of presentation). An internal consistency coefficient was computed by correlating the differential thresholds for the odd pairs with those for the even pairs. The resulting coefficient of internal consistency was .00. Thus, although judges agreed about the nature of the threatening and nonthreatening stimuli and about the scoring of responses, the subjects' scores were entirely unreliable. Individuals showed no consistency in "perceptual defense" (differential response thresholds) across supposedly similar hostile stimuli.

Conditionability

Classical learning formulations place great emphasis on conditioning as a basic process in learning. Consequently psychologists with an interest in both learning and individual differences have been especially interested in studying conditionability as a personality dimension. In spite of a great deal of research, however, there is no evidence for the existence of a general factor or trait of "conditionability" in either classical or operant conditioning paradigms.

Correlations among different measures and types of conditioning tend to be low or zero (e.g., Bunt & Barendregt, 1961; Campbell, 1938; Davidson, Payne, & Sloane, 1964; Eysenck, 1965; Franks, 1956; Lovibond, 1964; Moore & Marcuse, 1945; Patterson & Hinsey, 1964). Moore and Marcuse (1945) noted many years ago that "the concept of good or poor conditioners must always be with reference to a specific response." Reviewing the literature two decades later, Eysenck (1965) points out that correlations between conditionability measures depend on specific peripheral factors (sweat glands in the hand, pain sensitivity of the cornea). He also notes that even if these sources were eliminated correlations would still be affected by situational circumstances such as the sequence and massing of stimuli, the scheduling of reinforcement, the strength of CS and UCS, temporal intervals, and so on.

The evidence that learning variables like conditionability are unitary trait-like entities is no more convincing than the data for the consistency of personality traits couched in any other theoretical language. Whenever individual differences are elicited, however, the failure to demonstrate impressive reliability does not preclude the existence of extensive correlations with other response measures (e.g., Franks, 1961) as discussed in Chapter 4.

Moderator Variables

Wallach (1962), and Kogan and Wallach (1964), have called attention to the fact that "moderator variables" may influence the correlations found in research on behavioral consistency. By moderator variables Wallach and Kogan mean interactions among several variables that influence the correlations obtained between any one of the variables and other data. For example, correlations between two response patterns may be found for males, but not for females, or may even be positive for one sex but negative for the other. Thus, if the correlations between two response patterns are examined for both sexes combined, the different relations that might be obtained if each sex were taken into account separately could become obscured. Similarly, relations between two measures might be positive for children with high IQ but negative for those with low IQ. In other words, there are complex interactions so that the relations between any two variables depend on several other variables.

By analyzing their data to illuminate higher-order interactions of this kind, these investigators have been able to demonstrate significant associations among various measures of risk taking, and between risk taking and other variables. The resulting associations of course apply only to some subjects under a few conditions. This strategy of searching for interactions holds some promise. Since the interactions are obtained post hoc rather than predicted, however, considerable interpretative caution must be observed. Otherwise the analysis of the same data for many interactions provides many additional chances to obtain seemingly statistically significant results that actually monopolize on chance. That is, more "significant" associations occur by chance when more correlations are computed.

Temporal Stability

So far our discussion of consistency has focused on relationships among a person's behaviors across situations sampled more or less at the same time. Equally important, however, are data that examine how stable the individual's behavior remains in any one particular domain when he is reassessed at later times.

Results from the Fels Longitudinal Study give some typical examples of the stability of a person's behavior patterns over time (Kagan & Moss, 1962). The overall findings suggest some significant consistency between childhood and early adulthood ratings of achievement behavior, sex-typed activity, and spontaneity for both sexes. For certain other variables, like dependency, some consistency was found for one sex but not the other. Thus the rated dependency of girls at age six years to ten years correlated .30 with their adult dependence on family; the comparable correlation for boys was near zero. In the same longitudinal study of middle-class subjects the most highly significant positive associations were found between ratings of achievement and recognition strivings obtained at various periods of childhood and in early adulthood (Kagan & Moss, 1962; Moss & Kagan, 1961). Children who were rated as showing strong desires for recognition also tended to be rated as more concerned with excellence and with the attainment of high self-imposed standards when they were interviewed as young adults. Some of the many correlations between achievement strivings in childhood and comparable adult preoccupation with attaining excellence were exceptionally high, in several instances reaching the .60 to .70 range.

Apart from ratings the motive or need to achieve ("*n* Ach") has also been studied most extensively by scoring the subject's achievement imagery in the stories he tells to selected TAT cards. For example, if the person creates stories in which the hero is studying hard for a profession and aspires and strives to improve himself and to advance in his career, the story receives high *n* Ach scores. This technique, developed thoroughly by McClelland and his associates (1953), has become the main index of the motive to achieve and to compete against standards of excellence. As a result considerable attention has been devoted to studying the stability of this need by comparing *n* Ach scores obtained from the same individuals at different times. Moss and Kagan (1961) reported a stability coefficient of .31 for their sample over a ten-year period from adolescence to adulthood. They also reported a three-year stability coefficient of .32 for TAT achievement themes obtained at ages eight and eleven (Kagan & Moss, 1959). However, the correlation between *n* Ach at age eight and at age fourteen was only .22; the correlation between *n* Ach at age eleven and at fourteen years was a nonsignificant .16.

The stability of achievement motivation was also studied closely for shorter time intervals with other samples of people. Birney (1959) reported a coefficient of only .29 for *n* Ach on equivalent picture forms administered to college students within six months. He concluded that ". . . the *n* Ach measure is highly situational in character . . ." (p. 267). Similarly, a significant but modest coefficient of .26 was reported for a nine-week test-retest study with college students (Krumboltz & Farquhar, 1957). Higher correlations ranging from .36 to .64 have been found for shorter time intervals of three weeks to five weeks (Haber & Alpert, 1958; Morgan, 1953). Reviewing a great deal of information from many studies, Skolnick (1966a, b) reported extensive correlations between diverse adolescent and adult measures. Many correlations reached significance, especially for achievement and power imagery indices, although the associations tended to be extremely complicated and most often of modest magnitude.

Just as with consistency across situations, stability over time tends to be greatest for behaviors associated with intelligence and cognitive processes (e.g., Bloom, 1964; Gardner & Long, 1960; Kagan & Moss, 1962; Moss & Kagan, 1961). Most notably, extremely impressive stability over long time periods has been found for certain cognitive styles. Retest correlations on Witkin's rod-and-frame test (RFT), for example, were as high as .92 for time intervals of a few years (Witkin, Goodenough, & Karp, 1967). A time lapse of fourteen years was the lengthiest interval sampled in their longitudinal study. Even after such a long period, the stability correlation for boys tested with the RFT at age ten and retested at age twenty-four was .66. Data of this kind demonstrate genuine durability in aspects of cognitive and perceptual functioning.

A representative illustration of temporal stability comes from studies of behavior during interviews. Reasonable stability has been demonstrated for certain interaction patterns during interviews. These patterns were measured by an interaction chronograph devised to record selected temporal aspects of verbal and gestural behavior (e.g., Matarazzo, 1965; Saslow et al., 1957). In these studies the interviewer followed a standardized pattern of behavior, including systematic periods of "not responding," "interrupting," and other variations in style. The subject's corresponding behavior was scored on formal dimensions such as the frequency of his actions, their average duration, and the length of his silences. The results indicated that these interactions are highly stable across short time periods (such as one-week retests) when the interviewer's behavior remains fixed. The same interactions, however, were readily and predictably modifiable by planned changes in the interviewer's behavior, as later chapters discuss.

The trait-descriptive categories and personality labels with which individuals describe themselves on questionnaires and trait-rating scales seem to be especially long lasting. E. L. Kelly (1955) compared questionnaire trait self-descriptions obtained almost twenty years apart. During the years 1935–1938 several personality questionnaires were administered to 300 engaged couples, and most of them were retested with the same measures in 1954. The questionnaires included the Strong Vocational Interest Blank, the Allport-Vernon values test, and the Bernreuter personality questionnaire, among others. Self-reports of attitudes about marriage were highly unstable ($r < .10$), but the stability coefficients for self-descriptions of interests, of economic and political values, of self-confidence and sociability were high. The coefficients for these areas of self-reported traits ranged from about .45

to slightly over .60, indicating impressive stability, considering the long temporal delay between assessments.

As another example, the test-retest correlations on the California Psychological Inventory scales for high school students retested after one year, and for a sample of prisoners retested after a lapse of seven to twenty-one days, were also high (Gough, 1957). In general, trait self-descriptions on many personality questionnaires show considerable stability (Byrne, 1966). Studies of the semantic differential also suggest that the meanings associated with semantic concepts may be fairly stable (Osgood, Suci, & Tannenbaum, 1957).

Research on the temporal stability of personal constructs evoked by Kelly's Role Construct Repertory Test (Reptest) also indicates considerable consistency in constructs over time (Bonarius, 1965). For example, a retest correlation of .79 was found for constructs after a two-week interval (Landfield, Stern, & Fjeld, 1961). Factor analyses of the Reptest suggest that the first factor extracted has stable features, with an average retest correlation of .83, although the number of factors extracted is unreliable (Pedersen, 1958). Thus the trait categories people attribute to themselves and others may be relatively permanent, and may be more enduring than the behaviors to which they refer.

IMPLICATIONS

The data on cross-situational consistency and stability over time reviewed in this chapter merely provide representative examples from an enormous domain. The results indicate that correlations across situations tend to be highest for cognitive and intellectual functions. Moreover, behaviors sampled in closely similar situations generally yield the best correlations. Considerable stability over time has been demonstrated for some domains, and again particularly for ability and cognitive measures. Self-descriptions on trait dimensions also seem to be especially consistent even over very long periods of time.

As early as 1928 Hartshorne and May surprised psychologists by showing that the honesty or moral behavior of children is not strongly consistent across situations and measures. The Hartshorne and May data were cited extensively but did not influence psychological theorizing about the generality of traits. Similar evidence for behavioral specificity across situations has been reported over and over again for personality measures since the earliest correlational studies at the turn of the century. Considerable specificity has been found regularly even for syndromes like attitudes toward authority, or aggression and dependency, whose assumed generality has reached the status of a cliché in psychological writings.

The interpretation of all data on behavioral consistency is affected of course by the criteria selected. Consistency coefficients averaging between .30 and .40, of the kind obtained by Hartshorne and May, can be taken either as evidence for the relative specificity of the particular behaviors, or as support for the presence of underlying generality. Indeed, the Hartshorne and May data have been reinterpreted as evidence for generality in children's moral behavior, at least across related situations (Burton, 1963). Similarly, McGuire (1968) reviewed data on the consistency of suggestibility, persuasibility, and conformity and concluded that each has the status of a generalized, although "weak," trait. McGuire noted the tenuousness of the evidence, since the data consisted mostly of low but positive correlations which often reached the .05 statistical confidence level, sometimes did not, and which never accounted for more than a trivial proportion of the variance.

There is nothing magical about a correlation coefficient, and its interpretation depends on many considerations. The accuracy or reliability of measurement increases with the length of the test. Since no single item is a perfect measure, adding items increases the chance that the test will elicit a more accurate sample and yield a better estimate of the person's behavior. Second, a test may be reliable at one score level but unreliable at another. That is, the accuracy of the test is not necessarily uniform for different groups of people; a test that yields reliable achievement scores for ten-year-old children may be so difficult for seven-year-olds that they are reduced to guessing on almost all items. Moreover, different items within the same test do not necessarily yield uniformly reliable information (Cronbach, 1960). The interpretation of reliability coefficients is influenced by the relative homogeneity or heterogeneity in the tested behavior range of the sample of subjects. For example, if an ability test is given to a more or less uniformly bright group of college students, very slight errors in measurement could obscure actual individual differences. Any one set of observations provides merely a sample of behavior whose meaning may be confounded by numerous errors of measurement.

These and similar statistical considerations (Cronbach, 1960) caution us to interpret the meaning of particular coefficients with care. In spite of methodological reservations, however, it is evident that the behaviors which are often construed as stable personality trait indicators actually are highly specific and depend on the details of the evoking situations and the response mode employed to measure them.

It also is not necessarily justified to dismiss negligible correlations between measures because their component tests have low reliability. Low reliabilities of tests, subtests, and items may reflect true differences in the person across situations. To the extent that these changes really occur, the rationale that low coefficients result from the unreliability of the measures can be misleading and may serve to explain away instability on the grounds of instability.

It is important to distinguish clearly between "statistically significant" associations and equivalence. A correlation of .30 easily reaches statistical significance when the sample of subjects is sufficiently large, and suggests an association that is highly unlikely on the basis of chance. However, the same coefficient accounts for less than 10 percent of the relevant variance. Statistically significant relationships of this magnitude are sufficient to justify personality research on individual and group differences. It is equally plain that their value for making statements about an individual are severely limited. Even when statistically significant behavioral consistencies are found, and even when they replicate reliably, the relationships usually are not large enough to warrant individual assessment and treatment decisions except for certain screening and selection purposes, to be discussed in later chapters.

It is very easy to misunderstand the meaning of the findings on behavioral consistency and specificity surveyed in this chapter. It would be a complete misinterpretation, for instance, to conclude that individual differences are unimportant. To remind oneself of their pervasive role one need merely observe the differences among people's responses to almost any complex social stimulus under most supposedly uniform laboratory conditions. The real questions are not the existence of differences among individuals but rather their nature, their causes and consequences, and the utility of inferring them for particular purposes and by particular techniques, as later chapters discuss.

Consistency coefficients of the kind reviewed in this chapter are only one of several types of data pertinent to an appropriate evaluation of the empirical status of the main trait and state approaches to personality. It would be premature therefore to attempt to draw conclusions at this point; that task is deferred to later pages (Chapter 5). Sophisticated dispositional personality theories increasingly have come to recognize that behavior tends to change with alterations in the situations in which it occurs. They note, however, that the same basic underlying disposition (or "genotype") may manifest itself behaviorally in diverse ways in different situations so that heterogeneous behaviors can be signs of the same underlying trait or state. According to this argument, the dependent person, for example, need not behave dependently in all situations; indeed his basic dependency may show itself in diverse and seemingly contradictory overt forms. Although fundamentally dependent, he may, for instance, try to appear aggressively independent under some circumstances, and even may become belligerent and hostile in other settings in efforts to deny his dependency. Similarly, and in accord with psychodynamic theorizing, seemingly diverse acts may be in the service of the same underlying motivational force. For example, a person's overtly liberal political behavior and his overt social conservativism, although apparently inconsistent, may actually both be understandable as expressions of a more fundamental motive, such as his desire to please and win approval and recognition. These arguments for basic consistencies that underlie surface diversity are theoretically defensible, but they ultimately depend, of course, on supporting empirical evidence.

Apart from consistency evidence, trait and state theorists have diligently sought such supporting data in several other ways. One chief strategy has focused extensively on ratings of traits and states by people who know the subject or by the individual himself. That tactic has been closely integrated with the search for underlying dispositions through factor analysis and is at the crux of the psychometric approach to personality dimensions. Some of the main methods, findings, and issues connected with that approach are considered in the next chapter. Thereafter we shall turn to an equally important strategy of trait and state psychology: the search for validity evidence through investigation of the external correlates of test behavior. Studies in this vein investigate how inferences about dispositions from behavior in any one situation serve to predict the person's reactions under other different conditions. After that we shall consider issues relevant to assessing the utility of these assessment techniques and the dispositional constructs that guide them.

/3
TRAITS AND STATES
AS CONSTRUCTS

The last chapter showed that responses are not stimulus-free; behavior is always affected by the context in which it is evoked, and an individual's behavior in even slightly different situations may not be very consistent. But even if an individual's behaviors are specific to the particular situation, and vary across related situations, they generally are construed or interpreted as if they were signs of a consistent personality. People credit their own inconsistent behaviors with basic congruity. When they abstract, interpret, or construe another person they also tend to attribute consistency to him (Vernon, 1964). For many purposes, including the development of scientific theories, it is essential to construe underlying consistencies from heterogeneous events; sometimes, however, this process can also mislead the observer. The familiar "halo effect" in assessment is a common instance in which judges fail to discriminate between the diverse behaviors of the person being rated, and erroneously endow him with generalized characteristics that he does not show. This chapter deals with some of the issues that arise when people construe stable dispositions in others and in themselves.

The naive observer usually simplifies his observations, both about himself and about other people, by applying labels and constructs from a culturally shared trait theory. Even the simplest human behavioral sequences are readily interpreted as signs of generalized internal psychological states and attributes, and are construed as consistent motivated interpersonal actions.

Observers may even credit inanimate objects with human attributes and traits, and this tendency did not end with ancient animism.

41

In one study perceivers endowed moving geometric shapes with emotions and motivations ranging from anger through fear (Michotte, 1954). Likewise, when people watch a disc, a large triangle, and a smaller triangle moving about in and out of a large rectangle they tend to construe the objects as if they were humans engaging in interpersonal conflicts and rivalries: traits of aggressiveness are given to the larger triangle, while the smaller one might become heroic and the disc is timid and feminine (Heider & Simmel, 1944). From (1960) even claims that what we think we see always depends on the intentions we ascribe to others.

Of course, observers do not really believe that cartoons or moving shapes are living humans with psychological qualities. The findings only demonstrate the ease with which persons endow behavior with surplus meaning, especially when they are not provided with an alternative descriptive system, and when instructions and stimulus conditions are ambiguous. Persistent homunculi seem to be created in daily interpersonal relationships, and in the private and public personality theories developed by all people as well as by psychologists.

To invoke trait names as explanatory entities, however, confuses constructions about behavior with the causes of behavior. Traits are used first simply as adverbs describing behavior (e.g., "he behaves anxiously"), but this soon is generalized to describe the person ("he is anxious") and then abstracted to "he has anxiety." These descriptions are not problematic as long as their bases are recalled—namely, he is construed as behaving anxiously, and no more. Nothing is explained, however, if the state that *we* have attributed to the person from his behavior ("he has a trait or state of anxiety") is now invoked as the *cause* of the behavior from which it was inferred. We quickly emerge with the tautology, "He behaves anxiously because he has a trait of anxiety." This is the danger of trait-theoretical explanations, and it has been a problem since the days of faculty psychology.

THE CONSTRUCTION OF BEHAVIORAL CONSISTENCY

The intuitive conviction that persons do have consistent and widely generalized personality traits seems very compelling. The belief that people display stable generalized behavior across diverse situations is reflected in the continuing clinical practice of identifying, labeling, and categorizing individuals on such broad dimensions as anxiety or ego strength. For example, almost every clinical report attributes highly generalized traits to the client. Such reports abound with phrases like "passive, dependent behavior," "submissive personality," "aggressive behavior," "introverted," "rigid," "authoritarian," and so on. Often these statements are poorly qualified, with no detailed reference to the exact situation in which the behaviors are likely to be more or less present or altogether absent.

Why is the belief in the consistency of people's behavior across situations retained so persistently? In part this belief is strengthened by the actual existence of some consistency under some conditions. On the basis of generalization diverse stimuli may achieve equivalence and lead to similar behaviors (Chapter 6). Obviously a person does not have to learn everything afresh in each new or slightly different situation and his reactions to any novel situation are influenced by his past experiences. The empirically established behavioral consistencies, however, do not seem large enough to warrant the belief in very broadly generalized personality traits. The evidence reviewed in the last chapter seems to be discrepant with the enduring conviction that people show marked behavioral generality. The conviction that highly generalized traits do exist may reflect in part (but not entirely) behavioral consistencies that are *constructed* by observers, rather than actual consistency in the subject's behavior. This would place at least some trait consistencies in the interpretations, abstractions, or categories created by the observer rather than in the behavior of the observed. The observer's abstractions in many instances—but certainly not in all cases—may be related only tenuously to the behaviors of the persons they intend to describe. The fact that statements about the content and organization of traits may hinge on the observer's categories, and often are related only minimally to the actual behaviors of the observed person, is best revealed by research on trait ratings.

Trait Ratings as Observer's Constructs

Trait psychology has seen a long quest for a universal taxonomy of traits. This search has been based mainly on trait ratings. It was hoped that these ratings would reveal the underlying traits that exist in the rated persons. After several decades it seems that the resulting data often may be more relevant to the rater's categories than to the ratee's behavior.

One major psychometric strategy began with a search for all "trait names" in a standard English dictionary and produced some 18,000 terms (Allport & Odbert, 1936). Cattell (1947, 1957) culled from this list 4,504 terms which Allport had characterized as:

> . . . *most clearly "real" traits of personality. They designate generalized and personalized determining tendencies—consistent and stable modes of an individual's adjustment to his environment. . . . These terms do not imply merely temporary and specific behavior* . . . . (Allport, 1937, p. 306.)

As a next step, Cattell (1957) employed judgments of "just distinguishable" differences in semantic meaning to further reduce these items to 171 terms or "synonym groups" spanning the "personality sphere." The ratings obtained for these "trait elements" then were correlated and submitted to cluster analyses, yielding thirty-six clusters. These clusters, in turn, were converted into bipolar descriptions, and were named the "standard reduced personality sphere" rating scales.

A series of extensive and sophisticated factor-analytic studies investigated the degree of factor similarity obtained for diverse samples of subjects rated by their peers on scales drawn from a version of the reduced personality sphere (Norman, 1961, 1963; Tupes & Christal, 1958, 1961). Consistently the same set of five relatively independent or orthogonal factors appeared, and led to the conclusion that a "highly stable structure of personal characteristics has been identified" (Norman, 1963, p. 581). The five factor names and abbreviated descriptions of their twenty trait-rating scales are summarized in Table 4.

The conclusion that a stable, five-factor structure of personality exists seemed justified for several reasons. The results came from numerous, diverse samples of subjects and raters; the data included ratings based on interpersonal observations up to three years in length; and, most important, the same factors were found in different samples. For example, in one investigation the quantitative indices of similarity for the five factors across two samples were .990, .964, .910, .999, and .952 (Norman, 1963).

The belief that these data revealed a consistent, stable, generalized five-factor personality structure hinged on one basic assumption:

> *The structure obtained reflected the organization of these attributes in the ratees.* (Passini & Norman, 1966, p. 44.)

This assumption was in fact not justified. The factor structure that emerged when *complete strangers* were rated was highly similar to the five-factor structure from ratings of subjects that raters knew well (Passini & Norman, 1966). Judges in this study rated fellow college students with whom they had no previous experience. The judges' contacts with the ratees in the rating situation involved being

TABLE 4. Factor Designations for Twenty Trait-Rating Scales

Factor Names	Scale Dimensions
I. Extroversion or surgency	Talkative/Silent Frank, open/Secretive Adventurous/Cautious Sociable/Reclusive
II. Agreeableness	Good-natured/Irritable Not jealous/Jealous Mild, gentle/Headstrong Cooperative/Negativistic
III. Conscientiousness	Fussy, tidy/Careless Responsible/Undependable Scrupulous/Unscrupulous Persevering/Quitting, fickle
IV. Emotional stability	Poised/Nervous, tense Calm/Anxious Composed/Excitable Not hypochondriacal/Hypochondriacal
V. Culture	Artistically sensitive/Artistically insensitive Intellectual/Unreflective, narrow Polished, refined/Crude, boorish Imaginative/Simple, direct

(Adapted from Norman, 1963, p. 577.)

in the same room for less than fifteen minutes and there was no opportunity for verbal communication. The rating task was made plausible by asking the raters to judge the subjects as "you would imagine them to be." As the authors point out, the raters could not possibly have had direct knowledge of the ratee's attributes on dimensions like "sociable-reclusive," "cooperative-negativistic," and "responsible-undependable" since they were rating strangers. Nevertheless, the results yielded factors remarkably similar to the five factors obtained from ratings by groups of close acquaintances in previous studies. The investigators recognized that the main information available to the raters "was whatever they carried in their heads." Not surprisingly, such ratings by strangers showed little correspondence with the ratee's own self-descriptions (Passini & Norman, 1966).

D'Andrade (1965) asked college students to rate the similarity *in meaning* between all the possible pairs of words that described each of the poles on Norman's (1963) twenty bipolar scales. These similarity ratings for words were then factor analyzed. This analysis of ratings of meaning similarity yielded a five-factor structure essentially identical with the structure obtained by Norman for ratings of people. Thus the unities found in ratings of words alone corresponded with the unities obtained from ratings of people. This convergence suggests that so-called traits at least in part exist as components of the verbal terms used to describe the external world; they do not necessarily mirror the external world itself (D'Andrade, 1965).

A second major effort to identify basic traits through ratings was conducted by Lorr and his associates (e.g., Lorr, Bishop, & McNair, 1965; Lorr & McNair, 1963, 1965). These investigators undertook extensive factorial studies with rating scales of interpersonal behavior, adopting an approach based on Leary's (1957) dimensions of interpersonal behavior. Their inventories consist of many descriptive statements on which raters judge the extent to which the subject demonstrates the behavior. Examples are: bosses his friends and associates around; keeps aloof from his neighbors; takes the role of helper or supporter of authority figures; acts the clown or amuses others at a party (from Lorr, Bishop, & McNair, 1965, p. 469). On the basis of factor-analytic studies these scales have been grouped into "interpersonal categories" such as dominance, recognition, hostility, mistrust, and so on, and through an elaborate "typing process" persons are assigned into one of a number of types. Type I, for example, is described as an abasive, inhibited, submissive group characterized by the absence of dominance, competitiveness, and hostility. As with other psychiatric typologies (e.g., Phillips & Rabinovitch, 1958) there is considerable heterogeneity within types and overlap between them but some matching has been reported between the types isolated in different studies with similar scales. For example, Lorr, Bishop, and McNair (1965) indicate a good match between their types and three out of eight types which they found with a different sample (McNair & Lorr, 1965).

Descriptive efforts of this kind assume the existence of durable, highly general attributes in people, as reflected, for example, in the assertion that: "Characteristic interpersonal 'styles' or ways of relating to peers, authority figures and to subordinates are relatively enduring characteristics" (Lorr, Bishop, & McNair, 1965, p. 472). It should be recalled, however, that several years earlier Burwen and Campbell (1957) found no evidence for any generalized attitudes toward authority and peers.

D'Andrade (1965) also asked college students to rate on a meaning-similarity scale the words or phrases employed in the sixteen variable categories found in Leary's Interpersonal Check List. These variables were the basis of Lorr and McNair's (1963) rating scales. D'Andrade again found close correspondence between the ratings of meaning similarity in the words of the scales and the correlations among the interpersonal variables obtained from ratings of two hundred patients (Lorr & McNair, 1963). D'Andrade reports a correlation of .86 between the rating of meaning data and the checklist items. In another study, consistency in self-concept statements obtained from self-ratings with adjectives was found to result in part from individual differences in the meanings attributed to the words themselves (Loehlin, 1961, 1967).

Other evidence also suggests that ratings, and the factors identified by the analyses of trait ratings, often reflect the social stereotypes and conceptual dimensions of the judges. For example, three separate factor-analytic studies investigated the degree to which ratings reveal the subject's personality factors as opposed to the rater's conceptual or semantic factors (Mulaik, 1964). In one study the judges rated real persons including family members, close acquaintances, and themselves on seventy-six trait-rating scales. In a second study another group rated stereotyped persons like "suburban housewife," "mental patient," or "Air Force general" on the same scales. Still another sample of raters in the third study rated the "meaning" of selected trait words on the scales. The congruity between the trait factors that emerged from the three studies was compared using an index of factor similarity.

Five of the eleven factors from ratings of real persons were congruent with five of the ten factors from ratings of stereotyped persons. Moreover, these five comparable factors accounted for 70 to 80 percent of the variance in the first two studies. The same five congruent factors from these two studies were matched with four of the nine factors extracted from ratings of the meaning of the list of trait words. The author notes that:

> *These results suggested that "personality factors" based upon trait ratings of persons can be interpreted as distinct concepts*

implied by trait words rather than internal structural features of persons. (Mulaik, 1964, p. 506.)

To the extent that psychometric personality assessments are based on trait ratings they are similar to the data obtained from other research on person perception (e.g., Tagiuri & Petrullo, 1958). Person perception has been described as the:

> *... observations we make about* intentions, attitudes, emotions, ideas, abilities, purposes, traits—*events that are, so to speak, inside the person.* (Tagiuri, 1958, p. x.)

Person-perception ratings, however, like all trait ratings, really involve *interpretations* or *inferences,* not "observations," about the *hypothetical* internal states that may or may not be in the other person. Tagiuri realized the inferential nature of trait ratings:

> *The judgment that a person is "kindly" is not based on one specific stimulus constellation. Rather, an inference about a person's "kindliness" is based on the most diverse observations* .... (Tagiuri, 1958, p. xii.)

The actual existence of these traits or hypothesized states in the other person should not be assumed, because their locus may be in the constructs of the perceiver and not in the characteristics of the perceived. Indeed, research on person perception has led to the conclusion that the results depend far more on the perceiver than on the person perceived (Vernon, 1964). The same conclusion has been reached from a detailed review of research on trait ratings in psychometric personality assessment:

> *It seems best to regard ratings, not so much as summaries of objectively observed behaviour, as rationalizations abstracted from the rater's overall picture (his homunculus) of the subject.* (Vernon, 1964, p. 59.)

Nevertheless, the observer does not perceive a blank world, and surely there are congruences between his reports and the events he construes. For example, some unpublished results suggest reasonable validity for personality rating factors (Norman, 1966). In this study, students who had lived in the same fraternity for at least six months rated themselves and each other on virtually identical trait-rating scales. The data indicated considerable congruence between self-rating factors and similar factors from ratings by peers. That is, the construct clusters with which persons rated themselves corresponded to a significant degree with the ones their peers employed to describe them. Moreover, the correspondence for matched factors in self and peer ratings was far greater than for unmatched or dissimilar factors. These results are an important demonstration of congruence between subjects' trait constructs about themselves and their peers' constructs about them. The findings showed considerable agreement between a subject's stereotypes and constructs about himself and those that raters have about him. But neither the rater's nor the ratee's impressions may be closely related to nonrating behavior. For example, a member of a minority ethnic group may categorize himself verbally with the same labels that others employ for his group, but these labels may or may not describe his behaviors accurately.

Of course there also have been demonstrations of congruence between descriptions obtained from different raters in different contexts. For example, ratings by peers who know each other well can correspond with independent behavior ratings by other observers. This was demonstrated by congruences between peer nominations on clearly described dimensions of aggressive and dependent behavior and separate behavior ratings of actual aggressive and dependent behavior. The latter were reliably measured in experimentally structured life situations designed to elicit the relevant behaviors (Winder & Wiggins, 1964). On the basis of their peer reputations, subjects were classified into high, intermediate, and low groups on aggression and dependency. These groups were significantly different from each other in the amount of aggression and dependency they displayed overtly in the direct behavior assessments. Although the data demonstrate significant differences among the high, intermediate, and low groups, they do not provide information on the degree of association between the reputation and overt behavior measures, since no correlations were reported. It may be possible to predict group differences in overt behavior from group differences in reputation, but the degree to which an individual's behavior on one measure can be predicted from his position on the other cannot be assessed from these findings. In light of the data reviewed in Chapter 2 on behavioral specificity, it seems safe to expect that intraindividual consistency across situations would not be impressively high. Recall, in this connection, the preponderance of nonsignificant correlations among five behavioral dependency measures reported by Sears (1963).

A somewhat different approach has also been taken to determine congruences among independent ratings of traits. In this study, children gave free verbal descriptions of each other, and these descriptions were reliably coded into categories (Dornbusch et al., 1965). The data included descriptions in which one child described two others; two children described the same child; and two children described two different other youngsters. Descriptions with a common *perceiver* had the highest overlap of categories. Descriptions with a common perceived person had the next highest category overlap, and was "followed, surprisingly closely, by description with only a common culture" (p. 434). Description with "only a common culture" refers to the category overlap obtained between descriptions made by different persons of other *different* persons, with no overlap between perceiver and perceived. That is, A describes B and C describes D. In this paradigm the only commonality is that all persons are members of the same culture—in this case a summer camp. The increase in category overlap between this situation and one in which different perceivers describe the *same* individual was only about 7 percent. The authors noted:

> . . . the small difference introduced by specifying a common
> social object reinforces our finding of the greater impact of
> the perceiver. (1965, p. 440.)

In other words, agreement about the attributes of any particular child was virtually unaffected by knowing him. Thus congruences among independent ratings of traits may be more limited than has been assumed.

Trait Factors as the Researcher's Constructs

Some investigators try to arrive at "pure" measures of underlying discrete psychological traits through factor analysis and hope that factor analysis will isolate basic traits in persons. The results, however, depend on the items and subjects selected by the researcher, and on the details of his factorial procedures and decisions. Factor analysis helps to sort test responses into relatively homogeneous clusters, but it does not discover underlying personality traits. It has been claimed that factors correspond to the "real characteristics" or "primary dimensions" of the things being measured (e.g., Barlow & Burt, 1954; Cattell & Sullivan, 1962) and reveal the "incontrovertably known factor structure" of the measurement domain (Cattell & Dickman, 1962). In spite of these claims, however, factor analysis is not by itself a sufficient procedure to infer the determinants of test responses (Anastasi, 1961). Factor analyses of the physical dimensions of books demonstrate that there is no necessary correspondence between the factors obtained and the primary conceptual dimensions of the object (Overall, 1964). Overall devised twelve equations, each of which defined a complex measure as a linear function of the three conceptually primary dimensions of a book: height, width, and thickness. Included in the twelve variables thus defined were three pure marker variables that represented each of the three primary dimensions. He then measured one hundred actual books. The result was a matrix that contained the intercorrelations of the twelve complex book variables. He then performed a principle-axes factor analysis that yielded three factors. These factors, instead of representing the three primary dimensions, were in fact highly complex with regard to them. Conceptually the three factors were meaningful dimensions representing something like size, obesity, and squareness.

Factor analysis often proceeds on the basis of the assumption that the factors that are revealed represent the actual primary factors in the object or person being measured. As Overall points out, however, a single contrary demonstration like his is enough to call into question this basic assumption.

> *The important thing to consider is that if factor analysis results sometimes fail to correspond to primary dimensions of the objects being measured such a failure may occur when we attempt to use it as a method for discovering the "real structure of nature" in areas where the structure is unknown.* (Overall, 1964, p. 270.)

Factor analysis is a very useful tool for reducing a large set of correlated measures to fewer unrelated dimensions, and used as such it is a powerful method in psychological research. But there is no reason to assume that the procedure does more.

> *The results need not and do not have inherent in them any necessary relationship to "real" or "primary" characteristics of the objects or persons being measured.* (Overall, 1964, p. 270.)

And:

> *When we do not know beforehand what the primary dimensions are, it is difficult to justify the belief that factor analysis*

will somehow magically point them out to us. (Overall, 1964, p. 273.)

There is little reason to believe that factors correspond to the structure of nature in domains in which the dimensions are less apparent than the height, width, and thickness of books. Even so-called primary dimensions are human abstractions about objects or events rather than absolute intrinsic characteristics of nature. Traits identified by factor analysis simply reflect the correlations among particular measures. They are descriptive categories rather than underlying entities.

The belief that rating factors reveal the ratee's attributes is most seriously undermined by the lack of strong independent validity evidence. For example, Becker (1960) challenged the claims by Cattell and his associates (e.g., Cattell, 1957; Scheier & Cattell, 1958) that factors obtained from behavior ratings closely match those from questionnaires. Becker reviewed several factor-analytic studies in which attempts were made to find such cross-matches between behavior ratings and questionnaires. The first study (Cattell & Saunders, 1950) claimed to find five such cross-matches in data from several hundred college students. According to Becker, however, the correlations between the behavior measure and the questionnaire measure in each supposed match ranged from $-.44$ to $.26$, with a median of only $.02$. In a reanalysis of the data for women from the first study (Cattell & Saunders, 1955), fifteen personality factors were extracted. However, only one of these factors fully replicated a factor from the first study based on the same data. In the third study (Cattell & Beloff, 1956) eleven-year-old boys and girls were tested. Questionnaire (Q) and behavior rating (BR) data were obtained, correlations were computed, and a factor analysis was performed in which thirteen factors were extracted. Results were not encouraging: "In no case did both a Q factor and a BR factor load on the same factor." (Becker, 1960, p. 205.)

An unpublished study by Meeland (1952), included in Becker's review, attempted to distinguish between four extraversion-introversion factors. Behavior rating and questionnaire data from 102 college men were submitted to factor analysis. In this study, even when significant correlations occurred between "matched" behavior ratings and questionnaire factors, their meaning as evidence for traits in persons was dubious. The correlations across media for presumably *unrelated* factors turned out to be as strong (or weak) as the relationships found between ostensibly similar factors. For example, there was a correlation of $.37$ for "matched" factors from behavior ratings and questionnaires, but the average correlation for "nonmatching" factors was $.32$.

Trait-Rating Factors and Semantic Factors

If trait-rating factors reflect the rater's constructs they should also be similar to the factors that emerge from studies of the semantic meanings of words. This does seem to occur as the studies by Mulaik (1964) and D'Andrade (1965) indicated. Trait factors from ratings of persons also are often close to the meaning factors found in semantic differential studies. In semantic differential research the meaning of diverse words, phrases, and concepts were rated on many scales (Osgood, Suci, & Tannenbaum, 1957). The rater is supplied with a stimulus word like "feather" or "me," or a phrase like "my ideal self," and rates each stimulus on a graphic seven-point bipolar scale. Polar adjectives like rough-smooth or fair-unfair are the extremes of each scale. The rater is instructed to mark the point that shows how closely the stimulus concept is related to the points on the scale.

The results from diverse samples of stimulus content and raters repeatedly produced three main dichotomous semantic response factors. A primary *evaluative* (good-bad) factor accounted for approximately half to three-quarters of the extractable variance. The two other major factors were *potency*, represented by scale items like hard-soft, masculine-feminine, strong-weak; and an *activity* factor, tapped by scales like active-passive, excitable-calm, and hot-cold. As Mulaik (1964) and Vernon (1964) point out, these three semantic factors from studies of concept meanings are similar to the factors found in trait ratings of persons. Commenting on the two or three factors most consistently duplicated from Cattell's trait studies, Vernon (1964, p. 59) notes:

> *Thus there is usually a prominent good vs. bad factor including such traits as emotional stability and reliability, and an extravert-introvert dichotomy, or some variant of active-potent vs. passive-weak.*

Peterson's (1965) analyses of trait data also suggest that "the most dependable dimensions drawn from conventional factor analyses of ratings and questionnaires are simple, familiar dimensions of broad semantic scope" (p. 48).

Taken collectively, the foregoing evidence points to the critical role of the observer's concepts in the formation of impressions about personality. It therefore becomes important to understand how these concepts and categories in the perceiver function and influence his judgments.

53

CONSTRUCTED CONSISTENCIES

The data provided by judgments of others are restricted by the categories and the organizational limits of the judge. Constraints on the number of constructs or categories available to a perceiver may help to account for the constant coding of diffuse perceptual data into simpler forms: categorizations of events into fewer and simpler units places them within the limited scope of memory (e.g., Bruner, 1958). Without simplification of incoming data by assignment of labels and category codings it would be impossible to deal with the virtually endless flood of perceptions that impinge from the environment. Thus the construction of consistency, by relegating diverse events into a broader category that subsumes them, may be highly adaptive for many purposes, and may be dictated by limitations in the observer's organizing capacity.

Construction Limits

In 1956 George Miller called attention to the "magical number seven, plus or minus two," noting that seven categories (plus or minus two) seem to be the usual conceptual grouping limits for any "chunk" of information. In many cases, ranging from tasks involving absolute judgments of unidimensional variables in psychophysics to immediate memory, the limiting value seems to be 7 ± 2. Persons usually cannot remember more than about seven items from an input list, nor discriminate more than seven alternatives of an unidimensional variable. More recent work on memory (e.g., Mandler, 1968) leads to the speculation that the basic limit of the organizing system may be only about 5 ± 2 categories for any set of items.

These magical numbers, interestingly, are about the same as the number of main factors, categories, or dimensions usually extracted from factor analyses of judgments about persons and concepts. Similar magical numbers are found in the main factors or dimensions that emerge from studies of trait ratings (e.g., Tupes & Christal, 1958; Norman, 1963), of the semantic differential (Osgood, Suci, & Tannenbaum, 1957), of personal constructs (Bonarius, 1965; Crockett, 1965), and of clinical and social judgments (Bieri et al., 1966).

The fact that only a handful of factors usually accounts for the vast bulk of the variance in trait ratings is illustrated most clearly by Peterson (1965). It is inefficient to retain any factors beyond the first few because second factors usually account for less than half as much variance as the initial one, and after the first few factors the attributable variance becomes trivial. This is shown in Figure 1 which presents the discrepancy between the assumed variance function (Cattell, 1958) and the actual variance function that Peterson (1965) reports from his own empirical investigations of trait ratings.

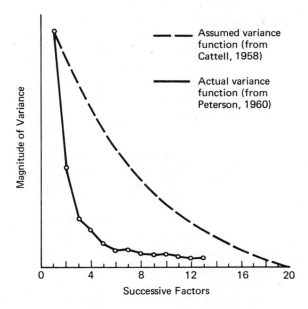

FIGURE 1.   *Assumed and actual variance functions. (From Peterson, 1965, p. 49.)*

Determinants of Constructed Consistencies

Many verbal constructions or interpretations about behavior tend to be quite stable over time. Recall that ratings of traits in people and ratings of the semantic meanings of words and concepts, evoked by paper-and-pencil tests, often show considerable temporal stability even over many years (Chapter 2). This tendency to construe stable personality consistencies in other persons and in oneself seems very pervasive and in some ways analogous to perceptual constancies. In perceptual size constancies, for example, an object's physical size may appear similar under many conditions. The stimulus object seems to have the same size, although its distance from the observer, and hence the size of the image on the retina, varies widely. Heider (1958), MacLeod (1958), and others have noted various parallels between these perceptual phenomena and aspects of person perception.

Both naive observers and sophisticated researchers frequently assume persistent dispositional or trait attributes in others, and in themselves, whether or not the confirming behaviors are actually displayed at a particular moment of observation. Moreover, behavioral inconsistencies are readily explained away: the person who has difficulty construing his discrepant behaviors as "fundamentally" congruent, or at least as all belonging to himself, rapidly encounters aversive consequences. The subjective impression that the same person behaves consistently in diverse situations may be facilitated by the ease with which we seem to recognize and identify him regardless of the context in which he is observed. This sense of recognition and identity may rest to a large extent on physical constancies—in appearance, speech characteristics, and movements—displayed relatively stably by the person. The impression of identity or constancy may be further reinforced by regularities in the environmental contexts and in the social roles in which the person typically is observed (as discussed in Chapter 9). For example, the subjective impression of behavioral constancy in others and in oneself may be strengthened by finding the person repeatedly in the same social-occupational role and in the environmental contexts associated with that role. Thus the college teacher ten years later may behave very differently in many contexts, but to the extent that he is still a teacher, and still spends most of his time on a campus, the impression of constancy is enhanced.

Perhaps the impression of behavioral constancy and consistency is most strongly maintained by the difficulty of obtaining disconfirming data. Most psychological constructs have such broad and ambiguous semantic meanings, and such diverse behavioral referents, that they are virtually impossible to disconfirm definitively. For example, the constructs that a particular woman is "very feminine," or "basically hostile," may be potentially supported by almost any kind of evidence about her behavior. Since the construct about what constitutes "real" femininity, or "real" hostility, may be modified and progressively elaborated as new evidence becomes available, it can be stretched so that diverse behaviors are taken as confirmation for behavioral consistency. Just as with any post hoc hypothesis, almost any data can be made to fit.

Both in daily relationships and in clinical contexts, the impression of behavioral constancy rests largely on the observer's anticipations or predictions about the subjects' homogeneous behavior, without the opportunity to assess the accuracy of the predictions. In psychiatric diagnosis, for example, the diagnostician assigns the patient to a category on the basis of familiar signs. The impact of the follow-up evidence for confirming or disconfirming his prediction is invariably minimized by being delayed, if indeed it ever does become available. Moreover, the evidence undermining the initial prediction can itself be disregarded—for example, by rejecting the measuring procedures as inadequate.

Voluminous research and theorizing on cognitive incongruity, on cognitive dissonance, and on cognitive balance indicates that persons generally reduce inconsistencies and discrepancies between incompatible cognitions (e.g., Abelson & Rosenberg, 1958; Festinger, 1957; Glass, 1968; Heider, 1958; Osgood, Suci, & Tannenbaum, 1957). People do minimize and avoid inconsistent cognitions about themselves and others and reconstrue discrepant events to impose compatibility upon them (e.g., Festinger, 1957). However, any tendency to provide consistency or order by cognitive realignments, in which the diverse behaviors of the same person observed at different times or places are made to seem consonant post hoc, should not be confused with actual convergences among the behaviors themselves.

Attempts to reduce dissonant impressions may be especially strong when the perceiver knows that he will have to communicate his reactions (e.g., Zajonc, 1960). In one study (Cohen, 1961), lists of contradictory traits were presented to many subjects. Half of them were told they would have to transmit their impressions of the described person to other people; the remaining subjects were informed that other people would give them their impression of the individual described by the traits. Those subjects who knew that they would have to transmit their reactions tended to polarize their evaluations and to suppress contradictory trait elements most strongly. Thus even the task of generating personality ratings or assessments for use by others may serve to pressure the individual into simplifying and reducing trait inconsistencies.

The generality or specificity of behavior is demonstrated by the strength of the relevant correlation coefficients. When constructs about trait generality are retained in the face of persistently low empirical correlations, it may be evidence for the tenacity and flexibility of our constructions and for the adaptability of our information-processing skills, but not necessarily for the generality of behavior.

Constructs Constrain Further Observation

To describe the events or behaviors that occur in nature or in the laboratory, observers must categorize, group, and label the phenomena that they observe. The observer must discriminate among the observed events and assign them to positions in categories. If the necessary discriminations are defined with clear referents, agreement among observers and accuracy is obtained readily. It is easy, for example, to score the frequency or rate of occurrence of such clearly discriminable events as a check mark on an inventory or a bar press in a Skinner box. Descriptive accuracy is good whenever there are clear bases for discriminating the event and for placing it on a dimension or category.

Traits and dynamics, however, usually involve broad categories with vague semantic referents, and the events that do or do not belong in particular state and trait categories tend to be difficult to discriminate. Under these ambiguous conditions special problems arise in the relations between events and the categories to which they are assigned. For one thing, once events are assigned into a global category, further observations about them tend to be biased. For another, these global categories tend to be assigned to behaviors even on the basis of little information, as the findings on trait ratings showed. After global labels are applied they may become difficult to disconfirm and to discard. Moreover, if broad trait categories are widely shared and commonly used in a culture, they may come to seem like intuitively appropriate descriptions for behaviors that they actually do not fit well.

It often has been found that after an individual categorizes or groups stimuli he tends to retain his category even in the face of contradictory evidence, paying less attention to the new information and focusing instead on information that confirms his category. This constraining effect of a category has been demonstrated for contexts as diverse as impression formation in person perception (e.g., Anderson, 1965; Asch, 1946; Wishner, 1960), hypothesis testing in problem solving (Davison, 1964; Wyatt & Campbell, 1951) and thinking (Bruner, Olver, & Greenfield, 1966), clinical diagnosis (e.g., Rubin & Shontz, 1960; Sines, 1959), and psychological research (Rosenthal, 1963).

Thus people often categorize each other rapidly even on the basis of little information and then adhere tenaciously to their categories. Psychotherapists are not exceptions; they also hold on to their initial categories, developing stable "images" of their patients within the first four hours of psychotherapy. The categories formed within the first few therapy sessions are retained more or less intact, and do not differ much from those found after twenty-four therapy sessions (Meehl, 1960).

The constraining effects of categories have become evident from several sources. Studies in one approach, for example, exposed subjects to a series of decreasingly ambiguous stimuli in the form of out-of-focus slide pictures. The focus became increasingly clear on successive presentations, and after each presentation the subject stated what he thought the picture was. The results suggested that the hypotheses the subject advanced during the early stages of inaccurate guessing constrained and retarded the development of more veridical perceptions of the stimulus (e.g., Blake & Vanderplas, 1950; Davison, 1964; Wyatt & Campbell, 1951).

PSYCHOMETRIC ASSESSMENT OF TRAIT CONSTRUCTS

Trait-rating studies usually employ an interpretative strategy in which the observer must make relatively global judgments about the meaning of behaviors. Moreover, he must rely on semantic referents whose meanings are multiple and ambiguous, rather than on nonverbal behavioral referents and operations. He is not supplied with clear steps to guide each phase of his descriptions and interpretations; consequently his own conceptions, stereotypes, and previous experience are his main guides. Note that these conditions are similar to the ones usually employed deliberately in projective testing.

An anomaly exists between the labels applied to psychometric personality rating tests and the data that they actually yield. These tests are called "psychometric," "objective," and "standardized." All these adjectives are appropriate descriptions, but only for the printed stimulus material, the scoring procedure, and the administration. The measurement conditions in psychometric personality trait ratings actually enhance interpretative subjectivity on the part of the respondent. In fact, trait-rating scales usually prevent detailed behavior descriptions; instead they tend to yield personal constructs. This feature of trait scales often may be obscured by the emphasis that most writers place on the "objectivity" of these tests. It is true that the stimulus materials are objective and standardized or reproducible in the sense that they usually are presented as printed items on questionnaires, inventories, or rating scales. Likewise, the scoring procedure is objective, because the respondent must react to each question or item with one of a limited number of prescribed or "structured" choices. For example, he selects from printed answers like "yes," "no," "strongly agree," "frequently," "don't know," and so forth. This contrasts with open-ended or unstructured tests, like the projective devices, on which the respondent may supply his own reactions from his repertoire of possible responses, making scoring agreement more difficult. Scoring agreement (reproducibility) is easy to attain when the response to each item is one choice from a limited number of experimenter-supplied alternatives. In turn, scoring agreement makes it more possible to achieve consistent interpretations about the relationships between particular score patterns and other data. Test reliability also is achieved more readily when the subject is confronted with the same limited range of response possibilities on every occasion.

In spite of the above "objectivity," both the stimulus questions and the instructions on psychometric tests usually require the respondent to extrapolate extensively from behavior, to go far beyond direct behavior observation, and to supply subjective inferences about the psychological meaning of behavior. Although the stimulus questions are standardized—that is, printed and therefore always the same on each occasion—their referents are unclear. Table 5 illustrates the diversity and ambiguity of psychometric personality questions with examples from two representative tests. As Table 5 shows, some questions inquire about what the subject typically does, whereas others ask what he is like, how he feels, or what he believes. Such ambiguous items require the respondent to interpret behavior and to provide inferences about psychological attributes. Hence he must construe, evaluate, and generalize about behavior, rather than describe particular behaviors in particular contexts on clear dimensions. When stimulus referents are vague it should not be surprising if the answers are more relevant to the respondent's personal interpretations than to his actual nontest behavior.

Accurate behavior description is increased when differences between subjects in their interpretation of the test stimuli are minimized; ambiguity in a test item produces interpretative subjectivity. Consider, for example, the interpretative variations that may be subsumed under a "yes" response to the statement "I am a happy person." When a response choice depends on highly subjective individual interpretations about the stimulus questions, the correlates of the "yes" as opposed to those of the "no" responses are likely to be diverse and confusing. The same considerations apply whether the data are elicited from the subject himself or from other persons who report about him. Ambiguous test items are appropriate stimuli for evoking rater's constructs, but not for providing behavior descriptions.

Likewise, ambiguity in *response* choices increases individual differences in subjective interpretation and reduces descriptive accuracy. The response choices, like the stimulus items on psychometric tests, are objective in the sense that they are printed and hence standardized. Their meanings, however, are usually ambiguous because different respondents define ambiguous terms like "strongly agree" in idiosyncratic ways. For example, how often is "often" and how frequent is "frequently"? Some self-report devices use response choices such as "al-

TABLE 5. SAMPLE ITEMS FROM PSYCHOMETRIC PERSONALITY
TESTS

Test	Items
California Psychological Inventory	I enjoy social gatherings just to be with people. I looked up to my father as an ideal man. I have a very strong desire to be a success in the world.
Wittenborn Psychiatric Rating Scales	No evidence that he imagines people (who probably are wholly indifferent to him) have an amorous interest in him. Believes (without justification) that certain persons have an amorous interest in him. Believes (without justification) that a sexual union has occurred or has been formally arranged for him.
	Not conspicuously lacking in self-assertiveness. General manner and verbal expressions mild. Desires and opinions can be overridden by a dominant personality. Appears to give in easily to the desires and opinions of others.
	No discernible psychological use made of physical disease symptoms. Use is made of physical disease symptoms to gain attention or to dramatize self. Use is made of physical disease symptoms for evading responsibilities, justifying failures, etc.

ways," "frequently," "seldom," and "never," whereas others provide a seven-point scale and ask the respondent to check the most appropriate point. The subject may be told, for instance, that "7" would indicate that the item is completely applicable to himself, that "1" indicates complete nonapplicability, and that he should check the point on the continuum that best describes his own reaction.

The fact that individuals differ in their referents for such response choices has been demonstrated often. Simpson (1944) asked students to indicate what percentage of the time would correspond to reports that they did something "usually," "often," "frequently," "sometimes," "occasionally," "seldom," and "rarely." As might be expected, a wide range of percentages was cited for each of these words. Twenty-five percent of the subjects applied "frequently" only to events occurring at least 80 percent of the time, whereas another 25 percent said that "frequently" applied to things that happen less than 40 percent of the time.

Confusion between Behavior Description and Interpretation

Many psychometric tests contain a heterogeneous mixture of items. Some items on the same test deal more with behavior description; other items evoke the personal interpretation of behavior. For example, on so-called "behavior-rating scales" some of the items do require the observer to rate the presence or absence of events, or their frequency, providing objective behavior descriptions. Scoring whether or not a patient enters the dining room, or how frequently he eats in particular settings, illustrates behavior descriptions. The same scales, however, also may include items that require the observer to interpret behavior, as in ratings of aggressiveness, hostility, dependency, or other inferred psychological attributes or traits. To the extent that these attributes are not completely specified with clear behavioral referents and operations, the ratings hinge on private definitions.

The instructions for psychometric ratings also tend to encourage subjective interpretations and minimize descriptive accuracy by emphasizing speed, first impressions, and "general" or global rather than discriminative reactions. For example:

> *Your first impression is generally the best so work quickly and don't be concerned about duplications, contradictions, or being exact.* (From instructions to the Leary Interpersonal Check List.)

Likewise, tests like the Bell Adjustment Inventory emphasize "There are no right or wrong answers"; or "Be sure to answer either TRUE or FALSE for every statement, even if you have to guess at some" (CPI directions).

Descriptive inaccuracy also is further increased when the investigator inquires about behavior in highly generalized or "typical" contexts, rather than in well-specified situations. The predilection for items dealing with reactions to general, rather than closely specified, situations is related to the concept that broad traits exist in persons and cause general and enduring behavioral consistencies. Researchers who believe this are likely to assume that a subject behaves consistently in many different situations, regardless of "minor" qualifying conditions. Consequently they select items that refer to relatively general or "hypothetical" typical situations. The research on behavioral specificity, discussed in the previous chapter, suggests that this practice is not justified.

The interpretational strategy that characterizes psychometric ratings and self-reports also has been used widely with many techniques other than questionnaires and paper-and-pencil ratings. Situational tests, "in vivo" behavioral samples, time sampling, role play, and other techniques usually begin with a description of specified directly observed behavior on predefined dimensions. For example, performance is described carefully in a simulated lifelike condition, such as building a small log bridge under stressful circumstances (Murray, 1948). These behavior descriptions, however, are then employed to generate higher-order inferences about the subject's personality; it is these ratings about unobserved attributes or traits, rather than the behavior description in the sampled situation, that enter into the assessment report and that become the bases for predictions. In this manner behavior samples and situational tests are actually converted into ratings of inferred traits.

Any evaluation of the merits and utility of an assessment technique must take into account not merely the method of data collection, but also the manner in which the obtained data are then treated. The information collected from any technique, whether a paper-and-pencil rating or a detailed work sample, can be treated either descriptively or interpretatively, serving respectively either as a sample or as a sign of behavior, as discussed in the following section.

Assessing Behavior and Categories about Behavior

Obviously the events or behaviors that occur in nature and the ways in which the observer who looks at the events perceives, abstracts, interprets, construes, or categorizes them are not identical. It is unnecessary for us to become involved in the philosophical and epistemological complexities of this issue; the discrepancy between behavior and its psychological construction is faced persistently. This discrepancy is found whenever observers of the same behaviors or events disagree about their stated interpretation of what actually occurred. Even when observers agree with each other their observations often are contradicted by independent evidence from other sources. Of course, all knowledge of the events or behaviors that occur in nature can come only through the perceptions of observers. As George Kelly (1955) put it, events and behaviors exist in the universe which "goes about its business of existing"—until observers come along and construe the events.

When the observer looks at behavior or events he can follow an interpretational-inferential strategy, or he can use more descriptive-behavioral tactics. These two emphases are matters of degree only. Although both foci are legitimate routes, they can lead to quite different assessments and serve different purposes: one illuminates to a greater extent the observer's categories, constructs, or abstractions about behavior; the other describes behavior in terms of the investigator's explicit predefined categories. The first involves mainly a higher-order inference process about the meaning of behavioral signs, whereas the second describes sampled events on clear, predefined dimensions supplied by the experimenter.

In personality assessment and research it is often unclear whether the constructions of the observer, or the stimulus properties of the observed behavior, are the focus of study. One may investigate the observer's reports about another person or object to clarify the subjective impressions and judgments that the other person or object creates in the observer. Alternatively, one can study the behaviors of the observed person in a manner that minimizes the observer's impressions and subjective judgments. The two strategies are quite different but in practice they get mixed up, as we have just seen with psychometrics.

To study personal responses to an observed object, person, or behavior, an interpretational strategy is used. The observer is given ambiguous information and must supply his own categories and subjective impressions and definitions to interpret the behavior he observes. For example he is not provided with a ruler or a clock, nor told precisely what and how to measure. In contrast, to investigate an object or behavior, a descriptive-behavioral strategy is more appropriate. The observer is assisted at every point by explicit steps. He is told exactly how to assign behavioral referents into experimenter-supplied categories. For example, he is given a dimension (like a ruler) and shown just how to make predefined discriminations on it. Depending on the exact conditions and purposes of the assessment procedure, events can be described and construed in highly diverse ways, and yield alternative descriptions and interpretations.

If a wide latitude of judgment enters into scoring decisions for a test, the transition from raw test response to score is not a straightforward clerical procedure. Interjudge agreement or consistency is the de-

gree to which different scorers or judges arrive at the same interpretative statements about the same test data. The transition from raw
response to score is usually most troublesome when there are many interpretative steps requiring higher-order inferences that are poorly
specified and ambiguous.

Observers may employ highly objective (clearly reproducible) steps
to arrive at shared conclusions. Both the steps and the conclusions may
be consistently replicated and consensually validated. Nevertheless,
these objective, reliable conclusions may not correspond to *independent*
evidence from other sources about the events that are being described.
Objectivity, in the sense of reproducibility, and accuracy or validity, in
the sense of agreement from *independent modes of observation* as well
as from independent observers, are not equivalent.

Members of the same culture often learn similar constructs or interpretations about the meaning of particular behaviors and events.
"Shifty" eyes, "tight" lips, high foreheads, and facial scars are examples
of cues whose meanings as signs of personality may be widely shared by
members of a given culture. Thus observers may agree with each other
about the meanings of such signs and produce similar interpretations
and labels from minimal cues. For example, if a person wears glasses he
is likely to be perceived as intelligent (Thornton, 1944). If "warmth" is
attributed to a person he is likely to be perceived as also being generous,
good-natured, happy, sociable, and wise (Wishner, 1960); if he has thin,
compressed lips he is likely to be rated low on the trait of "talkative-
ness" (Secord & Muthard, 1955).

The interpretations advanced by naive raters may be similar to
those generated by a psychological theory to the extent that the naive
observer's theory overlaps the psychologist's theory. Often it is difficult
to discriminate scientific personality theories from the personality
theories of the layman because both are rooted in the language and
stereotypes about behavioral meanings prevalent in the common culture. The trait theories that have guided most psychometric personality
research are not dissimilar from the common trait concepts found in
the Western cultures in which the theories arose. The concepts of nonobvious specialized psychological theories, like psychoanalysis, also have
come into common popular use, with many of the key terms and principles now customary parts of daily speech and interpersonal interpretation; consequently the naive rater and the expert may agree with each
other. Such agreement is evidence that the same behavioral signs are endowed with similar meanings by different observers, but does not necessarily support the accuracy of the interpretations.

Agreement among observers about the meaning of particular signs, but with no evidence for their accuracy, is found, for example, in many shared ethnic and attitudinal stereotypes (reviewed by Brown, 1965). It is equally evident from the results of psychometric trait research when persons rate or judge personality characteristics and the same factors emerge consistently, but often irrespective of the persons that are being rated, as reviewed earlier in this chapter. Similarly, clinicians may agree with each other about the dynamic meanings of a sample of behavior, but with little support from external evidence (Chapter 5).

A strategy for direct observation and descriptions of behavior on predefined dimensions is illustrated well in recent work by Lovaas and his associates (Lovaas et al., 1965a, b). These authors point out two main difficulties that have beset previous methods of recording people's behavior in an ongoing lifelike situation. First, the usual methods of writing or dictating an account of naturalistic behavior require the observer to direct a large part of his attention to the actual recording and thus restrict the amount of attention he can pay to the subject's behavior. The second problem concerns the lack of precision. It has been difficult to obtain a record which contains not only the behaviors that the subject performed but also the duration and the specific time of onset of each type of behavior. This latter information is necessary if one wants to determine the nature of any systematic covariations of an individual's specific behavior with his other behaviors, with the behavior of other persons, or with various changes in his environment.

Lovaas has devised an apparatus containing a panel of buttons which are depressed by the observer, each button representing a predefined category of behavior (Lovaas et al., 1965b). The button panel is attached to an Esterline Angus pen recorder so that when a button is depressed the corresponding pen on an automatic cumulative recorder is activated. The observer depresses the button when the subject begins to engage in the specific behavior designated by that button and does not release the button until the individual discontinues that behavior. After a minimal amount of practice the observer is able to devote his whole attention to watching what the subject is doing without looking at the button panel while recording up to twelve different behaviors. The procedure allows for a precise record that includes duration and the specific time of onset of each behavior. The method can then be used to determine covariations among the person's different behaviors and between his behavior and that of others in the situation.

Lovaas used the recording device primarily to record the behavior of autistic children, but the procedure can be used to observe the behavior of any person. The behavior categories chosen can be as specific or as global as is required by the particular purpose for which the observation is being made. Similarly, the behavior categories can be as descriptive or as interpretative as is desired. The only requirement is that the category be such that the records of independent observers show high agreement in their scoring of the particular behavior represented by the category. In this regard it seems reasonable to expect that the more descriptive the category is, the higher the agreement among the scorers is likely to be. This hypothesis is borne out by the experience of Lovaas who found it necessary to revise some of his categories in the direction of more precise behavioral descriptions in order to attain higher levels of reliability. The categories of "appropriate" and "inappropriate" verbal behavior, while valuable clinical categories, were found to require too much judgment on the part of the observers and thus did not yield high interscorer agreement. These categories were replaced by "Verbal I," defined as nonrepetitive intelligible behavior, and "Verbal II" defined as repetitious verbal behavior and nonintelligible verbalizations. Interscorer agreement was sufficiently high for these revised categories. In addition to Lovaas' method, a large array of ingenious observational techniques is available for recording diverse behaviors objectively and unobtrusively so that practically no distortion occurs from the measurement process itself (Webb et al., 1966).

As the preceding illustration shows, it is not too difficult to score accurately the occurrence, frequency, or rate of particular, directly observed, well-defined behaviors on a prescribed dimension. What a person *does* can be described reliably and accurately, but this description is different from how the person's behavior is subjectively *construed* by observers. Through direct observations one can accurately assess, for instance, the amount of money individuals leave as tips after a dinner, their financial response to charitable solicitations, the amount of time they spend listening to another person's troubles, and the like. These illustrations all involve descriptions of operationally defined events on predefined, objective dimensions such as units of money or time.

On the other hand, attribute or trait ratings obtained about the person, as when observers judge him on a seven-point scale of "generousness," or when the subject rates his own generousness, are more likely to provide data about the rater's constructs. To the extent that the exact behavioral referents for "generousness" are not explicitly given to the observer, his ratings about generosity hinge on his own definitions. If the particular behaviors that should serve as indices of generosity are not predefined and specified, the rater must use his own subjective judgments and supply his own personal referents and categories. His ratings then reflect subjective interpretations about the behaviors that are signs of generosity and depend on his own interpretation of generosity.

In general, consensus among judges is higher when interpretations require relatively little inference (as in ratings of verbal fluency) than when global and indirect complex inferences are requested, as in ratings of adjustment or psychotherapy prognosis (e.g., Howard, 1963). When elaborate interpretations or remote inferences to unobservables are required, reliability tends to be poor (e.g., Grosz & Grossman, 1964; Lewinsohn et al., 1963). As was noted at the start of this section, however, the differences between more inferential and more descriptive strategies are matters of degree rather than absolutes.

Implications of Traits as Constructs

As the preceding pages indicated, an important aspect of human behavior is that observers label and categorize both their own diverse behavior and the responses of others. Traits are categories of the observer who perceives and describes behavior and not necessarily properties of the observed behavior itself. Trait labels should not be confused with the antecedents and maintaining conditions of the behaviors to which they refer, nor with an accurate description of the behaviors themselves. In fact, this confusion does occur whenever trait descriptions are offered as explanations for behavior—for example, when inefficient, disorganized responses are "explained" by simply calling the performer "neurotic."

To the degree that personality evaluations, either about oneself or others, require judgments of poorly defined abstractions with vague referents, and are based on ambiguous, fragmentary data from the subject, accurate behavior description or prediction to nonverbal behavior should not be expected. An inexact match between events and their description occurs when observers summarize complex, lengthy, or diverse behavior sequences with broad terms that have multiple meanings. This inaccuracy happens if events are described in prose language, and as James Miller (1958) pointed out, occurs whenever statements exceed operational definitions. For many purposes imprecise verbal descriptions are not problematic. Often gross categorizations even have the enormous advantage of subsuming many events under commonly accepted, culturally shared abbreviations so that they can be communicated parsimoniously. Without such linguistic shorthand one would be left breathless from endless operational definitions, and the usual daily communication would become impossible. For many other purposes, however, the discrepancy between events and their verbal representations presents serious problems that can confuse the whole assessment enterprise.

To the extent that trait measurements reflect the preconceptions and constructs of the rater, it is not surprising if they do not correspond well to other nonrating data about the ratee. Although judges may agree with each other's interpretations, producing high consistency or reliability, their constructions may have little or no relationship to other evidence about the person whom they are evaluating (e.g., Mischel, 1965). Likewise, even when agreement between judges is low, Little and Shneidman (1959) found that expert clinicians interpreting projective test and other data "tend to make their interpretations in a stereotyped manner independent of the S" (p. 17). Data on the correlations between trait ratings and other independent information about the ratee are reviewed in the next chapter.

It has been widely assumed that poor correspondence between self-reports and actual nontest behavior, or poor correspondence between the subject's self-reports and ratings by observers, indicate that persons are either unable or unwilling to describe their behavior accurately. Inaccuracy has been attributed mainly to a variety of distorting motivational forces, including deliberate faking, lack of insight, and unconscious defensive reactions, all of which presumably produce inaccurate self-descriptions. Equally possible, poor correspondence between self-report and nontest behavior may reflect the fact that most self-reports elicit the subject's global interpretations about his typical behavior and his personal constructions about his psychological attributes or traits.

Weak associations between the subject's self-reports and ratings by observers also may be due to the fact that these two data sources often involve the matching of interpretations about behavior, as in the form of trait adjectives and other inferred attributes. Usually self-report tests do not deal with clear indices of the actual occurrence, frequency, or strength of particular behaviors and do not ask the subject to describe in detail his specific behaviors in concrete situations. In other words, much of what is called behavior rating in fact involves higher-order behavioral interpretation, and research on the correlations between diverse behavior ratings actually correlates diverse behavioral interpretations or constructions. These associations, however, say nothing about the ability of people to describe and predict behavior under more appropriate conditions. When persons are asked to describe, anticipate, or predict behavior, with minimal interpretation of its meaning, they may be as successful, or even more accurate, than other "experts" or tests (e.g., Mischel, 1965; Mischel & Bentler, 1965) as will be discussed in Chapter 5.

SUMMARY

This chapter has dealt with issues usually subsumed under "reliability," and particularly with the reliability of interpretations or categorizations about behavior. It has been stressed that agreement or reliability among raters in the labels put on behavior may spuriously create the impression that traits or dynamic states have been discovered in the people to whom the labels are applied. This kind of error is especially difficult to overcome because once a phenomenon is labeled or categorized new observations become constrained and disconfirmation of the label becomes more difficult. In turn, the labels that are applied to others, as well as to oneself, may persist over time with considerable tenacity, further enhancing the impression that the label fits the behaviors to which it has been applied.

Constructions about personality consistencies may be maintained in part by physical constancies in the person's appearance, speech, and movements. Regularities in the individual's environmental contexts, his social roles, and stable routines also enhance the impression of consistency. Moreover, it may be difficult to obtain disconfirming data for the belief in marked consistency because of the ambiguous semantic meaning of trait categories. The tendency to reduce behavioral inconsistencies and discrepancies between incompatible cognitions, and the organizational limits of observers, also may lead to the use of broad trait categories that may be maintained even in the face of contradictory evidence.

Diffuse perceptual data are constantly coded into simpler forms and categories according to the limits of the information-organizing capacity of the observer. The data obtained from trait ratings and personality questionnaires were interpreted as often reflecting raters' constructs rather than underlying traits. Factor-analytic studies have yielded similar factor structures for ratings of complete strangers and for subjects who are known well by the raters. However, analysis of ratings of the similarity of the meaning of trait names themselves yielded a factor structure essentially identical with that obtained for the ratings of people. Additional studies suggest that the personality factors based on trait ratings in part may be due to the meanings implied by trait words rather than internal characteristics of persons.

Two related strategies for assessment were outlined. The first discussed was an interpretational strategy that is used to study the personal, subjective interpretations of the observer. The observer is given ambiguous information and must supply his own categories to infer the meaning of behavioral signs. An example of this strategy is psychometric measurement based on trait ratings. The second strategy is a more descriptive approach in which the observer is assisted by explicit steps and supplied with clear categories to describe behavior on prescribed dimensions.

In the psychometric assessment of trait constructs the rater is usually required to extrapolate extensively from behavior and to supply subjective inferences about its psychological meaning. Ambiguity in the response choices further increases individual differences in subjective interpretation and reduces descriptive accuracy. Thus the printed stimulus material of behavior-rating scales is "objective" and "standardized," but to the extent that the attributes are not completely specified with clear behavioral referents and operations, the ratings hinge on the private ways in which the respondent construes or interprets behavior. Descriptive inaccuracy is further increased when the investigator inquires about behavior in highly generalized or "typical" contexts. This latter tendency stems from the belief that broad traits exist in persons and cause general and enduring behavioral consistencies.

Even when congruences are obtained between trait ratings by different observers, such consistency is not sufficient evidence to show that rated behavior is closely related to nonrated behavior. Judges may agree with each other but their interpretations may not be related closely to independent data about the person from other sources. Reports about psychological attributes such as traits and states require judges to describe verbally their own inferred characteristics or those of other persons. These personality ratings are susceptible to all the same variables that affect other personal constructs. They are, for example, easily and quickly generated from minimal information; readily and often erroneously generalized to events which they actually do not fit well; highly influenced by the details of the eliciting situation; and often firmly maintained in the face of contradictory evidence. All of these problems undermine the value of trait ratings, either of oneself or others, as accurate indices of behavior and as criteria for evaluating the efficacy of behavior predictions or the accuracy of behavior descriptions.

Although ratings and judgments about the psychological characteristics of people may not be strongly related to independent data about the subject's actual behavior, they can provide information about the rater's semantic and conceptual system. Statements about personality traits may help us understand the construct system of the respondent, as well as widely shared semantic stereotypes and pervasive judgmental halo effects, even when they do not yield reliable and accurate information about the behavior of the person who is being described. As such they may provide evidence about the personal constructs, stereotypes, semantics, or subjective "reasons" of the person who makes the statements (T. Mischel, 1964).

/ 4
PERSONALITY CORRELATES

Even if individuals show less cross-situational consistency in their behavior than has been assumed, numerous relationships do exist of course among a person's response patterns. Correlations frequently occur between a person's behaviors evoked under many different conditions, and therefore responses in any one situation can serve as signs of other things that the individual is likely to do in new circumstances. Personality psychology has studied these relationships extensively since the earliest work on individual differences began at the turn of the century.

Research of this kind seeks correlations among an individual's patterns of responses to different standardized eliciting conditions or tests. In this correlational strategy, test batteries are administered and the empirical associations between responses to these tests or stimulus conditions provide indices of how strongly an individual's behavior converges across situations. More recently, increasing attention is being given to the relations between individual differences (e.g., on a paper-and-pencil test) and responses to experimentally manipulated treatments. A typical question here might be how do people who have high scores on an anxiety scale differ in their reactions to failure from those who have low anxiety scores. Studies that explore relations among responses, either on formal tests or on laboratory measures, try to discover how an individual's behaviors in one situation serve as a sign of his behavior in other situations and attempt to illuminate the organization of behavior.

As long as statements are limited to operational descriptions of obtained responses and their empirical interrelations, there are no interpretative problems. Most personality psychologists, however, have not been interested in merely describing test behaviors and their correlates. Indeed there has been little interest in the sampled behavior itself. Instead, a sign approach has been pursued in which test responses are valued only as reliable indicators or signs of the traits and states that supposedly underlie them (Loevinger, 1957).

VALIDITY

The search for signs of personality, rather than for samples of the behavior of interest, has led to the selection of test responses that in themselves are trivial. The check marks on a paper-and-pencil scale, or doodles, figure drawings, or sentence completions obtained in trait-oriented assessments, are of little value as behavior samples. Understandably, therefore, interest has been less in the conditions that control changes in the test signs than in their correlates. The previous chapters have been concerned chiefly with issues of reliability. This chapter examines some of the main strategies to establish the value of an individual's responses as signs of his nontest behavior and hence with matters of validity.

As was noted before, the distinction between reliability and empirical validity becomes elusive in practice; it would be difficult to discriminate the point at which the measurement of a set of behaviors by a number of similar techniques in a reliability inquiry turns into an investigation of validity. The reliability-validity distinction is tenuous and depends on judgments about the degree of relatedness between the stimulus conditions in which responses are sampled. When the evoking stimulus conditions are closely related textbooks call it reliability research; when they appear largely independent the label of empirical validity is applied. The dimensions for judging relatedness between measures, beyond their actual empirical correlations, usually are unclear. Nevertheless, the consistency or reliability of any response measure automatically restricts the external validity correlates that it can yield (e.g., Cronbach, 1960). Therefore predispositional measures that provide relatively inconsistent response samples when even minor stimulus changes occur cannot be expected to supply impressive correlates with other data.

Responses Used without Extrapolating from the Sample

The least hazardous use of data is as self-contained samples, defined by the operations used to evoke them, without any inferences about their functions as signs or indicators of anything beyond themselves. For example, the subject's self-report on a ten-item questionnaire may be used as just that: *his* report about his *stated* reactions to the items under the specific circumstances of administration. Unless reliability studies are conducted to assess the extent to which the same responses are obtained under similar circumstances on other occasions, no statements are justified about the stability of the sampled behavior. Likewise, the sample cannot be interpreted as an index of unobserved behavior unless the links between it and other events are demonstrated.

To the extent that test behavior is a direct sample of the defined behavior of interest it is meaningful in itself and can be used without extrapolating to other events. For instance, if one is interested in a child's dependency behavior in relation to adult teachers in a nursery school, one can sample the dependent behavior directly (e.g., Heathers, 1953). Personality assessors, however, have traditionally required the subject to give a *verbal* self-report, usually in the form of "yes," "no," or a scale number to indicate intensity or degree of agreement, often to highly ambiguous items and under artificial testing conditions. When personality testing first began it was often assumed that such questionnaire responses provided an accurate index of typical nontest behavior. This assumption was consistent with the belief in highly generalized traits that express themselves pervasively across a multitude of situations.

In accord with these beliefs it was generally assumed by psychometricians in the 1920's and 1930's that what a person says he does reflects his typical overt behavior and that self-reports about traits therefore provide an accurate shortcut to the measurement of life behavior outside the test. But this "shortcut" may have turned out to be one of the costliest efforts to economize in the history of assessment. Scales to measure traits such as "friendliness," "extraversion," "confidence," "conservatism," "dominance," often were little more than poorly defined and arbitrarily labeled collections of items. The subject's trait score was simply the frequency with which he checked particular responses so that, for example, the more often he described himself as "friendly" the stronger was his trait of friendliness.

Hundreds of questionnaires and inventories appeared in the period between the two world wars, and many still flourish. Testers constructed trait lists more or less arbitrarily and labeled them according to the dispositions that they thought were involved, usually on the basis of the "face" features of the items. The result was that one man's introversion scale could be another's measure of independence or resistance to conformity pressures. Cronbach (1960, pp. 467-468) notes the confusion arising from freely labeling collections of items so that:

> *The meaning of "introvert" is twisted and turned so that it represents for one author a brooding neurotic, for another anyone who would rather be a clerk than a carnival barker. "Ascendance" ranges from spontaneous social responsiveness, in one theory, to inconsiderate and overbearing behavior in another. The verbal coinage has been so debased by popular usage and by questionnaire makers that some investigators try to free themselves by coining completely new terms. R. B. Cattell (1957) has succeeded in popularizing his word* surgency *to describe a certain pattern of energetic behavior, but he will surely encounter considerable resistance to such new-minted trait names as* parmia, premsia, *and* abcultion *(akin respectively to social extroversion, emotional sensitiveness, resistance to intellectual culture).*

Early psychometricians tended to follow the example of simple physical measurement, and took as their ideal models such measurements as table length with rulers or temperature with thermometers. The unquestioned assumption that mental traits exist as stable, generalized structures prevented them from paying much attention to the environmental determinants of behavior and to the variability of behavior as a function of the situations in which it occurs. Instead, attention was paid to standardization of measurement conditions, and concern with reliability usually overshadowed interest in validity. A notable exception was the empirically keyed Strong Vocational Interest Blank. Although these inventories sometimes had considerable value for screening decisions, they revealed little about the traits and states whose labels they bore.

Guided by trait theorists like Thurstone, Guilford, and Cattell, there developed in the 1940's an extensive effort to build homogeneous, "pure" trait scales, largely through factor analysis. When the limitations of this factorial approach began to be recognized, attention turned to the use of objectively scored personality inventories like the MMPI, and later the CPI, and to a search for the empirical external correlates of test behavior.

Correlations among Response Patterns

The bulk of trait-state personality research is based on a search for correlations among response samples or tests, providing vast networks of test-test correlations. Validity refers to the relationship between test data and other data, and specific validity coefficients are indices of the extent to which the person's particular verbal and nonverbal performances on the test are related to other data.

Interest may be in the correlation between test data and concurrently available criterion data (concurrent validity), or with criterion data available at a later time (predictive validity). Correlations may be with data that seem to have a strong, direct similarity to the content of the initial test sample (e.g., from arithmetic performance on the Wechsler-Bellevue to arithmetic success in a school course), or with data whose contents appear quite remote from the sample (e.g., from Rorschach achromatic responses to the psychiatric diagnosis of "depression"). Each of the dimensions discussed in Chapter 2, as well as many other behavior clusters, has yielded a network of correlates with other personality measures and with each other. These networks often have provided statistically significant associations and hence validity evidence, but the interpretation of the meaning of these relationships tends to become quite complex.

The experiences with the California F scale illustrate the typical problems regularly encountered with validity research on personality dimensions. Although the cross-situational generality of the authoritarian trait structure supposedly assessed by this instrument is dubious itself (Kenny & Ginsberg, 1958), a web of correlations has emerged from more than a hundred studies relating F scale scores to a multitude of variables. Correlations are with such diverse variables as tests intending to measure intelligence, xenophobia, family ideology, prejudice, anxiety, voting behavior, military reenlistment intent, cooperation in psychological experiments (Titus & Hollander, 1957), and even reactions to the U.S.-Soviet space race (Mischel & Schopler, 1959).

Most important, however, and typical of the fate of other personality measures, is the fact that the F scale is most strongly correlated with other paper-and-pencil measures, but much less systematically associated with nonquestionnaire measures of interpersonal behaviors sampled in diverse situations (Titus & Hollander, 1957). When correlations are computed with other questionnaires sampling similar attitude patterns, they sometimes reach impressive magnitude. For example, in the development of the F scale, correlations among verbal scales inquiring about various different negative characteristics of Jews—such as their "offensiveness," "intrusiveness," and "seclusiveness"—were found to range from .74 to .85 (Adorno et al., 1950). But these questionnaire-questionnaire correlations have to be interpreted with special caution, as later sections show.

The magnitude of the relationships obtained between the F scale and nonquestionnaire measures, on the other hand, is typically low.

Indeed, the phrase "personality coefficient" might be coined to describe the correlation between .20 and .30 which is found persistently when virtually any personality dimension inferred from a questionnaire is related to almost any conceivable external criterion involving responses sampled in a *different* medium—that is, not by another questionnaire. Generally such correlations are too low to have value for most individual assessment purposes beyond gross screening decisions. Moreover, the obtained networks of relationships often are too diffuse to be comprehensible theoretically. Finally, the correlations obtained among personality measures to some extent may simply reflect their common associations with intelligence and education. This point is illustrated in Table 6 which shows some differences in response to F scale items for groups differing in education. As that table reveals, the less education people have the more likely they are to agree with the assertions on the F scale.

TABLE 6.   RELATIONS BETWEEN EDUCATION AND RESPONSES
TO F SCALE ITEMS

Scale Item	Percentages Agreeing		
	College Education	High School	Grammar School
The most important thing to teach children is absolute obedience to their parents.	35	60	80
Any good leader should be strict with people under him in order to gain their respect.	36	51	66
Prison is too good for sex criminals. They should be publicly whipped or worse.	18	31	45
There are two kinds of people in the world: the weak and the strong.	30	53	71
No decent man can respect a woman who has had sex relations before marriage.	14	26	39

(Adapted from Hyman & Sheatsley, 1954, p. 94.)

As another example of correlational personality research, consider the relations among measures of personality and performance in a small group. Mann (1959) reviewed and surveyed the voluminous research on this topic conducted in the years from 1900 to 1957. The results again are fairly typical of the correlations found in research relating personality measures to behavioral criteria. The personality variables in Mann's survey included measures of adjustment, extraversion-introversion, dominance, masculinity-femininity, interpersonal sensitivity, and intelligence. Behavior in groups served as the criteria. These group behaviors were scored for leadership, popularity, activity rate, conformity, and other dimensions. Of the hundreds of correlations obtained, the median correlation between any aspect of personality and performance was never higher than .25, and in most cases the median correlation was closer to .15. Moreover, "The best predictor of an individual's performance in groups is intelligence" (p. 264). The median correlation of .25 was found for the association between intelligence and leadership; the usual median correlation for personality variables (other than intelligence) tended to be about .15.

Studies of how a person's self-reports correlate with what he actually does are also good illustrations of validity research. As the last chapter indicated, personality and attitude questionnaires generally require the subject to categorize his own behavior with trait-state terms and hence provide data about his verbal constructs. Surprisingly, relatively little is known about the empirical relations between a subject's constructs and his actual behavior toward the persons or objects described in his verbal statements.

Studies on this topic suggest that there are some congruences between measures of verbal attitudes toward an object or person and actual behavior to the relevant object or person, but the relationships are variable and not infrequently small or zero (e.g., Becker, 1960; Harding et al., 1954). LaPiere (1934), for example, long ago found little correspondence between the questionnaire answers about the lodging and restaurant services that would be offered to Chinese guests and the actual hospitality received when the guests arrived. On the mailed questionnaire 92.5 percent of the respondents indicated refusal of Chinese. However, a well-dressed Chinese couple, accompanied by a Caucasian, was refused accommodations in only .4 percent of the places they visited.

Statements about ideology do show correspondence with political choices. In one study among college students with high scores on the California *F* scale (suggesting strong ideological conservatism), 76 percent stated they preferred the Republican party whereas 65 percent of those low on the *F* scale preferred the Democratic party (Leventhal, Jacobs, & Kudirka, 1964). The relationships between *F* scale scores and stated voting behavior were statistically significant, students with high *F* scale scores choosing the more conservative political candidate. On the other hand, the discrepancy between stated voting behavior measured by simulations of voting choices in large-scale opinion polls and actual voting behavior in the polling booth in national campaigns is evident from the upsets not infrequently found in real elections.

In general, there often is some beyond-chance association between attitude statements or verbal descriptions about behavior and direct measures of the relevant behavior. A study by Brody (1965) on the relations between maternal attitudes and mother's actual behavior toward her child is fairly representative. Brody administered the Parental Attitude Research Instrument (PARI) and other measures to the mothers of preschool children. Thereafter, independent direct observations were obtained of interactions between the mothers and their children in a play setting. These interactions were reliably scored on dimensions relevant to those sampled verbally in the attitude scale (e.g., authoritarian-controlling, hostility-rejection). Of fifteen behavioral indices only seven showed a statistically significant relation with maternal attitude scores. Even the significant relations, however, were of moderate magnitude. The overall results led the author to conclude that there was no support for a strong relationship between expressed maternal attitudes toward child rearing and the direct observation measures of the mother's behavior toward her child.

Similarly, recall from Chapter 2 the poor correspondence between verbal reports about moral attitudes and nonverbal moral behavior found by Hartshorne and May (1928), as well as by later investigators (Aronfreed, 1961). To illustrate further, willingness to delay immediate rewards for larger but delayed gratifications in real choices is correlated only moderately with such preferences under hypothetical conditions described on questionnaires (Mischel, 1962). Results of this kind, and the previously reviewed data, typify the usual associations obtained between attitude and behavior measurement: some correspondence, but not very much, and never enough to warrant the assumption that verbal statements about behavior mirror the relevant behavior.

Consistent with the foregoing findings, thoughts and fantasies, as measured through projective and story-telling techniques, are correlated only marginally with measures of relevant overt behavior. For example, achievement concerns and ideations measured from TAT stories relate in limited ways to other measures of achievement. The same is true for other content areas, such as the associations between aggression imagery and aggression-relevant behavior. An enormously extensive tabulation of the correlations obtained between many kinds of motivational imagery (TAT themes) and behavior ratings documents these points (Skolnick, 1966). Sometimes measures of thought were found to be positively related to relevant actions, less often negatively, and most frequently not at all. McClelland (1966), reviewing this survey, noted that while the overall number of associations significant at the $p < .10$ level exceeded chance, ". . . the relationship is not close." Only about 25 percent of the predicted relationships were supported, generally at low magnitudes.

Within the same medium—for example, paper-and-pencil self-report tests—the correlations among anxiety questionnaires that deal with various topics, like test anxiety or more general anxiety reactions, often are substantial (e.g., Ruebush, 1963; Sarason et al., 1960). For instance, in one study (Sarason et al., 1960), the average correlation between scores on the Test Anxiety Scale for Children and the General Anxiety Scale for Children was .54 for girls and .61 for boys. It has also been found repeatedly, however, that physiological measures of anxiety tend to be unrelated to inferences about anxiety based on self-report inventories (Katkin, 1965; Martin, 1961; Raphelson, 1957; Rosenstein, 1960). Thus correlations among different paper-and-pencil self-report measures of anxiety tend to be fairly strong, but the associations become low or negligible when anxiety is measured by diverse methods.

Even when behavior is sampled exclusively on a questionnaire and subjects are merely asked to report how they would respond to different stimulus conditions, the variance due to individual differences may be more limited than that contributed by stimulus conditions. Endler, Hunt, and Rosenstein (1962) attempted to estimate on an inventory of anxiety the variance attributable to modes of response, stimulus situations, and individual differences. To accomplish this, they sampled on their inventory different situations as well as different subjects. They found that individual differences in anxiety accounted for only a very small proportion of the total variance, and, were led to conclude that:

> *The fact that a sampling of situations can contribute over 11 times the amount of variance contributed by individual differences among a sampling of Ss should give pause to clinicians, personologists, and psychometricians in general.* (Endler, Hunt, & Rosenstein, 1962, p. 12.)

There have been numerous research programs that have tried to identify individual differences on variables and to assess their relations to other things that the person says or does in different situations. The results often provide extensive networks of associations. One study, for example, investigated the relationship between cheating and willingness to delay immediate smaller rewards for the sake of larger but delayed gratifications (Mischel & Gilligan, 1964). In a first session sixth-grade school children had to indicate their actual choice preference for either an immediate smaller or a delayed larger reward in each of many choices. They chose, for instance, between getting a small notebook now or a larger notebook within one week, a small magnifying glass now or a larger one in one week, and 15 cents now or 30 cents in three weeks. In this same session their level of achievement motivation was assessed by McClelland's (1953) picture story-telling procedure.

In a second later session each child played a shooting-gallery game with a toy rifle. They were told that they would get special marksman badges if their scores were sufficiently high. Unknown to the children, their scores were controlled automatically so that they could not obtain enough points to get any awards through their own honest skill. Each child was left alone, however, to record his own hits and misses. This situation provided him an opportunity to falsify his scores in order to obtain the badges offered as achievement awards. The mechanical apparatus of course permitted the experimenters to score objectively the amount and latency of any cheating. As predicted, children who on the preexperimental tests showed more concern with achievement (in their stories) and less willingness to wait for delayed rewards also tended to cheat more and sooner in order to get the achievement prizes that they could not gain through their own skills.

The same program of research also has obtained significant correlations between preference for delayed larger rewards or immediate but smaller gratifications and numerous other behaviors. For example, children who chose to wait for rewards tended to have higher social responsibility scores (Mischel, 1961a), stronger achievement concerns (Mischel, 1961b), and greater intelligence (Mischel & Metzner, 1962) than children who chose immediate gratifications. It was also found that preference for delayed rewards increases with age, differs predictably across cultures, and varies as a function of certain rearing conditions in the home (Mischel, 1966b).

These preferences for delayed rewards in choice situations, however, are unrelated to the standards children set for rewarding their own behavior (Mischel & Masters, 1966), and to their choice of immediate as opposed to delayed unavoidable punishments of different magnitudes (Mischel & Grusec, 1967). Moreover, although often statistically significant, the relations between various individual difference measures and delay preferences generally were too low to account for more than a tiny fraction of the variance. A typical example is the correlation of .31 between total amount of cheating and unwillingness to wait for delayed rewards. Such small albeit statistically significant relations between individual difference measures and behavior tend to be the rule rather than the exception (e.g., Byrne, 1966). These weak associations, accounting for a trivial portion of the variance, become understandable when the enormous variance due to situationally specific variables that determine the consequences for behavior in any particular context is recognized. It has been shown that delay of reward behavior, for example, can be appreciably and predictably modified by the proper manipulation of cognitive and learning conditions (Mischel, 1966b), as later chapters will discuss. Although low response-response correlations are problematic for trait-state theories, they are consistent with, and expected by, social behavior theory (Chapter 6).

INTERPRETING PERSONALITY CORRELATIONS

Research on the correlates of individual differences in behavior usually has assessed differences between people on paper-and-pencil inventories and questionnaires. Individual differences on these personality tests have been correlated with responses to other paper-and-pencil tests and, much more rarely, with behavior elicited by other non-questionnaire techniques. The interpretation of the meaning of these correlations is beset with some special problems, as the following sections indicate.

Response Sets

Response sets refer to response consistencies irrespective of stimulus differences. Such "sets" have bedeviled much of the research on self-reports and ratings. One of the most studied response sets is the tendency to endorse socially desirable items.

The subject's expression of complaints and the degree to which he categorizes himself in socially undesirable terms may account for much of the variance on self-report inventories (e.g., Edwards, 1957, 1959, 1961). For example, on psychiatric inventories scores on scales depend on the respondent's willingness to endorse socially undesirable statements such as confessions about bizarre behavior, irregular bowel habits and somatic complaints, or eccentric and socially taboo thoughts. A person's scores therefore may reflect the degree to which he endorses socially desirable items rather than either autobiographical events or underlying traits. Consequently the associations found among different self-report measures may reflect commonalities due to the subject's endorsement of desirable items on diverse scales regardless of specific content. In light of these problems it can be quite misleading to interpret the correlations between inventories as evidence for covariations between the trait labels assigned to the tests.

Correlations between the rated social desirability value of items and the proportion of subjects who endorse them on personality questionnaires tend to be quite high, often exceeding .80 and sometimes even .90. Moreover, high correlations are found between the tendency to endorse socially desirable items (SD) and scores on most personality questionnaires. The correlation between SD and the Manifest Anxiety Scale, for example, was −.84 (Edwards, 1957). It is difficult to choose between the social-desirability interpretation and the characterological or trait interpretation of self-report scores on psychiatric inventories. The choice among interpretations is difficult because even an accurate self-report of problematic, idiosyncratic, or debilitating behavior invariably requires endorsing a socially undesirable item (Block, 1965).

A second widely studied response set is the tendency to either agree or disagree consistently with ambiguous statements regardless of their content. On self-report inventories, like the California *F* scale or the Minnesota Multiphasic Personality Inventory, the total scores are a direct function of the number of times the respondent agrees with or says "yes" to the items. This is because questions are worded so that agreement increases the trait score. For example, the more often the person answers "yes" on the California *F* scale the higher his "authoritarian" score will be. Hence it is difficult to distinguish the role of scale content from the effects of any tendency for subjects to say "yes" to items regardless of their content.

Agreement or acquiescence response sets refer to the tendency to agree with statements, especially ambiguous attitude statements, irrespective of their specific content. Agreement response sets may account for some of the variance on self-report and rating measures of personality dimensions, and also may contribute to the correlations obtained between these measures. Closely related response sets or styles of this type include the tendency to check extremes on rating scales, to give cautiously "doubtful" or "don't know" answers, to falsify responses, and to be consistent or inconsistent (Vernon, 1964). Numerous studies and surveys have claimed that the principal variance on self-report inventories is attributable to such response styles (e.g., Couch & Keniston, 1960; Jackson & Messick, 1958; Messick & Jackson, 1961; Wiggins, 1962).

On the *F* scale, for example, it has been argued that the tendency to answer "yes" and to acquiesce to *any* opinionated or doctrinaire generalizations about social issues, regardless of specific content, may account for as much as three-fourths of the reliable variance (Bass, 1955). Messick and Jackson (1958, 1961) likewise believe that acquiescence response sets have critical effects on inventories like the MMPI, and concluded that:

> *In the light of accumulating evidence it seems likely that the major common factors in personality inventories of the true-false or agree-disagree type, such as the MMPI and the California Psychological Inventory, are interpretable primarily in terms of style rather than specific item content.* (Jackson & Messick, 1958, p. 247.)

On the other hand, recent careful examinations of the logic and data of response-style investigations have seriously questioned the importance of agreement response sets on the *F* scale (e.g., Christie, Havel, & Seidenberg, 1958), and on all other self-report devices (Block, 1965; Norman, 1967; Rorer, 1965). These investigators note that tendencies to agree with items regardless of their content by no means account for all the systematic variance in scale scores and sometimes play a trivial role. Block (1965), for example, showed convincingly that the factor structure of the MMPI remained unchanged even when only scales balanced to eliminate the role of agreement response sets were employed.

There also have been some efforts to view individual differences in response sets as reflecting stable trait-like "stylistic" consistencies, rather than as measurement errors that require correction. In turn, these response styles have been conceptualized as trait-like properties and their personality correlates have been pursued. With some exceptions (e.g., Marlowe & Crowne, 1961), most attempts to describe the personality correlates of response styles have been based on correlations between response-style measures and other paper-and-pencil personality scales. These scales themselves are saturated with potential response-set influences. In a review of the literature McGee (1962) concluded that there is "little real defensible data to tie response styles to the criterion of independently measured behavior" (p. 293). Although agreement response sets sometimes may seriously affect answers to particular questionnaires, neither the generality of these response tendencies across measures, nor their stable correlates, has been established firmly.

Method Variance and Multitrait-Multimethod Analyses

As noted before, often the correlations among different personality inventories are very high. For example, the correlation between the

Taylor Manifest Anxiety Scale and neuroticism scores on the Maudsley Personality Inventory was .798 in one study (Spence & Spence, 1964). Correlations among such measures, however, are not necessarily evidence for associations among the traits and states whose names the tests bear. Tests are created and labeled with names designating the traits or predispositions that they are *intended* to measure, such as neuroticism, anxiety, defensiveness, anality, repression-sensitization, or ego strength. The correlations between measures by themselves cannot be interpreted as evidence for the associations between the labeled traits because diverse trait names often cover highly similar operations that require subjects to do similar things.

This overlap is most clear on paper-and-pencil inventories. Redundancy results from the fact that inventory constructors often borrow items from earlier inventories and therefore different tests may contain similar items presented in similar formats. Even within the same test the items overlap considerably among the subtests. For example, Shure and Rogers (1965) note that the basic thirteen scales of the MMPI consist of items that overlap 69 percent on the average with items on one or more other scales of the test.

Thus within particular response-eliciting techniques there are strong similarities in the stimulus conditions employed to evoke responses and in the response choices available to the subject. Although format similarity tends to be greatest among questionnaires, it also occurs within other media such as rating scales or story-completion techniques. Such similarities in the format of measuring techniques have been called method or apparatus factors by Campbell and Fiske (1959). These authors analyzed many of the correlations reported in the literature among personality measures and found that much of their common variance is attributable to similarity or overlap between the methods employed to elicit responses on them. That is, the correlations found among measures intended to tap various traits often result largely from similarities between the methods through which they were sampled (Campbell, 1960; Campbell & Fiske, 1959). For example, if three questionnaires are used to measure "dependency," the obtained correlations among them may be more attributable to the questionnaires than to the underlying trait consistency they intend to elicit.

The recognition that correlations often reflect method similarities among the measures led Campbell and Fiske to urge that the relative contributions of method as opposed to trait variance must be estimated. This can be accomplished by employing more than one method as well as more than one trait in the validation process. It is then necessary to show not only convergence between similar methods (e.g., questionnaires) intended to measure a particular trait, but also between *dissimilar* methods studying the same trait indicators. Research seeking to illuminate discrete traits or response predispositions therefore needs to study at least two hypothesized traits by at least two different methods.

When several ostensible traits are elicited by several techniques, a multitrait-multimethod matrix results. This matrix simply presents all of the intercorrelations found when each of several traits is measured by each of several different methods. The matrix then is analyzed to separate the extent to which obtained correlations reflect convergence due to common method factors, as opposed to convergence of a trait across diverse evoking conditions. These methodological cautions are now essential; supposedly different traits sampled by the same method may be as highly intercorrelated as is an ostensibly unitary, single trait when it is evoked by different methods (e.g., Campbell & Fiske, 1959; Goldberg & Werts, 1966). For example, the correlations found between supposedly discrete traits, like dependency and aggression, when both are measured by a similar method (such as questionnaires) may be of the same magnitude as the associations for a single trait, such as dependency, when it is measured by different methods (e.g., a questionnaire and behavior observations). On the basis of a review of illustrative multitrait-multimethod matrices available in the literature, Campbell and Fiske (1959) comment that the typical case shows an excessive amount of method variance, usually exceeding the amount of trait variance, and gives "a rather sorry picture of the validity of the measures of individual differences involved" (p. 93).

Discriminant Validity

Most test-validation efforts have tried to demonstrate that scores on a measure relate to scores on another measure, establishing networks of correlations among personality tests. To demonstrate that a test is measuring a new or different trait, however, one has to show that it is not mainly redundant with other widely available indices. Therefore it is important to establish the differences between any new trait measure and other sources known to account for large variance in test responses. In recent years it has become evident that many paper-and-pencil inventories are almost interchangeable in terms of the correlations they yield with external criteria. Different tests claiming to measure, for example, traits such as anxiety, self-esteem, neuroticism, ego strength, adjustment, or introversion often turn out to be more strongly related to each other than to criteria that might serve to differentiate them. Moreover, equally efficacious predictions often may be obtained from indices of intelligence, endorsement of socially undesirable items, or agreement with extreme or ambiguous statements. Thus whenever one claims to be measuring a novel trait or dimension one has to show what is *not* being measured as well as what is being measured. That is what is meant by "discriminant validation" and it (as well as positive correlations) is required to show that a test measures something new (Campbell, 1960; Campbell & Fiske, 1959). This need to demonstrate that measures are not largely redundant is especially evident when one considers the correlations between personality tests and measures of intelligence.

Correlations with Intelligence

In spite of the exceptions and qualifications noted in Chapter 2, measures of general intellectual ability, like the standard intelligence tests, yield the best available data for cross-situational consistency of behavior. Many measures that are construed as indices of personality are substantially correlated with tests of intelligence. Intelligence is correlated negatively, for example, with measures of authoritarianism and prejudice, and positively with certain cognitive styles, with honesty, with indices of impulse control, and with tests of creativity. The magnitude of these correlations is quite variable, but not infrequently it is as large as the associations between the personality test and the other external referents that serve to define it (e.g., Getzels & Jackson, 1962).

The correlations between measures of intelligence and personality indices raise the question of the degree to which the correlates of personality tests result from their common associations with intellectual abilities. For example, the obtained generality and stability, as well as the external correlates, of many cognitive-style measures may rest in part on their sizable correlations with indices of more generalized intellectual ability and achievement behavior (Crandall & Sinkeldam, 1964; Elliott, 1961; Mischel & Metzner, 1962). To illustrate, both the Witkin and Kagan measures of cognitive style are related to ability indices. The relationship between the Witkin Embedded-Figures Test and the Wechsler Intelligence Block Design subtest is so large that Witkin (1965) is willing to use Block Design scores when available as a substitute for other field-dependence measures.

In one study, the correlations between speed of finding the embedded figure in the Witkin test and Total Performance IQ and Block Designs on the Wechsler Intelligence Scale for Children (WISC) were

.55 and .51 respectively (Mischel & Metzner, 1962). Kagan likewise finds relations between his measure of analytic concepts and the Picture Arrangement WISC subtest, the associations being .58 and .55 in two samples of young children (Kagan et al., 1964). The correlations were slight, however, between analytic concepts and verbal subtests from the WISC.

Even when the effects of intelligence and age were partialed out, children's achievement behaviors, in the form of task persistence, time alone on tasks, and so on, predicted their behavior on the Witkin Embedded Figures Test. On the other hand, relations between Witkin "field dependence" and the children's actual social dependency behavior were negligible (Crandall & Sinkeldam, 1964). This suggests that Witkin's "field dependence" may have little relation to social dependency, but is related to intellectual and problem-solving persistence. Although research on cognitive styles may provide a clearer analysis of intellectual behavior, the cognitive-style responses themselves may reflect aspects of general intelligence and its correlates.

As a further illustration, tests intending to measure "creativity" sometimes have been no more closely associated with each other than with the usual indices of intelligence. Getzels and Jackson (1962) employed five procedures which they considered to be tests of creativity and administered them to large samples of school children. Yet the average correlation obtained among the creativity tests themselves was only .28, while it was almost as high (.26) between the creativity tests and IQ. Similarly, for girls the average correlation among the creativity tests themselves was .32, and it was .27 between the tests and IQ. Of course, the fact that scores on a creativity test are significantly associated with indices of intelligence does not itself necessarily undermine the creativity test and can even be taken as evidence for validity. The meaning of the creativity tests as measures of a novel trait, however, becomes obscure when the intercorrelations *among* them are no greater than the relations between them and intelligence.

In another study seven creativity tests were devised (Flescher, 1963). These tests were essentially independent of an IQ index ($r = .04$). The average of the twenty-one correlations among the seven creativity tests themselves, however, was only .11. Wallach and Kogan (1965), recognizing these shortcomings in purported creativity measures, recently developed tests of cognitive modes in a way that takes account of, and minimizes, the correlations between the new tests and standard intelligence measures. These investigators restricted their definition of creativity to the number and uniqueness of different answers or associations that children supplied to questions. For example, one test required the children to name as many things as they could that were related to a stimulus phrase like "round things," or things "that will make a noise." On another test the subjects named alternate uses for objects like a newspaper or a knife. In a third test they were asked to name all the ways in which two objects (e.g., potato and carrot) might be alike. Responses to five tests of this kind were scored for frequency and for uniqueness. The correlations for the frequency and uniqueness of responses given across these tests ranged from .07 to .74 and on the whole provided reasonable consistency evidence within the relatively narrow domain sampled. Moreover, the consistency data for these tests were not very dissimilar from the generality evidence obtained for ten indices of IQ in the same study. Most important, the associational measures of creativity were essentially unrelated to the intelligence test scores, providing the necessary evidence for discriminative validity.

Correlations between intelligence and indices of personality are not restricted to tests like cognitive styles and creativity on which some relations with IQ might be both expected and acceptable. For example, reviewing the literature on "authoritarianism," Christie (1954) estimates that the correlations between California F scale scores and either IQ or years of education range between $-.50$ and $-.60$.

Intelligence may play an especially important role in self-report inventories and other paper-and-pencil personality questionnaires that intend to assess maladaptive behavior. High scores on neuroticism and anxiety questionnaires, for example, are obtained to the extent that the subject expresses complaints and admits deviant or socially undesirable behavior. If more intelligent subjects respond more acutely and discriminatively to the aversive consequences of self-derogatory reports, they are less likely to report negatively about their own behavior. A tendency for brighter persons to express more socially appropriate responses on questionnaires may be reflected in the fact that brighter and more educated individuals tend to endorse less "authoritarian" and antidemocratic beliefs on attitude questionnaires (Brown, 1965; Christie, 1954). Similarly, Hartshorne and May (1928) found that the correlation between IQ and honesty was .344—about as high as the average consistency of honest behavior itself.

As the foregoing examples illustrate, the correlations between personality tests and intelligence tests sometimes are as high as the correlations between the personality tests and their intended criterion referents. In some cases the correlations among diverse forms of the same personality-test battery are no higher than the associations between the tests and intelligence measures. In light of such facts, Campbell and Fiske (1959) have rightly urged that investigations of all traits therefore should include correlations between the hypothesized trait and measures of intelligence. If an ostensible trait covaries largely with intelligence, and if its correlations with other indices simply reflect the shared variance due to intelligence, it adds little to invoke it as a new trait.

Trait or Construct Validation

Personality assessors guided by trait and dynamic theory usually want to infer and describe a person's traits and states from his test responses. *Construct* or *trait validation* is the effort to elaborate the inferred traits determining test behavior (Campbell, 1960). The concept of "construct validity" was introduced by trait psychologists for problems in which the assessor has:

> no definite criterion measure of the quality with which he is concerned, and must use indirect measures. Here the trait or quality underlying the test is of central importance, rather than either the test behavior or the scores on the criteria. (Technical Recommendations, 1954, p. 14.)

The fundamental characteristic of construct validation is the simultaneous validation of the test and of the trait construct. The psychometrician interested in the traits supposedly accounting for test responses must commit himself, however tentatively, to some theory about the underlying hypothesized dispositions or traits that he believes determine responses on his test. Through a variety of methods the investigator tries to establish a network of relationships intended to illuminate what is related to his category about the underlying attribute, trait, or personality disposition and what is not. Although construct validity only recently has come to the attention of psychologists as a specific validation style (Cronbach & Meehl, 1955), it is as old as the first attempts to clarify conceptually what determines test responses, and to ascertain with appropriate follow-up the soundness of the conceptualization (Bechtoldt, 1959).

Traditionally, construct validity involves the following steps, illustrated in Sarason's (1966) recent discussion of the procedure. The investigator begins with a hunch about a category dimension on which individual differences can be compared, for example "submissiveness." He might regard submissiveness as a "tendency to yield to the will and suggestions of others" (Sarason, 1966, p. 127), and to study this tendency he devises a measure of submissiveness. He has no one definite criterion, however, and instead may use diverse behavioral samples as indices of the subject's underlying trait of submissiveness. He then proceeds to generate and test hypotheses about how submissiveness, manifested on his tests, does and does not relate to other behaviors in particular situations, revising his construct on the basis of his findings.

As this example illustrates, construct validation is similar to the usual procedure of testing and revising hypotheses about relations by examining the empirical associations among responses evoked in situations. Construct validation is primarily distinguished from other strategies on the grounds that in construct validity the investigator's construct is not fully *equivalent* to any *one* behavioral measure or criterion. Indeed, the investigator may not be sure about the particular criteria that are most appropriate for the construct. For example:

> *The word construct (validity) is used rather than either predictive or concurrent (validity) because there is no one criterion of submissiveness. . . . Submissiveness . . . permeates a great many activities.* (Sarason, 1966, p. 127.)

A distinguishing feature of constructs, whether they are personal or theoretical, and whether they are expressed by the client or by the clinician, is that they have multiple referents. A researcher interested in the category of "attitudes," for example, usually means more than check marks on a particular inventory, just as a client talking about "inferiority" means more than the particular example of it that he cites at any one moment. The same applies to most trait terms: they have multiple meanings rather than single referents. In this sense adequate referents for a category or construct may require many behavior samples and may never be complete. "Anxiety" for example, can be said to be more than self-reports, or GSR measures, or sampled behavior under conditions designed to induce stress, and so on; instead it refers to all these and many more. Any one measurement (or even many of them) does not exhaust all possible referents for a category and that is true also in fields other than personality. In research on "memory," for example, the investigator likewise has many possible ways of measuring the phenomena of interest. Neither "recall" nor "recognition" nor numerous other techniques are entirely equivalent to "memory." Thus the fact that no single criterion can be found for personality constructs is not a unique situation and entails no special procedures. Construct validation is simply hypothesis testing and theory building with imperfect and incomplete operations for the investigator's categories.

The fact that any category or construct can have multiple behavioral referents, and that these change as a function of the stimulus conditions in which they are evoked, has led to some confusion. Two main problems are selecting the behavorial *referents* for the construct and attributing a *causal* role to the construct.

As long as a construct is viewed as so complex that no referents can be found for it the construct remains unstudiable. In the area of personality it is often argued that adequate criteria or behavorial referents for the most important constructs are not available. In all fields, however, criteria are never revealed automatically by nature and always must be devised by the researcher. To accomplish this, the researcher must *define* his category and *specify* observable behaviors that serve as referents for his definition. The utility of a construct cannot be assessed until its behavioral referents are publicly specified, albeit tentatively. These public referents for a construct are supplied by the person who uses it—only people can supply definitions; nature consists of events, not of abstractions, and does not provide scientists with categories. Rather, the scientist selects and defines his categories and tests their usefulness by determining their consequences for understanding, controlling, and modifying events in nature.

This point was made vividly at a symposium when George Kelly (1958) noted that we often erroneously look for the meaning of words in their objects of reference rather than in their subjects of origin. For example, if a teacher complains that a child is "lazy," or poorly motivated, or anxious, the assessor may turn automatically to the child to determine whether or not the teacher was right. He thus may try to check the construct (e.g., lazy) against the child's behavior before he knows what the construct is. "We hear a word and look to what is talked about rather than listen to the person who utters it." (Kelly, 1958, p. 40.) He elaborates his point this way:

> *According to this dogmatism, when I say that Professor Lindzey's left shoe is an "introvert," everyone looks at his shoe as if this were something his shoe was responsible for. Or if I say that Professor Cattell's head is "discursive," everyone looks over at him, as if the proposition had popped out of his head instead of out of mine. Don't look at his head! Don't look at that shoe! Look at me; I'm the one who is responsible for the statement. After you figure out what I mean you can look over there to see if you make any sense out of shoes and heads by construing them the way I do. It will not be easy to do this, for it means abandoning one of the most ancient ways of thinking and talking to ourselves.*

As the foregoing quotation suggests, the utility of a construct can be assessed only after its referents are defined; otherwise one searches the world for evidence to answer a question without knowing the question. On the other hand, as is most evident when statements deal with the physical properties of an event (the shoe is black, the shoe is moving) it is also necessary to look at the event and to consider the shoe as well as the speaker.

Limited referents for a construct restrict its scope. For example, a definition of ego strength exclusively equivalent to voluntary delay behavior in specific conditions obviously is very narrow. Multiple referents for a construct broaden its meaning or range, as when ego strength is defined to encompass particular patterns of voluntary delay, self-reward, and reactions to transgression.

Categories are abstractions that sometimes are treated as if they were realities, as is evident from disputes about what a particular sequence of behavior "really is." Often these disputes involve no more than a semantic quarrel, as every clinician and researcher has witnessed. Much time is spent in both research meetings and case conferences discussing, for example, whether a particular behavior is *really* a sign of anxiety, or of guilt, or of shame, or of hostility, or of repressed dependency. Likewise, the research literature abounds with controversies whose crux is a definitional dispute about the "real meaning" of terms like identification, incorporation, internalization, or imitation. Sometimes the protagonists seem to forget that they are merely matching observations of behavior with their own constructed definitions about the behavior category. This process permits judgments about how well observations fit particular categories or definitions, but a "true" glimpse of "real" aggressive, hostile, healthy, or whatever behavior is never revealed. Behavior simply occurs, oblivious to the constructions and definitions placed upon it by observers, except insofar as these constructions themselves lead to behavioral consequences. The question of "what is mental health," for example, can be answered with any number of definitions, illustrating again that such categories involve abstractions from particular viewpoints for particular purposes, rather than absolute revelations of realities (e.g., Scott, 1958).

Hazards in the Misuse of Personality Constructs

It is perfectly appropriate to infer the characteristics of an organism and the underlying mechanisms that mediate between observable stimulus inputs and the responses to which they lead. Indeed, this is a basic technique for attempting genotypic explanations. Investigators may invent abstractions freely, but their usefulness should be demonstrated. In spite of the many strong reminders that constructs about inner traits and states are in the theoretician's head and not inside the person he describes (e.g., Kelly, 1955), assessors sometimes employ speculative constructs as if they were demonstrated causes, rather than abstractions whose value has to be proved.

Few psychologists would be misled into believing that high scores on a color-sorting task are explained adequately by the statement, "He did well because of his excellent color-sorting ability." But more esoteric versions of the same error persist, and mere abstractions, like the personality, the self, the ego, the self-image, are turned into living things that exist in persons or even possess them and become independent of the behavioral consistencies that supposedly justify their having been postulated in the first place. Constructs continue to be animated and vitalized in spite of repeated admonitions against turning them into quasi-explanatory ghosts and fictions which soon come to pursue autonomous lives of their own.

Sometimes mental traits and states are invoked as if they were the causes of behavior while their own antecedents are ignored or forgotten. Unfinished causal sequences are found whenever mental states (cognitions, affects, motives, etc.) are employed as explanations of behavior while the determinants of the mental states themselves are omitted from the anaylsis. Skinner (1964, p. 93) calls this the use of "mental way stations" for unfinished causal sequences and comments:

> *A disturbance in behavior is not explained by relating it to felt anxiety until the anxiety has in turn been explained. An action is not explained by attributing it to expectations until the expectations have in turn been accounted for.*

Clearly, an adequate analysis must encompass the *variables* that control the behavior of interest and not merely the hypothetical stops along the route.

Trait and state validation research tends to dwell on response-response associations; the resulting correlations help to clarify the patterns of behavior that "go together" beyond chance, thereby illuminating the organization of response systems. However, the causal or controlling factors that determine the obtained correlations of course remain uncertain. Correlations among response patterns do not reveal their controlling conditions; the latter can be clarified through experimental investigations, as later chapters discuss.

The fact that correlations among measures by themselves provide no evidence for the causes of their association is too obvious to require much comment. A droll illustration should suffice. An anonymous report (cited in Webb et al., 1966, pp. 116-117) found a strong correlation between the methodological disposition of psychologists and the length of their hair. The investigators observed the hair length of psychologists attending professional meetings and they also coded the methodological orientation of the meetings. For example, the length of hair was compared between those who attended a series of experimental papers and those who attended a set of papers on ego-identity formation. The results clearly showed that the "tough-minded" psychologists have shorter hair than those who attended the more "tender" meetings. As Webb and his associates (1966, p. 117) commented:

> *Symptomatic interpretations, psychoanalytic inquiries as to what is cut about the clean-cut young man, are not the only possibilities. The causal ambiguity of the correlation was clarified when the "dehydration hypothesis" (i.e., that lack of insulation caused the hardheadedness) was rejected by the "baldhead control," i.e., examining the distribution of baldheaded persons (who by the dehydration hypothesis should be most hardheaded of all).*

To illustrate some of the interpretative hazards just discussed, a typical correlational study of "ego strength" will be considered at length. In this study (Shippee-Blum, 1959), high school students were divided into three groups on the basis of their citizenship course grades, teachers' rankings, and presence or absence on the dean's blacklist. The blacklist contained the names and offenses of students who had not responded to disciplinary measures from the teachers and who displayed the most serious disciplinary problems. Those with combined antisocial scores on all three measures in the highest third of the distribution were classified as "rebels," whereas children with zero scores were called "cooperators."

All subjects then answered a questionnaire designed to "measure ego-strength as a function of the individual's capacity to bind tensions, i.e., to control impulse gratification." The items involved statements such as "I sometimes open presents before I'm supposed to," "I am always calm and cool," and "I lose my temper easily." In addition, to assess "self-regarding attitudes and ego-ideal formation," the children checked a list of adjectives whose positive or negative value implications had been established by pretesting. The adjectives were words like well-dressed, confident, thoughtful, timid, and good-natured. Each subject checked the list under three conditions, respectively marking true the adjectives that described him, then those that described his father, and finally those that described his mother. The "ego-ideal" was defined as the ratio between the child's esteem for his parents and his own self-esteem. Weak ego-ideal was defined operationally as a ratio of fewer favorable adjectives applied to the parents than to oneself. Either the reverse, or an equal ratio of positive adjectives applied to parents and self, constituted a strong ego-ideal. These procedures were introduced with psychodynamic theorizing, for example:

> *Ego-strength refers to the ability to withstand tension without resorting to various defense mechanisms such as distortion, repression, displacement, uninhibited attack or flight. Such an ego should be able to make use of and enjoy opportunities maximally without undue anxiety, guilt, avoidance, etc.* (p. 44.)

Note that the ego is endowed with relative independence and has its own experiences. Moreover:

> *In this study the major hypothesis of decreased ego-strength in the rebellious adolescent was tested by comparing the tension-binding-capacity of a group of rebellious adolescents to an equated group of cooperative adolescents.* (p. 45.)

This statement implies that the answers to the questionnaire tap the respondent's "tension-binding capacity," for which there is no evidence.

> *Such a frustration tolerance requires a strong ego. Consequently, a person lacking the prerequisite ego-strength, as exemplified by the rebellious adolescents, will show low frustration tolerance. Low frustration tolerance may manifest itself in various ways; for instance, in a narcissistic orientation toward the self.* (p. 45.)

The respondent's favorable self-ratings thus become a sign of "narcissistic orientation to the self." Further:

> *But the ego of the rebellious adolescent is weak and cannot tolerate tension. The rebel is impulsive. His impulsiveness demonstrates his ego weakness. If his ego is too weak to bind tensions it should also be too weak to allow the internalization of parental demands which constitute the growth of the super-*

> *ego. . . . Thus it can be expected that the superego formation of rebels is defective. That is the hypothesis tested here.* (p. 46.)

Relatively less favorable ratings of the parents are thus interpreted as a sign of defective superego formation.

The actual findings revealed significant associations between membership in the rated antisocial-behavior category "rebels" and questionnaire scores. Children who had been rated as having severe disciplinary problems and who obtained poor citizenship grades also more frequently described themselves as less "calm and cool," more likely to lose their temper, and so on.

In addition, the "rebels" checked more positive adjectives in their self-descriptions than did the cooperators. This result is interpreted as support for the hypothesis that "unrealistic" self-esteem as defined by extreme scores on a self-esteem measure is a function of "rebelliousness" (p. 49). This interpretation may create the erroneous impression that "rebelliousness" caused the more antisocial children to rate themselves less modestly than the "cooperators." The remaining empirical finding is introduced with the statement:

> *A weakened ego-ideal in the rebel was predicted from the hypothesis of impaired ego-strength underlying asocial behavior and the consequent defective superego functioning.* (p. 49.)

The data, however, only showed that fewer of the "cooperators" compared to the "rebels" tended to rate their parents more unfavorably than themselves. The author acknowledged the possibility that the parents of the "rebels" actually might be less pleasant and that the children might simply have been correct in their evaluations. There is, however, a more parsimonious interpretation: the "cooperators" may have achieved their prosocial label in the first place in part because they may be more likely to say nice, socially appropriate things to and about adults, including their teachers and their parents. Conversely, poor citizenship grades and teacher's ratings, as well as presence on the dean's blacklist, are more likely outcomes for children who do not say nice things about adults. The discussion continues:

> *The psychoanalytic construct "impaired ego-strength" presented itself as a convenient unifying principle, whch allowed us to order divergent behavior manifestations into one system. The positive findings of this study substantiated psychoanalytical theory at several levels of abstraction. By extrapolating from*

the data, the primary explanatory principle was confirmed to the extent that the study affirmed the lower order hypotheses derived from the construct "impaired ego-strength." (p. 49.)

The paper concludes with the statement:

The results supported the psychoanalytic thesis of ego-weakness in the rebel. Implications for further research were discussed. (p. 50.)

These statements may create the impression that the findings support the conceptual framework. In fact, the study indicates only that "rebels" rated themselves less modestly than "cooperators," and also tended to rate their parents less favorably in relation to themselves than did the "cooperators." The point is not that studies of this kind are vulnerable; the author meticulously specified the operations. There is nothing wrong, for example, in calling favorable self-ratings "a narcissistic orientation to the self" and less favorable ratings of parents than of self "a defective superego." It is the reader who may be vulnerable, to the extent that he misses the gap between the constructs and their operations. Perhaps the most difficult and critical task for the student is to discriminate clearly between the investigator's theoretical statements and his operations and data. Otherwise the same data used one day as evidence for the construct validity of "ego strength," "ego-ideal," and so on, may soon become the evidence for "social approval motives," "conformity," "affiliation," "acquiescence," "social desirability," "response sets," or other constructions favored by the particular investigator. In this manner correlational networks keep being relabeled with little gain in cumulative knowledge.

Of course theory serves to guide the investigator and helps him to ask questions and to select operations. The utility, however, of construing or interpreting behavior with a particular category, or with a set of related categories in a theory, is assessed by the empirical relationships that are illuminated. Usually the utility of a category is best seen from external validity data and by the efficacy of the constructs for producing behavioral control and modification.

Construct Validity and Construct Utility

Much has been written about systematic validity research (e.g., Campbell, 1960; Campbell & Fiske, 1959; Cronbach & Meehl, 1955), and some research programs have carefully investigated particular theoretical constructs, like anxiety (e.g., Spence & Spence, 1964), conditionability (Eysenck, 1965), extraversion-introversion (Eysenck, 1956), or achievement motivation (Atkinson & Feather, 1966). The results usually provide some evidence for the research value of the construct. These construct validity studies often have theoretical interest, and may lead to intriguing controversies of interpretation. For example, correlations between personality measures and performance in the eyeblink conditioning situation have been interpreted as due largely to the relation between extraversion and conditionability by some researchers (e.g., Eysenck, 1956, 1965); other researchers have interpreted the same correlations as mediated by the subject's drive level, inferred from Manifest Anxiety Test scores (e.g., Spence & Spence, 1964). Definitive interpretations are complicated by the fact that generally the intercorrelations among variables depend on numerous other moderating considerations, such as the sex of the subjects and of the experimenters, their status and age, and a host of specific factors in the particular experimental situation (e.g., Sarason, 1966). Moreover, impressive external correlates usually are not found since behaviors subsumed under terms like anxiety or conditionability tend to be specific, depend on the particular stimuli in the situation, and do not constitute highly generalized behavioral syndromes. Instead the associations tend to be unstable, generally low, and usually occur only with large samples preselected for extreme scores on the personality scales. Most important, the personality measures in most cases are questionnaires which are often as strongly correlated with each other as with the new construct indices. As a result the data, although often interesting, have little relevance for facilitating assessments, for generating individual predictions, or for designing treatments.

The results of construct-validation research should provide evidence for the *utility* of categorizing behavior in accord with the particular construct. The evidence about a construct—either a personal or a theoretical construct—may best be evaluated with respect to the *consequences* produced by categorizing behavior with the construct, by showing what one can *do* with the construct, and not by trying to establish the absolute truth value of the category itself. A key test for any construct is its range of convenience—what the user can say and do with the construct and the empirical consequences it yields. It may be more meaningful to talk about the utility of both constructs and tests than about their validity. The utility of a trait-state construct can be assessed by the degree to which the obtained correlations facilitate the predictions and decisions faced by the assessor, therapist, and researcher, as discussed in the next chapter.

100

SUMMARY

A behavior sample cannot be interpreted as an index of unobserved behavior unless the links between the sample and what it represents are demonstrated. It is least hazardous to use test data as self-contained samples defined by the operations used to obtain them. Correlational personality research, however, has sought to establish the validity of response samples as signs of personality. A test (or any other behavior sample) may not measure anything beyond itself. A plausible content relationship between test items and the domain they are supposed to represent does not guarantee the stability of a measure, nor does it demonstrate any relations between test responses and hypothesized underlying states or traits. Criterion validity assesses the relationship between the obtained sample and other criterion data, either concurrently or predictively. Construct validation tries to elaborate the inferred traits determining test behavior. The strategies and problems involved in these tactics were discussed in detail.

The results of research on the correlates of individual differences provide a great many overlapping networks of relations among variables. These associations tend to be of high magnitude chiefly when behaviors are measured by redundant methods, such as questionnaires whose formats and content are similar. On the other hand, when diverse behaviors are sampled by different measures, the association, although often beyond chance, generally tends at best to be of very modest strength. The interpretation of personality correlations was shown to involve special problems, particularly when these associations are based on questionnaires. The issues discussed included response sets, method variance, discriminant validity, correlations between personality measures and indices of intelligence, and the use of multitrait-multimethod matrices.

The value of the investigator's construct lies in its demonstrable utility, established through empirical relations between observables. The relationships obtained by correlational personality research are large enough to demonstrate that personality is not capricious. However, while people may construe themselves and each other as characterized by consistent dispositions their behavior across settings is far from homogeneous. The results reviewed suggest that personality organization is much more subtle than broad unitary trait theories of personality would indicate. The next chapter explores the empirical utility of both trait and psychodynamic constructs.

$/5$

UTILITY

As discussed in the last chapter, validity can be demonstrated by the degree to which statements converge with information obtained from other independent, concurrently available data sources, or from criterion events observed at a later time. If a test (or any other response sample) provides a reliable statement that corresponds reasonably with descriptions from other data sources, the question then becomes: what is the value of the statement?

Statistically significant outcomes indicate that a difference between groups or a relationship among measures has occurred, and that it probably is not attributable to chance. Reliance on statistical significance is misleading, however, when interpreting the utility of a procedure. Attainment of a beyond-chance prediction in itself tells us nothing about the relative value of the predictor data, nor about the increment provided over other less costly possible predictors.

There is no point in employing a lengthy, expensive personality test or inference process to generate descriptions or predictions that are readily available from cheaper concurrent sources. It would not be useful, for example, to demonstrate that clinicians can accurately describe a person's sex, occupation, or marital status on the basis of his Rorschach protocol. Test-derived statements also are trivial if they merely correspond to routinely available data. Thus if a clinic regularly obtains behavior ratings from clinical personnel, test-derived inferences that match these ratings add little. This conclusion would not be true to the degree that the test-derived descriptions can be obtained more economically or can be shown to be more accurate or comprehensive. Similarly, the costs of test-based descriptions might be justified if they provided nonobvious statements much more rapidly than alternate, routinely available sources. Test-derived personality descriptions are valuable to the extent that they provide significant increments in valid information over other less readily available or less economical sources. That is what is meant by "incremental validity."

It is hard to separate the validity of a test from the validity of the personality construct it supposedly measures (Cronbach & Meehl, 1955). The utility of statements about unconscious motives, defenses, conflicts, and other constructs of psychodynamic theory, for example, depends on the value of the predictions and treatment decisions to which they lead in the individual case. The utility of the results reflects both on the theoretical constructs and on the test procedures from which these results are generated. Some of the issues and the evidence relevant to the value of personality tests and trait-state constructs are considered in detail in this chapter.

AN ILLUSTRATIVE PSYCHODYNAMIC ASSESSMENT

Before looking at the research evidence it may be helpful to examine a report that illustrates fairly representatively the type of clinical interpretations made in individual assessments. This report provides a concrete instance of many of the issues discussed more abstractly throughout the rest of the chapter. The client was a male veteran, thirty-six years of age. The report is based on a psychodynamic interpretation of his Rorschach and TAT protocols, his answers to a sentence-completion test, and the basic "face sheet" or intake information about the client (Rogers, 1955).

> *Test results emphasize a basically characterological problem with currently hysteroid defenses. Impairment of his ability to make adequate use of independent and creative fantasy, associated with emotional lability and naivete, are characteristic of him. He has difficulty in repressing his unacceptable feelings and wishes, and is in the unfortunate position of being unable to make adequate use of fantasy as an alternate control. In fact, it appears that the very attempt to use fantasy typically results in preliminary success followed often by hopelessly inadequate endings that seem not to reduce, but to increase his anxiety.*
>
> *Anxiety is easily evoked and seems to be primarily related to problems arising from his difficulty in developing close interpersonal relationships. Due to a markedly passive-aggressive*

character make-up, in which the infantile dependency needs are continually warring with his hostile tendencies, it is not difficult to understand his current conflict over sexual expression. Sexually, he is probably basically passive, and yet may be as demanding of his sexual partner as he is in other types of relationships. It is apparent that such behavior, which in this patient is likely to be marked, would lead to difficulties with, and probable rejection by, any long-term sexual partner. There is a strong element of fearfulness in his conception of sex.

It is possible that much of his difficulty is historically connected with his early relationships and identifications with his parents. Although the father is perceived as a satisfying figure, there are many indications that his relationship with an apparently aggressive, demanding and dominating mother was most difficult for him. His current relations with his wife do not appear to represent an improvement from the earlier ones with his mother. Any failure on her part to give in to his demands probably leads to hostile feelings on his part—hostile feelings that he finds most difficult to express for the fear of loss of love. In general, his attitude toward women as a whole is a hostile one. His relationships with them have probably never been satisfying to him.

Feelings of inadequacy are coupled with strong status needs and with many indications of self-doubt and deprecation. Some increase in self-esteem is sought through fantasy, often frankly sexual in nature. No matter how satisfying the beginning, however, conflict and guilt often prevent a satisfactory consummation of the fantasied situation. No evidence of paranoid thinking was found. (From Lawrence Rogers, in Burton & Harris, 1955, pp. 167–168.)

This case report illustrates some of the main features of traditional clinical assessment. Note, for example, the focus on inferences about hypothesized underlying characterological states; the implicit assumption that these underlying processes exert fairly pervasive, generalized effects on behavior and particularly on feelings; the relatively global, undifferentiated statements about his behavior; the psychodynamic emphasis on sexual and aggressive impulses and defenses for coping with them; and the attempt to link current sexual and aggressive problems to relations with the parents, especially the mother, in early life.

The confidence that one can reasonably have in reports of this kind depends on the supporting evidence provided by research on clinical judgment and on the techniques upon which the clinician relies in generating his inferences. In addition, one must evaluate the utility of each individual assessment and this can be accomplished by attending to several criteria, as discussed in the following sections.

INCREMENTAL VALIDITY

Increments over Base Rates and Clinical Stereotypes

The incremental validity of every bit of assessment information depends on the degree to which it adds to information available from the *base rates* for the appropriate population. For example, if 95 percent of the in-patients of a particular hospital are diagnosed "schizophrenic," a test-derived statement that predicts this label correctly 80 percent of the time is less useful than automatically calling every patient in the hospital schizophrenic. The same considerations apply when the base rates for a variable are extremely low in the relevant population. Meehl (1956), for example, comments on the futility of scoring MMPI keys, or content on the Rorschach, to predict suicide in an out-patient clinic in which 5000 patients were treated during an eight-year period and not one committed suicide. Although correct predictions generated from tests or clinical inference might be impressive in some contexts, they may be a waste of time when population base rates are extremely high or low (Meehl & Rosen, 1955). A test that yields descriptions or predictions which are supported far more often than chance may still generate less useful statements than those available from base rates alone. Tests are least likely to improve base-rate statements when the behavior that is being described or predicted is extremely frequent or infrequent in the population.

Personality descriptions or predictions that can be applied to virtually all people in a given population have little discriminative value and are merely elaborations of base rates. Little is gained and much time may be wasted if, for example, a hospitalized psychiatric patient is described as having troubled interpersonal relations, problems with his self-concept, and sexual difficulties. Nor is it enlightening to learn that an adolescent boy is "unsure about his masculine role." Such stereotyped descriptions of highly common conditions can create the illusion that something is being said, whereas in actuality they do not discriminate between any persons within the given population and hence they illuminate nothing unique.

106

Increments over Simple Self-ratings and Self-predictions

The utility of an assessment procedure also should be evaluated against simple self-ratings. Mischel (1965) related self-reports by Peace Corps volunteers during their training in the United States to their later performance as teachers in Nigeria. The volunteers' self-reports on the *F* scale and other direct questionnaires significantly correlated with later ratings by supervisors of their behavior in Nigeria. Correlations ranged from .34 to .45 and were unsurpassed by such more expensive predictors as staff ratings and interviews. Costly personality inferences, based on interviews (*r* = .13) and on pooled assessment board ratings (*r* = .20), did not even reach statistical significance (Mischel, 1965). The correlations with self-reports, if replicated, would have considerable value for screening decisions based on extreme scores. Similarly, Marks, Stauffacher, and Lyle (1963), in a study attempting to predict outcomes for schizophrenic patients on the MMPI, found that simple self-report attitude scales, like the California *F* scale, yielded better predictions than "factorially pure scales" (p. 126).

Peterson (1965) pressed the point for simplicity of self-report data even further. He found that two simple and direct self-ratings, one on "adjustment" and one on "introversion-extraversion," each on a seven-point rating scale, may be as useful as time-consuming second-order factor scores calculated from Cattell's 16 P-F test and from cumbersome personality-rating schedules. The mean correlations of the two self-ratings of adjustment and introversion-extraversion respectively with the comparable second-order factors from the 16 P-F were .56 and .66. In addition, the simple self-ratings showed appreciable temporal reliability over a five-week span and better discriminant validity than data from factor analyses.

In another study a simple fifteen-item checklist of activity preferences was developed to discriminate empirically between high school students with high and low school accomplishments (Holland & Nichols, 1964). In cross-validation studies this scale yielded correlations with criterion measures of college achievements that ranged from .19 to .64 (with an average *r* of .37). Multiple-regression formulas also were established dealing with numerous personality test scores (e.g., Super Ego Scale, Independence of Judgment, Aspirations and Goals) after comprehensive screening of more than 200 potentially useful inferred personality variables. The resulting cross-validated multiple correlations with the criterion ranged from .12 to .44 and averaged .31, providing poorer predictions than those from the simple checklist.

Four traits were studied with five methods in a sophisticated multitrait-multimethod design (Wallace & Sechrest, 1963). The traits selected were hostility, somatic concerns, achievement concerns, and religious concerns; the methods for measuring these areas included self-reports (in the form of self-descriptions), reputation ratings by peers, projective techniques (incomplete sentences, Rorschach, and TAT), and behavioral indices such as scholastic average and number of visits to health services. The results showed that the convergent and discriminant validity of self-descriptions were not exceeded by any other source; self-descriptions and peer reputations provided consistently better correlations than any other combination of methods.

A great deal of effort has been expended to try to improve the techniques of scale construction in the hope of increasing the predictive efficacy of tests. A careful study (Hase & Goldberg, 1967) used a common item pool (from Gough's 1957 California Psychological Inventory) for all scales and then compared different scale-construction strategies that drew from this pool. Specifically, they compared the relative validity of personality-inventory scales developed by each of six main strategies of item selection. These strategies of test construction included the factor-analytic as well as empirical and theoretical psychometric techniques. The results indicated that the particular scale-construction strategy made little difference. The authors concluded that:

> *procedures of item grouping are probably* not *a cause of the relatively low coefficients typically reported in the psychometric literature, and therefore the guilty culprit might well be the inventory items themselves . . . .* (p. 243.)

The results also clearly showed that the individuals' own simple self-ratings were the best predictors of how their peers rated them. The self-ratings exceeded the predictions generated by *any* of the scales, including the best regression equations based on the best scale combinations. In sum, often the simplest, gross self-ratings relate to external criteria at the same level as, and often better than, more sophisticated complex psychometric tests designed to infer underlying personality.

If the assumption that dynamic-motivational factors make people unable or unwilling to predict their own behavior accurately is suspended, it becomes reasonable to ask the person directly how he will behave. Lindzey and Tejessy (1956) scored the TAT stories of college students for ten "signs" of aggression—aggressive turns in themes, death from external sources, avoidance of the gun on card 3BM, etc. These signs were correlated with the following criterion measures of aggression: diagnostic council ratings based on situational tests and extended observation, interview and autobiography, scores on Rosenzweig's Pic-true-Frustration Study (P-F), and self-ratings of aggressiveness by the subject himself. None of the ten TAT signs of aggression was cor-related significantly with diagnostic council ratings; one TAT sign cor-related significantly with observer ratings, three with P-F extrapunitive scores, and three with P-F intrapunitive scores. In contrast, the sub-jects' own self-ratings were significantly associated with seven of the ten signs of aggression. The data suggest that "signs" reflect information about the subject which could be obtained more directly by simply ask-ing him.

Self-predictions have fared relatively well in many contexts—for example, the prediction of hypnotizability. Self-predictions of hypnotiz-ability were no less accurate than indirect measures, although the pre-dictive accuracy of all measures was modest (Melei & Hilgard, 1964). Likewise, exploratory research on a Peace Corps group suggested that volunteers were able to predict whether or not they would be rejected at the end of training better than indirect inventories, interviews, and projective tests (Mischel, 1965).

In another context, the directly expressed interests of college sopho-mores in 1939 predicted their actual occupations in 1953 at least as well as, and sometimes better than, their 1939 scores on the Strong Voca-tional Interest Blank (McArthur & Stevens, 1955). Similarly, occupa-tional predictions based on the announced vocational choices of college freshmen would have been better than those from the psychometrically sophisticated Strong test (DuBois & Watson, 1950).

Lasky and his associates (1959) asked open-ward psychiatric patients to predict their own behavior and the behavior of the other patients on their ward. In this study patients generally were unable to predict accurately their own future long-term adjustment. One hindrance may have been the possibility that patients distorted their self-predictions in the hope that more favorable predictions would influence the staff's decisions about their actual fate. Of considerable interest, however, is the fact that the psychiatric patients were able to predict the behavior of other patients as accurately as did the professional psychiatric staff. Patients predicted the future rehospitalization as well as the work, fam-ily, and health adjustment of other patients with an average accuracy of 70 percent. The staff members predicted with exactly the same average accuracy.

The relative utility of the self-prediction of college grades was investigated by Mischel and Bentler (1965). The results of two studies showed that college students can predict their own course grades as well ($r = .62$) as the best available predictor (previous grade average,

$r = .63$). Moreover, even when students were led to believe that their self-predictions would be seen by their instructor, the accuracy of their self-estimates remained unaffected. The results demonstrated that at least under some circumstances persons can predict their own outcomes on a complex criterion with reasonable accuracy. Direct self-predictions of grades in these studies compared favorably with predictions obtained from achievement, aptitude, and personality measures in other research (e.g., French, 1963). The success of self-predictions seems especially noteworthy in view of the relative unreliability of the criterion measures and the fact that final course grades were based on a composite of performance measures (e.g., essays, objective tests) which were far from perfectly intercorrelated and some of which were scored with considerable subjectivity. Recent research to predict achievement and affiliation behaviors also shows that self-reports can do as well as projective tests (Sherwood, 1966).

Assessors might seriously consider arranging conditions so that subjects can report honestly about their expectancies without incurring negative consequences. The assessors then could investigate the utility of the subject's own predictions. These predictions might be especially useful if they require the subject to anticipate his own behavior, to say what he does and will do, rather than to interpret his own traits and to judge what he is like.

Increments from Projective Data

Perhaps no search for important information about personality has been as extensive as the one conducted for more than two decades by means of projective tests. Hundreds of studies exist on the predictive, concurrent, and, to a lesser extent, construct validity of major projective techniques. The literature has become so voluminous that it defies comprehensive review even in books devoted to that purpose (e.g., Murstein, 1963; Zubin, Eron, & Schumer, 1965). Psychodynamic theories rest on the belief that personality is revealed by highly indirect behavioral signs—that reactions to inkblots, or free associations, or seemingly casual expressions provide key clues revealing core features of the individual's psyche. Consequently, evidence for the value of indirect signs of personality is essential to justify this widespread assumption.

All the conditions that lead to descriptive inaccuracy in responses to psychometric inventories are deliberately maximized in the elicitation of projective data. The structure of the eliciting situation in projective testing is ambiguous because, in accord with psychodynamic theory, it has been widely assumed that under ambiguous conditions the subject's responses will reveal, at least in part, his unconscious processes and his core personality. As MacFarlane and Tuddenham (1951) point out, projectivists usually assume that because the projective test "offers the subject wide latitude to reveal himself, the particular sample of responses supplied by the protocol mirrors the subject's basic personality organization." (MacFarlane & Tuddenham, p. 34.) This view is similar to the psychoanalytic belief that basic and enduring personality structure is revealed by all behavioral manifestations, especially in minimally structured situations because unconscious material can then slip through the defenses more readily.

Projective tests merely confront the subject with an ambiguous situation with little structure; whatever sense is made out of the resulting data depends on the interpreter. Projective tests are far from the "X-ray technique" that early enthusiasts thought they paralleled. The projective situation elicits a profusion of verbal responses; the tasks of bringing order into the data, of quantifying and categorizing them, and of inferring the variables suggested by the theory remain the assessor's.

In the personality ratings obtained from psychometric tests the respondent must judge subjectively the meaning of each test statement and then indicate how the description applies to him (or to the person he is rating). On projective tests this interpretative subjectivity is doubly compounded. Not only must the respondent interpret an ambiguous set of stimuli, but also the scorer or test interpreter must intepret an ambiguous set of resulting responses. Although scoring and categorizing of responses on psychometric tests is objective and straightforward, it is highly interpretative with projective data and depends on the clinician's categories.

The inference process for relating observables to unconscious meanings and dynamics is largely intuitive with few if any explicit relational rules provided by psychodynamic theory. Moreover, the constructs themselves frequently are ambiguous and difficult to specify operationally. The psychoanalytically oriented assessor therefore is extremely dependent on his own intuitions and clinical inferences, although the reliability and utility of his interpretations of course can be assessed objectively.

The overall results from validity research on the major projective techniques suggest that low but statistically significant correlations often are found between various test patterns and other responses serving as criteria. These associations are difficult to interpret because the studies often have been marred by methodological problems. Among the difficulties are uncontrolled variations in protocol length and response frequency, inappropriate subject samples, inadequate control groups, poor external criteria, interpretations facilitated by test-irrelevant responses, and spurious impressions of convergence between judgments based largely on stereotypes shared by the raters. These and other flaws have been documented elaborately (e.g., Cronbach, 1949; Vernon, 1964; Zubin, Eron, & Schumer, 1965), and a few illustrations suffice here.

For example, even when obvious identifying data are removed from the protocol, the subject's vocabulary and other test content may provide test-irrelevant clues about his occupation, education, ideational bizarreness, interests, achievements, and so forth. Such information affects the judge's interpretations, but reveals nothing about the singular powers of the test itself as a personality measure. Likewise, the homogeneity of subjects in the sample and their similarity to the control groups affect the difficulty of generating statements that discriminate among them. For instance, it would not be impressive to demonstrate that judges can reliably discriminate the Rorschach protocols of ten college students from those of ten acutely disorganized and hospitalized schizophrenics. Similarly, clues like the number of responses in the protocol may be correlated with the respondent's intelligence or verbal fluency and serve as a basis for prediction apart from the content of the responses or other protocol features on which the interpretation ostensibly hinges.

Even if the methodological inadequacies that spuriously inflate correlations and the failures to replicate were to be completely ignored, the obtained relationships still are generally so low that they have little appreciable utility for individual assessment decisions or for the design of individual treatments. At best, when the correlation coefficients do reach statistical significance, they tend to be in the .20 to .40 range, or lower, accounting for only a small fraction of the criterion variance.

To illustrate, the conclusions from an extensive Rorschach validation study still fit the facts from hundreds of studies conducted since then:

> *The ordering of relationships between the Rorschach variables and the criteria is not dissimilar from chance expectation. Further, not only are most of the relationships of zero order, but the only ones in which this is not the case involve intelligence, which can be approached more efficiently by other instruments.* (Eschenbach & Borgatta, 1955, p. 272).

112

In general, predictions based on personality inferences from projective data tend to be less accurate than those more easily available from cheaper and simpler data. Attempts to combine personality inferences from projective data with objective test scores usually reduce predictive efficiency, as later sections show.

Psychodynamically oriented psychologists have pointed out, appropriately, that evaluations of the practical utility of personality constructs cannot be based only on the predictions generated by tests alone. Clinicians often note that their assessments, in accord with psychodynamic theory, require highly individualized judgments of the meaning of the person's total pattern of behavior, apart from discrete test scores and response samples. Therefore it is argued that the total personality configuration must be evaluated. This kind of global personality assessment involves intuitive judgments about the meaning of behavior patterns and their relations. Usually the clinician tries to infer the motives, goals, and conflicts that supposedly underlie the person's behaviors and then predicts overt behavior on the basis of his inferences about these dynamics. Global assessment requires experienced clinicians guided by their theory, as well as by intuitions and subjective inferences which cannot be verbalized. Indeed, it has become evident that research on the clinical use of test data actually is inseparable from research on clinical judgment; interpretations about the meaning of test responses as signs usually depend on the clinician and his own subjective inferences. In the last decade much attention therefore has been devoted to investigations of clinical judgment. The results are especially important because the efficacy of personality assessments depends in large part on the utility of the judgments and predictions that clinicians can generate from their inferences about underlying personality and its effects on behavior.

Increments from Clinical Judgment

Research on clinical judgment has been devoted to several main questions: the effects of training on predictive accuracy; the effects of the information available to the judge on his accuracy; the generality-specificity of judgmental accuracy; the correlates of "good" judgment; and, most recently, the situational variables affecting the judgment process.

Global judging ability has been assessed by a variety of methods, summarized by Taft (1955) and more recently by Cline (1964). Perception of emotional expressions in photographs, drawings, models, and movies sometimes has been used in clinical skill research, and even more commonly in person-perception studies. In addition, clinical judging skills have been tested by asking judges to rate and rank traits, to write personality descriptions, to match persons with data about them, and to predict behavior or to postdict history. Predictions may be about highly specific behavior, like responses on a personality inventory, or as general as predicting the person's future professional success. The sources for criterion information have included the subject's own responses (e.g., self-ratings, test scores), as well as data about him obtained from observers (e.g., peers, experts). Some of the main results are reviewed in the following paragraphs.

Research on clinical ability has compared the relative accuracy of judges who had varying degrees of clinical training with those who were untrained. Since most psychological or psychiatric training deals mainly with psychodynamic inferences and nonspecific relationship therapies, the results should not be generalized to all clinical training. Studies of this kind compare the judgmental accuracy of psychologists, psychiatrists, psychiatric social workers, or other trained clinicians with the judgments of clinically inexperienced groups (e.g., nurses, secretaries, college students). Sometimes these studies also examine the effects of amount of training, usually by comparing the accuracy of judges who have attained different degrees of clinical experience. The influence of experimentally introduced training programs on subsequent judgments also has been assessed.

A study by Crow (1957) illustrates research on the effects of clinical training on global judgmental skill. Senior medical students were divided into two groups. An experimental group received extensive instruction on physician-patient relationships and obtained experience in such relationships through prolonged contacts with patients. A control group of medical students remained unexposed to this intensive interpersonal training. Tests of interpersonal perception were administered at the beginning, during, and at the end of the training year. These tests permitted comparisons of the accuracy with which the judges predicted the self-ratings and actual test responses (on the MMPI) of patients whose interview behavior they observed on films.

Contrary to the investigator's expectation, the clinically trained students tended to become *less* accurate than those in the control group. The trained judges became significantly more variable in their estimates than those in the control group and, additionally, assumed significantly less agreement between the patients' self-ratings and their actual test responses. The more the judges tried to take account of individual differences among patients by increasing the amount of variability they placed in their predictions for different patients, the less accurate they became. That is, accuracy scores were negatively associated with variability scores, and increased variability reduced predictive accuracy.

Judges, because of their clinical training, became more sensitive and responsive to what they perceived to be individual differences. As a result they also became less accurate than if they had based their predictions on relatively undifferentiated stereotypes. Training programs devoted to enhancing accuracy of interpersonal perception therefore may actually decrease accuracy by sharpening the trainee's attentiveness to individual differences. The implications for clinical training traditionally devoted to intensive interpersonal experiences are clear. Relationship training may improve relationships, but it does not seem to contribute to predictive accuracy.

Sechrest, Gallimore, and Hersch (1967) studied the effects of various kinds of feedback on predictive accuracy for two traits, anxiety and "pleasantness." The criteria for these traits were the subjects' scores on MMPI anxiety scales and peer-nomination ratings of pleasantness, the subjects being preselected for extreme scores on these dimensions. Judges attempted to predict these traits from the subjects' responses to a version of the Incomplete Sentence Test. Feedback had a slightly positive effect on the judges; those who received feedback made somewhat better predictions. This effect was entirely motivational, however, since feedback had similar effects regardless of whether or not the feedback information was accurate. Although "knowledge of results" facilitates performance on most tasks, global inferences about traits do not seem to improve markedly from feedback to the judge.

Laboratory research on accuracy of interpersonal perception and global judgment often is criticized because it uses artificial situations that do not represent the actual diagnostic problems confronting the practitioner. Moreover, in practice the clinician is free to base his inferences on data from his favorite diagnostic technique and is not constricted by the experimenter's techniques. Acknowledging these objections, a number of investigators have studied the effects of training on accuracy in common diagnostic tasks typical of those used in the clinic.

Goldberg (1959), for example, compared the diagnostic judgments of organicity made by psychologists and nonprofessional judges (secretaries) from Bender-Gestalt protocols. This study eliminated some of the criticisms of previous attempts at assessing clinical judgments. The investigation involved a problem typically encountered by the practicing clinician, used a highly favored diagnostic technique, and independently validated diagnostic inferences against acceptable clinical evidence (independent diagnosis by a competent neurological team).

Goldberg found that the professional judges were not better than the nonprofessional in their ability to diagnose organic brain damage from the Bender. Although many clinical and nonprofessional judges diagnosed better than chance, their predictions from the test were not as good as predictions without any diagnosis guided only by knowledge of the base rates for the percent of organic patients in the clinic population. Although a foremost national authority on the Bender test was more accurate in his diagnosis than anyone in the original study, his judgments were not markedly better than predictions from knowledge of the base rates alone. Ratings of confidence from the judges also showed that there was no relationship between degree of confidence and diagnostic accuracy on this task.

Horowitz (1962) compared clinical judgments against base-rate personality descriptions. In this study psychotherapists described their patients with Q-sort items to provide a validity criterion. Base-rate predictors were computed by averaging the Q-sort descriptions for a sample of these patients. These averaged descriptions were compared with the individualized descriptions for the remaining people in the sample. The mean validity for the base rate or averaged descriptions was .43. In contrast, when twelve clinicians judged each case individually from biographic identifying data, plus the Rorschach, TAT, and sentence completions, they achieved only a mean validity coefficient of .35. When the clinicians worked solely from biographical identifying data the mean coefficient was .32. A mean validity of .21 was obtained by sixty introductory psychology students, each rating one patient only on the basis of the biographic data. The difference in accuracy between clinicians and college students when both used only biographic information did not reach significance.

In general, studies show no clear advantage for trained judges; psychologists are not consistently better or worse than nonpsychologists (e.g., secretaries, college students, nurses), and clinical training and experience usually does not improve the accuracy of global judgments (e.g., Danet, 1965; Goldberg, 1959; Kremers, 1960; Luft, 1951; Soskin, 1959). If anything, clinical training and experience may be somewhat detrimental and reduce judgmental accuracy, or at least introduce systematic biases such as a greater emphasis on pathology and less favorable prognoses (e.g., Soskin, 1954, 1959; Taft, 1955). Sarbin, Taft, and Bailey (1960), in their review of studies comparing trained and untrained judges, reach a similarly negative conclusion.

The Generality of Judgmental Accuracy

For any judgment task there are, of course, sizable individual differences in accuracy. But judgmental accuracy is not strongly consistent across diverse situations so that one cannot generalize confidently about relatively good or poor judges. One set of investigations (Cline, 1964) claims evidence for considerable generality in judgmental accuracy. The results are mainly in the form of modest although often statistically significant correlations among criterion measures (e.g., trait ratings, postdictions). All data, however, were collected in the same single session and based on observing the assessee in one situation (a filmed interview). Cline recognized that even in this restricted context judgmental "ability" was factorially complex, not unidimensional, and involved several orthogonal factors rather than a large general factor. Moreover, stereotypes in judging were the major variable that contributed significantly to predictive accuracy apart from any other variable (Cline, 1964, p. 280). Other studies (e.g., Crow & Hammond, 1957) have found no support at all for any consistency in the accuracy of clinical judgments. Thus, Krech, Crutchfield, and Balachey (1962) concluded from their extensive review that ". . . there is no clear evidence for a generalized ability to perceive others correctly . . ." (p. 65).

The generality of judgmental accuracy across tasks or situations is as doubtful as the generality of other personality traits (Chapter 2). Attempts to study judgmental accuracy are beset by the same problems characterizing all trait research that deals with ratings. Rating variance often is attributable to systematic biases like rating response sets (extremeness, tendency to use the middle of the scale, to agree with items regardless of content, etc.), to semantic ambiguities in the judges' interpretation of trait terms, and to ratings based on the judges' stereotypes.

In addition, person-perception studies have been prey to special sources of error arising from the correlations between the judge's own self-description on a variable, his estimate or prediction of the assessee's position on that variable, and the assessee's actual responses. Predictive accuracy is affected by the extent to which the responses of the judge and assessee are alike and by the degree to which the judge attributes his own responses to the assessee. These problems of interpersonal perception, discussed at length elsewhere (e.g., Cline, 1964; Cronbach, 1955; Gage & Cronbach, 1955; Vernon, 1964), have undermined the conclusions that can be drawn from many studies in the area.

In view of the relative specificity of judgmental accuracy it seems unlikely that many stable characteristics can be found that would discriminate among better and poorer judges "in general." Perhaps the most promising dimension of differences among judges involves aspects of intellectual ability. Watley and Vance (1964), for example, found that a mean difference of about two sigma (27 raw points) on the Miller Analogies Test separated counselors who predicted accurately from those who did not.

Some recent research on categorizing behavior has focused on how the categories a person employs affect the ways in which he interprets new information about another person or object. People who use many categories tend to distinguish more clearly among other individuals in the impressions they form of them. They also are less likely to assume that other people are similar to themselves (Crockett, 1965). Cognitive complexity, however, seems to be unrelated to predictive accuracy, so that the predictions generated by judges who use many categories are no better than those who use only a few (Sechrest & Jackson, 1961). Indeed, as research on clinical judgment shows, judges who use more categories may predict less well than those who rely on a couple of stereotypes.

A few studies have investigated the relationship between an observer's cognitive complexity (the number of categories he employs) and the ways in which he integrates potentially contradictory information in his impressions of another person. In general these studies have tried to test the hypothesis that cognitive complexity facilitates the assimilation of potentially contradictory information into a unified impression. Alhough this hypothesis has received some support (e.g., Mayo & Crockett, 1964), other studies provide only partial confirmation (Rosenkrantz & Crockett, 1965), and some experiments fail to support the hypothesis at all (Crockett, 1965; Leventhal & Singer, 1964). Considering the fact that neither judgmental accuracy nor the personality correlates to which it has been related are broad dispositions, strong and consistent correlations seem unlikely. The complexities of the information processing that underlies all social judgment processes in general, and clinical inferences in particular, are being recognized increasingly (Bieri et al., 1966; Levy, 1963).

Increments from Standard Diagnostic Sources

Although the outcomes from studies of accuracy in clinical judgments generally have been negative, it might be that to achieve better results the clinician needs to draw on his total arsenal of diagnostic aids. In practice, clinicians have come to rely heavily on a fairly standard battery of personality tests and techniques which they use regularly for the assessment of most problems in the majority of clinical situations. This array of procedures typically consists of the Rorschach inkblots and often also the TAT and the MMPI. A client also is likely to be asked to complete a series of unfinished sentences, to draw some pictures, and to participate in a short interview. His reactions to all these queries then are interpreted clinically. It has been widely believed that each of the components of the assessment battery might shed light on at least some central aspects of personality and that the resulting combination would permit the clinician to both formulate and test important hypotheses about the individual. Clues coming from any one technique thus could lead to hypotheses whose truth could be tested from other evidence contained in another part of the total assessment information.

A battery of this kind is the core of most traditional personality assessments. The emphasis on these procedures also is reflected in the fact that most clinical training programs devote a great deal of time (usually several years) to teaching graduate students how to administer and interpret this standard battery which has come to define in large part the clinical psychologist's role. In light of this emphasis, research on the value of the total battery is of special importance. There have been many studies of the efficiency of predictions generated from these standard diagnostic procedures routinely administered in clinical settings. These investigations help to clarify the relative contributions of the different parts of the total procedure.

Kostlan (1954) investigated which of the most popular data sources and data combinations permit the clinician to make the most valid personality inferences. For this purpose he selected four favorite sources of clinical information: the social case history, the MMPI, the Rorschach, and an incomplete-sentence test. Twenty experienced clinical psychologists served as judges, and each was assigned data from five out-patients in a large mental hospital. The clinicians worked under each of five conditions. In four conditions *one* of the data sources was missing. For example, the clinician obtained the MMPI, sentence completions, and social history but not the Rorschach. In a fifth condition the clinician saw only a face sheet with minimal identifying information: age, marital status, occupation, education, and referral source. After the judges studied and used the diagnostic data as they would normally, they made their psychological inferences about the patient on a specially devised 283-item checklist. The two criteria of accuracy for these inferences were degree of agreement with a panel of criterion judges who used all four sources of clinical information and congruence with progress reports from the patient's therapists.

The inferences permitted by the minimal identifying data (age, marital status, etc.) exceeded chance. Most striking, these inferences were not surpassed by judgments based on any other data source or combination, unless the clinician also had the social case history. In other words, only inferences from data that included the social history were more accurate than those from the identifying data alone. The only source of information that could not be removed without loss of accuracy was biographical data in the form of the case history. Sines (1959) also reports that biographical identifying information "held its own" relative to test data. In addition, Sines found that the interview contributed to greater descriptive accuracy, especially when it was conducted early in the diagnostic sequence.

Clinicians have often suggested that the combination and integration of clinical techniques, rather than the use of single instruments in isolation, is important for effective assessment. A recent study (Golden, 1964) investigated the incremental effects of combining the Rorschach, TAT, and MMPI tests as opposed to using them singly. Neither the reliability nor the validity of clinical inferences increased as a function of the number of tests, nor were there any differences among tests or pairs of tests. Again the clinicians were experienced, having interpreted a median number of 200 MMPIs, 250 Rorschachs, and 200 TATs. The range of experience extended from about 40 to 2500 administrations for each of these tests.

Similar findings come from a study by Soskin (1959) with different criteria, different judges, and additional data sources. None of the test information improved predictions beyond the level attained from biographical data alone. Moreover, student nurses predicted as well as clinicians when both used only the basic biographical information. These findings on the relative utility of simple biographical information, which permits the judge to make stereotyped statements from the subject's occupation and his overall socioeconomic and marital role status, are similar to results by Gage (1952), Crow (1957), Farina, Garmezy, and Barry (1963), and others.

Soskin's study also provided additional confirmation (e.g., Sines, 1959) that after conceptualizations or categories are formed they restrict the use of new data. After judges formed their hypotheses about the subject by studying his biographical data, they observed him in nine role-playing situations. The clinical judges employed this additional information chiefly to confirm their initial conceptualizations.

Another type of evidence that is highly pertinent in evaluating clinical inferences about traits and states involves their reliability. Many careful studies have examined the degree to which experienced clinicians reach agreement with each other in the inferences that they derive from standard data sources. In a classic study of the reliability of clinical judgments Little and Shneidman (1959) examined the inferences made by expert clinicians from each of five sources: the Rorschach, TAT, MMPI, Make-a-Picture-Story, and case history data. Diagnostic agreement was only slightly better than chance, and agreement about personality dynamics was at best modest. Commenting on their findings, Little and Shneidman (1959, p. 26) noted:

> *The results are even somewhat more distressing when one considers the magnitude of correlations obtained even when they were significant. A small decrease in chance variation is a legitimate goal for screening instruments but relatively useless for tools such as projective techniques where individual prognosis is desired.*

Statements about "deep-seated unconscious anxieties," "latent homosexual tendencies," "reaction formations," and other similar inferences about inferred covert dynamic processes or structures pervade diagnostic reports. Such statements may provide intriguing reading. No matter how fascinating personality descriptions may seem, however, they have little value when competent judges cannot agree about them.

A sophisticated study of judgmental reliability by Goldberg and Werts (1966) employed the multitrait-multimethod matrix design (Campbell & Fiske, 1959). Experienced clinical psychologists independently ranked each of four sets of ten neuropsychiatric patients on one of four traits: social adjustment, ego strength, intelligence, and dependency. The clinicians based these rankings on one of four data sources: the MMPI, Rorschach, Wechsler Intelligence Test, or a vocational history. Thus the consensus about traits inferred from the same data sources could be separated from agreements based on diverse data sources.

The average correlations between judgments of the *same trait* made from *different data* sources (monotrait-heteromethod) reflect the degree to which the clinicians agreed with each other. These average correlations were .17 for social adjustment, $-.01$ for ego strength, .25 for intelligence, and .03 for dependency, providing an overall mean of .11.

These trivial associations are even more undermined when compared with the average coefficients among all correlations for *different* traits (average total heterotrait). Ideally, the latter values should be low, whereas the monotrait-heteromethod convergences should be high. Among the four traits studied, only intelligence gave an average coefficient of convergence ($r = .25$) higher than the average heterotrait correlations ($r = .16$).

While this tiny a degree of convergence for a trait as significant as Intelligence seems incredible, the results for the other three traits were even worse! Social Adjustment yielded an average co-efficient of convergence of .17, exactly equal to its average heterotrait correlation. . . . In general, the monotrait-hetero-method correlations averaged only .11, while the heterotrait cor-relations averaged .16! (Goldberg & Werts, 1966, p. 204.)

Moreover, judgments of *different* traits based on the *same* data source (heterotrait-monomethod) provided correlations (mean $r = .37$) that were uniformly greater than the average heteromethod correlations. This finding of highest correlations for judgments across *diverse* traits from the same data source illustrates again "how instrument-bound clinical judgments can become" (p. 205).

The overall results showed that "the judgments of one experienced clinician working from one data source bear no relationship to the judg-ments of another clinician working from another data source" (p. 204), even when the different clinicians are all experienced and are diagnosing the same patient on what is supposed to be the same trait. The results are especially compelling because four patient samples were used; they were deliberately selected to span a very wide range of traits to avoid constraining judgmental convergence by a restricted trait range in the sample. In addition, ranking procedures were employed so that the re-sults could not be attributable to artifacts from coarsely grouped trait ratings, and both the traits and instruments were drawn from among those most widely employed in clinical settings. Perhaps most striking, essentially similar results have emerged from numerous other investiga-tions. Howard (1962), for example, found the average clinical interjudge agreement correlation was .05 for inferences from the Rorschach, TAT, and sentence-completion protocols.

Marks (1961) conducted an elaborate assessment of the diagnostic process in a child guidance clinic. He found that the collection, com-bination, and integration of massive clinical data in the manner usually done in the clinical situation "does not enable the clinician to make in-ferences about personality which are significantly more accurate" (p. 35) than inferences from blind interpretation of limited data like MMPI responses. Marks concluded that current standard diagnostic procedures may be an "extravagant waste of time" (p. 35).

Confronted by results of this kind, many clinicians have become increasingly disillusioned with personality tests. Generally, however, they have construed the negative research data as reflecting on the specific assessment techniques rather than on the basic assumptions of the psychodynamic and trait approaches that guide their interpretations. As a result they often still use and rely on techniques like the Rorschach and the TAT, claiming that they employ them more as an interview than as a standardized test. They point out that these devices simply provide a set of ambiguous stimuli to which the client reacts; the clinician then bases his assessments, in part, on his interpretations about the dynamic meanings revealed by the client's behavior. The justifiability of this practice depends, however, on the evidence supporting the value of clinical inferences and judgments about dispositions from indirect behavioral signs and, as we have seen, the data are negative.

Psychiatric Diagnosis

Traditionally much time has been devoted to assessments aimed at finding a formal psychiatric diagnosis for clients especially if they come to mental hospitals. To a large extent this focus has resulted from the widespread psychiatric belief that psychological problems reflect distinct underlying mental disease processes. The classification of the American Psychiatric Association (1952) dichotomizes disorders into the organic and the functional, and further subdivides these two into additional subcategories. Mental deficiency, diagnosed primarily on the basis of the individual's scores on intelligence tests, stands outside the dichotomy, midway between the organic and functional groups.

Several different dimensions, rather than a single systematic classificatory principle, emerge in the resulting nosology. Although organic disorders are classified on the basis of probable etiology (pathological brain conditions), mental deficiency is diagnosed by scores on intelligence tests. The functional disorders, on the other hand, are classified according to descriptive symptom syndromes mixed with speculations about their psychodynamic etiology. The subcategories in this scheme are remarkably imprecise and ambiguous. Therefore it is hardly surprising that psychiatric diagnoses have little utility. Clinicians may achieve fair and even good agreement when they classify heterogeneous groups of people into a few major categories like "organic," "psychotic," and "characterological" disorders. Agreement tends to be poor, however, and even at a chance level when more specific diagnoses are attempted (e.g., Ash, 1949; Hunt, Wittson, & Hunt, 1953; Schmidt & Fonda, 1956).

For example, Ash (1949) investigated the agreement between individual psychiatrists who diagnosed the same fifty-two male patients. Each patient was examined at least by two, and in many cases by three, psychiatrists. A full nosological scheme was employed with five major divisions (e.g., mental deficiency, psychosis, neurosis), and each subsumed minor categories, with a total of sixty specific categories. For specific categories agreement was obtained only in 20 percent of the cases judged by three psychiatrists and in from 31 to 44 percent when there were two judges. For the five major divisions there was 46 percent agreement for cases judged by three psychiatrists and 58 to 67 percent for cases judged by pairs.

Higher percentages of agreement were found in one study (Schmidt & Fonda, 1956) in which pairs of psychiatrists independently diagnosed a large sample of state hospital patients. When patients were grouped into three major categories (organic, psychotic, and characterological) the pairs of judges agreed on an average of 84 percent of the cases. Agreement within specific diagnostic subtypes of the psychiatric classification scheme was found only for about half the cases, and was virtually absent for psychoneuroses and "personality-pattern-and-trait disorders."

The utility of clinical diagnostic judgments is undermined further when base-rate data are considered for specific psychiatric categories at particular hospitals. For example, Boisen (1938) found that hebephrenia was diagnosed 76 percent of the time in one Illinois hospital and only for 11 percent of the cases in a second. Predictions based on the percentages of the diagnosis used in a given hospital therefore would probably be much better than individual clinical diagnoses. The literature on the temporal stability of diagnostic labels is more scanty. However, a large-scale study (Masserman & Carmichael, 1938) revealed, not surprisingly, that after one year 41 percent of the follow-up cases required a major revision in their nosological classification.

The utility of psychiatric diagnostic categories is most limited because people who bear different diagnostic labels in fact display greatly overlapping behavior. For example, Zigler and Phillips (1961c) investigated the frequency of occurrence of 35 psychiatric symptoms among 793 patients who had been diagnosed into psychoneurotic, schizophrenic, manic-depressive, and character disorder categories. The 35 symptoms (e.g., depressed, withdrawn, irresponsible behavior, lying) refer to descriptions of a patient by the psychiatrist or referring physician at intake (Phillips & Rabinovitch, 1958). Of the 35 symptoms 30 were found in the diagnosed manic-depressives, 34 in the character disorder group, and all 35 in both the neurotic and schizophrenic groups. The finding that the same behaviors occur in a remarkably high proportion of patients assigned to diverse diagnostic categories is consistent with earlier data on the heterogeneity of behavior displayed by persons labeled with the same psychiatric terms, (e.g., Freudenberg & Robertson, 1956; Wittenborn, Holzberg, & Simon, 1953).

Zigler and Phillips (1961c) also assessed the frequency with which each of the 35 symptoms occurred in each of the four diagnostic categories. For this purpose they evaluated the tendency of each of the 35 symptoms to appear or not to appear in each of the four broad diagnostic categories. Accordingly, they constructed 140 2×2 contingency tables recording the frequency of occurence or nonoccurrence of each symptom for each group in comparison to the other three groups combined. Evaluated by chi square, 67 of the 140 contingencies were significant, suggesting that some symptoms tend to be associated with particular diagnostic categories beyond chance expectations. However, the magnitude of these associations (in the form of contingency coefficients) was less than .10 for half the cases and exceeded .30 in only one instance. These trivial relationships indicate that assignment to a particular diagnostic category supplies minimal information about the patient's behavior.

Recognizing the deficiencies of the standard classification scheme, a number of investigators have developed behavior rating scales for psychiatric patients. These studies search for more homogeneous, stable descriptive dimensions and clusters mainly through factor analysis of ratings (e.g., Wittenborn, Holzberg, & Simon, 1953; Phillips & Rabinovitch, 1958; Wittenborn, 1962; Zigler & Phillips, 1960, 1961c; Lorr & McNair, 1963, 1965; McNair & Lorr, 1965; Lorr, Bishop, & McNair, 1965). The same problems that beset all ratings and categorizing efforts apply in ratings of the behavior of psychiatric patients: the clusters that are obtained may reflect the shared categories and stereotypes of the raters and not necessarily the behavior of the ratees (Chapter 4).

In a good example of these studies a psychologist and an aide observed and rated 150 male hospitalized psychiatric patients on a set of 115 scales (Wittenborn, 1962). Ratings were made on scale items like "claims can't sleep," "lies or steals indiscriminately," "overreacts to overtures," "behavior has no function," "unaware of others' feelings," and "fears impending doom." The ratings were based on observations and/ or interviews during a two-week period. Since many of these scales required the raters to infer the patients' inner states (rather than to describe their behavior), it is not surprising that agreement among raters often tended to be very low and that interrater correlations reached .25 or higher on only 72 scales. Nevertheless, the data for 98 scales were intercorrelated and submitted to an independently programmed factor analysis. The orthogonal factors that emerged were described with labels corresponding closely to familiar psychiatric terms, like "schizophrenic excitement," "depressive retardation," "manic state," or "paranoid schizophrenia."

In addition to problems of poor interrater reliability, the previously discussed limitations of factor analysis of ratings as a technique for "discovering" dimensions (Chapter 3) restricts the utility of such classifications. As Wittenborn (1962) recognized, the factorial studies of symptom intercorrelations are affected by the specific patient population, the content of the rating scales, and the factorial model, and all of these make cross-study comparisons difficult. These dimensions may have some descriptive value and can supply observers with a taxonomy of trait labels. They do not, however, provide information either about the etiology of the behaviors or about the treatments required to modify them therapeutically. Moreover, the studies do not provide information about the consistency with which the labels assigned to the patients fit their behaviors across situations. Considering the situational specificity of behavior it is not surprising that the labels assigned to psychiatric patients have to be changed often and that psychiatric diagnoses are exceedingly unstable. Although the standard psychiatric classification system may have some value for gross initial screening decisions, it seems to have little utility beyond that.

Incremental Speed

Most clinicians have become very dubious about formal diagnoses and instead seek to convey a "portrait" of the salient features of the individual's personality, as the report at the start of this chapter illustrated. A main purpose of such assessments has been to supply the therapist with a sketch of the client's ostensible personality structure rather than with a diagnosis. Hopefully the therapist then can form his plans for the client in the light of this characterization.

Therapists tend to arrive very rapidly at their own stable notions about the patient's psychodynamics and personality. Meehl (1960), for example, reports that the therapist's "image of his patient," assessed by repeated trait descriptions in the form of Q sorts, crystallizes and stabilizes somewhere between the second and fourth therapeutic hour; this picture is not very different after twenty-four therapy sessions. Thus, curiously, many assessments employ tests that consume more of the clinician's time to obtain a personality description than the clinician needs to arrive at his own formulation if he uses the time for psychotherapy with the patient. The Rorschach, for example, takes about four hours of the clinician's time (Odom, 1950). Oddly, the therapist's ratings often are the key validity criteria, but more time is used to approximate them in assessments than is taken by the clinician to develop them in the course of therapy itself.

As noted before, the bulk of research on impression formation also shows that interpersonal stereotypes are developed rapidly from minimal information and constrain the way in which later new data are interpreted (Anderson, 1965; Asch, 1946; Bruner & Tagiuri, 1954; Tagiuri & Petrullo, 1958; Wishner, 1960; etc.). The same tendency is seen in clinical work (e.g., Sines, 1959). For example, Parker (1958) found no increase in the diversity and richness of hypotheses generated by the clinician in the third as compared with the first interview. Moreover, agreement between diagnosticians and therapists does not seem to be influenced much by the amount of contact that the therapist had with the particular patient (Sines, 1959). Rubin and Shontz (1960) found that clinicians showed great diagnostic tenacity and adhered to their initial categories, largely ignoring new information. After the perceiver has categorized the other person he tends to employ new data to confirm his hypotheses rather than to generate new impressions.

Clinical Self-confidence

One of the main justifications for retaining clinical-inference techniques is the subjective faith that clinicians have in the utility of their judgments. Unfortunately, confidence about the validity of inferences is unrelated to their empirical accuracy (e.g., Goldberg, 1959). Oskamp (1965) found that judges became increasingly confident in their own judgments as they obtained increasing information about a case. But although self-confidence soared with information, accuracy did not. Clinicians also may agree with each other strongly and confidently about the meaning of cues although the presumed connection between the cue and criterion behavior is not valid (e.g., Holtzman & Sells, 1954; Mischel, 1965).

Results from more than twenty years of research provide no objective reasons to employ the trait-state judgments of either skilled clinicians, or other judges, to predict behavior. Studies of clinical inference have led to almost uniformly negative conclusions. Clinical inferences have little or no predictive validity (e.g., Goldberg, 1959; Holtzman & Sells, 1954; Kelly & Fiske, 1951). Experienced clinicians usually are no more accurate than inexperienced nonprofessionals such as secretaries (Goldberg, 1959; Crow, 1957; Soskin, 1959). Clinical training does not enhance the accuracy of trait inferences; predictions may even become less valid when the judge departs from common stereotypes (e.g., Crow,

1957; Stelmachers & McHugh, 1964). These conclusions have been reached regardless of the type and amount of information on which judges base their interpretations (e.g., Stelmachers & McHugh, 1964). Clinical inferences have no incremental validity relative to simple actuarial procedures (e.g., Danet, 1965; Goldberg, 1965; Gough, 1962; Marks, 1961; Meehl, 1954; Oskamp, 1962). Clinical judgments thus provide considerably poorer predictions than those readily available from cheaper and simpler sources.

These findings make it hard to understand why confidence in clinical inferences about dynamics and traits tends to persist so tenaciously. In part, clinical self-confidence may be bolstered by what Meehl (1956, p. 266) has called "personality description after the manner of P. T. Barnum." He urged that:

> . . . *we adopt the phrase* Barnum effect *to stigmatize those pseudo-successful clinical procedures in which personality descriptions from tests are made to fit the patient largely or wholly by virtue of their triviality; and in which any nontrivial, but perhaps erroneous, inferences are hidden in a context of assertions or denials which carry high confidence simply because of the population base rates, regardless of the test's validity.*

In one study, college students were administered personality tests and then were given written personality interpretations (Ulrich, Stachnik, & Stainton, 1963). Although the interpretations supposedly were based on their psychological test results, in fact each of the fifty-seven students obtained the identical report, illustrated by the following excerpts (p. 259):

> *You have a strong need for other people to like you and for them to admire you. . . . Your sexual adjustment has presented some problems for you. . . . Disciplined and controlled on the outside, you tend to be worrisome and insecure inside. . . . Some of your aspirations tend to be pretty unrealistic.*

The overwhelming majority of the students indicated the reports captured their personalities very well. Of the fifty-seven students, fifty-three rated the report as either excellent or good, only three giving it an average rating, one calling the interpretation poor, and none very poor. Their general enthusiasm was also reflected in open-ended comments of great praise and excitement (p. 260). For example, "I agree with almost all your statements and think they answer the problems I may have." Or,

128

"On the nose! Very good. I wish you had said more, but what you did mention was all true without a doubt. I wish you could go further into this personality sometime." Other students indicated they felt they had been helped substantially by the interpretations.

Considering the warm reception that psychological cliches receive, and the difficulty of ever disconfirming Barnum personality statements, it is understandable that they tend to be retained. Although similarly vague Barnum personality generalizations are dismissed more readily if offered by palmists and fortune tellers, they are exceedingly difficult to reject when made by prestigeful authorities.

Actuarial Description and Prediction

An alternative to relying on clinical judgment is to turn, instead, to more objective, statistical techniques for organizing information about the individual. Meehl (1954) discriminated assessment styles primarily by the methods they employ to combine and weight data. According to Meehl, the statistical, mechanical, or formal combination of data characterizes *actuarial* prediction; the informal, nonmechanical, impressionistic, or subjective methods of combining data mark *clinical* predictions. This distinction rests entirely on the *method of combining data* and has nothing to do with the data sources. Both actuarial and clinical predictions can be based on the same data; they differ only in how the inferences are generated from the data to yield predictions and descriptions.

In the strategy favored by clinicians and mainly influenced by psychodynamic theory, the clinician himself enters heavily into the inference process by interpreting test responses or other observations as indirect signs of personality. In this clinical inference process the clinician weights and combines data as signs of personality in accord with his own intuitions to arrive at a behavior description or prediction. For example, predictions about future behavior are based on clinical judgments about test scores from an extensive battery of measures, and scores are assigned differential weights and meanings intuitively. The validity of these inferences is then assessed by studying the accuracy of the clinician's statements. On the other hand, in actuarial prediction or description test data are combined and weighted mechanically by fixed, explicit statistical rules, as in multiple-regression equations.

Meehl's articulate analyses of clinical versus actuarial approaches, and his "box score" for tallying their relative predictive efficacy, led to a flood of studies comparing the utility of the predictions produced by clinical versus statistical methods of data combination. To illustrate, an extensive study compared the efficacy of clinical inferences with results from empirically obtained response-response relations (Goldberg, 1965). Diagnostic judgments along a neurotic-psychotic continuum were made by twenty-nine clinical judges for each of numerous MMPI profiles. Fairly simple actuarial indexes were more accurate than the *best* diagnostician. Linear composites of single scale scores ($L + Pa + Sc - Hy - Pt$) outperformed all diagnosticians and provided the most effective single predictor of neuroticism-psychoticism for the total cross-validated sample (the validity coefficient being .44). Most impressive, and consistent with previously cited data, such simple linear combinations were more accurate than complex sophisticated configural models, including the Meehl-Dahlstrom Rules.

About fifty empirical studies have compared the efficiency of attempts to combine information by the human judge with the efficiency of a formalized statistical procedure. Meehl (1965) noted that these investigations, ranging over extremely diverse content domains, showed significantly superior predictive efficiency for the actuarial method in approximately two-thirds of the studies and essentially equal efficiency in the rest with only a single exception (Lindzey, 1965). For many years there was a heated controversy between proponents of intuitive as opposed to formal statistical data combination, including some articulate and sensible pleas for a sophisticated integration (e.g., Holt, 1958). The cumulative empirical results on the scoreboard, however, leave little doubt that, although both techniques generally yield far from ideal predictions, those generated informally are less adequate as well as more expensive.

Recognizing the predictive inefficiency of traditional personality assessments, clinicians have pointed out that much of their activity really is aimed at personality descriptions and not at behavior predictions or formal diagnosis. Sundberg and Tyler (1962), for example, indicate that the clinician seeks an overall image of the patient so that he can generate "working hypotheses" about him. As the case report at the beginning of this chapter illustrated, most of the clinician's statements are descriptions of hypothesized dispositions rather than specific predictions about future behavior. The bulk of current clinical diagnostic activity probably consists of such personality descriptions and these portraits can be formulated either clinically or actuarially, as Meehl (1954) has pointed out.

The realization that informal personality inferences by the clinician are no more accurate, and often less valuable, than those generated actuarially has led to several impressive attempts to supply clinicians with "cookbooks." These cookbooks contain empirically obtained personality descriptions and outcome predictions for clinical use. The basic strategy is illustrated in handbooks or "atlases" prepared by Marks and Seeman (1963) and by Gilberstadt and Duker (1965).

The construction of an "atlas" of either actuarial description or prediction involves several steps. First, a number of test response patterns are selected and various test profiles are identified, yielding a set of mean profiles. Most actuarial studies depend on MMPI response patterns, although any other sample of behavior of course could be used. Ultimately, mechanical rules are specified to group or code responses into code types. These code types involve patterns of elevations on subtests as well as differential weightings of component scores. The rules may be developed in any number of ways, including intuitively, but in the final phase they must be formalized and fixed mechanically. The code types are matched empirically with whatever external data the cookbook creator selects. For instance, for each code type a descriptive atlas might contain examples of the personality descriptions that are *most* and *least* applicable; typical case history characteristics, symptoms, and complaints; diagnoses; typical psychometric characteristics on other tests and rating scales; and predictive statements about the probable course in treatment (for example, mean length of stay, general prognosis).

The essence of the actuarial procedure consists of matching predictive and descriptive information with test response patterns and cross-validating these associations. The investigator begins with a pool of items which he administers to a group known to differ on an external criterion (e.g., males versus females, hospitalized or nonhospitalized). The test scales are constructed so that ultimately the items are retained that best discriminate among people who differ on the selected external criteria. Or the assessor can work with a fixed large pool of items, as on the MMPI, but the meaning of scales and test profiles is established empirically by their external correlates. Gradually the scales become defined by the discriminations and associations they yield empirically with external criteria. Cross-validation is essential to assure that only the relatively stable associations between configurations of test behavior and external data are retained. Q-sort personality descriptions by psychotherapists or other clinicians are a favorite source for external data. The Q-sort descriptions that best discriminate among persons with different test code types provide the prototypic descriptions for the atlas.

To illustrate, a particular atlas code begins with a figure of the mean MMPI profile identifying the code type for males and females (Marks & Seeman, 1963). A set of simple rules identifies whether or not any profile fits the code type. For example, scales 2, 7, and 4 might have to be above a score of 70.

After the person's code type has been identified one simply looks up the descriptive information available for that type. The atlas lists the Q items that are most and least descriptive for persons whose MMPI profiles fit the identifying rules for each code type. In addition to many Q-item characteristics, each atlas code also contains representative case history information about the typical presenting problems, personal history, mental status, treatment prognosis, and psychometric test characteristics. Obviously numerous other kinds of descriptive and predictive information also could be collected and included, and there are no limits on what an atlas can contain. Gilberstadt and Duker (1965), for example, provide short descriptive statements in their atlas that are the essence of the usual diagnostic report. By flipping to the appropriate profile the clinician can save many diagnostic hours and read within moments that a client has the following "cardinal features" (p. 48):

> High standards of performance and achieve well. Capable of emotional ties. Chronically anxious and striving to do well. Vulnerable to accumulated increments of stress from pregnancy of wives, purchases of new houses, illness in families, etc. When unable to tolerate additional anxiety, become depressed, clinging, dependent, self-depreciatory, lose confidence, feel inferior, become overwhelmed. Have somatic manifestations of anxiety (e.g., diarrhea, chest pain, nervous stomach, dizziness, etc.).

Clinicians interested in this kind of personality profile can achieve it more readily, inexpensively, and at least as adequately (or inadequately) by consulting the cookbook as by attempting the inferences on their own. Of course the same questions that are raised with all other descriptions must be asked about actuarially obtained personality statements: once they are obtained, what is their value? At the least, however, the actuarial description has the value of freeing the clinician's time for therapeutic and research activities.

Since test profiles on questionnaires tend to be reasonably stable over time there is a good chance that the individual's code type will not change drastically on each retest. On the other hand, the descriptive statements and external correlates found for individuals with particular profiles may or may not remain stable. Actuarial "cookbook" assessments can easily become outdated and people may be described with "recipes" that no longer fit them. Therefore the correlates of atlas code types require constant cross-validation.

A similar empirical strategy was employed to delineate the external correlates that discriminate people who are high from those who are low on the main factors of the MMPI (Block, 1965). As a first step, Block employed only the test scales balanced for agreement response tendencies so that the role of acquiescence sets was eliminated. He found that the internal consistency and factor structure of the MMPI remained unchanged, still yielding two main factors, tentatively called Alpha and Beta. Next, on the basis of various kinds of observations (e.g., interviews, tests, an intensive three-day assessment), clinicians described the hypothesized traits of subjects in five samples by means of Q-sort statements. Finally, Block categorized the Q items that best discriminated the highs from the lows on each factor in each sample. To illustrate, in one sample an item more characteristic of Alpha Lows was "tends to feel guilty"; an item more characteristic of Beta Lows was "has social poise and presence; appears socially at ease."

The Q-sort items that discriminated persons high and low on the two factors suggested some similarity to Eysenck's "adjustment" and "introversion-extraversion" factors respectively, although Block prefers the terms "ego-resiliency" for the first factor and "ego-control" for the second factor. Quite apart from the names given to the factors, the results can have considerable value for screening decisions and for the description of group differences. The utility of inventories or other response samples depends, of course, on the adequacy of the external behavioral criteria selected. To the extent that differences in score patterns—whether on subtests, on profile configurations, or on factors—discriminate persons on meaningful external criteria, they provide a basis for selection and screening procedures. The value of any technique for these purposes depends on the increments it provides over other cheaper procedures when both the costs of the prediction process and the value of the incremental predictive accuracy it provides are taken into account.

The emphasis in the actuarial-clinical dispute on the method of combining data should not obscure the important theoretical difference between most studies conducted in these two traditions. Actuarial predictions are based on previously obtained cross-validated associations among response patterns on tests and criterion behavior. Prediction involves statements about response-response associations (linking test patterns and criterion information) established empirically, sometimes by virtually random trial and error, and then cross-validated for a new sample of people in similar settings. For example, if people who say on self-reports that they like strawberries differ reliably on an external criterion from those who report they dislike this fruit, predictions are made solely from the empirical association between test response and criterion. No inferences are made about the meaning of the reported preference as a sign of underlying states or traits. The investigator may search afterward of course for mediating processes that might have accounted for the obtained response-response associations (e.g., Gough, Wenk, & Rozynko, 1965). However, the prediction process usually does not take these theoretical inferences into account, and they do not enter into the prediction equations.

Thus in actuarial assessments test responses do not serve as signs of personality, but serve rather as empirical indicators of other responses with which they were found to be associated in previous population samples. In this sense, actuarial assessment is a radically empirical search for response-response associations; no inferences are made about underlying mediating states that might link the associations. Actuarial assessment differs from trait-state assessment by using test response patterns not as signs of underlying personality but as empirical signs of other response patterns.

Empirically keyed tests, established actuarially to discriminate between persons exclusively on the basis of criterion behavior, have clear potential for screening and selection decisions. The value of these actuarial instruments depends in large part on the usefulness and relevance of the criterion behaviors selected. Moreover, the value of such selection procedures depends on their cost. A judgment about their value must take into account the expense of generating the predictions as well as the value of increasing correct predictions beyond cut-off points available from alternative cheaper data or from base rates alone.

Empirically keyed actuarial procedures are especially susceptible to the danger that changes in the relevant population, or in the determinants of criterion behavior, may go unnoticed. When such changes occur they render the actuarial response-response predictions obsolete. For this reason it would be more appropriate to use actuarial predictor data based on samples of relevant behavior, rather than to rely on blind empirically keyed signs that have neither theoretical nor logical relevance to the criterion.

An encouraging step in this direction has been taken by Wiggins (1966), who has begun to isolate the substantive content dimensions of self-reports to MMPI items. It would also be valuable, as Wiggins recognized, to go beyond the pool of MMPI items. In the initial selection of a stimulus pool the assessor could seek items and situations that are similar to the situations involved in the outcomes that he is trying to predict. These conceptually relevant items then could be submitted to empirical validation, so that only those that discriminate between people on criterion behavior in cross-validation would be retained.

134

Actuarial predictions thus need not be a blind search for any items that turn out to discriminate among people on criterion behavior. The same basic strategy can be applied to many stimulus situations that are components of criterion performance. For example, tests directly sampling responses to fear-provoking stimuli can be validated actuarially to predict relevant fears in life situations. Tests sampling on-the-job performance can be validated actuarially to predict future job success. Tests sampling responsivity to particular change procedures can be validated actuarially to select the best predictors of future change in relation to specific treatments. In addition, considering the previously described value of straightforward self-predictions and direct, simple self-reports, these should be included in any validation program. Now that high-speed computers are a reality all these possibilities are becoming increasingly feasible (Kleinmuntz, 1963, 1967).

The clinician who relies exclusively on actuarial prediction is, of course, at a loss when he must predict to a new situation for which no empirical data are available in his cookbooks and for which base rates are unknown. In this case, he is often tempted to turn to his clinical intuitions. An alternative to that risky course, however, is to seek information from indices of the individual's directly relevant past behavior or to ask the person directly.

Increments over Indices of Past Behavior

A person's relevant past behaviors tend to be the best predictors of his future behavior in similar situations. It is increasingly evident that even simple, crude, demographic indices of an individual's past behaviors and social competence predict his future behavior at least as well as, and sometimes better than, either the best test-based personality statements or clinical judgments. Such "demographic" variables as occupation, previous marital history, educational attainments, socioeconomic status, and other indicators of social competence generally yield predictions that equal and sometimes excel those based on inferences about underlying personality. The fact that past behavior tends to be the best predictor of similar future behaviors is consistent with data on temporal stability in personality, reviewed in Chapter 2, showing some significant stability in what people do when retested later in similar situations.

A good illustration of the relative predictive efficacy of past behavior comes from a study of parole outcomes (Gough, Wenk, & Rozynko, 1965). This study investigated the predictive utility of a "Base Expectancy" experience table developed for the California Youth Authority. The table was constructed empirically and provided actuarial weights for variables that previously had discriminated between thousands of offenders who successfully completed a parole year and those who violated their parole. The expectancy table was composed of seven variables, including the occurrence of prior commitment and frequency of previous delinquencies, type of offense, and age at first admission. The predictive utility of this simple record of past behavior was compared with scores from the scales of the MMPI and CPI personality inventories. Table 7 summarizes the mean differences between several hundred parole violators and nonviolators on these measures in a cross-validating sample. The base expectancy index was clearly the best single predictor, yielding the largest differences and excelling all personality scales. As Table 7 shows, the mean difference between parole violators and nonviolators was 4.62 on the base expectancy index: no other measure yielded a difference even half that size.

TABLE 7. MEAN DIFFERENCES BETWEEN PAROLE VIOLATORS AND NONVIOLATORS (CROSS-VALIDATING SAMPLE)

Variable	Mean Difference	Variable	Mean Difference
Base Expectancy	-4.62^a		
MMPI Scales:		CPI Scales:	
L	0.01	Do	0.06
F	1.53	Cs	0.92
K	0.25	Sy	0.03
Hs + .5K	0.52	Sp	0.61
D	0.32	Sa	0.67
Hy	0.98	Wb	-0.15
Pd + .4K	1.33	Re	-0.61
Mf	0.79	So	-2.07^a
Pa	0.39	Sc	-1.84^b
Pt + K	0.52	To	-0.30
Sc + K	1.80	Gi	-0.63
Ma + .2K	1.44^b	Cm	-0.81^b
Si	0.50	Ac	-1.07
A	0.37	Ai	0.20
R	-0.15	Ie	0.36
Es	-0.26	Py	-0.24
		Fx	0.72
		Fe	0.24

(Adapted from Gough, Wenk, & Rozynko, 1965, p. 436.)
[a] $p \leq .01$.
[b] $p \leq .05$.

Six multiple-regression equations in the original sample also were designed to maximize predictive utility. In the cross-validating sample these equations all differentiated violators from nonviolators well beyond chance, the t values for half the equations exceeding those obtained from base expectancy alone. Somewhat larger or smaller mean differences of this kind of course provide no information about the relative utility of the techniques, nor about the increment over base-rate predictions. To answer this question the investigators computed additional estimates from the information that about 5000 boys are paroled yearly in the state and 56 percent of these youngsters have a successful parole period. Based on this 56 percent success base rate alone there would be 2800 accurate forecasts yearly if one simply predicted success for all of them. The prediction from the base expectancy table alone would be correct 2950 times; the best equation, combining base expectancy data with the CPI, would be correct in 3150 instances.

To evaluate the utility of the increments provided by each data source over the base rate it is necessary to consider the cost of obtaining the data for each predictor and the value of each additional correct and incorrect prediction. Although some of these cost functions can be computed with money units, others require value judgments beyond finance. In the parole study just discussed, for example, the costs of the base expectancy data or of the additional equations can be computed readily in terms of the time, staff, and money required. The value of each increment in predictive accuracy, or of each loss of a correct forecast, is less straightforward. For example, if even a single instance of incremental prediction can prevent the loss of life, as in the prognosis of suicide and homicide, it could offset formidable costs incurred in the prediction process. Judgments of this kind pit the costs of the predictions against various probable changes in accuracy. Such assessments must calculate the value of the alternative outcomes to society and to the decision-making institutions, as well as the costs of the predictions themselves. Cronbach and Gleser (1965), casting this problem into the framework of decision theory, have applied mathematical procedures to practical personnel decisions so that the costs of measurement and the loss from erroneous decisions can be taken into account systematically. Applications to typical clinical situations should be feasible since the main decisions involved in most clinical and selection assessments actually are quite limited (e.g., Dailey, 1953).

Relevant past behavior also has been found to be the best predictor of future behavior in many other applied prediction projects. Empirical studies of the correlates of poor as opposed to more favorable prognosis for neuropsychiatric patients suggest that even gross indices of overall past adjustment are the best predictors of future adjustment. With pa-

tients diagnosed as schizophrenic a distinction often has been made between "process" and "reactive" types (e.g., Becker, 1956, 1959; Garmezy
& Rodnick, 1959; Kantor & Winder, 1959). The distinction rests mainly
on estimates of the degree of premorbid adequacy, the speed and sud-
denness of the onset of schizophrenic behavior, and the relative favor-
ableness of prognosis. Persons called reactive as opposed to process
schizophrenics have better premorbid adjustment. They also are more
likely to behave more adaptively in the future.

Zigler and Phillips (1961a, b; 1962) investigated the relationship
between patterns of behavior problems and the degree of adjustment
or social competence achieved before hospitalization. Their index of
premorbid adjustment involved the degree of attained education, tested
intelligence, and occupational skill. In addition they included measures
of the stability of previous employment, the occurrence and maintenance of marriage, and the age reached before onset of debilitating
behavior. Persons with high premorbid adjustment scores computed
from these measures have a better prognosis than those with poor histories (Zigler & Phillips, 1961d).

Lindemann and his associates (1959) differentiated neuropsychiatric patients who stayed in the hospital for short as opposed to long
periods on the basis of simple indices of current and past behavior such
as rated severity of incapacity, legal incompetence, and history of alcoholism. Repeatedly, such variables as the rated severity of deviant
behavior and the length and frequency of prior neuropsychiatric hospitalizations tend to be the best predictors of subsequent outcome ratings (Fulkerson & Barry, 1961). Some of the variables that best predict
length of community stay and employment of released psychiatric patients were found in an extensive study by Lorei (1967). Success in staying in the community after release from the mental hospital was associated with several direct indices of current and previous social competence. To illustrate, the ex-patients who remained longer in the community tended to be those who had not been hospitalized during the
two years before their last admission, did not have a drinking problem,
reported themselves to be less disabled, and evaluated their own families
less negatively. The correlates of maintaining a job in the community
also reveal some of the reality considerations and environmental supports that enhance adjustment. Employment tended to be more stable
for ex-patients who were white, married, did not "profess disability,"
had less history of past hospitalizations, had held jobs recently, and were
rated as more competent.

In sum, the best prognostic index of future adjustment generally
is previous adjustment (e.g., Fairweather et al., 1960). The fact that

the individual's past record of maladjustment and hospitalization is a good index of the future probability of similar behaviors is dramatically apparent from a study by Lasky and his associates (1959). Correlations from .33 to .61 were found between the weight of the patient's file folder and various measures of problems after release. The mean correlation was .52. The incidence of rehospitalization, for example, had a .61 correlation with the folder's weight! This study also serves to illustrate that a correlation coefficient is not evidence for a causal relation between variables.

Studies of academic and professional achievement also have shown that relevant past behavior is the best predictor of future behavior. For example, E. L. Kelly (1966) found that the best predictor of grades throughout the four years of medical school was the average of pre-medical grades. This simple index of relevant past behavior was an appreciably better predictor than scores from several personality tests and other personality indices and supports the previously cited results by Mischel and Bentler (1965). The ability of people to predict their own behavior reasonably well may be because they know their own relevant past behavior better than anyone else.

Although simple indices of past behavior may offer the best available predictors of relevant future behavior, it is hardly surprising that they often account for only a very small fraction of the criterion variance (e.g., Lindemann et al., 1959; Lorei, 1964). Predictions of long-term outcomes for persons in heterogeneous and completely uncontrolled environments tend to be especially poor. For example, Marks, Stauffacher, and Lyle (1963) found that demographic indices of behavior, such as length, frequency, and severity of previous neuropsychiatric hospitalizations, legal hospital commitment and judged legal incompetence, and time since first hospitalization, are among the best available indicators of average adjustment ratings of psychiatric patients one year after their release. However, to predict which patients would remain outside the hospital for a full year and which ones would be rehospitalized within the year, only one variable (behavior ratings) out of 114 was significant.

Long-term outcomes like hospitalization largely depend on uncontrolled environmental conditions. Although demographic indices of past behavior (or weight of file folders) may provide a gross estimate of the overall future adjustment, they cannot define the details of the environment in which the patient will find himself many months later. The specific relations between samples of past and future behavior, and the contingencies that affect these associations, are discussed in subsequent chapters on behavior assessment.

139

The assessor who tries to predict the future without detailed information about the exact environmental conditions influencing the individual's criterion behavior may be more engaged in the process of hoping than of predicting. If there is no choice, however, and the assessor is faced unavoidably with the task of trying to predict outcomes from current or past indices with no information about the future conditions governing criterion behavior, his best predictions are likely to come from measures of directly relevant behavior. Predictions should be most accurate when the past situations in which the predictor behavior was sampled are most similar to the situations at which predictions about future behavior are aimed. Antisocial parole behavior should be best predicted by past antisocial behavior, future job success should be best predicted by prior job success, future academic achievements should be best predicted by past academic achievements, and assessments of future adaptive behavior should be best predicted by prior social competence and social adjustment history.

Personnel psychologists have recognized the utility of specific behavior sampling and indices of directly relevant behavior far more keenly than personality psychologists. Not surprisingly, direct performance measures such as absenteeism rate, sales records, past salary, and promotions tend to be better predictors of future job performance than more indirect inferences about personality dynamics. Even personnel selection, however, has not infrequently relied on personality tests, trait ratings, and indirect inferences about a candidate's characterology rather than on samples of his relevant performance. Nevertheless, there are many instances of reasonably satisfactory job outcome predictions and personnel decisions based on behavior samplings obtained in special situations or during probationary periods in the first few trial weeks of work (e.g., Guion, 1965). Recently Webb and his associates (1966) have compiled an impressive collection of "nonreactive" measures that are especially useful for unobtrusively sampling behaviors relevant to all kinds of activities and outcomes.

The view that assessment should sample directly the behaviors of interest is not novel and in most fields is the standard procedure. The performance of products like machine tools or automobiles is tested under conditions that sample and approximate some of the actual conditions for which these objects are intended. Concert performers are more likely to be hired for their performance in an audition than for checking responses on a paper-and-pencil inventory. Likewise, laboratory psychologists who wish to extrapolate from their findings to life situations select as their dependent measures samples from the class of behaviors they seek to predict. For example, the researcher interested in the effects of particular variables on learning rate is likely to make learning rate his dependent measure.

The measurement of intellectual performance by "mental ability tests" is probably the most sophisticated and advanced area of traditional testing and provides the most adequate predictions generated by psychometricians. The relatively great success of measurement and prediction in this area, contrasted to the failures of "personality testing," may partly reflect the frequently overlooked fact that intellectual or mental ability tests sample *directly* the behaviors of interest.

As early as 1905 the innovators in this area studied intelligence by a method they considered "the most direct of all," consisting of "experiments which oblige the subject to make an effort which shows his capability in the way of comprehension, judgment, reasoning, and invention." (Binet & Simon, 1905, cited in Anastasi, 1965, p. 36.) Also interesting, and rarely recognized, is the fact that these originators of ability tests were concerned with the direct *assessment* of the subject's current intellectual functioning to "measure the state of the intelligence as it is at the present moment" (p. 36) and not with either predictions or postdictions.

Although intelligence tests elicit work samples that are not necessarily identical with the criterion tasks, they do sample content or operations *relevant* for performance on the criterion. These direct sampling procedures employ test stimuli that are either similar to those in the criterion situation, as when responses to arithmetic questions are the predictors for school grades in mathematics, or that require the subject to engage in operations similar to those needed for success on the criterion (e.g., subtle and rapid visual discrimination).

Some outcomes are particularly difficult to predict because directly relevant past behavior may not have occurred. Suicide is a key example: it can occur only once, so how can it be predicted from past behavior? Indices of relevant past behavior, however, often are available even for suicide. For example, there are likely to be previous suicide attempts, verbalizations about suicide, suicidal threats, and the presence of people in the family who have modeled suicide behavior by actually committing it (e.g., Farberow & McEvoy, 1966). Even the statistically rare event, or the one that occurs only once for an individual, may be more predictable from relevant behavioral evidence than from personality inferences.

The reluctance to sample relevant criterion behavior directly in personality assessment probably relates to the assumed but unestablished practical difficulties of doing this effectively and economically. There have been many efforts of course to sample behavior directly

141

in the past. Because of the preoccupation with trait-state inferences, however, behavior samples usually have been interpreted as *signs* of personality, rather than validated empirically as *samples* directly relevant to criterion behavior. Most so-called "situational tests" actually have not been used as criterion samples but rather have served as signs to infer personality, with criterion predictions based on inferences about the subject's dynamics as supposedly revealed through the situational test (e.g., OSS Assessment Staff, 1948).

The most important barrier to behavior assessment is the prevalence of the psychodynamic dictum that the proper foci of assessment are inferences about presumed underlying processes rather than behavior itself. This reflects the psychodynamic belief that behavior is merely the surface manifestation of underlying causes and should be used only as a clue to detect the underlying deep-rooted problems. Indeed, this view holds that indirect assessment has the important advantage of bypassing the assessee's defensive distortions. To justify that belief, however, would require compelling evidence that inferences to these hypothesized underlying states can be made reliably and that they have utility.

Utility for Planning Individual Treatment

It is commonly believed that detailed personality assessments are of great value to psychotherapists. Indeed, a major rationale for the large expenditure of time and money required to obtain personality descriptions, either clinically or actuarially, is the assumption that such assessments help to plan treatment programs. We have already seen that psychotherapists get their own stable "images" of their clients very rapidly so that assessment reports do not appreciably hasten the impressions that the therapists can form themselves. In spite of that, personality descriptions could have value if they help the clinician to formulate treatment objectives and strategies.

A study by Dailey was addressed to this critical issue of the relationship between personality evaluations and actual decisions. Dailey (1953) examined the effects of clinical diagnostic reports on the clinician's choice of treatment in a hospital in which there were ostensibly thirty-two possible decisions about how to treat patients. Clinicians were given a list of these decisions and indicated the treatments they would recommend for the average or typical patient admitted to the hospital. Although thirty-two decisions supposedly were possible, in fact a very few treatments, like group therapy and occupational therapy, were almost routinely recommended for everyone. Other treatment questions, such as "Should he receive vitamins?," were irrelevant to most psychological reports. After their hypothetical recommendations for "typical" patients were elicited, the clinicians read diagnostic case reports for nine patients and were asked to select treatments for each of them. Only about a fourth of the treatment recommendations made without any diagnostic data and for any "average" patient would have been changed by reading the actual case reports.

Even if most people get the same general treatment (e.g., relationship therapy), it might be valuable to have individual assessments, provided that these permitted the therapist to tailor the general treatment more specifically to the particular needs of the individual. Most traditional forms of psychotherapy, however, are nonspecific relationship therapies in which the client's diverse verbalizations are interpreted by the same set of principles (Bandura, 1968). To the extent that diverse problems are treated by the same nonspecific techniques, it is idle for assessments to be concerned with the particulars of treatment. It becomes understandable, therefore, that a traditional schism exists between psychological diagnosis and treatment.

Most traditional psychotherapists do not believe that assessment facilitates therapy. Meehl (1960) reports a survey of 168 medical and nonmedical psychotherapists, representing Freudian, neo-Freudian, Radovian, Sullivanian, Rogerian, eclectic, "mixed," and other orientations. The therapists answered a questionnaire that included the item "it greatly speeds therapy if the therapist has prior knowledge of the client's dynamics and content from such devices as the Rorschach and TAT." Only 17 percent of the therapists indicated that they believed that such prior knowledge of the client's personality greatly speeds treatment. A survey by E. L. Kelly (1961) tends to corroborate this picture.

Moreover, in the survey of psychotherapists reported by Meehl (1960), 43 percent stated that "warmth and real sympathy are much more important than an accurate causal understanding of the client's difficulty." Eighty percent believed that the personality of the therapist is more important than the theory of personality he holds, and two out of five even said that "under proper conditions, an incorrect interpretation, not even near to the actual facts, can have a real and longlasting therapeutic effect." This attitude is consistent with the fact that there are no specific psychodynamic therapies for specific problems (e.g., Patterson, 1948). Commenting on this point Wallen (1956, p. 337) noted, "We may expect to find certain distinctive difficulties in the treatment of, say, obsessives, but that fact probably does not change our therapeutic approach." He goes on to assert, "The events taking place in the therapy sessions are better guides for the therapist's activity than an abstract account of the patient's personality given by tests and case history" (p. 337). Thus traditional psychotherapists may be indifferent to any descriptive or predictive evidence about the client from sources outside the therapy relationship. Indeed the majority of therapists ignore the assessment report, frequently preferring to be completely dissociated from, and ignorant of, the diagnostic data. Elaborate, time-consuming personality reports therefore may be an extravagant waste of time not only because of their limited reliability and validity but also because they generally remain unused.

Rogerian client-centered therapists even explicitly disavow the value of assessments altogether. Generally, the client-centered therapist "would use the same approaches no matter what psychological study revealed about the patient" (Wallen,1956, p. 337). Freudian psychotherapists, however, often do take diagnostic data into account, at least in making decisions about the client's suitability for psychotherapy. For the psychoanalytically oriented assessor a number of criteria are available to guide judgments about the client's potential for psychotherapy. Even when specific prediction is not intended the attributes of the ideally psychoanalyzed individual are likely to serve as an abstract standard of psychological health. Freud maintained that the major aim of psychoanalytic treatment should be to make the person's unconscious become conscious. Hence, psychoanalytically oriented assessment tries to infer the individual's capacity for insight—that is, for learning to recognize his unconscious impulses and their expressions and to "accept" them. This practice reflects the assumption that insight, by making the unconscious conscious, ultimately results in a reduction or disappearance of symptoms and is a prerequisite for durable behavior change.

In assessment this belief leads to attempts to judge the person's ability to accept unconscious material without "resisting," by erecting further defensive maneuvers, or going altogether to pieces and becoming "swamped" with unconscious material. To appraise the potential for insight, the assessor makes inferences about the strength of various defenses and globally judges the overall strength of the ego. It should be recalled, however, that empirical evidence indicates little consistency in the behaviors used as indices of ego strength (Chapter 2). Since "insight," and the entire psychoanalytic therapeutic transaction, involves the ability to verbalize, the assessor pays special attention to the assessee's intellectual level and verbal skills and tries to appraise his adequacies in this respect.

In accord with the foregoing psychodynamic assumptions, assessors

144

tend to spend much time appraising the client's potentials for insight and for accepting probing into the unconscious and its consequences. Prognoses for psychodynamic therapies supposedly are based on judgments about the client's intelligence, degree of anxiety and discomfort, his motivation and insight, as well as his age and, to a lesser extent, inferences about his past adjustment and ability to relate (Garfield & Affleck, 1961). This judgment may sound complex, but typically it involves no more than the prediction that people who are most well off socioeconomically and least disturbed will profit most from treatment. This is consistent with Freud's beliefs that the good prospective patient should "possess a reasonable degree of education and a fairly reliable character" (Freud, 1959, Vol. I, p. 257), should be young or at least not much older than fifty, and should be sufficiently distressed by his problems to want to change, but not too severely confused, depressed, or debilitated (Freud, 1959, Vol. I). Considering the unreliability of inferences about personality it seems likely that decisions about the client's suitability for insight therapy could be made most efficaciously from simple measures of social competence—for example, socioeconomic level. In fact, the type of treatment individuals actually do get is closely related to their socioeconomic status (Hollingshead & Redlich, 1958).

THE TRAIT-STATE APPROACH: CONCLUSIONS AND IMPLICATIONS

In sum, the data reviewed on the utility of psychometrically measured traits, as well as psychodynamic inferences about states and traits, show that responses have not served very usefully as indirect signs of internal predispositions. Actuarial methods of data combination are generally better than clinical-theoretical inferences. Base rates, direct self-reports, self-predictions, and especially indices of relevant past behavior typically provide the best as well as the cheapest predictions. Moreover, these predictions hold their own against, and usually exceed, those generated either clinically or statistically from complex inferences about underlying traits and states. In general, the predictive efficiency of simple, straightforward self-ratings and measures of directly relevant past performance has not been exceeded by more psychometrically sophisticated personality tests, by combining tests into batteries, by assigning differential weights to them, or by employing more complex statistical analyses involving multiple-regression equations. These conclusions for personality measures apply, on the whole, to diverse content areas including the prediction of college achievement, job and professional success, treatment outcomes, rehospitalization for psychiatric patients, parole violations for delinquent children, and so on. In light of these findings it is not surprising that large-scale applied efforts to predict behavior from personality inferences have been strikingly and consistently unsuccessful (e.g., Kelly & Goldberg, 1959).

The main themes emerging from these results were becoming apparent more than a decade ago. Findings during the last few years serve primarily to turn the themes into sharp conclusions and to make their implications more unavoidable. Reviewing diagnostic activities in 1960, Meehl commented:

> *Personally, I find the cultural lag between what the published research shows and what clinicians persist in claiming to do with their favorite devices even more disheartening than the adverse evidence itself.* (Meehl, 1960, p. 26.)

The "cultural lag" that Meehl deplores is probably in part due to the fact that "Barnum" statements and other clinical truisms tend to be highly reinforcing. Barnum statements, whether achieved from clinical hunches or statistical formulas imbedded in cookbooks, are hard to discredit because, as we saw, even the person who is described with personality clichés tends to congratulate the writer for his perceptively penetrating insights (Ulrich, Stachnik, & Stainton, 1963).

The results of trait-state assessments reviewed in this and the preceding chapters, taken collectively, lead to clear conclusions. With the possible exception of intelligence, highly generalized behavioral consistencies have not been demonstrated, and the concept of personality traits as broad response predispositions is thus untenable. Referring to the trait and factor approach after reviewing the evidence, Vernon (1964, p. 239) comments:

> *The real trouble is that it has not worked well enough, and despite the huge volume of research it has stimulated, it seems to lead to a dead end.*

Often the poor correlations found in personality research have been attributed to measurement errors. Increased sophistication about measurement techniques, however, has produced even sharper and stronger evidence to question the generality of personality traits and the usefulness of inferring such broad dispositions. Many of the response consistencies obtained across measures turn out to be due to the commonality of the test stimuli or methods used to elicit the responses and to other sources, like response sets, that undermine the interpretation of data as indicators of personality traits. Hunt (1965) has summarized the overall status of trait generality aptly:

> . . . *individual differences have been conceived typically after the fashion of static dimensions and have been called traits. Those who have attempted to measure personality traits, however, have all too often found even the reliability and validity coefficients of their measures falling within a range of 0.2 and 0.5. If one takes the square of the coefficient of correlation as a rough, "rule-of-thumb" index of the proportion of the variance attributable to persons, it would appear to be limited to somewhere between 4 and 25% of the total. This is incredibly small for any source which is considered to be the basis of behavioral variation, but we personologists have blamed our instruments rather than our belief in the importance of static dimensional traits . . . .* (Hunt, 1965, p. 81.)

The initial assumptions of trait-state theory were logical, inherently plausible, and also consistent with common sense and intuitive impressions about personality. Their real limitation turned out to be empirical —they simply have not been supported adequately. Investigators guided by them have shown remarkable ingenuity, creating a variety of research strategies in efforts to discover broad dimensions of personality. Their concerted labors over many decades have produced some major contributions. Perhaps most striking, research in this tradition consistently has called attention to the prevalence of great individual differences in almost all aspects of behavior and has described those differences on many dimensions, providing extensive taxonomic systems. In addition, the trait orientation has fostered key developments in the measurement of intelligence and cognitive functions. Its contributions to large-scale preliminary screening decisions for many problems of personnel selection and placement have also been notable. In historical perspective, perhaps equally important, the long search for broad personality traits has explored intensively an avenue of study that had to be pursued so that its possibilities could be evaluated empirically. If there had never been a thorough search for generalized personality dimensions, then we would probably have to start one now.

The historical debt due to global trait and state theories of personality must not obscure their empirical failures. Such conclusions are difficult to accept, however, especially unless a better alternative can be found. Usually the failure to predict behavior incrementally from inferences about underlying traits and states has been interpreted as resulting from inadequacies in the particular judges or clinicians, in the tests and samples they employ, in the criterion measures, or in the particular trait-state personality construct and theory that guided them. Each of these objections undoubtedly has merit. But while the findings on the inutility of trait-state inferences often are dismissed as reflecting deficiencies in measurement techniques, the data actually are consistent with the results found in experimental studies of human behavior and social learning processes, as subsequent chapters will show. From the viewpoint of social behavior theory the results reviewed in this and the previous chapters reflect the empirically unjustified assumptions of trait and state theory and not merely the limitations of measurements.

It has often been acknowledged that a viable approach to personality must bridge the gap between the principles and methods of general experimental psychology and the problems confronting the personality psychologist concerned with the assessment and modification of complex human behavior. The remainder of this book extends and develops principles and methods from the experimental study of social behavior to problems of personality assessment and change, and pursues alternatives to the traditional trait-state strategies for personality study.

/6
PRINCIPLES OF
SOCIAL BEHAVIOR

This chapter considers some of the basic processes through which social behaviors are learned and the manner in which they can be changed. It will become evident that the findings reported in the preceding chapters are consistent with the results and expectations from experimental studies of behavior reviewed here. Therefore the findings on the limited utility of responses as signs of underlying personality and on behavioral specificity should not be dismissed as resulting from the methodological inadequacies of a young science. Rather, their implications for behavior assessment and change will have to be explored seriously. In this chapter, first we shall present some basic concepts about behavior; then the data on the cross-situational specificity and consistency in behavior provided by trait-state research will be analyzed from the perspective of social behavior theory.

The term "social behavior theory" is used here to refer to a synthesis of theoretical principles from the experimental study of social behavior and cognition. Rather than attempting to define the nature of social behavior theory abstractly, it will be delineated by focusing on the determinants of human learning and behavior change, as viewed from this perspective and discussed in this and the following chapters. These chapters will examine the implications of social behavior theory with special attention to its relevance for the assessment and modification of personality.

Social behavior theory differs fundamentally from trait and state theory in its conceptualization of the determinants of behavior. Trait and state theories look for stable response predispositions in persons as the generalized and enduring causes of their behavior. In contrast, social behavior theory seeks the determinants of behavior in the conditions that covary with the occurrence, maintenance, and change of the behavior. A useful trait or state theory depends on demonstrated major cross-situational consistencies in behavior, whereas social behavior theory neither assumes nor requires such broad consistencies. Instead, social behavior theory depends on the discovery of independent variables or stimulus changes that produce and maintain modifications in behavior. While trait and state theories search for consistencies in peoples' behavior across situations, social behavior theory seeks order and regularity in the form of general rules that relate environmental changes to behavior changes. This concern with independent variables— with the observable causes of behavior—dictates that major attention be paid to the manner in which experiences change and regulate behavior, and leads one to focus on the learning and cognitive processes that govern these changes.

ACQUISITION OF BEHAVIOR

Observational Learning

Learning, or the acquisition of behavior, can occur without any direct reinforcement to the learner (e.g., Bandura & Walters, 1963; Campbell, 1961; Hebb, 1966; Mischel, 1966a). People learn through their eyes and ears by noting the experiences of others and not merely from the outcomes they get directly for their own behavior. Learning without direct reinforcement is sometimes called "perceptual," sometimes "cognitive," sometimes "vicarious," and sometimes "observational" or "modeling." All these labels refer to an individual's acquiring new behavior through observation with no direct external reinforcement. Behaviors may be learned observationally by watching what others (models) do, or by attending to the physical surroundings, to events, and to symbols such as words and pictures. Through observation individuals learn about the structure of the environment and the behavior of others. They learn not only what people do, but also about the characteristics of the physical and social universe (Bruner, Olver, & Greenfield, 1966). A great deal of human learning is mediated by perceptual-cognitive processes and depends on observation of environmental contiguities rather than on direct reinforcement for the person's own behavior. Indeed, learning can occur even when the learner makes no overt response during the observational learning experience (Deutsch & Deutsch, 1966).

By simply observing behavioral sequences the observer can learn entirely novel response patterns that previously were unavailable to him (Bandura & Walters, 1963). The acquisition of such wholly new response patterns through observational processes is most apparent in language learning (e.g., Bandura & Harris, 1966). Undoubtedly observational processes are also important in the learning of trait names for oneself and for other people, and in the acquisition of dispositional concepts and stereotypes.

In addition to facilitating new learning, observation of the behavior of others may have eliciting or inhibiting effects on the observer's present performance of previously learned behaviors. The manner in which these effects occur is illustrated in the vicarious transmission of delay behavior without any direct reinforcement (Bandura & Mischel, 1965). It was hypothesized that self-imposed delay of reward would be determined in part by the delay patterns displayed by social models. The study also compared the relative magnitude and stability of changes in delay-of-reward behavior as a function of exposure to real-life and symbolic modeling cues.

In the initial phase of this experiment many children were administered a series of paired rewards. In each of these pairs they were asked to select either a small reward that could be obtained immediately, or a more valued item contingent on a delay period ranging from one to four weeks. For example, children chose between a smaller, immediately available candy bar and a larger one that required waiting. From the total pool of subjects those falling in the extreme top and bottom quartiles of the delay-score distribution were selected for the succeeding phases of the experiment.

Children in these extreme groups (who exhibited predominantly either delayed-reward or immediate-reward patterns of behavior) were then assigned randomly to one of three treatment conditions. One group of children observed live adult models who exhibited delay-of-reward responses counter to the group's self-gratification pattern; a second group was similarly exposed to a model displaying the opposite delay-of-reward behavior, with the exception that the modeling cues were presented only symbolically in written form; a third group had no exposure to any models. Immediately following the experimental procedure the children's delay-of-reward responses were measured in the absence of the model. In order to test the generality and stability of changes in delay behavior, the subjects were reassessed by a different experimenter in a different social setting approximately one month after completion of the experimental phase of the study.

As predicted, the modeling procedures altered the children's delay-

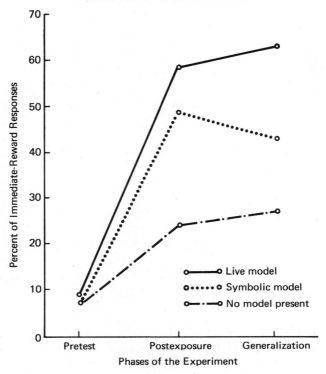

FIGURE 2. *Mean percentage of immediate-reward re-*
sponses by high-delay children on each of
three test periods for each of three experi-
mental conditions. (From Bandura & Mis-
chel, 1965, p. 702.)

of-reward behavior substantially in the direction of their model's choice
patterns. Figure 2, for example, shows the mean percentage of immediate-reward responses produced by the high-delay children on each of the
test periods as a function of treatment conditions. Children who had
shown a predominantly delayed-reward pattern displayed an increased
preference for immediate and less-valued rewards as a function of observing models favoring immediate gratification. Conversely, those who
had exhibited a marked preference for immediate rewards increased and
maintained their willingness to wait for more highly valued delayed
reinforcers following exposure to models displaying high-delay behavior. The results of this investigation provided support for the in-
fluential role of live and symbolic modeling cues in the transmission of

socially significant response patterns like self-control. Both short-term and long-term generalization effects were found.

This study also provides an interesting contrast between traditional psychodynamic theories of voluntary delay behavior and the approach of social behavior theory to the same phenomenon. According to the psychoanalytic theory of delay behavior (Freud, 1959; Singer, 1955), aroused impulses press for immediate discharge of tension through overt motoric activity. The capacity to delay or inhibit motor discharge by substituting ideational representations presumably reflects the gradual shift from primary-process activity to reality-oriented, secondary-process thinking. The psychoanalytic approach, like all trait and state formulations, thus leads one to seek determinants of delay behavior in such hypothetical internal events as ego organizations and energy-binding ideations. In contrast, social behavior theory, as illustrated in the foregoing experiment, views manipulable social-stimulus events as the critical determinants of self-controlling behavior. These changes were produced on measures whose "ego strength" construct validity, in the form of associations with other indices of self-control, had been elaborated previously (Chapter 4). Changes of this magnitude in children who were initially so extreme in their delay-of-reward orientation help to document the dependence of personality indices on stimulus conditions.

The foregoing experiment likewise illustrates that some of the same considerations that limit correlational studies also constrain experimental investigations. Although the independent variables exerted strong effects, they still did not account for more than a limited portion of the total variance in delay behavior. It is true that over the three phases of the study the percent of immediate-reward choices made by subjects who initially preferred delayed rewards increased from less than 10 percent at the beginning to more than 60 percent on the generalization task a month after initial exposure to the live model. Nevertheless, in spite of this high and predicted amount of change, within each condition and at each phase there still were considerable differences among children. As a result of the children's prior experience the experimental manipulations presumably had different meanings for them and exerted different effects on different youngsters. Moreover, the fluctuation in delay behavior shown in the control group seems to reflect the same kind of behavioral instability abundantly discussed in previous chapters.

Similar experiments on the effects of observation have demonstrated that many complex verbal, emotional, and motoric behaviors are learned, maintained, elicited, inhibited, and modified, at least in part, by modeling cues. Behaviors affected by exposure to models include

153

maladaptive psychotic syndromes, fears and avoidance behaviors, as well as aggressive patterns, prosocial responses, and linguistic and judgmental styles (e.g., Bandura, Grusec, & Menlove, 1966; Bandura & Walters, 1963; Chittenden, 1942; Lovaas et al., 1966). By simply watching the verbal and nonverbal behavior of live or symbolic models, the observer can change his own language, abstractions, and social judgments, as evidenced by changes in his subsequent verbal and nonverbal behavior. Modification of abstractions through observational learning without direct reinforcement has been demonstrated for the standards people use for their own self-reward (e.g., Bandura & Kupers, 1964; Carlin, 1965; Mischel & Liebert, 1966; Staub, 1965); the moral judgments that they render about behavior (Bandura & McDonald, 1963); and the language categories they employ in speech (Bandura & Harris, 1966).

The characteristics of a model effect the degree to which his behavior is adopted by observers. For example, there is a positive association between the rewardingness and power of social agents and their effectiveness as models (e.g., Bandura & Huston, 1961; Mischel & Grusec, 1966; Mussen, 1961). A nurturant relationship between the observer and the model who displays the behavior tends to facilitate observational learning. When models vary in their power or control over resources, the behaviors of the more powerful model tend to be imitated and adopted most (Bandura, Ross, & Ross, 1963). Moreover, people adopt in varying degree the behaviors of more than one model, even when one is decidedly more powerful and rewarding than the other (Bandura, Ross, & Ross, 1961). The observer's resulting behavior therefore is a novel patterning of the behaviors from many observed events and is not merely a copy of a single model. Since people almost invariably are exposed to many models and observe a multitude of behavioral possibilities, they can create almost endless new combinations of behavior.

Of course modeling effects depend not only on the attributes and behavior of the model but also on the particular individual who observes them. Among the many subject variables found to influence responsivity to social models are the observer's age and sex in relation to the model's, his immediately prior social reinforcement experiences, and his history of reinforcement for independence or for matching behavior (Bandura & Walters, 1963). Within many studies the effects of the experimentally manipulated stimulus conditions interact with the particular attributes of the subject and with his emotional state.

The components of observed behavior tend to be learned even if the person was the object, as well as the witness, of the behaviors and experienced direct *aversive* consequences from the modeled behaviors. In one study (Mischel & Grusec, 1966), preschool children were exposed to an adult female whose noncontingent rewardingness and future control over the child were varied. Rewardingness was manipulated by varying the degree to which the model provided the child with both material and social noncontingent reward (e.g., games, treats, praise, attention) in a preexperimental interaction. In the high-reward condition the model spent twenty minutes with the child during which she dispensed all these resources generously, playing with the youngster warmly and showing affectionate interest in him. In the low-reward condition, in contrast, during this same time period the child was ignored by the model who busied herself with her other "work" while the youngster was left to amuse himself with a few old broken toys. Power or control over both positive and negative outcomes was manipulated cognitively by varying the model's role. For half the children the model was introduced as a visiting out-of-town teacher who would never reappear, whereas for the other half she was introduced as the child's new school teacher.

Thereafter the children participated with the model in a "special game" that involved playing with a cash register, making change with play coins and bills, and so on. During this interaction the model was aversive to the child in novel ways ("aversive" behavior), and she exhibited novel behaviors with no direct reinforcement consequences for the child ("neutral" behaviors). More specifically, the aversive acts consisted of making the child wait for rewards, removal of reward, and sharp criticism. The modeling of neutral behaviors consisted of emitting distinctive verbal and motor behaviors (e.g., marching around the room while saying "March! March! March!"). The aversive behaviors were designed to have direct negative consequences for the subject, whereas the neutral behaviors were merely modeled without any direct reinforcement consequences for him. In the former instances the child was the object of the behavior, whereas in the latter he was only the observer of the displayed behaviors.

The child had a chance to play the game with the model and then was left alone briefly (while observed through a one-way mirror). Any of the model's neutral or aversive behaviors reproduced by the child, either in the model's presence or while alone, were scored as "rehearsals." In the next phase the subject's task was to show another person who was dressed as a clown how to play the cash register game in the model's absence. Measures were taken of the transmission of the modeled neutral and aversive behaviors to the "clown" in her absence.

Figure 3 shows the number of subjects in each treatment condition who *rehearsed* neutral and aversive behaviors. Significantly more children rehearsed both the model's aversive and neutral behaviors when

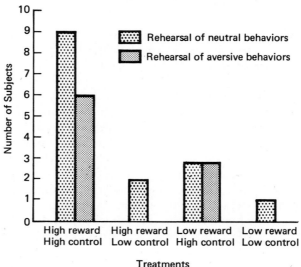

FIGURE 3. *Number of subjects rehearsing neutral and aversive behaviors as a function of the model's rewardingness and future control. (From Mischel & Grusec, 1966, p. 201.)*

the model had been both highly rewarding and had future control than when her rewardingness and control were low. The model's future control was especially important for the children's tendency to rehearse her aversive behaviors. As Figure 3 indicates, in the two conditions in which the model's control had been low not a single child rehearsed her aversive behaviors. On the other hand, rewardingness significantly affected the rehearsal of neutral but not aversive behavior, although the trend was in the same direction. The model's rewardingness also led to greater *transmission* by the children of her aversive behaviors to the clown but did not affect the transmission of her neutral behaviors.

On the whole the results demonstrated that observed behaviors may be reproduced and transmitted to others without external reinforcement for their actions, even when the observer was the object of the modeled behaviors and received aversive consequences from the model. Indeed, the percent of aversive behavior transmitted exceeded the percent of neutral behavior transmitted. Moreover, the extent to which the model's behaviors were reproduced was affected by her rewardingness and her future control over the subject. The overall results support the view that the rewardingness of a model and his power are determinants of the degree to which his behavior is adopted. The findings suggested, however, that these two variables have different effects as a function of the type of behavior (neutral or aversive) displayed by the model and of the stimulus situation in which the subject reproduces it (rehearsal or transmission). These results again highlight the specificity of the determinants controlling behavior and show that the effects of independent variables depend on the particular behavior and situation involved.

The degree to which the observer *attends* to the model determines in part how accurately he learns the model's behavior. Attention to the model is affected by such variables as the observer's previous reinforcement history with similar models, as well as by the model's social characteristics such as his prestige. For example, the model's power and rewardingness strongly increase the attention paid to him (Grusec & Mischel, 1966). The observer's constructs about any of the attributes of another person may constrain the information to which he attends, as was described in Chapter 3.

Conditioning of Stimulus Valences

Like observational learning, classical conditioning depends on contiguous associations among stimuli rather than on reinforcement for responses. Neutral stimuli acquire valence and reinforcing powers when they become associated with other stimuli that already have reinforcing powers and emotion-arousing properties. The process through which an initially neutral stimulus acquires valence or affective value is best illustrated in classical conditioning.

In the familiar classical laboratory paradigm, when a buzzer (CS) is presented repeatedly as the animal receives food (US), the buzzer may come to elicit by itself autonomic responses similar to those initially produced by the food. In *aversive* classical conditioning, on the other hand, the US is a pain-producing stimulus. If, for example, a light and an electric shock occur contiguously for several trials, the light itself can come to evoke components of the emotional pain reaction to the shock. Neutral stimuli which are associated contiguously with an aversive US thus may become aversive conditioned stimuli capable of eliciting fear and avoidance responses. The processes of positive and aversive classical conditioning help to explain the acquisition of intense emotional reactions to previously neutral stimuli.

A previously neutral stimulus, once conditioned by contiguity with an unconditioned stimulus (e.g., food, pain-producing shock), also can serve as the basis for further higher-order conditioning (e.g., Mowrer, 1960). Higher-order conditioning occurs when a conditioned stimulus modifies the power of new neutral stimuli with which it becomes contiguously associated. Through higher-order conditioning words and other symbols can become potent conditioned stimuli with the capacity to elicit autonomic responses. In turn, these words or symbols affect the value of additional previously neutral stimuli with which they become associated (Insko & Oakes, 1966; Staats & Staats, 1957, 1958, 1963).

When symbols and words with negative connotations, such as "ugly" or "bitter," are associated with other labels, such as the names of persons or nations, these latter words become viewed as unpleasant. In contrast, when the same names are paired with positively conditioned words like "sweet" and "pretty" they become rated as pleasant. Activities, goals, interests, and so forth, achieve differential value by being differentially associated with positive or negative outcomes and labels. For example, words like "sissy," "pansy," "tough," or "sweet" acquire differential value for the sexes, and the application of these labels can easily affect the value of other neutral events.

Even if a person has not had a directly aversive experience with a stimulus he may learn intense emotional responses to it *vicariously* through observation of the emotional reactions displayed by others. In vicarious conditioning the person receives no direct positive or aversive stimulation and merely observes repeated contiguity between a stimulus and an emotional response exhibited by another person (Berger, 1962). In one study adults repeatedly observed the sounding of a buzzer paired with feigned fear responses displayed by an experimental confederate. Gradually the observers themselves developed conditioned psychogalvanic responses to the sound of the buzzer alone (Bandura & Rosenthal, 1966).

Vicarious classical conditioning helps to account for the development of emotional behavior toward people and objects that were never directly associated with noxious or positive outcomes in the individual's history. Consider, for example, the development of strong fears of dogs or snakes. Even if a person was never bitten or otherwise directly traumatized by the animal, he may come to fear it intensely as a result of witnessing the emotional upset of other people when they had encounters with the animal.

In clinical contexts, when clients complain of emotional arousal and intense avoidance behavior to particular classes of stimuli (e.g., snakes), the clinician often begins by searching for some direct traumatic experience, like a snake bite, that might account for the genesis of the disorder. If he cannot find evidence of a direct traumatic experience the clinician might assume either that the episode was repressed, or that the stimulus objects evoking the client's emotional response have unconscious symbolic meanings. The snake, for example, according to dynamic theories, might be a phallic symbol, and the client's emotional reactions to it might reflect displacement and other unconscious interventions. A more parsimonious interpretation of the same phenomenon, however, may be that the reaction was acquired vicariously through observation of the emotional behavior of others.

As another illustration, the girl whose mother repeatedly displays inhibited attitudes toward men and sexual matters can adopt many of her mother's attitudes without ever having a traumatic sexual experience directly. Once these negative emotional reactions have been acquired they also constrict the person's actions toward the emotion-provoking events. The girl who fears men is unlikely to relate well to them sexually. As these examples illustrate, on the basis of vicarious as well as of direct classical conditioning processes, previously neutral stimuli may come to elicit strong emotional responses.

Observational learning and classical conditioning both involve a change in behavior as a result of the contiguous association among stimuli. Although both processes depend on sensory contiguity between stimuli, in classical conditioning no new response is learned. Rather, an autonomic reaction or "respondent" already present in the organism's repertoire becomes associated with new stimuli. In observational learning, on the other hand, new responses, with no necessary autonomic accompaniments, may be acquired as a result of attending to sensory events.

Distinction between Acquisition and Performance

It is useful to distinguish between the learning or acquisition of behaviors and their performance. A person does not perform all the behaviors he has learned; there are discrepancies between what he has learned or knows and *can* do, and what he actually *does* in particular situations. Individuals of course learn a multitude of potentially antisocial or deviant, as well as prosocial, behaviors. For example, most adolescent boys know how to throw rocks, wield knives, and break windows. But even among boys who have acquired these skills to the same degree there are striking individual differences in the extent to which they perform them. Similarly, although both men and women in our culture know how to apply lipstick or face powder, or to insert cigars in their mouths, the sexes differ in the frequency with which they perform these activities. For any one individual there are major discrepancies between what he is able to do in any given situation and what he actually does.

According to the present social learning formulation, learning or the acquisition of novel responses is regulated by sensory and cognitive processes; learning may be facilitated by reinforcement but does not depend on it (e.g., Bandura & Walters, 1963; Hebb, 1966). Direct and vicarious reinforcement are, however, important determinants of response selection in *performance*, as later sections show.

A recent study of imitative behavior illustrates the potential discrepancy between what persons have learned and what they perform. Children watched a film of an adult who displayed novel aggressive responses (Bandura, 1965a). The consequences produced by the adult's aggressive behavior were manipulated experimentally in the film. In one condition the film sequence showed the adult's aggressive behavior punished; in a second it was rewarded; and in a third it was left without consequences. On tests after the films, children who had watched aggressive behaviors punished imitated them less than those who had observed the model's novel aggressive responses rewarded or left without consequences. But it would be erroneous to conclude that these performance differences mirrored differences in learning. Additional posttests revealed that when attractive incentives were offered to the children contingent upon reproducing the model's responses, the differences between the conditions were wiped out. These findings suggested that the children in all conditions had learned the model's behavior equally well. The observation of different response consequences, however, had inhibited or facilitated their subsequent performance, probably by influencing their expectations about what would happen to them if they were to try the behaviors.

On the other hand, learning as well as performance can be affected by prior experiences with the model who is the source of the behavior. In one study (Grusec & Mischel, 1966) the model's rewardingness and control over resources was varied *before* the children observed her display a novel sequence of behaviors. Her manipulated attributes not only affected the children's willingness to perform her behaviors, but also the degree to which they had learned them. This became apparent in a postexposure test in which the children were offered incentives contingent on reproducing her behavior. As a function of the model's attributes, significant differences were found in the extent to which children *recalled* her behavior, as well as in their spontaneous imitative performances. Presumably her social characteristics had affected the observer's attention and learning, as well as his readiness to adopt her behaviors.

Whether or not a person has learned a response pattern can be known only from his performance. A behavior may not be performed because it was never learned in the first place. On the other hand, a response pattern may be potentially available currently to the person but not elicited by the particular stimulus conditions. For example, the response may be inhibited, and the incentive conditions in the situation may not be strong enough to elicit it, but the introduction of more potent incentives may readily lead to the desired behavior.

The only way one can know whether the absence of a particular behavior under given eliciting conditions reflects that it has not been learned or that, in contrast, it was acquired but is simply not being performed, is by varying the evoking conditions and introducing incentives designed to produce the behavior. Take, for example, poor results on a vocabulary test obtained when the assessor has created what he considers optimum testing conditions. The assessor may conclude that the subject has not learned how to define a series of vocabulary items, rather than that he is able to do so but that the performance is inhibited or that he is attending to something else. The assessor's conclusion should be restricted, however, to the variations in eliciting and incentive conditions with which he actually experimented.

RESPONSE-REINFORCEMENT RELATIONS

Most human social behaviors may be viewed as voluntary, instrumental response patterns or "operants" (Skinner, 1953). The reinforcements that follow these response patterns change the future likelihood of similar responses. Reinforcers, contrary to some common misconceptions, are not restricted to gastronomic and sexual pleasures, nor to such banal outcomes as food pellets, candies, nods, and grunts of social approval. The almost endless events that can be identified as reinforcers include such cognitive gratifications as information (Jones, 1966) or the attainment of competence. Reinforcing events may involve either the presentation of positive reinforcers or the removal or reduction of aversive stimuli. Any conditions that alter the reinforcers to which a response pattern leads also change the probability that similar behavior will occur. If, for example, parents respond with prompt solicitous attention to loud crying tantrums from their child, the probability that the child will perform similar tantrums in the future increases. If, on the other hand, the behavior is ignored and unrewarded its future likelihood diminishes.

Direct Response Consequences

The reinforcing outcomes or consequences produced by an individual's behavior change the likelihood that he will show similar behavior subsequently in related situations. This is demonstrated most clearly in studies designed to change behavior systematically. The basic steps are illustrated in a study that was planned to reduce the maladaptive social isolation of a nursery school girl (Allen et al., 1964).

Ann, a bright four-year-old girl from an upper middle class background, increasingly isolated herself from children in her nursery school. Simultaneously she developed various techniques to gain the prolonged attention of adults. These latter efforts generally were successful since teachers accorded her much warm recognition for her many mental and physical skills. Her efforts to maintain adult attention, however, led to extreme isolation from other children and became increasingly problematic.

An assessment of the amount of time Ann spent with children, with adults, and by herself during nursery school showed that she was isolating herself extensively from the other youngsters. Most of the attention that adults were giving her was contingent, unintentionally and quite inadvertently, upon behaviors from Ann that were incompatible with her playing with other children. Her teachers unwittingly were reinforcing precisely those activities that led Ann away from play with her own peers. Indeed, the more problematic her behavior became, the more it elicited warm concern and close attention from adults. To untangle this increasingly morbid circle a plan was formed to give Ann minimum adult attention for her isolate behavior and for her attempts at solitary interactions with adults. Simultaneously she would receive maximum adult attention contingent on her play with other children.

To assess any changes in Ann's behavior two observers continuously sampled and recorded her proximity and interactions with adults and children in school at regular ten-second intervals. After five days of baseline data had been recorded the new plan was instituted. Now any approximations to social play, such as standing or playing near another child, were followed promptly by teacher attention. Whenever Ann began to interact with children an adult quickly attended to her as a participating member of the group. For example, "You three girls have a cozy house! Here are some more cups, Ann, for your tea party." Attention was withdrawn whenever Ann began to leave the group or attempted solitary adult contacts.

The effects of the change in the consequences to Ann for isolate behavior versus social behavior with her peers upon her interactions with

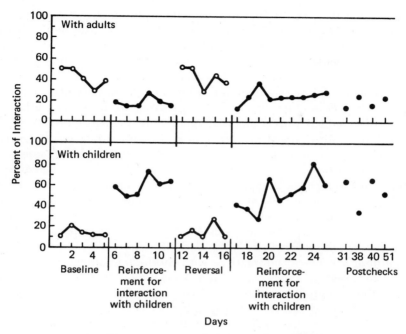

FIGURE 4. *Percentages of time spent in social interaction during approximately two hours of each morning session. (From Allen et al., 1964, p. 515.)*

children are summarized in Figure 4. As the figure shows, in the baseline period before the new response-reinforcement contingencies were instituted, Ann was spending only about 10 percent of her school time interacting with children and approximately 40 percent with adults. She was altogether solitary for about half the time. When the contingencies were changed and warm attention from adults was given only when Ann was near children or interacting directly with them, her behavior rapidly changed in accord with the new contingencies. On the first day of this new arrangement (day six) she spent almost 60 percent of her time with peers. Simultaneously, since her interactions with adults were no longer reinforced, they quickly diminished to less than 20 percent.

The most compelling evidence that behavior depends on the reinforcing consequences it yields comes from data showing the effects of reversing the contingencies back to the conditions that held during the baseline period. On the twelfth through the sixteenth days the teachers again used their traditional nursery school procedures and became attentive to Ann for teacher-dependent behavior. As the figure shows, Ann quickly resumed the patterns that characterized her baseline behavior, ignoring contacts with children and turning to solitary activities where teachers would attend to her alone.

Starting on the seventeenth day the therapeutic contingencies were restored; peer contacts again led to attention while solitary behavior and lone contacts with adults were ignored. As the figure reveals, Ann's behavior again changed rapidly in accord with the new contingencies. In this phase, the teachers gave less frequent, intermittent, nonsystematic attention for interactions with children. Similarly, the schedule of nonreinforcement for adult contacts was gradually relaxed. These changes became possible as Ann's play with her peers became increasingly rewarding for its own sake apart from the adult attention to which it had led initially. Postchecks of Ann's behavior after termination of systematic reinforcement by adult attention showed Ann continuing to maintain her new social relations with children. Her new play patterns with her peers now presumably were being maintained by the gratifying consequences produced by the play behavior itself.

As Figure 4 shows, Ann responded very rapidly to changes in the consequences that her behavior produced. She was able to change back and forth from isolated to socialized patterns not only rapidly but also with no direct tuition. That is, Ann apparently had the skills necessary both for play with children and for isolated contact with adults. Although she knew how to engage in both kinds of activity, the one she chose depended on the reinforcers available in the situation.

Similar studies, discussed in later chapters, have shown repeatedly that systematic alterations in response consequences predictably alter a wide range of behaviors, from psychotic talk, criminal delinquency, and maladaptive sexual behavior to nursery school interactions of the kind just described. These studies have been concerned mainly with the therapeutic modification of problematic behavior. Simultaneously they also demonstrate that predictions about individual behavior can be generated accurately from knowledge of the environments in which the behavior occurs. Ann's social behavior at nursery school, for example, could be predicted with considerably greater precision from knowledge of her *teachers'* behavior on any particular day than from inferences about her own dynamics or traits.

The fact that the response pattern selected by an individual in a situation is affected by the previous reinforcing consequences or reinforcement history of similar responses in earlier related situations has been borne out by numerous laboratory studies. For example, Davitz

(1952), working with ten small groups of children, rewarded half the groups with praise and approval for making aggressive and competitive responses during a series of brief training sessions. The remaining groups were rewarded for cooperative and constructive behavior during the training periods. Thereafter all children were frustrated by exposure to a film that was interrupted just as it approached its climax. At this point the children also were forced to return a candy which had been given to them earlier, and their reactions to these frustrations were recorded immediately on motion picture film in a free-play situation. Analyses of the filmed behavior showed that children who had been rewarded previously for constructive alternatives responded more constructively to the frustration. On the other hand, those children who had been rewarded for aggression in competitive games during the training sessions now reacted more aggressively to the frustrating experience.

Probably the most extensive research on learning has dealt with direct manipulation of response consequences, as in operant conditioning. In this approach new response patterns are acquired through a "shaping process" of "successive approximations." Response elements approximating the terminal behavior are positively reinforced, whereas dissimilar behaviors are unrewarded, until the final desired response pattern is produced (e.g., Skinner, 1953, 1956, 1960). The operant paradigm usually is arranged so that the subject emits responses freely. Operant-conditioning research has investigated the effect of manipulating the reinforcing consequences produced by responses on the subsequent occurrence of similar responses. Studies of this kind have focused on the importance of discriminative stimuli and of reinforcement for the "shaping" or modification of behavior. These studies have demonstrated repeatedly the critical role of specific environmental response-reinforcement contingencies for the support, maintenance, and change of behavior (e.g., Ferster & Skinner, 1957).

The *patterning*, sequencing, or scheduling of the reinforcing consequences produced by a performance affect its future occurrence and strength (e.g., Ferster & Skinner, 1957). For example, continuous reinforcement usually facilitates the speed with which responses are learned. Intermittent reinforcement, on the other hand, tends to produce more stable behavior that is more persistently maintained under conditions of nonreinforcement or extinction. Under some circumstances the scheduling of reinforcement is even more important than the nature of the reinforcer. This was found, for example, in animal studies in which performances under complex schedules of punishment termination were compared with performances under similar schedules of food presentation. Performance was more affected by the schedules of reinforcement than by whether the reinforcer was food presentation or shock termination (Morse & Kelleher, 1966). During human socialization many potentially maladaptive or deviant behaviors are unintentionally rewarded on schedules that lead to the development and persistence of undesirable reactions that are exceedingly resistant to extinction.

Self-administered Response Consequences

The reinforcing consequences incurred by behavior are dispensed not only by the external physical and social environment. A striking characteristic of human behavior is that people judge and evaluate their own behavior and reward and punish themselves. In the typical laboratory situation the animal performs while the experimenter or his mechanical equipment dispenses preplanned reinforcing outcomes contingent on the organism's behavior. People, in contrast, exert considerable control over the rewarding and punishing resources available to them. They congratulate or deprecate themselves for their own attributes and actions; they praise or abuse their own achievements privately as well as publicly; and they self-administer social and material rewards and punishments from the enormous array of reinforcers freely available to them.

Whether or not an individual rewards or condemns himself hinges not only on what he does, but also on the exact context and detailed circumstances of his performance. The standards that a person observes other people using, the relations between his performance and the performance levels achieved by others, and the incentives available to him all affect his choice of self-reward or self-punishment on any occasion (e.g., Bandura & Kupers, 1964; Bandura & Whalen, 1966; Kanfer & Marston, 1963a, b; Marston, 1965; Mischel & Liebert, 1966). The conditions that control the choice of self-administered rewards and punishments, and their relevance for the maintenance and modification of behavior, will be discussed in later chapters.

Indirect (Vicarious) Response Consequences

The consequences a person expects depend not only on the outcomes he has received for his own behavior in similar situations, but also on the outcomes he has observed other people obtain. By observing the consequences produced by the behavior patterns of others, the observer presumably learns about the outcomes that he would probably encounter if he were to attempt similar behaviors himself.

In one study nursery school children watched an adult model who

was forced to wait for a reward dispensed by a vending machine apparatus (Carlin, 1965). While he was waiting for his reward the adult in one
condition displayed cues indicating that the delay was aversive for him.
He paced about impatiently, and when the machine finally dispensed a
treat he tasted it with visible annoyance and displeasure, quickly
throwing it away. In a second condition the model waited patiently and
calmly, and when his treat arrived he evidenced pleasure and satisfaction. Children in a third condition knew the model was waiting for his
treat, but the model was hidden from view so that they could not observe his waiting and consummatory behavior.

After exposure to these treatments children in all conditions chose
from the vending apparatus between a series of immediately available
but smaller rewards and larger rewards that required waiting. Children
who had observed the model's aversive reactions to the waiting period
and his displeasure at receipt of the delayed treat now were least willing
to wait for larger rewards. By simply observing the model's waiting
behavior the children's own choice behavior was affected. The children
also showed sharp discrimination. They were unwilling to wait for
rewards similar to the one for which the model had waited with displeasure, but their choice of less similar rewards was less affected, and
their choice of dissimilar rewards was entirely unaffected.

Observation of positive reinforcing consequences for a response
pattern tends to disinhibit the observer and to increase the probability
that he will engage in similar behavior. For instance, observing encour-
agement and praise encountered by people who display a pattern of
behavior (e.g., aggressiveness) increases the observer's own tendency to
behave in similar ways (i.e., aggressively). Conversely, when social
models are punished for their behavior, observers tend to show greater
inhibition of similar behavior (Bandura, Ross, & Ross, 1963).

Thus vicarious as well as direct reinforcement consequences for
performances affect the individual's subsequent behavior. A person does
not have to perform particular behaviors himself to learn their consequences. For example, a man does not have to be arrested for wearing
dresses in public to learn some of the consequences of transvestism. Any
information that alters the person's anticipations about the probable
outcomes to which a behavior will lead should also change the likelihood that he will engage in the behavior (e.g., Rotter, 1954, 1960).

The role of vicarious response consequences is illustrated clearly in
the study by Bandura, Ross, and Ross (1963). In that study, it will be
recalled, children watched a film of an adult who displayed novel aggressive responses. The adult's behavior in the film was either punished,
rewarded, or left without consequences. After seeing the films, children

who had observed punishment for aggressive behaviors imitated them less than those who had observed the model obtain either rewards or no consequences for aggression.

INSTRUCTIONS, RULES, AND PERSUASIVE COMMUNICATIONS

Any information, direct or indirect, about response-reinforcement relations can greatly shorten the learning process and affect performance. Obviously, for example, directions on how to reach the nearest exit in a fire are more effective than trial-and-error gropings in the dark. Likewise, informational feedback about past performance and instructions about the situation and contingencies that will confront the subject in the future critically affect his behavior (e.g., Mischel, 1958a; Mischel & Grusec, 1967; Rotter, 1954).

Our discussion of observational processes has dwelt mainly on effects that occur when people watch live or filmed models directly. Behavior also can be dramatically modified, however, as a result of symbolic and cognitive processes not dependent on actual observation of the model's activities. For example, individuals may change their attitudes and preferences after either reading or hearing about the relevant behavior of others (e.g., Bandura & Mischel, 1965; Duncker, 1938). The potency of these symbolically produced effects often is striking.

In one study (Duncker, 1938) preschool children were told an exciting, vivid story in which the hero, Eaglefeather, violently abhorred a pleasant-tasting food while he supposedly relished a more noxious food. After listening to the exploits and emotional reactions of the hero, the children tended to adopt his food preferences. Moreover, these dramatic changes in the children's subsequent food preferences remained fairly stable over time.

Abundant research on social influence through persuasive verbal communications also attests to the importance of cognitive alterations evoked by instructions and language in producing verbal and nonverbal behavior change (e.g., Hovland, Janis, & Kelly, 1953; Leventhal, Jones, & Trembly, 1966; Leventhal, Singer, & Jones, 1965; McGuire, 1960; Schachter, 1964). Most of these efforts have been devoted to changing attitudes and feelings on a great variety of topics by means of various types of social influence pressures and verbal persuasion.

The attributes of the communicator who delivers the communication tend to affect the degree of attitude change. Thus prestigeful and attractive communicators tend to exert greater social influence. Similarly, even the pleasantness of the situation in which a communication is received tends to affect an individual's reactions to the communication (e.g., Razran, 1940). For example, Hovland and Janis (1959) report that the effectiveness of a persuasive message was enhanced if it was communicated while the subjects were eating a pleasant snack.

A good deal of the research on social influence has been guided by a broadly eclectic form of reinforcement theory. Investigations in this framework have found that attitude change is influenced by such variables as the prestige and credibility of the communicator, the behavior of peers and other social models, and the incentives offered for opinion change. Of course, the individual's attention to, and comprehension of, the communication content is also a critical determinant of his subsequent behavior.

A second stream of social psychology research, guided by dissonance theory (Festinger, 1957), has found that individuals tend to reduce cognitive inconsistency. Studies on this topic suggest that when a person has behaved in a way that seems seriously inconsistent with his other cognitions about himself, he tends to modify his cognitions and to rationalize his behavior in a manner that makes what he did seem congruous with his beliefs (e.g., Brehm & Cohen, 1962).

Verbal instructions come to regulate both verbal and nonverbal behavior rapidly in the course of human development, although the mechanisms are still largely unknown (e.g., Birch, 1966; Lovaas, 1964a, b; Luria, 1961). Verbal events acquire signal properties and may exert their effects primarily through the information they convey to the learner (Egger & Miller, 1962; Postman & Sassenrath, 1961). Studies of the informational properties of verbal and nonverbal events, although still scarce, document the importance of verbal instructions as determinants of the effectiveness of both verbal and nonverbal stimuli (e.g., Cairns, 1967).

An investigation of how words can influence subsequent verbal and manual responding was conducted by Lovaas (1964b). It was found that the content of a verbal response affects the rate of verbal output. For example, when subjects repeatedly emit the word "slower" they pronounce it slowly with lengthening time intervals between the words. The opposite effects were found with the word "faster." Most interesting, the rate of verbal output controls the rate of nonverbal output. Thus, children were trained to respond with the word "slower" to one stimulus light, and with the word "faster" to another. After these discriminations were established, latencies of a *nonverbal* response (lever pressing) were observed under alternate presentations of the stimulus lights. The discriminative stimulus porperties of these two words were apparent in the fact that nonverbal responses to the light previously associated with "slow" had much longer latencies and slower rates than those to the "fast" light.

Studies of this kind, relating changes in nonverbal behavior to the modification of verbal responses, are in the minority. Many more studies have shown attitude or verbal change through reward of speech (Scott, 1957), including modification of psychotic and psychosomatic verbalizations through appropriate reinforcement (Ayllon & Haughton, 1964). Although the relations between verbal and nonverbal behavior have not yet been explored thoroughly, it seems likely that either class of behavior can serve both as reinforcing and discriminative stimuli for the other.

Regardless of the underlying mechanisms, it seems plain that the meaning of a stimulus, and its effectiveness as an elicitor and reinforcer of behavior, may be modified readily by associating it with new information conveyed through language and symbols. The meaning of verbal instructions, like the exclamation "Fire!," in turn depend on the larger structure and context in which they occur (Braine, 1963) as well as on the individual's previous associations with the symbols. For example, "Fire!" may lead to a dash for the exit or a volley of rifle bullets. Instructions from others as well as self-instructions may produce rapid change. The maintenance of such symbolically evoked change, however, is affected by the actual consequences produced when the subject practices the new actions (Chapter 9).

In accord with his emphasis on the principle of operant conditioning and direct reinforcement, Skinner has criticized investigations that employ verbal instructions or convey information about contingencies as when, instead of "shaping a response," the subject is simply told to respond in a particular way, or when a schedule or pattern of reinforcement is described rather than imposed. He calls this a "circumvention of an operant analysis" (Skinner, 1966).

It may be true, as Skinner (1966) suggests, that verbal instructions, descriptions, and observations do not affect behavior in the same way as direct exposure to the actual contingencies. For example, the poker player who learns his game from the rule book may play differently from the one whose behavior has been "shaped" by the actual contingencies encountered in playing the game. Indeed it is doubtful that the poker player who is shaped exclusively by contingencies without instructions or nonparticipant observation would financially survive the first hundred trials. Since most human learning occurs with the aid of instructions and observations, and not merely by direct shaping through reinforcement for successive approximations, it seems both arbitrary and unnecessarily restrictive to limit investigations and assessments to those in which the actual contingencies are imposed and enacted. On the other hand, it is important to recognize, as Skinner insists, that the manner in which behavior is acquired and maintained—through instructions, observation, or direct experience with contingencies—may affect the subsequent course of the behavior in different ways when new contingencies are introduced.

In most operant conditioning situations with human subjects, direct instructions about the response-reinforcement contingencies would lead almost at once to the desired terminal response. This seems especially evident in the verbal-conditioning situation in which the experimenter emits sounds or gestures signifying social approval ("uhum") contingent on the subject's saying items from a preselected class of responses, such as personal pronouns (e.g., Krasner, 1965). It has become increasingly clear that subjects in verbal-conditioning situations who become aware of the response-reinforcement contingency rapidly say the appropriate words. Indeed, until the subject can verbalize the contingency he tends to show little or no verbal conditioning (e.g., Farber, 1963; Spielberger & DeNike, 1966).

Especially under ambiguous performance conditions, verbally transmitted rules greatly facilitate learning and performance. For example, if a training agent verbalizes the rules on whose basis he is administering reinforcing outcomes, subjects can more readily adopt the standards that he is trying to transmit (e.g., Aronfreed, 1966; Liebert & Allen, 1967). Thus when children are told that particular performance patterns are good, while other outcomes are unsatisfactory, they adopt for themselves the appropriate standards more quickly than when such verbal rules are absent or ambiguous (Liebert & Allen, 1967).

Symbolic and cognitive processes also may play a critical role in classical conditioning paradigms. In laboratory studies of human classical conditioning the development and maintenance of autonomic conditioned reactions seems to depend on the subject's recognizing the connection between the conditioned and the unconditioned stimulus (Chatterjee & Eriksen, 1960, 1962; Fuhrer & Baer, 1965; Grings, 1965). In experimental studies of aversive conditioning, for example, conditioning tends to occur only with those persons who later can verbalize the CS-US contingency. Moreover, when subjects are simply told about the CS-US contingency their autonomic reactions tend to shift accordingly. For example, after aversive conditioning has been established, if subjects are informed that the conditioned stimulus will not be followed again by the aversive stimulus, their emotional reactions to the condi-

171

tioned stimulus can extinguish rapidly and even without any overt extinction trials.

On the other hand, in life situations intense conditioned emotional reactions often become firmly established and clearly are not under such ready cognitive control. These cases are best illustrated in "irrational," intensely emotional fears whose hallmark is their resistance to corrective information designed to assure the hapless person that the events he fears actually are harmless. Therefore the analysis and treatment of such abnormal conditions is especially challenging and theoretically important, as discussed in later chapters.

GENERALIZATION AND DISCRIMINATION

The degree to which an individual responds consistently across situations depends on processes of generalization and discrimination. Sometimes the conditions controlling the occurrence of generalization and discrimination are predictable readily, especially when the stimuli can be grouped on psychophysical dimensions of similarity. Outside the limits of the laboratory, however, and with more complex stimuli, generalization and discrimination phenomena become more difficult to predict.

The principles of stimulus discrimination and generalization apply to emotional responses acquired observationally and through classical conditioning as well as to the instrumental behavior patterns discussed in preceding sections. The case of Albert is a familiar example of the generalization of classically conditioned responses (Watson & Rayner, 1920). In a laboratory experiment a severe phobia was induced in Albert, a young child, by simply pairing the presentation of a white rat with aversive stimulation. Just as Albert reached for the animal a loud, fear-producing noise was made and these contiguous presentations of rat and unpleasant noise were repeated several times. Soon Albert developed an intense phobic reaction to the rat. When later presented with a wide range of new furry stimuli, including cotton, fur coats, human hair, wool, and other animals, he showed strong fear toward them, although they themselves had not been paired with noise.

Through primary and higher-order direct and vicarious conditioning, many maladaptive or deviant behaviors, characterized by painful emotional reactions and pervasive avoidance responses, come to be associated with diverse stimuli that were previously neutral. Likewise, through generalization processes new stimuli that share components of the conditioned stimuli may come to evoke similar reactions. General-

172

ization phenomena of course are not restricted to aversive emotional reactions and avoidance responses; similar effects occur with positive affective arousal and approach behavior. Thus an individual for whom homoerotic stimuli have become attractive may become aroused by, and subsequently seek, diverse homoerotic objects and activities including photographs, garments, odors, and the like. Similarly, in fetishisms a host of related stimuli typically acquire the power to evoke strong arousal reactions.

Extensive stimulus generalization may occur regardless of the exact learning mechanisms through which the particular conditioned responses were acquired initially. For instance, responses acquired either through operant conditioning or classical conditioning, or vicariously in observational learning, may generalize to many related situations. Dependent attention-seeking syndromes initially acquired through observation and reinforced by a parent, for example, may generalize to persons and contexts outside the home.

Generalization effects depend on the similarity among stimulus situations. A failure experience on an arithmetic task, for example, results in a decrement in stated expectancy for success on closely related academic tasks, but the effect is smaller or even zero on expectations for success in dissimilar areas like verbal reasoning or athletics (e.g., Chance, 1952; Jessor, 1954; Mischel & Staub, 1965). Likewise, a model's negative reactions toward a delayed reward reduced children's willingness to wait for rewards, but only when the rewards were similar to those toward which the model showed his impatience (Carlin, 1965).

The functional similarity among situations arises from more than their physical similarity; generalization occurs not only to physically similar stimuli (Grant & Schiller, 1953), but also to those that are contextually (e.g., Braine, 1963) and semantically related (e.g., Lacey & Smith, 1954; Lang, Geer, & Hnatiow, 1963). Semantic generalization of conditioned responses has been demonstrated often. For example, when subjects receive an electric shock during exposure to rural words like "barn" or "cow," they later show GSR fear reactions to other words connected with farming (Diven, 1937; Lacey & Smith, 1954). The mechanisms of higher-order generalization are incompletely understood, and direct and indirect first-order and higher-order conditioning influence both affective and instrumental responses in a multitude of different and complex ways (e.g., Braine, 1963; Feather, 1965). The effects depend on the exact circumstances of the individual's history with the particular stimuli and on the details of the eliciting situation, but the processes are far from clear.

Learning formulations of semantic generalization rely on the con-

173

cept of response-mediated associations (e.g., Mowrer, 1960; Staats & Staats, 1963). Every stimulus attribute—for example, a distinctive tone—elicits a sensory (or representational) response in the observer. If a new word—call it "ilg"—is repeatedly paired with the tone, it comes to elicit a portion or component of the mediating sensory response made to the tone (as well as the sensory response made to "ilg" itself). Gradually the word comes to elicit part of the response that the sensory stimulus or object with which it was associated elicits. Most important, other words that are associated with ilg, even if they were never paired with the tone, may come to elicit some of the components of the mediating response evoked by the tone. The more semantically similar the words are to "ilg," or the more closely they have been associated with "ilg," the more likely they are to produce a mediating response similar to the one elicited by "ilg" itself.

Internal response-mediated associations also are hypothesized in the phenomenon of sensory preconditioning (Hebb, 1966). In that process two sensory events, such as a light and a sound, repeatedly are presented contiguously. Then one of the two stimuli—say the light—is made the CS for a specific avoidance response by pairing it with the onset of shock. If the other stimulus (the sound) then is presented, it elicits an avoidance response similar to the one produced by the light, although the sound and shock have never been paired together directly. Presumably the original pairing of light and sound produced a connection between their corresponding internal mediating processes. Presentation of either stimulus alone subsequently evokes a component of the representational mediating responses for both stimuli.

Thus, through a process of contiguous associations previously neutral stimuli, including new words and symbols, become capable of eliciting new representational and affective internal responses that in turn lead to external responses. This occurs through the association of the new stimuli with other stimuli that previously achieved evoking power through their contiguity with unconditioned positive or aversive stimuli (e.g., food, pain-producing events).

Although contiguity may alter the meaning of words through conditioning, the contextual and grammatical structure in which the contiguity between words occurs also influences the meanings that are created (Braine, 1963). For instance, Mowrer (1960) gives an example of the classical conditioning of the meaning of words through contiguity. He deals with the association between the words "Tom" and "thief" in the sentence "Tom is a thief." There are many ways, however, in which these two words could be closely contiguous without producing a more negative meaning reaction to "Tom." As Mandler (1961) noted, this is apparent, for example, from the sentences "I have a friend called Tom. A thief once stole his wallet." It is very unlikely that this contiguous association between "Tom" and "thief" would elicit a more negative emotional reaction to Tom. The manner in which the structural features of language modify the meaning of words is now under extensive investigation in psycholinguistics (e.g., Miller, 1965).

There have been relatively few inquiries into generalization effects between verbal behavior and nonverbal behaviors relevant to the verbalization (e.g., Luria, 1961). One series of studies suggests that nonverbal instrumental behavior could be altered appreciably through reinforcement of the relevant verbal behavior. The following procedure was employed (Lovaas, 1964a). Nursery school children were reinforced by a puppet for saying food words like "carrots" or "celery" preselected by the experimenter. In individual sessions with each child a cowboy puppet seated on a puppet stage made comments such as "When you say the name of a snack, that word helps move my hand. . . . Say the name of a snack and make my hand move." (Lovaas, 1964a, p. 675.) When the child pronounced the name of the food that had been preselected for reinforcement by the experimenter, the puppet's hand moved, depressing a miniature lever which dispensed a trinket to the child. After repeated operations of this kind, changes in the children's actual consumption of the named foods were carefully assessed during snack times at the nursery school. Comparisons of the amounts of named foods consumed on days before verbal reinforcement with food intake after verbal reinforcement yielded highly significant differences.

It was very difficult to separate the discriminative from the reinforcing functions of the manipulated stimuli (the puppet's behavior). That is, the puppet's response of "good" to the child's "carrots" may have served as a signal or "implicit command" for eating carrots as well as (or instead of) exerting reinforcing functions (Lovaas, 1964a). Similar studies have demonstrated an increase in aggressive behavior following reinforcement for aggressive verbal behavior (Lovaas, 1961), changes in motor performance after verbal conditioning of attitudes (Krasner, Knowles, & Ullmann, 1965), and changes in group therapy behavior after verbal conditioning (Ullmann, Krasner, & Collins, 1961).

Considerable generalization occurs if a response pattern, like aggressive or dependent behavior, is reinforced uniformly in relation to highly diverse stimuli. On the other hand, discrimination occurs when a response pattern is reinforced in the presence of one stimulus property and nonreinforced, or extinguished, in the presence of other stimulus

175

properties. On the basis of the individual's direct and vicarious experiences stimulus properties come to signal the probable consequences to which behavior will lead in a particular situation. These cues serve as discriminative stimuli.

When discriminative stimuli change so does behavior, and without such adaptability human survival would be difficult indeed. Behavioral consistencies irrespective of discriminative stimuli would result, for example, in automobile traffic independent of road signs, pedestrians, and roads, and in social relations independent of social settings, social cues, and the persons to whom one is relating. Obviously behavior without environmental cues would be absurdly chaotic, as is recognized in every laboratory experiment with either humans or animals. The fact that environmental cues produce enormous variations within the behavior of the same person, however, has been less obvious to trait theorists, in spite of the evidence on relative trait specificity yielded by trait research, as the earlier chapters documented.

In sum, the repertoire of potential behaviors available to an individual depends on his past direct and vicarious learning experiences. In the present view, his choice among the numerous behavioral alternatives available to him in any given situation depends on the probable reinforcing consequences to which each available alternative is most likely to lead in that particular situation (e.g., Rotter, 1954). The anticipated consequences to which a behavior pattern leads in any situation depend on the person's direct and vicarious past experiences in similar situations. Even subtle verbal and nonverbal changes in the situation alter the cues that signal the probable consequences of behavior. When the probable reinforcing outcomes produced by a behavior pattern change, the probability of the behavior itself changes. For this reason, cross-situational consistencies in behavior cannot be expected when behavior yields discrepant consequences in different situations.

The implications of the foregoing concepts about the determinants of behavior for understanding consistency and specificity in personality have not been recognized clearly. The following sections apply these concepts about the conditions controlling social behavior to the data that have emerged from correlational studies of traits and states.

THE INTERPRETATION OF BEHAVIORAL SPECIFICITY AND GENERALITY

In 1928 the authors of the Character Education Inquiry interpreted their data on the specificity of moral conduct in a way that fits equally well the results on most of the traits and states that have been studied so exhaustively during the many years since their original work:

> *It may be contended of course that as a matter of fact we rarely reach a zero correlation, no matter how different may be our techniques, and that this implies some such common factor in the individual as might properly be called a trait. We would not wish to quarrel over the use of a term and are quite ready to recognize the existence of some common factors which tend to make individuals differ from one another on any one test or on any group of tests. Our contention, however, is that this common factor is not an inner entity operating independently of the situations in which the individuals are placed but is a function of the situation in the sense that an individual behaves similarly in different situations in proportion as these situations are alike, have been experienced as common occasions for honest or dishonest behavior, and are comprehended as opportunities for deception or honesty.* (Hartshorne & May, 1928, p. 385.)

Several main findings have emerged from the data on traits and states reviewed in the preceding chapters, and it is now instructive to summarize them briefly. First, behavior depends on stimulus situations and is specific to the situation: response patterns even in highly similar situations often fail to be strongly related. Individuals show far less cross-situational consistency in their behavior than has been assumed by trait-state theories. The more dissimilar the evoking situations, the less likely they are to lead to similar or consistent responses from the same individual. Even seemingly trivial situational differences may reduce correlations to zero. Response consistency tends to be greatest within the same response mode, within self-reports to paper-and-pencil tests, for example, or within directly observed nonverbal behavior. Intraindividual consistency is reduced drastically when dissimilar response modes are employed. Activities that are substantially associated with aspects of intelligence and with problem-solving behavior—like achievement behaviors, cognitive styles, response speed—tend to be most consistent.

There are, of course, many correlations among an individual's behaviors even in response to diverse situations. Individual differences occur on almost all measures of behavior; extensive networks of correlations can be, and have been, found for response patterns on a multitude of tests. These vast networks of test-test correlations are, however, of limited utility, mainly because of the situational specificity of behavior and the consequently low magnitude of the associations. The foregoing results are consistent with the principles of social behavior summarized in this chapter as the following sections discuss.

The facts of behavioral specificity point to the importance of considering specific stimulus conditions and contingencies for the accurate prediction and control of behavior. Behavior tends to be extremely variable and unstable except when stimulus conditions and response-reinforcement relations are highly similar and consistent (Fiske, 1961). Assigning the same label to diverse behaviors that are elicited in different contexts and through dissimilar methods—as when checking responses on inventories, motoric acts directed at persons, and verbal reports to inkblots are all called "aggressive responses"—can obscure the fact that the covariations among the responses are a function of the similarities in their evoking and maintaining conditions. For example, whether dependency toward peers at school covaries with dependency toward teachers is a function of the extent to which the response consequences and maintaining conditions for these activities are correlated.

The Specificity of Response Consequences

We should not expect a person to show similar behavior across situations if the consequences produced by the same behavior pattern in different situations are discrepant. If reinforcement consequences for the performance of responses are largely uncorrelated, the responses themselves should not be expected to covary strongly, as they indeed do not in most empirical studies (Chapters 2 and 4).

Consider, for example, the differences in the typical outcomes to an American adolescent girl for wearing slacks on a family picnic or wearing the same garment to her high school graduation ceremonies. The object at which behavior is directed, and numerous other details of the situation, all may influence the consequences of the behavior and hence the probability for its future occurrence. Young girls, for example, may be expected to be dependent on others in many situations and circumstances, but rarely toward strange males on park benches at night. To the extent that dependency is sanctioned in one context, but not in the other, cross-situational consistency should not occur.

To illustrate, boys whose parents encouraged them to be aggressive with peers, but who were punished for aggression in the home, behaved aggressively at school but nonaggressively at home (Bandura, 1960). Similarly, Trinidadian lower-class Negroes rarely choose to wait for promised delayed rewards and usually prefer immediately available albeit smaller gratifications (Mischel, 1958a, 1961a). Promises of future rewards have been broken frequently by promise-makers in their past experience, and these people participate in a culture in which immediate gratification is modeled and rewarded extensively (Mischel, 1961b, c). Nevertheless, they save money, plan elaborately, and give up competing immediate gratifications to make long-term preparations for annual feasts, religious events, and carnival celebrations (e.g., Mischel & Mischel, 1958).

As the foregoing illustrations point out, reinforcing consequences in naturalistic life contexts depend not only on the content of the behavior but also on the particular circumstances in which it occurs. This fact is perhaps most apparent if one considers the variables that influence social judgments about behavior and hence the social consequences and the social rewards and punishments which the individual receives. The social consequences produced by any pattern of action depend not only on what a person does but also on who does it, on the conditions in which he does it, and on the observers who evaluate the behavior. The consequences for shoving, pushing, and hitting, for example, depend on who does it (a four-year-old boy or a forty-year-old minister), to whom he does it (an attacker, a child), the details of when and how he performs the behavior, as well as on the evaluative standards of any observers who judge his actions.

Or consider how the social consequences of sexual acts hinge on the persons and exact circumstances involved in the behavior and on the people who evaluate it. Considerations like the age and social conditions of the participants, as well as the locale of their activity, may make the difference between whether the sexual behaviors lead to a jail sentence, a confinement in a mental hospital, or a wedding. Or take the area of moral behavior and resistance to temptation. When the probable reinforcing consequences for cheating differ widely across situations—depending on the particular task and circumstances, the behavior of others, the likelihood of detection, the probable consequences of being caught, the value of success, and so forth—impressive generality in moral conduct is not to be found.

The dependence of behavior on precise stimulus conditions and on the probable reinforcing consequences to which the behavior leads is illustrated most clearly in the detailed study of the single case. In this context recall again Ann's nursery school behavior. As Figure 4 showed, when the consequences for Ann's behavior changed, she rapidly changed accordingly.

Just as with behavior that is controlled by externally administered reinforcement, self-reinforcing processes also depend on specific environmental cues. The standards people employ to evaluate themselves, and the stringency or leniency with which they subsequently reward themselves, all are influenced by highly situational considerations (e.g., Mischel, 1966b). Because individuals also make their own self-rewards highly contingent on very specific situational considerations, broad behavioral consistencies across tasks and contexts are reduced even more. It would be hard to find a person who regularly reacts to his own behavior in the same ways irrespective of just what he has done and how it stands in relation to what others do in similar situations.

In accord with the principles of stimulus generalization and discrimination, behaviors become widely generalized only when they are reinforced uniformly across many stimulus conditions. Since the bulk of social activities yield positive outcomes in some contexts but negative consequences in other situations, the behaviors tend to become remarkably specific. As a result, poor associations among response patterns even in seemingly similar situations are found, it will be recalled, quite ubiquitously (Chapters 2 and 4).

Consider once more the intercorrelations among measures sampling, for instance, dependent behaviors, such as "touching, holding, and being near." If a child has been rewarded persistently for "touching, holding, and being near" with same-sex peers at nursery school but not with adults at home, a strong positive correlation between dependency measured in the two situations will not be obtained. Individuals discriminate between contingencies to a great degree even in behaviors often used as referents for supposedly stable generalized traits like dependency, aggressiveness, self-control and "ego strength." This fact, ignored so frequently in personality formulations, in research, and in assessment, has now been demonstrated too often to be controversial.

Recognizing the specificity of behavior, some proponents of trait and dynamic theories nevertheless still argue for genotypic or underlying unities that exist beneath the surface. They adhere to the familiar distinction between overt "acts" and covert dispositions and maintain that beneath the diversities of observable behavior lie more basic consistencies in the form of motives, goals, needs, or other state and trait genotypes. Commenting on this pervasive concept of genotypic unities as an explanation for overtly inconsistent behavior, Brim (1960) notes:

> . . . *studies which first assume the existence of such a genotypic trait in a sample of individuals, then stipulate what the evidence of its existence (and absence) will be in a variety of situations, then actually gather the data to validate the conception are not*

at hand. The genotypic conception of personality, if one were to take a harsh view, appears as a bit of legerdemain in which the theorist snatches identity from diversity by distracting attention from what one actually sees to something the theorist says is there, whether one can see it or not. (Brim, 1960, pp. 136–137.)

Several years after Brim's sharp conclusions, the evidence, as reviewed in preceding chapters, seems to remain equally weak.

If one assumes, as do trait-state theorists, that people have highly generalized dispositions, then seemingly discrepant behaviors from the same person require special interpretations to explain why he behaved inconsistently. The issues here may be illustrated by a hypothetical clinical example. Consider a man who is judged by the assessor to be "basically passive" and to have strong dependency motivation. Having decided that passivity is a basic consistent disposition in the client, any behavior from him that seems inconsistent with his passivity and dependency needs must be explained with special constructs and mechanisms. Evidence that he is aggressive or hostile in some situations, or seemingly self-sufficient and independent in others, for example, might be interpreted as reflecting his defensive maneuvers and his conflictful struggle against his underlying "basic" dependency motivation.

As discussed earlier (Chapter 3), both the layman and the scientific theorist persistently seek interpretative consistency in the face of incongruous, inconsistent data, and one way to reduce dissonance is to invoke constructs about consistent underlying states or motives when behavioral inconsistencies become apparent. The argument that underneath the surface or "phenotypic" diversities of an individual's social behavior there exist underlying "genotypic" unities of personality is unimpeachable in the abstract, but its utility is empirically unsupported. On the other hand, the social behavior theory formulation emphasizes the discriminations that come to regulate behavior in very subtle ways. As such it does not need to invoke special mediating mechanisms to intervene between hypothesized dispositions and supposedly discrepant surface behaviors; it interprets the diverse behaviors themselves as the predictable, expected results of socialization processes in which discrimination training plays an enormously important role. If in the course of an individual's development dependency is modeled, expected, and rewarded in some situations but self-reliance and independence is learned and supported in other settings, then he will display both kinds of behavior. No special defense mechanisms, conflicts, displacements, or other underlying processes need to be invoked to account for these "inconsistencies," since the hypothesis of generality was not made in the first place.

Consistency of Intelligence and Related Skilled Behaviors

As noted in earlier chapters, intellectual and cognitive behaviors tend to be more consistent across situations than most personality dimensions. The consistency of these patterns may arise in part from the relatively uniform consequences they produce across situations. That is, discrimination training for achievement-related accomplishments and intellectual behavior may be less sharp than for dependency or sexual behavior. If the consequences for intellectual and achievement activities were more uniform across many situations they would lead to less discrimination and greater consistency of these behaviors in diverse settings.

The relative consistency of intellectual and achievement-related behaviors probably also reflects their dependence on basic skills and aptitudes, some of which hinge on genetic endowment. Moreover, intellectual skills and competencies involve long chains of interdependent components that are required for effective functioning across many situations. For example, if an individual has not mastered the fundamentals of a foreign language he is likely to perform uniformly poorly on all the many tasks for which that language is an essential component or prerequisite. A Frenchman who has not learned English is likely to fail tests of English reading, writing, conversation, comprehension, and so forth, regardless of the incentive conditions and reinforcement manipulations offered to him at the time of testing. Likewise, a child who cannot read is unlikely to do well on vocabulary and spelling tests.

Specificity and Consistency in Response Modes

In any one response mode a good deal of consistency may often be found. Recall the durability of the traits and states that people attribute to themselves (and others) on personality questionnaires. Often these broad concepts, labels, and stereotypes may be applied by the person to many behaviors and over long time periods (Chapters 2, 3, and 4). These constructs, sometimes based on only a few features of behavior, may be retained tenaciously even in the absence of further confirmatory evidence, as we have seen.

On the other hand, such consistency is much more rare across different response modes. The response mode in which behavior occurs influences the consequences to which the behavior leads. An individual's thoughts, stories, self-reports, daydreams, and overt enactments all dealing with the theme of murder, or of sexual acts, rarely lead to the same consequences or even to highly correlated consequences. To the extent that the outcomes for behavior in different response modes and eliciting conditions are uncorrelated, consistencies across these response modes should not be expected.

To illustrate, when there is little discrepancy between the probable consequences and maintaining conditions for verbal reports and their parallel nonverbal behaviors, considerable congruity is found between them. Thus, for example, political attitudes and actual voting tend to be consistent with each other (Chapter 4). On the other hand, when there are major discrepancies in the evoking and maintaining conditions for verbal statements about someone or something and for direct relations toward the person or object, the statement about behavior and the actual behavior may be highly inconsistent. Recall, in this connection, the discrepancy between the biased private verbal attitudes and the actual hospitality toward a minority group shown by motel owners (LaPiere, 1934).

Usually the consequences for similar content expressed in different response modes are drastically different. A person whose stories on a projective test abounded with aggressive themes would be credited with a healthy, active fantasy life, but the same individual probably would be incarcerated if he enacted similar content in his interpersonal relations. Hence it should not be unexpected that even seemingly slight diffrences in the response medium used to sample behavior have provided relatively unrelated results, and that trait scores from one medium (e.g., questionnaires) show limited relations to scores for the same trait elicited in any other different medium (e.g., Campbell & Fiske, 1959; Skolnick, 1966a).

The Specificity of Stimulus Valences and Emotional Behavior

Emotional reactions, just like instrumental responses, also tend to be far more specific than trait and state theories have assumed. The specificity of emotional behavior is most clearly illustrated in clinical contexts when detailed individual assessments are available. Clark (1963) described a woman who had been terrified of birds and feathers for many years. Her fears were so intense that she was unable to go on outdoor walks, avoided zoos and seaside holidays, and became constrained in many ways. A closer assessment revealed that she was able to think about the objects of her fear, and to even imagine them vividly, without upset. She could easily tolerate verbal descriptions of the stimuli without experiencing any disturbance; her fears seemed restricted to actual encounters with the real objects and only then did she react with terror.

As another example, Lazarus noted the specificity of the conditions controlling sexual fears in frigid women (1963). One woman, for instance, was calmly able to imagine herself engaged in certain sexual caresses, but only if they occurred in the dark. Or White (1964) describes a pilot who became debilitatingly anxious when flying, but only whenever his plane exceeded an altitude of 9000 feet. In another context, Metcalfe (1956) found asthmatic attacks occurred in a young woman primarily after she had contacts with her mother.

These examples of specificity in the conditions producing emotional arousal illustrate the fact that emotional reactions and stimulus valences also may involve quite subtle discriminations. Affective reactions, like all other responses, are rarely oblivious to environmental cues. Just as the probable consequences of any behavior pattern depend on numerous specific situational considerations, so does the affective value or valence of any stimulus hinge on the exact conditions in which it occurs.

This specificity is true even for primary or unconditioned reinforcers. For example, whether or not food has positive incentive value or aversion-producing effects depends on the food deprivation or hunger of the consumer. Hunger can be turned into nausea easily by even a subtle change in stimulus conditions (e.g., a comment about the ingredients of the meal). Similarly, conditioned reinforcers, like praise or censure, depend on numerous situational variables that control their effects, as well as on the organism's arousal state at the moment.

Among the many variables known to affect the meaning and valence of a stimulus is the sequencing and patterning of the stimulus (e.g., Buchwald, 1959, 1962; Crandall, Good, & Crandall, 1964; Helson, 1964; Spence, 1966); the subject's prior direct and vicarious experiences with it (e.g., Carlin, 1965; Mischel & Grusec, 1966); social comparison processes (e.g., Festinger, 1954); and the cognitive labels the person assigns to his own emotional arousal state (Schachter & Singer, 1962). Moreover, as later chapters show in detail, the valence of any stimulus can be altered readily by associating it directly or symbolically and cognitively with stimuli of opposite valence.

Response Consequences and Performance on Personality Tests

Clinicians have sometimes acted as if responses to personality "tests" are exempt from the variables that affect behavior. But it is naive to believe that behavior on psychological tests ostensibly measuring personality reflects a pure X-ray-like version of the respondent's durable underlying psyche and is somehow immune to response consequences and situational cues. Research results on the determinants of both projective and objective test responses shatter any illusion about the independence of test behavior and eliciting conditions (e.g., Masling, 1960).

A heterogeneous and seemingly chaotic collection of variables has been found to affect performance on psychological tests that were intended to measure personality. This array includes instructions about the test itself and a host of details in the testing situation. The assessor's behavior, the procedures of administration, the subject's experiences immediately before the test, as well as the attributes of the test materials all affect the test response (e.g., Murstein, 1963). These findings have made it plain that personality tests do not reveal a situation-free glimpse of the individual and cannot distill persons independent of stimulus conditions. However, the interpretation of just how these "situational" variables affect test performance has been unclear.

In the present view, the situational variables that affect responses on personality tests exert their effects in large part by modifying the probable consequences to the subject for particular test behaviors. This occurs in exactly the same way that modification of the outcomes produced by behavior, both directly and vicariously, has been shown to determine behavior in nontest contexts. The unnecessary divorce between experimental personality research and clinical assessment may have served to obscure this similarity and to dichotomize erroneously answers on personality tests and all other systematically sampled behavior.

Findings from experimental personality research show that performance on a variety of measures—including tests of achievement and aggressive, dependent, and self-control behavior—is affected by the direct and observed response consequences for similar performance in related situations (e.g., Bandura & Walters, 1963; Mischel, 1966a; Rotter, 1954). In light of these results, it should not be unexpected that conditions in a testing situation that provide cues about probable response consequences for particular test responses in turn affect the subject's actual test performance, producing great behavioral specificity.

Any cues that modify the probable consequences for making particular test responses alter the behavior that occurs. The examiner's mere presence itself may inhibit the expression of responses by modifying the probable consequences for their performance. For example, TAT stories told in the presence of the examiner tend to be more guarded, the themes reflect less affective involvement, and story content is happier and has more optimistic outcomes than when stories are composed privately (Bernstein, 1956).

In a similar vein of research, Mussen and Scodel (1955) examined differences in sexual content of TAT responses as a function of the type of examiner. Two groups of college students were sexually aroused by viewing photographic slides of attractive nude females before taking the TAT. In one group the session was conducted by a stern professorial man in his sixties, whereas in the second group a permissive graduate student presided. The manifest and implied sexual contents of the test responses were rated and combined into a single score for each subject. These scores revealed significantly higher sexual content for subjects tested under the more disinhibiting conditions. Presumably the expression of strongly sexually tinged stories would be less sanctioned and less positively received by a stern academician than by a permissive fellow student.

Instructions about the nature and purpose of testing also can affect the probable response consequences for test behaviors and thus change performance on the test. Instructions which imply that certain test patterns may produce negative consequences by resulting in critical evaluations of the respondent tend to inhibit and constrict responsivity on projective tests like the Rorschach and TAT (e.g., Henry & Rotter, 1956). Moreover, test responses, like all other behaviors, are modifiable readily, even by subtle cues and reinforcements emitted intentionally or unintentionally by other persons including the examiner (e.g., Wickes, 1956).

Social Desirability and Response Consequences

One of the most consistent findings illustrating the close correspondence between probable response consequences for test behavior and actual test performance comes from data often construed as "error" by psychometricians. Perhaps the strongest correlations consistently found in psychometric assessment research are for the relationship between the rated social desirability of response alternatives on tests and the actual probability of endorsing or choosing the response (e.g., Edwards, 1959, 1962). These extremely strong and reliable associations, discussed in Chapter 4, generally have been taken as evidence for discrete "social desirability response sets." Moreover, extensive psychometric efforts have been made to control, partial-out, and eliminate them. In the present view, the social desirability ratings of test response items provide an index of the reinforcement value of endorsing them. The strong correlations between this value and the probability of selecting the item

186

reflects that response selection on personality tests, as elsewhere, is determined by the probable reinforcing consequences of the choice. If endorsing X is likely to lead to more positive consequences for the subject than endorsing Y, then, not surprisingly, he will endorse X.

Response Sets as Failures in Discrimination

One common instance of stimulus generalization encountered in personality assessment and research involves response "sets" of the kind frequently found in answers to personality questionnaires (Chapter 4). Response consistencies—for example, in answering yes or no to diverse, ambiguous questions regardless of content—reflect a failure to discriminate item content. The person instead answers consistently with either "yes" or "no" regardless of the stimulus item. Agreement response sets, like other response consistencies that ignore stimulus differences, are examples of stimulus generalization. Understandably, such failures to discriminate occur most readily when the test items are extremely ambiguous, are phrased vaguely, and when no objectively right or wrong answers are possible. Usually sharp discriminations are hindered by the structure and instructions of the personality tests and questionnaires themselves (Chapter 3). Precisely under these ambiguous conditions it is most difficult to discriminate clearly the different reinforcing consequences likely to occur for different responses across items. Since stereotyped, highly generalized verbal descriptions and broad cliches about traits tend to be sanctioned and reinforced pervasively in the culture, subtle discriminations in answers to trait questionnaires should not be expected. Indeed such questionnaires yield fairly global interpretative categories and stereotypes about behavior, rather than objective descriptions (Chapter 3).

Method Variance or Stimulus Variance

A main finding of trait research is that similarities in the format of measuring techniques account for a great portion of the correlations obtained among personality measures, as when several questionnaires are used to measure ostensibly different traits (Chapter 4). "Method variance," or the common variance resulting from the use of measuring techniques that employ similar or overlapping formats or apparatus, has been construed as "error" by psychometricians. To counteract this error new statistical techniques to control and minimize method variance are sought perpetually (e.g., Block, 1965; Campbell & Fiske, 1959; Norman, 1966). From the present viewpoint, however, method variance is not error; it simply reflects "stimulus variance" or the response commonality expected when common eliciting stimulus conditions are employed. Just as would be anticipated from findings on stimulus generalization, response consistency across situations in assessment diminishes to the extent that the situations are dissimilar, and increases to the extent that they share common features.

IDIOGRAPHIC PEOPLE AND NOMOTHETIC ANTECEDENT PROCESSES

In the uncontrolled conditions of any person's life a multiplicity of specific variables combine in idiosyncratic patterns. The resulting unique circumstances in turn lead to the unique, idiographic patterns that constitute an individual's personality. Although every individual, and indeed every response pattern, is in a sense unique, the basic processes that determine his behavior are not.

The kinds of antecedent processes discussed in this chapter—observational learning, conditioning, direct and vicarious reinforcement, generalization, and discrimination—lead to diverse social behavior patterns which then are endowed with different labels by observers. For example, the same general principles that account for the learning and performance of dependency apply to aggression (e.g., Bandura & Walters, 1963). Moreover, the same processes that account for the development of extreme maladaptive dependency also permit us to understand the development of prosocial patterns of self-control and voluntary delay of reward (e.g., Mischel, 1966a, b). The same basic antecedents that determine all these behaviors should also determine, say, attitudes toward an authority. In social behavior theory the variables that control the development and modification of prosocial behavior are no different from those that govern "abnormal" syndromes. Regardless of the value and trait labels applied to social behaviors, the basic processes that account for their acquisition and modification have been found to be the same.

It would be very surprising if the various patterns of social behavior to which investigators assign different labels were actually controlled by basically different processes. It would be odd, for example, if observational learning were an important determinant of relations with peers but not of attitudes toward foreign countries, or if reinforcement patterns influenced behavior in small groups but not attitudes toward teachers in large classrooms. In research directed at particular units of behavior the specific type and content of reinforcers, models, and contingencies might be different for each unit, but the underlying processes would be the same. Thus although the specific aggressive behaviors displayed by a mother would differ of course from her submissive behaviors, the variables that determine how readily a child adopts the modeled events would be the same.

The same general principles would apply whether one is investigating the "construct validity" of, for example, submissiveness in research with a group of college students, or the conditions controlling the disadvantageous extreme submissiveness of a troubled client in a mental hospital. Once submissiveness is considered to be submissive behavior rather than an internal entity it can be defined with observable response referents and studied. Responses, albeit many different ones, sampled through different media (verbal, symbolic, direct) become the referents for the behavior. The task then involves studying the conditions that control submissive behavior in its various forms. Obviously it would be most inefficient to conduct such an inquiry randomly. In addition to specifying his response units, the investigator seeks "if . . . then" relationships, in which the "if" is a stimulus change and the "then" is an alteration in the response pattern. The elaboration of these "if . . . then" or "stimulus change/response change" relations gradually becomes his account of the determinants of submissiveness. In each analysis, whether it deals with a response pattern in a single individual or with group data, it becomes necessary to identify the precise stimulus conditions that are controlling the behavior of interest—the specific models, the substantive reinforcers, the exact discriminative signals in the particular situation of concern. Such analyses are the chief task of social behavior assessments, whether they deal with the individual client or with groups.

The Acquired Meaning of Stimuli

The phenomena of discrimination and generalization lead to the view that behavior patterns are remarkably situation specific, on the one hand, while also evokable by diverse and often seemingly heterogeneous stimuli on the basis of generalization effects. The person's prior experiences with related conditions and the exact details of the particular evoking situation determine the meaning of the stimuli—that is, their effects on all aspects of his life. Usually generalization effects involve relatively idiosyncratic contextual and semantic generalization dimensions and are based on more than gradients of physical stimulus similarity.

In animal laboratory research it is feasible for the investigator to know in detail most of the organism's environmental history from direct observation, but this is never possible in human assessment. Even with a simple stimulus, like the onset of a light, it is impossible to predict behavior unless the respondent's prior history with the stimulus is known, or unless his current response is sampled. Accurate predictions about a rat's behavior in reaction to a signal light in a controlled, restricted environment depend on the predictor's knowledge of the rat's previous history with the light: one must know the properties or meaning that the stimulus has acquired for the subject. If the history is unknown, the response has to be assessed directly. The same stimulus could lead to running right or left, or jumping, or crouching, or leaving the compartment, depending on the organism's history, as well as on the total context in which the event occurs. The same problems apply, obviously even much more complexly, if one ventures statements about human responses.

The conditions under which particular stimuli acquire their meaning or power in the life of any person are often both adventitious and unique. It therefore may be futile to seek common underlying dimensions of similarity or generalization on the basis of which diverse events come to evoke a similar response pattern for all persons. Instead it would seem more profitable to assess the exact conditions that regularly lead to increments or decrements in the problem-producing behaviors for the particular person.

Behavior assessments *do not* label the individual with generalized trait terms and stereotypes, sort him into diagnostic or type categories, pinpoint his average position on average or modal dimensions, or guess about his private reasons and motives. Instead the focus is on sampling the individual's relevant cognitions and behaviors. In this sense, behavioral assessment involves an exploration of the unique or idiographic aspects of the single case, perhaps to a greater extent than any other approach. Social behavior theory recognizes the individuality of each person and of each unique situation. This is a curious feature when one considers the "mechanistic S-R" stereotypes not infrequently attached by critics to behavioral analyses. Assessing the acquired meaning of stimuli is the core of social behavior assessment, and is inextricably linked with behavior change, as is discussed in the following chapters.

SUMMARY

Three social learning paradigms were considered: observational (cognitive, perceptual) learning, classical conditioning, and response-contingent reinforcement. Observational learning is based on contiguity and can occur in the absence of any direct reinforcement to the observer. The main factors that affect observational learning were reviewed. Many complex cognitive, semantic, emotional, and motoric behaviors, both adaptive and maladaptive, are learned, elicited, or inhibited, and maintained by modeling cues.

A distinction was made between learning (or the acquisition of behavior) and performance. By varying the eliciting conditions and introducing incentives designed to evoke a particular behavior, one can determine whether its absence under given eliciting conditions indicates that it has not been learned or that the behavior was acquired but is not being performed. The manner in which the direct and vicarious reinforcing consequences for behavior affect the future occurrence of similar behavior was discussed. The important role of instructions, language, and cognitive processes in complex behavior was emphasized. Then the data on response-response associations, reviewed in earlier chapters, were analyzed in light of the processes of generalization and discrimination.

The concepts presented in this chapter were shown to be compatible with the findings reviewed in the preceding chapters: behavior depends on the exact stimulus conditions in the evoking situation and on the individual's history with similar stimuli. The studies reviewed in this chapter illustrate some of the many variables whose effects account for behavioral specificity. Simultaneously studies of this type also suggest that orderly relations between stimulus changes and consequent response changes can be predicted under reasonably controlled conditions. Studies of the precise ways in which behavior comes to depend on stimulus conditions, and of how alterations in stimulus conditions are followed regularly and consistently by predictable behavior changes, reveal basic lawfulness. Moreover, although behavior is complex and depends on a multiplicity of situation-specific variables, for many practical and theoretical purposes meaningful predictions and control can be achieved when a few key variables are properly arranged.

BEHAVIOR CHANGE

/7

If behavior is regulated by highly specific stimulus variables and contingencies, then both assessment and psychotherapy need to be much less global and far more pinpointed enterprises than they usually have been. It also becomes clear why global estimates of the overall strength or frequency of broad response dispositions, as in trait-state descriptions of people as generally "hostile," "aggressive," "passive-dependent," "neurotic," or "anxious," have turned out to have little utility beyond gross screening. Instead, a more useful type of assessment would have to deal with behavior in relation to specific contingencies and discriminative conditions. For example, it would have to specify for the "hostile" man just when and how he is hostile, and just when he shows more, and when less, of his hostile behavior. In this manner it becomes possible to go beyond mere global characterizations of another person and, instead, to discover the conditions that influence his behavior. Then, if desired, these conditions can be altered so that more advantageous behavior becomes possible for him.

Behavior assessments are not intended to assign the individual into a diagnostic category, nor to infer his traits and dynamics, nor to predict his position on a personality dimension or in an unknown situation. Instead, the main purpose of social behavior assessment is to design treatments that most appropriately suit the particular client's objectives .As a starting point we must consider the meaning of problematic behavior. Then the remainder of this chapter, and the next one, will examine how the principles discussed in the previous chapter guide the conduct of behavior change and assessment.

DEFINING PROBLEMATIC BEHAVIOR

Clinical assessment usually has been practiced in medical settings and since its inception has been linked with the medical profession and its traditions. This medical history has greatly reinforced the psychiatric disease model which holds that maladjustments reflect underlying disease processes rather than socially acquired behavior problems.

The Disease View

In the disease approach to abnormal behavior the person is seen as a "patient" victimized by his mental "illness" as if it were a physical disease in the same sense as mumps or cancer. Hypothesized mental diseases are conceptualized in terms of medical constructs for pathology like "schizophrenia," "manic-depressive psychosis," "obsessive-compulsive neurosis." Psychiatric constructs of this kind are part of the heritage of the Kraepelinean classification system in which psychological problems were interpreted as manifestations of unitary disease entities that supposedly possess relatively unique characteristics.

In the disease viewpoint interest in behavior itself is bypassed in favor of inferences to underlying mental diseases, the behaviors being seen as mere "symptoms" of the underlying pathology. Traditionally "diagnosis" implies that there is some concrete thing, like an organ defect, an invading germ, or some definite psychic entity within the person, that exists internally and is the source of his behavioral troubles. The diagnostic search is to find the pathology so that it can be treated. "Differential diagnosis" is the search for the exact disease responsible for the symptoms.

There is little evidence to support the value of the disease approach to the modification and assessment of psychological problems (e.g., Eysenck, 1960; Hobbs, 1966; Rotter, 1954; Szasz, 1961). Agreement is poor about the relations between patterns of psychological behavior and the hypothesized diseases of which they are supposed to be the symptoms. As Chapter 2 showed, behavioral patterns themselves have little cross-situational consistency. Attempts to categorize people into psychiatric disease classifications also have been unsuccessful and the behaviors subsumed by different categories overlap greatly (Chapter 5). It is possible to achieve reasonable agreement among raters for very broad categories of deviant behavior ("organic," "psychotic," "characterological," e.g., Schmidt & Fonda, 1956), but less gross classifications into the usual psychiatric syndromes generally cannot be made reliably.

Even if it were possible to classify "symptomatic" behaviors reliably into relatively discrete and consistent categories, the consequences for designing psychological treatments still would be unclear. The designs of current traditional psychotherapy programs are largely unaffected by the personality descriptions and by the trait-state labels assigned to patients (Chapter 5). A notable exception is that some psychiatric labels (like psychosis or organicity) may prevent their bearers from receiving special individualized attention and psychotherapy. In addition, those labeled organic receive more phenothiazines and far more "nonspecific" treatments (Bannister, Salmon, & Leiberman, 1964).

In the disease approach, the term "mental ill health" has been stretched to refer to such diverse behavioral manifestations as juvenile delinquency, schizophrenia, suicide, unhappiness, and passive acceptance of an unbearable environment (Scott, 1958a, b). As a result the terms mental health and mental illness have become so unclear that they serve mainly as the foci for semantic quarrels about the nature of psychological health and illness. Szasz has been one of the most articulate critics of what he calls the "myth of mental illness" and of the disease approach to problems of social-psychological behavior. As he contends, "problems of living," rather than "demons, witches, fate, or mental illness," are our adversaries (Szasz, 1960, p. 118).

The disease model is appropriate for the analysis and treatment of physical illness in medicine, but it has little utility for conceptualizing psychological problems. As long as there are no identified discrete organic pathologies that can be tied clearly to social behavior, speculations about them have little value for the assessor. On the contrary, adherence to medical analogies, and labeling people with the names of diseases whose disease properties and physiological bases are not established, can distract the assessor from concentrating on the psychological conditions controlling the behavior of concern. The medical model also leads to an emphasis on individual psychotherapy and on psychiatric hospitalization, rather than on relearning experiences in life settings and social reeducation for disturbed individuals. The limitations of practices guided by the disease model are being recognized increasingly. In the context of helping severely disturbed children, for example, Nicholas Hobbs (1966) commented:

> *We have become increasingly convinced that a major barrier to effective national planning for emotionally disturbed children is the professional's enchantment with psychotherapy. Everything in most model institutions revolves around getting the*

child to his therapist 1, 2, or maybe 3 hours a week. A few superb treatment centers combine psychotherapy with a program of daily activities conducive to personal growth and integration. But these are rare indeed. It is not uncommon to find children locked 15 stories high in steel and glass, with a caged roof to play on, drugged to keep them from doing too much damage to the light fixtures and air conditioning, while they await their precious hour, guarded by attendants who think disturbed children must scream, fight, climb walls, cower in a corner. Most frequently, of course, therapy is not available; most hospitals hold children hoping somehow they will get better. . . .

An overcommitment to individual psychotherapy seems to us to stem from an uncritical acceptance of "cure" as the goal in working with a child, a consequence of defining the problem initially as one of "illness." That some disturbed children are "ill" in the usual sense may be accepted, but to define them all as such leads, we think, to a host of unvalidated and unquestioned assumptions; to a preoccupation with the intrapsychic life of the child, with what goes on inside his skull; to an easy use of drugs without knowledge of their long-term effects on character development; to the extended isolation of children from their families, the presumed source of contagion; to a limitation of professional roles; to the neglect of schools and of schooling; and so on (p. 1108).

The view that behavior problems are symptomatic surface manifestations of underlying diseases appears to have had as little utility as the belief that prosocial behaviors are merely superficial indicators of basic underlying traits and dynamic states. As we have seen, the assumption that behaviors (deviant or otherwise) are surface manifestations or overt indicators of generalized, underlying dynamic and motivational predispositions (either diseased or healthy) has led to a long search for stable, consistent intrapsychic predispositions. Inferences based on these hypothesized traits or dynamic forces have had little predictive utility. Moreover, even highly skilled clinicians generally are unable to agree with each other about the particular dynamics, motives, and dispositions that characterize a given individual (Chapter 5). Consequently one might be skeptical about the value of the insights into these motives, dynamics, and dispositions that therapeutic relations are supposed to impart to clients. The value of traditional therapeutic activities aimed at modifying these underlying entities is most seriously questioned by the data on the outcomes obtained from the standard forms of insight and relationship psychotherapy.

Eysenck's review of treatment outcomes in 1952 pointed out that the improvement rate (about 64 percent) for patients who received intensive and prolonged psychotherapy did not exceed the improvement rate (72 percent) for similar patients who were treated only custodially or by general practitioners. Almost ten years later Eysenck (1960) found no evidence to change the picture. On the contrary, even more data appeared to indicate that untreated patients did not seem to fare worse than those who received intensive psychotherapy, both groups showing some improvement. Eysenck's conclusions of course have been challenged (e.g., Rosenzweig, 1954) and the methodological limitations of most research on treatment outcomes have been so formidable that firm conclusions could not be reached. Some of the main assumptions guiding most studies on the effectiveness of psychotherapy also have been criticized sharply (Kiesler, 1966).

Although the literature on the outcomes of traditional psychotherapy is often confused and difficult to interpret, a few themes emerge (Bergin, 1966). The only school of traditional interview psychotherapy that has received any systematic validating support is client-centered therapy (e.g., Truax & Carkhuff, 1965a, b). Client-centered therapy does seem to produce significant alterations. Usually these changes are measured by the self/ideal correlation obtained from Q sorts or from other verbal self-categorizations on trait scales before and after therapy. Bergin's extensive review of outcome research indicated that on such measures some clients improve significantly but others deteriorate significantly during treatment. The overall mean effect therefore tends to be similar to the mean for controls whereas the variance for treated groups often is greater. Bergin concluded, appropriately, that psychotherapy may cause clients to become either significantly better or worse than controls. Gendlin (1962), for example, reported detrimental effects from relationship therapy for some clients, especially those diagnosed schizophrenic. The evidence that psychotherapy can hurt some people is as compelling as the data that it can help them.

The total results of outcome studies for traditional treatment methods raise basic doubts about the appropriateness and effectiveness of the most widespread current forms of interview psychotherapy (Bergin, 1966). As Freud (1959) recognized in 1918, it is clear that treatment alternatives are sorely needed for the traditional forms of insight and relationship therapy. Such alternatives, in the form of social behavior therapies, are inextricably linked with behavior assessment.

The Social Behavior View

In the view of social behavior theory, such terms as mental illness, maladjustment, and abnormality all refer to social judgments about a person's behavior rather than to hypothesized diseases or to traits or states that reside in the person who displays the behavior. Statements about "appropriate" socialization or adjustment involve judgments about the extent to which the individual performs socially expected and approved behaviors. These judgments often also hinge on inferences about the degree to which the person values culturally sanctioned goals and behaviors. Statements about maladjustment, deviance, personality disturbance, in contrast, involve inferences about the extent to which an individual's behaviors generate aversive or nonoptimal outcomes for himself and others.

Behaviors can be evaluated psychologically by the immediate and long-range consequences they produce for the individual and for other people. Problematic behaviors may be construed as response patterns that engender consequences judged to be disadvantageous or aversive for others in the society and/or for the person who displays them. These judgments about behavior, like all social value judgments, depend on the specific circumstances in which the behavior occurs and on the social role and status of the individual (Hollingshead & Redlich, 1958).

Judgments about the consequences of an individual's behavior are made both by the individual and by the members of the community who observe and evaluate him. Frequently a person labels himself and reacts to his own behaviors very differently than does the bulk of society. A successful criminal, for example, may experience few aversive immediate personal consequences although his activities lead to severe distress for others. On the other hand, a successful executive may receive the blessings of society while he is privately unhappy enough to contemplate suicide.

Rather than becoming embroiled in social judgments about the client's behaviors, or in speculative reconstructions about their hypothetical origins and motivational roots, behavior assessment begins with an attempt to select reasonable treatment objectives. The effort to specify the treatment objectives that should be attained is the least studied and often the most difficult phase in behavior assessment.

In some clinical situations the most urgent and highest priority goal is apparent readily. Consider the case of a young woman (5 feet, 4 inches tall) who previously had weighed up to 120 pounds, but who stopped eating until her weight had dropped to 47 pounds (Bachrach, Erwin, &

Mohr, 1965). She was in extreme danger of death and had no detectable causal organic diseases. The historical reasons for the weight loss were unknown but there could be no doubt about the behavioral problem. Behavior assessment in this case was automatically directed at identifying the most effective environmental manipulations that could restore her eating and increase her body weight. To help this woman regain weight, eating was reinforced with a varity of incentives whose attainment was made contingent on her food consumption. Although medical and other treatments had failed to alter her condition, a careful program of reinforcement for eating, initiated in the hospital and maintained after her discharge, served to almost double her body weight and to save her life.

Lazarus (1963) provides another illustration of relatively clear objectives in his report of women who were completely frigid sexually. In these cases the assessment consisted of identifying a broad range of sexual situations that engendered varying degrees of emotional upset. In the treatment itself profound relaxation responses, induced hypnotically or by suggestion, were paired with increasingly anxiety-provoking sexual thoughts. As a result of these carefully planned presentations, sexual thoughts and sexual acts gradually become more and more pleasurable.

The foregoing cases illustrate readily apparent treatment objectives. It is more difficult to select the initial goals when the case is not so dramatically extreme. Clients have many problems, and the most urgent objectives are not always obvious at the outset. Moreover, the client frequently does not specify direct and reasonably precise referents for his difficulties. Clients are not necessarily more immune than psychologists to theoretical preconceptions, and they too tend to put their constructs before their behavior. Often clients discuss the hypothetical causes of their problems before describing them, or assume that trait terms like anxiety, feelings of insecurity, and depression simultaneously describe and explain their difficulties.

Although most clinical assessments are concerned primarily with detecting the motives underlying the client's statements, a social behavior analysis requires elaboration of just what is being referred to, and of the consequences of the described behavior for the person. If the consequences are aversive, the questions become what requires change and how change can be accomplished best. Perhaps the largest barrier to achieving this objective occurs when the assessor prematurely assumes that he understands adequately the sensory and evaluative referents, and the consequences, involved in the client's statements. The discovery of appropriate referents for these personal statements and private, personal constructs is one of the critical steps in behavior assessment, as discussed in the next chapter.

Behavior may yield disadvantageous consequences because of many different inappropriate reactions to diverse stimuli. It is convenient to simplify this great diversity by grouping the problem-producing stimuli into a few major categories.

First consider stimuli that are problematic primarily because they evoke disadvantageous emotional reactions in the person. Stimuli may produce aversive emotional reactions and avoidance in an individual, although they evoke neutral or even positive affective reactions from most members of the community. Emotional reactions may be in the form of somatic disorders, such as functional gastrointestinal, cardiovascular, and respiratory problems, muscle tensions and fatigue states, or intense anxiety complaints. Common examples are intense fear reactions to seemingly neutral objects, like kitchen knives or birds, or to routine interpersonal situations. On the other hand, stimuli may have acquired the opposite effects; some stimuli evoke positive emotional arousal and approach although most people in the culture react to them neutrally or even with aversion. Typical examples are sexual attraction to one's own sex or fetishistic behavior.

There is still another basis for grouping stimuli. In these cases the problem is not primarily a disadvantageous conditioned emotional reaction. Rather, the individual's response to particular stimuli is incorrect, inappropriate, or otherwise deficient. The stimuli, however, do not necessarily evoke intense or disturbing conditioned emotional reactions in him. For instance, the criminal who refuses to abide by probation rules and the child who is persistently inattentive to the teacher and aggressive in the classroom illustrate such problems. Closely related are problems resulting from behaviorial deficits. In these cases the individual encounters disadvantageous consequences primarily because he has never learned the skills and competencies necessary for effective functioning in particular situations. Individuals with deficient educational, vocational, social, and interpersonal skills (so often found in "underdeveloped" areas), abundantly illustrate the paralyzing social and personal disadvantages resulting from severe behavior deficits.

Inappropriate emotional reactions and behavior patterns may have been initially acquired mainly through observational learning, direct reinforcement, classical conditioning, or most likely through a combination of processes at work for a long time. Although it may be possible in the laboratory to generate and observe clear differences between antecedent processes ultimately producing inappropriate response patterns, the assessor faces the client after the deviant pattern has been established. Regardless of theoretical orientation it is usually impossible to reconstruct accurately the unobserved historical genesis of behavior. Consequently, it may be wiser in assessment to identify disadvantageous emotional reactions, performance deficits, and inappropriate behavior by isolating the stimulus conditions in which these problems occur. Assessment then can focus on the current maintaining conditions for problems and the manipulations most likely to modify them effectively. As later sections will illustrate, lasting and significant therapeutic alterations in behavior have been achieved repeatedly in the absence of any knowledge of the historical antecedents of the individual's troubles.

Research, assessment, and treatment are truly integrated in the social behavior approach. Assessment identifies the problem-producing stimuli; treatment modifies the disadvantageous responses evoked by the stimuli and helps the individual to develop more optimal coping techniques. These modifications are achieved by changing the power of the problematic stimuli, either by associating them with other stimuli or by changing the consequences obtained by the responses they evoke, in accord with the principles discussed in the previous chapter. Alterations in previously problematic behavior are also supplemented by the development of more advantageous alternative behaviors.

A focus on the psychological conditions that govern disturbed behavior, and on the rearrangement of psychological variables that can change them therapeutically, in no way preempts the role of physiological and genetic variables. The latter undoubtedly are absolutely critical in the genesis of behavior, and ultimately may be harnessed effectively to achieve many changes in psychological problems. Moreover, there may well be limits on the kinds of changes that even the most potent psychological techniques can achieve—for example, in the reeducation of brain-damaged patients. All that can be expected of an approach is that it concentrate on the variables with which it deals and that it try to go as far as possible with them. The following sections explore the treatment and assessment of psychological problems from the perspective of social behavior theory.

MODIFICATION OF VALENCES

Almost any initially neutral stimuli may acquire the power to evoke phobic and anxious emotional responses if the stimuli have been associated directly or vicariously with aversive events or outcomes. Aversively conditioned emotional reactions also may generalize extensively to new stimuli. These generalizations may be based on dimensions of semantic and contextual, as well as physical, stimulus similarity, as noted in the last chapter.

Common clinical examples of aversive arousal and avoidance include phobic and anxious reactions to particular objects, people, and social and interpersonal situations. Not only external events, but also their symbolic representations in the form of words or of thoughts and fantasies, may engender these aversive emotional responses in the person. Thus the individual's own covert and overt behaviors often serve as the stimuli for negative emotional reactions from himself. For example, thoughts about masturbation, as well as the act of masturbation, may evoke anxiety in the person for whom these events have been aversively conditioned. On the other hand, as a result of discrimination learning, sharp differences in the emotions aroused by covert and overt responses often occur. Thoughts about marital infidelity or murder might be tolerated easily by an individual for whom the act itself would generate severe guilt and self-punishment. Painful emotional reactions are not limited to fears. Functional somatic disorders, muscular tensions, fatigue, other psychosomatic complaints, and anxiety states illustrate the diverse reactions that may result when stimuli persistently evoke acutely distressing emotional arousal.

Following intense arousal all kinds of avoidance behaviors generally ensue rapidly. Many of these escape efforts may be maintained persistently since they provide powerful reinforcing consequences, chiefly by terminating the painful autonomic emotional state. For example, elaborate obsessive-compulsive rituals, such as handwashing for several hours, may be maintained by reducing the anxiety generated by diverse conditioned stimuli (e.g., Wolpe, 1963). Other reinforcing consequences, such as attention and sympathy from relatives and friends, or relief from noxious duties, can also serve to maintain the avoidance patterns once they become established. As a result, increasingly self-paralyzing behaviors may occur that inadvertently lead to more and more disadvantageous and crippling outcomes. In one case a woman's fear of birds and feathers led her to avoid all walks out of doors because of the possibility that birds might come near her, greatly constricting many aspects of her life (Clark, 1963a). Persistent fears and avoidance behaviors initially are probably mediated by classically conditioned autonomic responses. After these avoidance responses are established, however, their occurrence may be governed primarily by central nervous system processes and environmental cues independent of autonomic arousal (Bandura, 1968; Black, 1959; Wynne & Solomon, 1955).

All of the foregoing examples have dealt with inappropriate aversive emotional reactions and avoidance behavior. Conversely, inappropriate positive arousal occurs when stimuli and behavior sequences that are neutral or even unpleasant for most people in the community have acquired the power to produce positive emotional arousal in an individual. These emotional responses in turn are accompanied by instrumental approach behavior. Common examples here include fetishism and the bizarre rituals that often are associated with it. Sadistic and masochistic behaviors likewise reflect activities and fantasies that have become positively valenced for the individual while they are abhorred by the majority. There are many less extreme but more common instances of disadvantageously intense attractions and addictions that society either does not tolerate or permits only under highly limited conditions. Homosexual behavior constitutes one frequent clinical problem of this kind, and alcoholism and drug addiction are others.

Behavior therapy for disadvantageous emotional reactions, regardless of whether they are positive or negative in affect, is based on the same basic learning principles, as the following sections illustrate.

In accord with classical conditioning, the valence of stimuli can be changed by pairing them repeatedly with other stimuli that elicit even stronger emotional reactions of the opposite valence. For example, if a stimulus that evokes some fear is repeatedly associated with one that elicits an even stronger incompatible reaction, such as profound relaxation or highly intense pleasure, the valence of the fear-provoking stimulus gradually changes. The previously feared stimulus begins to acquire some of the calming or pleasurable emotion-producing powers of the strong relaxing or pleasure-evoking stimulus. Conversely, if a stimulus that evokes positive emotional arousal is repeatedly paired with one that elicits an incompatible reaction, such as intense pain, displeasure, or aversion, some of these latter unpleasant emotional reactions gradually become elicited by the formerly positive stimulus.

The approach of Wolpe and his associates exemplifies the use of counterconditioning therapy to neutralize aversive emotion-arousing stimuli (e.g., Lazarus, 1961; Wolpe, 1958). First the stimuli or situations that evoke marked emotional arousal and avoidance are identified. These events then are graded on a hierarchy of severity, ranging from the least disturbing to the most intensely anxiety-provoking events. In the next phase the client is taught deep muscle relaxation, mainly through a technique of progressive body relaxation (Jacobson, 1929). While the individual is comfortably seated and calm the therapist demonstrates and teaches him how to tense and then deeply relax different muscle groups. Relaxation training proceeds in a gradual sequence that finally leads to a state of diffuse and total calmness. Often the suggestions to relax are presented under hypnotic sets of varying depth. Sometimes relaxation training is also facilitated by the use of appropriate relaxing drugs.

After a few sessions with the therapist the client generally is able to learn to relax to his own cues and to practice relaxation under his own control outside the therapy room. This self-training is helped by a phonograph or tape-recording of the relaxation instructions which the client can play in his home under the proper calm conditions. The person thus can practice on his own the relaxation exercises as he listens to the audio instructions, providing him with greater autonomy while also saving therapy time in the clinician's office.

In the critical phase of counterconditioning treatment the relaxation responses now are paired with the least anxiety-arousing stimulus from the previously established hierarchy. Usually the stimulus event is presented symbolically or verbally while the client is profoundly relaxed and calm. The therapist merely says the words for the item while the subject concentrates on the item cognitively, generating the most vivid, lifelike image of it that he can form in his imagination. Whenever the subject experiences even the slightest diminution in his relaxed state he immediately signals the therapist. He is instructed promptly to discontinue the image of the stimulus until he reachieves his relaxed state. Thereafter the next lowest (less severe) item on the hierarchy is presented. After the client can concentrate in imagination on this item without loss of relaxation the next more severe item from the hierarchy is introduced. Through careful use of these procedures it is possible to neutralize increasingly aversive stimuli by eliciting relaxation responses to them. Since relaxation is inherently incompatible with anxiety, the former tends to prevent the latter if conditions are arranged properly.

Thus in Wolpe's counterconditioning procedure the individual is exposed cognitively to mild (but increasingly severe) samples of aversive or fear-arousing stimuli. Simultaneously he is helped to make responses that are incompatible with anxiety, such as muscle relaxation. The empirical principle of counterconditioning is simple, as schematically represented in Figure 5. If responses strongly antagonistic to anxiety can be made to occur in the presence of mild anxiety-evoking stimuli, the incompatible response at least partially prevents the anxiety response. Consequently the association between the aversive stimulus and anxiety becomes reduced, while the association of the stimulus with the relaxation reaction becomes strengthened (e.g., Guthrie, 1935; Wolpe, 1958). The crux of a proper arrangement is insuring that the aversive stimuli are carefully presented in a graded sequence of in-

Phase 1 — Before Counterconditioning:

Phase 2 — After Counterconditioning by Contiguous Presentations of:

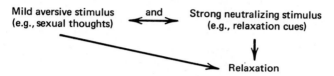

FIGURE 5. *Schematic representation of counterconditioning procedure.*

tensity. This sequence must present items that do not evoke excessively severe emotional reactions. Otherwise the person may become so overwhelmed that he cannot make the incompatible (relaxation) response. Through repeated contiguous associations between mild aversive and strong oppositely valenced responses, the valence of the former is changed in the direction of the latter.

Wolpe's counterconditioning technique should shatter any stereotypes that behavioristic therapies confine themselves to mechanical S-R relations that ignore the individual's cognitive and affective internal processes. Far from denying cognitive and emotional inner states, behavior therapy utilizes cognitions and emotions deliberately in treatment to achieve behavior change and to help the client gain better control over his own disturbing intrapsychic experiences. During stimulus neutralization treatments the client thus *imagines* the presence of symbolically presented emotion-provoking stimuli; imagining is hardly a mechanical procedure, nor would it fare well with an "empty organism."

Wolpe's own theoretical formulation has drawn extensively on neurological speculation whose validity has been questioned seriously by many critics. The counterconditioning technique to which his theorizing led, however, has been studied extensively and has been applied to many problems. Counterconditioning or stimulus neutralization procedures have effectively modified not only phobias but also the instrumental avoidance patterns and obsessive-compulsive behaviors that often are developed to reduce anxiety. Wolpe (1963), for example, reported the case of an adolescent boy who had a severe hand-washing compulsion. Assessment indicated that after urination the boy spent up to forty-five minutes in an elaborate ritual to clean his genitalia. These ablutions generally were followed by another period of up to two hours devoted to washing his hands. Traditional psychodynamic therapists might concentrate on the exploration and interpretation of the boy's sexual fears and relate them to Oedipal problems and to his psychosexual history. Wolpe instead noted that urine and urination appeared to be the precipitating stimulus for the youngster's obsessive-compulsive rituals. Consequently, the boy was desensitized to stimulus hierarchies dealing with urine and urination, presented under deep relaxation. According to Wolpe, excellent and rapid progress occurred under this regimen. Similar treatments for obsessive-compulsive disorders were reported to be successful by Eysenck and Rachman (1965), and Davison reported the successful application of counterconditioning techniques to the treatment of sadistic fantasies (1967b) and of somatic delusions (1966). Thus the valence of virtually anything that can be imagined—and not merely simple objects or physical situations—can be altered under the proper conditions.

Relying on the client's ability to visualize in his imagination a realistic, vivid image of the problematic stimuli has some striking advantages. This symbolic procedure permits treatment of diverse covert responses to a wide range of stimuli when the performance of the overt motoric behavior would be either impractical or impossible. It is far more feasible, for example, in the neutralization of sexual fears (Lazarus, 1963) to have a woman imagine herself in various erotic relations with her husband than to enact the behavior in the clinician's office.

In addition, these symbolic or cognitive presentations make it possible to deal in miniature form with stimuli whose live presentation would provoke overwhelming anxiety and avoidance. Through appropriate verbal description, sometimes aided by pictorial cues, almost any situation can be presented in a way that makes it simultaneously vivid but not emotionally debilitating. Wolpe (1961), for example, described the successful desensitization of a woman's fear of automobiles through the presentation of imaginary scenes in a fictitious context, accompanied by relaxation. Her intense terror reaction to cars made it clearly impossible to use actual automobiles as stimuli, at least in the early treatment phases. In the same manner one can also change feelings and attitudes toward anxiety-provoking interpersonal situations and relationships.

Although clinical testimonials about the therapeutic successes achieved by these techniques are encouraging, they do not supply firm evidence regarding their utility when compared to various alternative treatments and controls. In addition, case studies cannot discriminate the components of any technique that are truly essential for its success from those components that are irrelevant. Only controlled studies can help to identify the critical ingredients of any particular technique for behavior change and can assess its relative efficacy. In recent years a number of such experimental studies, mainly dealing with systematic desensitization, have become available.

Several experimental studies have demonstrated that systematic cognitive desensitization can effectively eliminate many phobias (e.g., Lang & Lazovik, 1963; Lang, Lazovik, & Reynolds, 1965; Lazarus, 1961; Paul, 1966, 1967; Rachman, 1967). In these studies snake fears have been highly favored not only because they are common fears but also because of the symbolic sexual significance that psychodynamic theories attribute to snakes (Brill, 1949). According to psychodynamic theory, such phobias as snake fears represent symbolic manifestations of an underlying core problem. A basic cure of the phobia cannot be achieved without an alteration in the unconscious dynamic conflicts supposedly symbolized by the phobic symptom. Consequently, the fact that these phobias can be eliminated without any exploration of their possible unconscious meanings and their historical etiology has considerable theoretical importance. Psychodynamic theory suggests that unless insight into the ostensible unconscious origins of the symptoms is achieved no lasting improvement can be expected. In fact, follow-up studies reveal that the gains from behavior therapy tend to be retained or even increased and give no evidence of symptom substitution (Lang & Lazovik, 1963; Paul, 1967; Rachman, 1967; Wolpe, 1958, 1961).

A carefully designed study investigated the relative efficacy of cognitive desensitization for treating intense public-speaking anxieties. College students who dreaded public speaking were assigned into one of four conditions (Paul, 1966). In one group they were exposed to Wolpe's cognitive desensitization procedure and were systematically relaxed to progressively more threatening imagined situations connected with public speaking. In another condition subjects received brief, traditional, insight-oriented psychotherapy from an expert clinician. Students in a third condition served as "attention-placebo controls," obtaining placebo "tranquilizers" and bogus training allegedly designed to help them "handle stress." Subjects in each of these conditions had five contact hours over a six-week period for their treatments. The final group was a no-treatment control which took the pre- and post-treatment assessment battery but received no special treatment.

The assessments before and after treatment included tests, ratings, and behavior observations to measure public-speaking anxiety cognitively through self-report, physiologically, and behaviorally. In the latter assessments the subject's actual public-speaking behavior under stress conditions was directly observed and scored. The results are summarized in Figure 6. Systematic desensitization was found to be consistently the most superior treatment on all cognitive, physiological, and behavioral indices of anxiety. Brief, insight-oriented psychotherapy did not differ from attention placebo, but both these conditions yielded greater anxiety reduction on nonphysiological measures than the no-treatment controls. On the physiological measures, however, only the desensitization group showed a significant reduction in anxiety when compared to the no-treatment controls. A follow-up on the test battery six weeks later showed that improvement was maintained and no indications of symptom substitution were found.

Similarly, another follow-up study two years after termination also revealed that these improvements continued to be maintained stably (Paul, 1967). The people who had received systematic desensitization still showed the greatest improvement. In spite of a search for possible symptom substitution no evidence was found to suggest that it occurred; on the contrary, further beneficial generalization effects seemed to result from the reduction of the anxiety problems.

Lazarus (1961) and Paul and Shannon (1966) also successfully extended counterconditioning procedures to small groups. In the study by Paul and Shannon (1966) highly anxious college students received group desensitization cognitively to social-evaluative situations dealing with public speaking. Just as in Paul's other study (1966), the desensitization technique was clearly effective and again produced results consistently superior to those from brief, insight-oriented psychotherapy and control conditions. Desensitization in groups seemed to be at least as effective as individual desensitization, plus being obviously more economical, requiring an average of less than two hours of therapist time per client. Students who received the counterconditioning treatment not only became desensitized to public-speaking stresses but also showed a significant increment in overall college grades when compared to students in the other conditions.

A study by Davison (1967a) showed that actual contiguity between presentations of the graded aversive stimuli and the incompatible response (in the form of relaxation) is essential for effective systematic desensitization. In this experiment people with intense fears of nonpoisonous snakes were assigned into one of four conditions. In the "desensitization" group a graded series of snake-relevant aversive stimuli

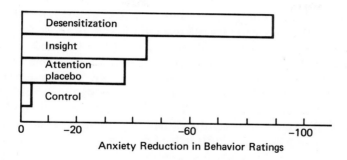

Anxiety Reduction in Behavior Ratings

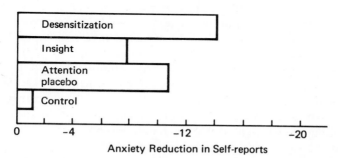

Anxiety Reduction in Self-reports

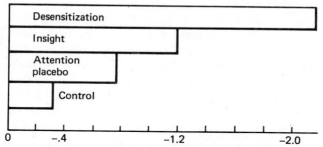

Anxiety Reduction in Physiological Measures (Composite)

FIGURE 6. *Mean reduction in anxiety from pretest to post-test found for each group on each of three measures. (Adapted from Paul, 1966, p. 33.)*

were paired cognitively (in imagination) with deep muscle relaxation, as in Wolpe's standard clinical technique. The second condition was a "pseudo-desensitization" treatment designed to control for the effects of relaxation itself, as well as for any relationship factors and expectations for success. Persons in this group received the identical treatment as those in the first condition except that neutral stimuli, entirely irrelevant to snakes, were paired with relaxation. The third or "exposure" condition exposed subjects to the series of graded snake-relevant aversive items but in the absence of deep relaxation. Finally, those in a "no treatment" control participated only in the pre- and post-treatment assessments. In the assessments before and after treatments all people were tested for actual approach behavior to a live snake as well as for self-reported anxiety. The results clearly supported the hypothesis that systematic desensitization effects indeed depend on the contiguous pairing of the graded conditioned stimuli with the anxiety-competing response (relaxation). Only subjects in this genuine desensitization condition showed any significant reduction in avoidance behavior.

Another experiment included a detailed investigation of the role of relaxation in the desensitization process (Schubot, 1966). This study compared presentations of graded aversive stimuli under hypnotically induced, deep muscular relaxation and under the normal state. Subjects who were not intensely fearful at the outset showed significant improvement regardless of the depth of relaxation employed during the counterconditioning process. On the other hand, extremely avoidant individuals showed significant improvement only after counterconditioning under deep relaxation.

Wolpe and his colleagues have relied largely on relaxation as the favorite incompatible response to be paired with emotionally aversive stimuli. However, relaxation may be difficult to induce in some persons. In these cases other responses incompatible with anxiety and avoidance, such as sexual arousal and assertive behavior, can be evoked (Wolpe, 1958; Wolpe & Lazarus, 1966). In one of the earliest applications of this method, eating appetizing food was the anxiety-incompatible response (Jones, 1924). The subject was a boy who had developed severe fear reactions to furry animals and especially to rabbits, as well as to furry objects, cotton, wool, and feathers. In counterconditioning the youngster was fed attractive foods in the presence of a caged rabbit. The rabbit was always kept sufficiently far from the table to insure that the boy's eating would be undisturbed and the rabbit was brought successively closer to the boy each day. Ultimately it was possible to place the rabbit on the table and even in the child's lap without disturbance. Moreover, the boy's fear responses were eliminated, through generalization, to all the additional previously indicated fear-arousing stimuli. Presumably some of the positive responses involved with eating became associated with the formerly aversive stimuli and served to neutralize them.

During the counterconditioning treatment itself some people, especially children, may find it difficult to generate vivid images of the items presented verbally from the stimulus hierarchy. Vivid imaginal concentration on stimuli can be enhanced by presenting them as realistically as possible. To achieve this, the stimulus can be described verbally in compelling detail. Still better, the stimuli often can be presented pictorially, on films, in fictitious contexts (stories), or they can actually be presented directly, as the following case illustrates.

Clark (1963a) attempted systematic desensitization with a woman who had developed a socially debilitating fear of feathers and birds. She could not go for walks out of doors, or visit parks or zoos with her child, or go near the seaside, because birds might come near her. Assessment revealed that for this woman thinking about birds was not problematic; encountering them, however, was nearly catastrophic. Consequently, desensitization had to deal with graded exposures to live stimuli, rather than to thoughts about them.

As a first step all the events and situations that elicited her self-reported anxiety were collected and listed with the usual verbal techniques. These items then were ranked in a hierarchy of severity through a process of paired comparisons. Thereafter she was confronted gradually with the actual stimuli in the order of increasing severity. The items included a variety of feathers (large and small, stiff and downy), as well as a bag full of feathers, a 4-inch by 1½-inch bundle of feathers bound with black thread, and an assortment of stuffed and live birds. Among the birds was a stuffed pigeon with outstretched wings, a caged budgerigar, pheasants, chickens, park ducks, and so on. These materials were gradually presented to the client at increasingly close distances over a series of desensitization sessions, beginning with a feather at a space of twelve feet.

Her reactions to these events were inferred not merely through her own reports but also by autonomic measurement of GSR changes. The latter measures served as cues to guide the programming of the materials. Clark noted that several times when a stimulus was brought too close GSR changes were noted well before the client reported any increments in anxiety. Most interesting, this woman claimed from the outset that she was able to visualize clearly the anxiety-provoking stimuli in imagination without undue upset. Even vivid verbal portraits by the psychologist of the feared objects did not disturb her. Actual encounters with the real stimuli (e.g., birds' wings), however, were completely terrifying for her and had been a problem for about twenty-five years. Graded exposure to the actual stimuli, paired with relaxation, effectively eliminated this woman's phobia and the associated avoidance patterns.

The effects of desensitization during therapy sessions were enhanced further by carefully planned exposure to increasingly severe samples of the feared objects in naturalistic situations. For example, her visits to the therapist were interspersed deliberately with visits to a museum containing small and large stuffed birds. Later she visited an aviary with live birds behind wire screens, and afterward a public park with tame ducks and birds that could be fed. This case underlines the specificity of anxiety-evoking stimuli and consequently the need to deal in therapy with stimuli that approximate as closely as possible the ones that elicit problems outside the therapy room.

Similarly, Freeman and Kendrick (1960) successfully treated a woman who feared cats and furry objects by exposing her directly to stimuli that were, in very small steps, more and more similar to cat fur. Specifically, she was confronted with pieces of material that were graded in texture and appearance to range from velvet to catlike fur. After touching these materials she progressed to toy kittens and pictures and ultimately to a live kitten followed by a mature cat.

Another interesting innovation comes from Lazarus and Abramovitz (1962) who used "emotive imagery," a symbolic modeling procedure similar to Duncker's (1938), to treat a ten-year-old boy. The child was referred for treatment because of an excessive fear of the dark. This boy became extremely anxious whenever his parents went visiting at night; even when they stayed at home he would not enter any dark room alone. He began to have nightmares, and his school work showed some deterioration. He also became afraid to be alone in the bathroom and only used it if a member of the household remained there with him.

On questioning, the boy indicated that he invariably became tense and afraid toward sunset although he was not anxious during the day. A discussion of the child's interests and activities revealed his passion for two radio serials, "Superman" and "Captain Silver." These heroes were employed in the therapy as follows:

> *The child was asked to imagine that Superman and Captain Silver had joined forces and had appointed him their agent. After a brief discussion concerning the topography of his house he was given his first assignment. The therapist said, "Now I want you to close your eyes and imagine that you are sitting in the dining-room with your mother and father. It is night time. Suddenly, you receive a signal on the wrist radio that Superman has given you. You quickly run into the lounge because your mission must be kept a secret. There is only a little light coming into the lounge from the passage. Now pretend that you are all alone in the lounge waiting for Superman and Captain Silver*

to visit you. Think about this very clearly. If the idea makes you feel afraid, lift up your right hand."

An ongoing scene was terminated as soon as any anxiety was indicated. When an image aroused anxiety, it would either be represented in a more challengingly assertive manner, or it would be altered slightly so as to prove less objectively threatening.

At the end of the third session, the child was able to picture himself alone in his bathroom with all the lights turned off, awaiting a communication from Superman. (Lazarus & Abramovitz, 1962, pp. 192—193.)

Treatment for inappropriate positive arousal, as in fetishism and homosexuality, is the converse of the counterconditioning procedure just discussed for aversive emotional arousal and avoidance. Here samples of the inappropriately positive stimulus are presented contiguously with stimuli that evoke extremely intense aversive reactions. After repeated pairings the previously positive stimuli acquire some of the aversive emotional properties evoked by the noxious stimuli with which they have been associated.

In one case a man had been persistently aroused sexually by the sight of perambulators and ladies' handbags. He reacted by compulsively trying to attack and destroy these objects (Raymond, 1956), and as a result he was often jailed. On one occasion he deliberately ran into a perambulator with his motorcycle, and at other times he smeared oil on them. He was also hospitalized for smearing mucus on a lady's handbag. In turn, he suffered extreme employment and marital difficulties. Extensive psychoanalytic therapy and interpretations about the psychosexual meaning of his strange behavior were of no help. His compulsion became so severely distressing that surgery, in the form of an irreversible brain operation on his frontal lobes, was considered seriously. Instead, the far less drastic alternative of aversive counterconditioning was employed. Repeated presentations of the fetishistic objects (handbags, perambulators) were paired with the onset of drug-produced nausea. These counterconditioning sessions were conducted regularly in the hospital for a week, with a follow-up series shortly after his discharge and again after a half year. An assessment eighteen months after the start of treatment indicated elimination of the fetish as well as dramatic improvement in the client's social, sexual, and vocational adjustment.

As another example, a young married man developed a passionate attachment to girdles and experienced great anxiety unless he wore one constantly during the day (Clark, 1963b). Increasingly his relations with his wife suffered because he compulsively wore her undergarments. Naturally his strange fetish had fairly pervasive debilitating effects on his social and vocational functioning. As part of the assessment some of the main fetishistic objects that he found stimulating were identified. These items included stockings and girdles as well as photos of girdle-wearers. The client next voluntarily hospitalized himself for about a week. During this time drug-induced nausea was paired repeatedly with presentations of the fetishistic paraphernalia. He was encouraged to wear the undergarments and to gaze at the plethora of fetishistic pictures while he became increasingly sick from the medication. As nausea progressed, he also heard a recording which he had made earlier and on which he had vividly elaborated his fetishistic pleasures. These treatments occurred about twice daily for seven to ten days. Follow-up after three weeks and again after three months indicated that the client was back at work again "enjoying a normal sex life and symptom free" (Clark, 1963b, p. 405).

MODIFICATION OF RESPONSE PATTERNS

Behavior therapists often distinguish between treatments based on either aversive or positive classical conditioning and those employing the mechanisms of operant or instrumental learning. This distinction is useful, especially for research, because it permits studies that attempt to produce and modify behavior experimentally with two different paradigms. The classical conditioning paradigm is used experimentally to generate new emotional reactions to stimuli by altering the contiguity among stimuli, as the last section showed. Operant or instrumental conditioning is typically employed to investigate and alter experimentally the consequences produced by response patterns. Applied to avoidance behavior, for example, this treatment technique requires that the stimulus conditions and reinforcement consequences be rearranged deliberately so that new adaptive responses are progressively emitted and reinforced while the previous avoidance behaviors and maladaptive emotional responses are extinguished.

The distinction between the classical and instrumental learning paradigms in clinical practice, however, and especially in assessment, often becomes less sharp. In the first place, it is usually impossible to establish the mechanisms by which the deviant behavior was acquired historically. When an individual's learning history was not observed

214

and recorded it cannot be reconstructed with certainty. Second, highly similar, if not identical, behaviors may be generated by diverse learning histories. Furthermore, the same principles of behavior modification generally can be applied effectively regardless of the mechanisms through which the behavior was acquired. Choices among alternative behavior modification techniques therefore may be made most appropriately on the basis of the client's current suitability for them, rather than from inferences about the history of the behavior. For example, whether cognitive desensitization or extinction through actual approach is the more suitable treatment depends largely on the ease with which the approach behavior can be evoked and its consequences controlled.

Extinction

Several ingenious clinical applications have been reported in which the avoidance patterns associated with aversive emotional reactions have been extinguished by having the client successfully approach and thus gradually master previously dreaded situations. Recall, for example, that in Clark's (1963a) case the woman who feared birds was desensitized to them not merely by relaxation to birds in imaginary situations. Gradually her treatment also included carefully planned visits to a museum containing stuffed birds, confronting caged live birds in an aviary, and ultimately facing unconfined birds in a public park.

Walton and Mather (1963) treated a 34-year-old store manager who had anxiety and psychosomatic reactions when he thought people were looking at him. These feelings were especially strong in stores and cafes. A hierarchy of routes was developed to include those on which more and more shops and people would be found. The client began his walks at night so that he would encounter very few people. When he had gradually mastered his route, the time was changed to the noon hour. After two months of this regimen the problematic behavior was eliminated and a one-year follow-up revealed no recurrence.

A similar approach procedure on graduated tasks was used by Herzberg (1941) to treat a woman who was afraid to go into the street. Likewise, Grossberg (1965) reports successfully treating a woman who feared public speaking by exposing her gradually to more and more demanding public-speaking situations. In early sessions she simply read prepared speeches under circumstances designed to assure that no adverse consequences would occur; later she improvised under increasingly difficult conditions in the presence of more and more listeners.

Contingent Reinforcement

The discussion so far has centered on the modification of those disadvantageous behaviors in which conditioned emotional reactions have an especially important part. As previously noted, however, many disadvantageous behaviors are primarily a function of inappropriate response-reinforcement relations. Treatments to modify response-reinforcement relations in behavioral therapies seek to alter the consequences produced by disadvantageous behaviors, thereby changing the individual's responses so that they lead to more advantageous outcomes. To accomplish this goal situations are created in which the inappropriate behavior is deliberately nonreinforced, and thus extinguished, while more advantageous alternative behaviors are carefully reinforced.

Some of the most systematic efforts to assess and modify the reinforcing conditions that maintain problematic social behavior and interpersonal relations have been reported by Bijou and his associates (e.g., Bijou, 1965). The case of the isolated nursery school child, Ann, discussed in Chapter 6, is but one example of their extensive work. Their programs generally contain a series of clear stages that reflect the close integration of behavioral assessment and treatment procedures. First, the problem behaviors are observed and defined and their frequency or duration in a naturalistic context are assessed. Then the reinforcing consequences that seemingly maintain the behavior are observed and recorded. On the basis of this analysis new response-reinforcement contingencies are substituted for the naturally occurring observed contingencies. Thereafter the resulting response rates are again assessed. Next the original naturalistic response-reinforcement contingencies are reintroduced to establish with certainty the causal conditions maintaining the deviant behavior. In the final phase the therapeutic contingencies are reinstated, the prosocial behaviors reinforced, and the problematic behavior extinguished.

These steps have been applied to assess and modify diverse mild and severe problems manifested by children in nursery schools and other nonclinical and clinical settings. Through systematic application of these techniques, jumping, walking, running, and related motoric behaviors were reinstated in a three-year-old girl who had regressed to crawling (Harris et al., 1964); social interactions with peers were increased in children who had been isolated, withdrawn, and overdependent on adults (Allen et al., 1964); extensive operant crying was reduced while prosocial responses were strengthened (Hart et al., 1964); and the self-destructive, schizophrenic behavior of a child was analyzed and controlled (Lovaas et al., 1965a).

The naturalistic contingencies that control the behavior problems of hospitalized adult patients diagnosed as chronic schizophrenics have been assessed and modified with especially great care (e.g., Ayllon, 1965; Ayllon & Azrin, 1965; Ayllon & Haughton, 1962; Ayllon & Michael, 1959). The essential features of this program were to identify and define the individual's undesirable behaviors and the currently incompatible but more desirable response patterns that ultimately could replace them. The patients often had been hospitalized continuously for many years, were highly disorganized, frequently mute, and too disturbed to participate in the formulation of reasonable treatment goals. Consequently decisions about the definition of undesirable behaviors and more valuable alternatives were guided largely by the staff. Because these patients generally resided on "back wards," which are infrequently or irregularly visited by professional staff, many of the observations and decisions were made by ward staffs. These ward staffs were primarily nurses and attendants, who functioned under the guidance of the senior personnel.

To identify and define undesirable or inappropriate behaviors the nurses described the duration and frequency of the patients' most problem-producing activities. After the nurses had been oriented to the investigator's behavioral approach it was also reasonable to ask them to describe the kind and frequency of naturally occurring reinforcement obtained by the patient and the possibility of controlling these reinforcements by environmental manipulations. These preliminary descriptions were supplemented by direct, systematic observation to obtain more detailed and objective information about the duration and frequency of the defined problem behaviors emitted by each patient.

After baseline measures for undesirable behavior and for more prosocial alternatives were established, the treatments commenced. They consisted of extinguishing the deviant behavior and positively reinforcing the prosocial alternate. This phase also was conducted by the nursing staff, with over 100 nurses participating in the project. The type of instruction conveyed to this vast personnel is illustrated by the informal definition of reinforcement:

> *Reinforcement is something you do for or with a patient, for example, offering candy or a cigarette. Any way you convey attention to the patient is reinforcing. Patients may be reinforced if you answer their questions, talk to them, or let them know by your reaction that you are aware of their presence. The common-sense expression "pay no attention" is perhaps closest to what must be done to discourage the patient's behavior. When we say "do not reinforce a behavior," we are actually saying*

"ignore the behavior and act deaf and blind whenever it oc-curs." (Ayllon & Michael, 1959, p. 325.)

In the next phase the nurses deliberately reinforced prosocial behavior when it occurred during the time sample; when undesired behavior occurred it was simply recorded without reaction by the nurse. This basic paradigm was used to modify a multitude of long-standing problems ranging from bizarre rituals to the psychotic talk of delusional patients.

One study changed the disturbed eating behavior of an entire ward of chronic schizophrenic patients (Ayllon & Haughton, 1962). A whole hospital ward was the unit, including patients who previously had been spoonfed, tubefed, and submitted to electric shock in efforts to induce eating. In the new program, these extreme treatments were discontinued: patients were no longer coaxed, coerced, reminded, or helped to eat. Instead the nurses were kept away during mealtimes to prevent inadvertent reinforcement for refusal to eat. In order to eat meals patients now had to independently enter the dining room without assistance and at the appropriate time. Initially an interval of thirty minutes was allowed for the patients to enter the dining room, but this was reduced gradually to five minutes over a period of fifteen weeks. The dining room was locked except during the appropriate time period, whose commencement was announced to the patients. Each patient's entry or nonentry into the dining room was recorded and it was found that those who entered invariably ate. Although initially the staff had feared some patients might starve themselves, these fears proved to be quite unfounded. The program was successful and no negative consequences were observed. Similar programs, using more complicated reinforcers contingent on increasingly appropriate social behavior in a clear system of steps, have been applied by Atthowe and Krasner (1967); Ayllon and Azrin (1965); Fairweather (1964, 1967); and others, to large groups, wards, and special communities.

In one extensive hospital ward experiment psychotics received tokens similar to money contingent upon their engaging in therapeutic activities (Ayllon & Azrin, 1965). In return for such functions as self-care, productive work, and rehabilitative jobs, both on and off the ward, the patients obtained tokens which they could exchange for desirable activities and outcomes available from a large array of alternatives (discussed in Chapter 8). In accord with expectations from operant conditioning research, the patients worked successfully at their jobs and behaved adaptively when the attainment of tokens depended on adequate performance and on prosocial activities. However, when receipt of the desired rewards and privileges was not made contingent upon their own adaptive functioning, the patients quickly abandoned their jobs and resumed their more usual psychotic hospital patterns. The clear dependence of the patient's prosocial behavior on the reinforcement operations is illustrated in Figure 7.

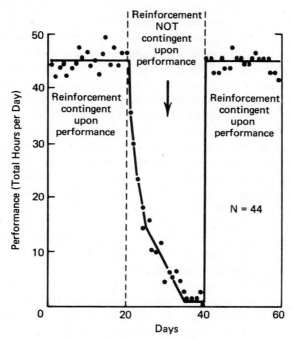

FIGURE 7.   *The total number of hours of on-ward performance by a group of forty-four patients.* (Ayllon & Azrin, 1965, p. 373.)

The work of Ayllon and his colleagues shows the challenging innovations that are possible in spite of the practical limitations encountered by measurement and change efforts in large, complex ward settings. Their work not only produced striking results but also illustrated the economy of behavioral assessment and modification techniques since the bulk of these activities can be conducted by nonprofessional staff. The staff time required should be amply compensated by the more self-controlled, adaptive adjustments of the patients, especially when far more drastic procedures, like physical restraints, electroconvulsive shock, or brain surgery, become unnecessary. In most behavior change programs, paid volunteers, ward attendants, nursery school personnel, and classroom teachers can conduct assessments and treatment programs of the kind just described so that the demands on professional time need not be great. The professional staff serves primarily as consultants, using their knowledge of learning principles and research to design the measurement and modification procedures.

Although the preceding reinforcement studies generally demonstrate compelling treatment effects achieved at fairly low costs, their designs usually make it impossible to assess their *relative* value or utility compared to alternative treatments and controls. This limitation occurs in all one-subject or one-group designs: they have pre- and post-treatment assessments but no comparison groups. These studies therefore leave many questions unanswered. For example, as the last chapter indicated, most operant conditioning effects with people seem to occur only when the individual also knows and can verbalize the contingent relation between his behavior and reinforcement. Moreover, instructions and modeling procedures can convey insight rapidly into the pertinent response-reinforcement contingencies. Individuals learn the outcomes of behavior quickly and, if incentive conditions warrant it, adapt their actions accordingly. Consequently it would be important in any behavior change program to determine the relative efficacy of therapies in which the new response-reinforcement contingencies are described verbally to the subject (rather than simply imposed and instituted with no explanations of the relevant rules).

Studies without control groups cannot identify and isolate the critical components of the particular change technique and the relative contributions of each component. In spite of these considerations, the demonstration that restoring the pretreatment response-reinforcement contingencies produces a return to the previous behavior shows the causal role of the treatment variable in generating change. By now, however, the more interesting question is not "do reinforcement manipulations change behavior" but, rather, just how do they work and how does their efficacy compare with other change techniques and with appropriate control groups.

One behavior therapy program that has demonstrated its utility impressively is the special therapeutic community to rehabilitate chronic psychotics developed by Fairweather and his colleagues (1964, 1967). This program, based on social learning principles, consists of a series of clear steps and contingencies that mark every phase of the patient's progress through the hospital and then out into a specially designed patient lodge located in the larger community. The therapeutic lodge was developed in response to the fact that many psychotic patients who have experienced more than two years of hospitalization continue to remain in the hospital enduringly and, if discharged, are returned to the hospital within a few months (Fairweather, 1964). In light of these data Fairweather tried to develop small social systems that could be transplanted into the community itself and provide the special supportive environments required by chronic psychotics.

As a first step a patient group was organized in the hospital and lived and worked together in a special ward. To encourage group responsibility and to approximate the conditions of a realistic society, the patients were given maximal autonomy over their own lives and daily activities throughout the program. They themselves had to make increasingly complex and difficult decisions about their collective behavior, the entire group being held responsible for the behavior of all its members at each stage. Progress to the next step was always made contingent upon success at the prerequisite step. While still in the hospital this group was presented with problems of the kind they would later have to confront in the community. These challenges involved, for example, organizing the lodge itself, caring for each other, planning and securing job employment, and so on. After a few weeks it was possible to move the group to the lodge, and after another month there they began to function as a basically autonomous, self-sufficient subsystem. For example, they organized and maintained a janitorial and yard service employing their own members, kept their own records, arranged their transportation, and assumed responsibility for their own living and working arrangements. Staff help, in the form of professional consultants to the lodge, gradually was replaced by lay volunteers, and then slowly was withdrawn completely. The patients themselves learned and assumed fully such responsible roles as nurse and work manager; within three years it was possible to withdraw all external help to the lodge, ex-patients now remaining together freely as a completely autonomous, self-sufficient group absorbed into the community (Fairweather et al., 1967). The only remaining contacts with the hospital were follow-up visits from a member of the research staff at six-month intervals and even that visit depended upon the approval of the ex-patients.

The utility of the lodge programs is apparent when the outcomes for lodge members are compared with matched control patients who were released into the larger society. As Figure 8 shows, patients in the lodge remained in the community far longer, and were employed much more enduringly, than controls who did not have the lodge available to them. Most impressive (Figure 9), the costs of the community lodge average less than five dollars daily, whereas the cost of hospitalizing these individuals tends to be about three to ten times more expensive for every day of care, depending on the type of hospital. When the income earned

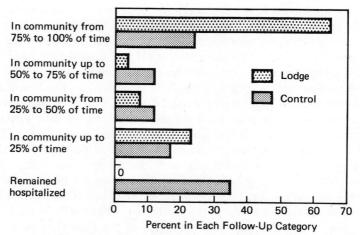

In community from 75% to 100% of time

In community up to 50% to 75% of time

Lodge

In community from 25% to 50% of time

Control

In community up to 25% of time

Remained hospitalized

0   10   20   30   40   50   60   70

Percent in Each Follow-Up Category

FIGURE 8. *Comparison of the percentage of time in the community for the lodge and control groups for six months of follow-up. (From Fairweather et al., 1967.)*

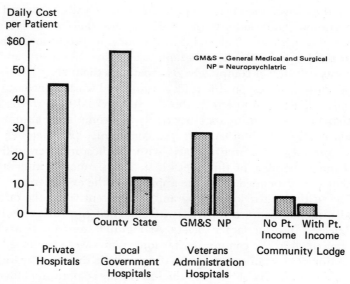

Daily Cost per Patient

GM&S = General Medical and Surgical
NP = Neuropsychiatric

County State   GM&S NP   No Pt.   With Pt.
                                   Income   Income

Private   Local   Veterans   Community Lodge
Hospitals   Government   Administration
                    Hospitals   Hospitals

FIGURE 9. *Comparison of treatment costs in California Bay Area, 1966. (From Fairweather et al., 1967.)*

by the people in the lodge through employment is taken into account, the economic advantages of the lodge system become even more striking.

Traditional psychotherapy tends to focus on emotional and motivational problems. Many people, however, are characterized as deviant or maladjusted mainly because they have not learned the coping patterns necessary to meet effectively the social or vocational demands of their environment. The problems of socially deprived, underprivileged persons, reflected in school, vocational, and interpersonal difficulties, may result in large part from their never having acquired in sufficient strength the response patterns needed to obtain reinforcement and to avoid aversive consequences from the environment. These people, like many of the chronic patients in Fairweather's programs, rather than being improperly motivated, may be virtually unable to live satisfyingly because they have not learned the skills and essential components required for successful functioning. Behavior deficits, rather than motivational or incentive considerations, are especially evident when individuals simply cannot perform behaviors adequately although potent incentives are offered to them. Such failures to perform widely expected behaviors produce unfortunate consequences, both in the form of negative reactions from others and insufficient positive reinforcement for the person who has the deficit. This, in turn, can lead to many other problems, including severe emotional reactions and avoidance patterns.

When a person has not mastered commonly expected and important interpersonal and vocational skills, the appropriate treatment is a learning program designed to remedy the deficits. These programs try to teach the individual increasingly complicated skillful behaviors. For this purpose the subject is presented with a series of graded tasks, his responses at each step are elicited, and he is reinforced when correct. Often the procedure is most efficient when the appropriate response at each step is modeled explicitly for the individual either directly or through symbols. Lovaas and his associates (1966) have modified the deficient speech and social behaviors of severely autistic children in this manner. To teach these mute children to talk the therapist first models sounds and rewards the child only for vocalizing within a specified time interval. As the child's proficiency increases the therapist proceeds to emit more complicated verbal units, gradually progressing from sounds to words and phrases. When the training proceeds further, rewards from the therapist become contingent on the child's reproducing more elaborate verbalizations with increasing speed, accuracy, and skill. Ultimately, combinations of modeling and reinforcement procedures help the child to learn increasingly complex meanings and complicated naturalistic speech.

Similar training procedures helped to develop vocalizations in a mute three-year-old girl whose clinical diagnoses included retardation at a mental age of nine months, cerebral palsy, epilepsy, and emotional disturbance (Kerr, Meyerson, & Michael, 1965). The procedure here entailed repeated elicitation and selective reinforcement of the child's initially faint vocal grunts.

Complex learning programs have been designed to teach people a variety of problem-solving strategies and skills, as well as to convey information efficiently. Many studies have explored the conditions affecting conceptualizing behavior in normal and retarded children. Some investigations also have developed programs to increase the young-sters' discrimination skills (e.g., Bijou, 1965; Bijou & Orlando, 1961), to improve their classroom learning (Birnbrauer et al., 1965), to teach reading and language skills (Staats, 1965; Staats et al., 1964; Staats & Staats, 1963; Staats & Butterfield, 1965), and to rehabilitate autistic children (Ferster & DeMyer, 1961).

The utilization of basic learning principles to correct behavior deficits was also evident in a project to reeducate severely emotionally disturbed and socially deprived children (Hobbs, 1966). Project "Re-Ed" employed naturalistic situations and ecological contingencies to increase the social and educational competence of severely disturbed youngsters. In this program, groups of children, selected from among the most severe custodial cases in state institutions, lived in carefully designed communities under the guidance of resident teacher-counselors. The programs stressed the rapid development of constructive social relations coupled with guidance in school skills and in other areas of deficiency. A main part of the training involved a schedule of carefully planned social behaviors and contingent rewards. The staff in this project, just as in most of the previously cited studies, consisted largely of inexpensive and readily available personnel, such as college students.

Advances in the application of learning principles to education have not been restricted to people with severe behavior deficits. Recent developments in automated and computer-assisted learning aids have facilitated self-instruction for specialized groups and content areas, as in the education of talented students from the preschool years on through college (Atkinson & Suppes, 1967; Leib et al., 1967). For example, Atkinson and Hansen (1966) developed computer-assisted instructional programs for initial reading. Their computer arrangement is designed so that each child progresses at his own pace through a subset of materials tailored to his own particular learning needs. The great advantage of computers in such learning programs is that they permit rapid sequencing of the appropriate instructional material on a highly individualized basis.

Modification of Response Patterns Vicariously and Symbolically

As the last chapter indicated, behavior can be modified effectively through vicarious, observational, or cognitive symbolic processes as well as through direct reinforcement. Direct reinforcement itself is unlikely to have powerful effects unless the individual is capable of making the responses on which the attainment of reinforcement depends (Bandura, 1965b). An effective behavior change program therefore must assure that the person learns the necessary response patterns, and that the environment provides the cues necessary to evoke those responses. Exposure to the behavior of appropriate models is one of the most effective ways to enhance the acquisition of new behavior patterns and skills. At the same time modeling also provides discriminative cues and vicarious reinforcers that help to guide the individual's choices (Chapter 6). In fact, most behavior change programs combine live and symbolic modeling cues, instructions, and direct reinforcement procedures, as was seen in the instructional programs that were discussed earlier.

The potency and efficacy of observational learning is illustrated clearly in the modification of response patterns that involve intense emotional reactions, as in severe phobias and their accompanying avoidance syndromes. It has been demonstrated that avoidance behaviors can be extinguished vicariously by observing models fearlessly approaching the aversive conditioned stimuli. In one study, groups of preschool children who were intensely afraid of dogs observed a fearless peer model who displayed progressively stronger and more positive approach behavior to a dog (Bandura, Grusec, & Menlove, 1967). In the course of eight brief sessions the model exhibited increasingly longer and closer interactions with the dog in accord with a prearranged program of graduated steps. The model progressed from briefly petting the dog while the latter was safely confined in a play pen to ultimately joining the dog in the playpen and hugging and feeding the animal wieners and milk from a baby bottle. The results revealed significantly greater approach behavior on the part of children who had watched the nonanxious model when compared to their peers in control groups.

In a second study Bandura and Menlove (1968) presented the model's behavior on film, creating even more economical treatments. They found that observation of the film-mediated fearless model likewise produced significant decrements in the observer's fearful behavior.

Film-mediated modeling procedures of this kind may be a highly effective and economical means for preventing, as well as modifying, the development of disadvantageous reactions to widespread problematic situations in the culture. Recent work on the modification of snake phobias by modeling and desensitization procedures (Bandura, Blanchard, & Ritter, 1968) suggests that a combination of observing the model's fearlessness plus receiving direct guidance for approach behavior from the fearless model is considerably more potent than cognitive desensitization.

The studies by Bijou, Ayllon, and others cited in the last section on contingent reinforcement illustrated the impressive behavior control that can be achieved in highly structured environments when external constraints closely regulate the person's behavior. Effective and enduring behavior change, however, requires that the troubled person himself ultimately comes to regulate his own behavior appropriately apart from constant immediate surveillance and control by others.

Behavior-change techniques that do not depend on the complete and almost constant control of the environment by therapists have obvious advantages. Rather than seeking to control the client's environment forever, effective long-term change depends on altering the valence and meaning of stimuli and hence the person's own choice behavior in naturalistic situations. For example, the cognitive and affective meaning of stimuli can be modified as was illustrated in the direct and vicarious extinction of emotional reactions.

Recent research (Bandura & Kupers, 1964; Kanfer & Marston, 1963a, b; Mischel & Liebert, 1966, 1967) shows how such phenomena as the internalization of standards, in which persons learn to regulate their own behavior, can be understood by social learning principles without recourse to postulated unobservable intrapsychic entities. To illustrate this, and to show the interaction between observational and direct training experiences in the modification of complex behaviors such as constructs, standards, and self-control patterns, one of these studies (Mischel & Liebert, 1966) is described in some detail below.

People evaluate their own performance, as well as the activities of other persons, and frequently set verbal and performance standards that determine, in part, the conditions under which they self-administer or withhold numerous readily available gratifications and a multitude of self-punishments. For example, they may evaluate their own test results, their financial and social status, and their sexual prowess. Failure to meet widely varying self-imposed performance standards often results in self-denial or even harsher self-punishments, whereas attainment of difficult criteria more typically leads to liberal self-reward and a variety of self-congratulations. The same objective performance may be a signal for joy in one person but for self-flagellation in another. There are, of course, wide individual differences in the kinds of standards and the levels on which persons make their own self-reward contingent, and these criteria influence their behavior in many contexts.

In life situations standards usually are transmitted by individuals who exhibit their own criteria and also reinforce the observer's adherence to particular standards. The modeled and directly reinforced behaviors may not be congruent; the criteria used by social agents for administering rewards and punishments to themselves often are discrepant with the standards which they directly impose on others. Consider, for example, the father who tries to influence his child toward self-denial and work while he simultaneously and persistently indulges himself. Although frequent reference is made to the importance of "consistency" in child-rearing practices, usually this refers to consistency in the use of direct training techniques across different situations, rather than to the effects of consistency or discrepancy between direct training and modeling procedures. Mischel and Liebert (1966) investigated the effects of discrepancies in the stringency of the self-reward criteria used by an adult and the standards he imposed on a child.

Children participated with a female adult model in a task that seemingly required skill but on which scores were experimentally controlled. The model and subject both had free access to a plentiful supply of tokens which could be exchanged for attractive rewards. In one experimental group the model rewarded herself only for high performances but guided the subject to reward himself for lower achievements; in a second condition the model rewarded herself for low performances but led the subject to reward himself only for high achievements; in the third group the model rewarded herself only for high performances and guided the child to reward himself only for equally high achievements. After exposure to these experimental procedures the children's self-reward patterns displayed in the model's absence were observed and scored through a one-way mirror. The results are summarized in Figure 10.

It was expected that the reward criteria privately adopted by the children would be a function of both the criteria they had observed the model use for herself and those she had imposed on them directly. The results showed that when the observed and imposed criteria were consistent they were adopted and maintained readily by all children. Thus, those children who had been held to a stringent standard and also observed a model who was stringent with herself became uniformly stringent in their own self-reward. These children also used higher

227

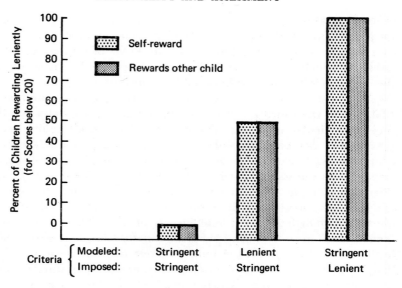

FIGURE 10. *Self-reward and transmission of standards as a function of the stringent or lenient initial criteria exhibited by the model and imposed on the child during training. (Adapted from Mischel & Liebert, 1966, p. 49.)*

standards for reward than either children who had received the same stringent direct training but observed a lenient model or those who were permitted leniency themselves. When the observed and imposed criteria were discrepant, and the criterion leading to more reward was the one that subjects were directly trained to adopt, they rewarded themselves generously in the model's absence and maintained the lenient criterion on which they were trained. In contrast, among those who had been trained to be stringent but had observed a more lenient model, only about 50 percent subsequently rewarded themselves liberally when there were no external constraints. Children adopted lenient criteria more frequently when they had been permitted greater leniency themselves than when they had observed it in another.

In a post-test the children demonstrated the game to another younger child, still in the absence of external constraints and the experimenter herself. The children consistently imposed on their peers the same standards that they had adopted for themselves, hence transmitting their own learned self-reward criteria. As this study illustrates, the appropriate manipulation of variables produces alterations not only in what individuals do under direct surveillance and external controls but also in the standards and behavior patterns that they come to adopt privately for themselves and that they subsequently transmit to other people.

Perhaps most interesting is the fact that children who were trained on a stringent criterion, by a model who was similarly stringent with herself, adopted and transmitted more stringent reward standards than those who received the identical direct training but from a model who exhibited greater leniency in her own self-reward. The results of this experiment showed how self-evaluations, in the form of patterns of self-reinforcement, may be affected jointly by the criteria displayed by social models and the standards directly imposed on the observer, with the resultant behavior determined by a predictable interaction of both processes. The potency of these effects is shown in Figure 10 which indicates that in two of the conditions the experimental manipulations exerted their effects uniformly on every single child; in these two conditions the behavior of each child could be predicted completely by simply knowing the condition to which he was assigned.

Many seeming paradoxes in the relationships between child training practices and the child's subsequent behavior may reflect insufficient attention to the discrepancies between the behaviors the child observes used by powerful and successful models and those which he is directly trained or guided to perform. In most life situations people are exposed to diverse demands and influences. It should not be surprising, for example, if a mother who tries to train her daughter to become "feminine," while she herself behaves in a "masculine" fashion, rears a child whose scores show conflict on masculinity-feminity measures. Similarly, when the ideals modeled and supported by an adolescent's parents conflict with those valued and encouraged by his peers, apparent inconsistencies should be expected in the youngster's behavior. Traditionally such seeming inconsistencies tend to be interpreted as reflections of deep-seated conflicts. On closer inspection, however, if the multiple contingencies influencing the child's behavior are discovered, then his seeming conflicts should more readily become explicable in terms of multiple observational and reinforcement influences without any need to invoke hypothetical intrapsychic mechanisms.

Often a person's performances are appropriate and adequate; his problems mainly involve inappropriate evaluation and self-reinforcement for objectively adequate achievements. Proper assessment of these problems requires analysis of the performance criteria and conditions that guide the person's self-rewards and self-punishments. When the referent behaviors are appropriate but the constructions about them are problem producing, alterations in the constructions (standards, labels, self-reactions), rather than in the behavior to which they refer, may be required.

As has been emphasized repeatedly (e.g., Chapter 3), people label and categorize behavior (their own as well as other peoples') in addition to behaving nonverbally. Although the label may not fit the condition to which it refers, the label itself generates consequences. For example, the labels that people apply to their emotional states may influence their subsequent reactions (Schachter & Singer, 1962; Schachter & Wheeler, 1962). In many instances the label may also function as an exceedingly potent aversive reinforcer, as in "homosexual," "queer," or "crazy," both when one applies it to oneself privately and when one employs it as a public description; application of the label can have powerful emotional consequences regardless of its representational accuracy. Consequently the replacement of negative labels with words and cognitions that have more positive evaluative meanings may yield some therapeutic gain, as when a man who has categorized himself as a drunken failure comes to call himself a passive-dependent personality. A major function of verbal psychotherapies may be to substitute less aversive labels and cognitions from the therapist's theory to describe conditions that were previously categorized by the client with less neutral, more aversive, verbal tags.

Some of the most imaginative approaches to assess and modify personal categories or constructs were developed by George Kelly (1955). Kelly stressed that although a person might be unable to change a particular event he could always reconstrue or reinterpret the event in an alternative, more convenient way. The same event can be categorized or abstracted in terms of more than one stimulus element, as is especially evident in language behavior. For example, one might categorize an event as "blue," but also as "sad," "ugly," "essential," "priceless," or "lovable." In life contexts most events can be categorized in numerous alternative ways; a woman might construe her husband as insufferable, impossible, hostile, unbearable—and also as indispensable and essential. To summarize such a description as evidence of ambivalence is an unenlightening truism. Rather than searching for what people "really are," Kelly sought ways of helping them to categorize themselves, and each other, more conveniently.

Kelly emphasized the importance of personal constructs for behavior and viewed man as an hypothesis maker who should be credited with the same theory building and categorizing capacities sometimes reserved for the scientist. Man, however, is not left completely immersed in his constructs and hypotheses: Kelly recognized that expectations can be expressed only in terms of behavior. As he put it, the personal-construct psychologist takes the position that "a person is what he does" (1955, p. 403). Therefore his therapy, while emphasizing constructs, also includes extensive role rehearsals. These rehearsals help the client to practice and test new behaviors and then to redesign his role and his actions in the light of the consequences that he experienced. One of Kelly's procedures, fixed-role therapy, illustrates the use of symbolic modeling to affect changes in personal constructs and in behavior patterns consistent with those constructs.

In fixed-role therapy a role sketch is written describing in detail a new "make-believe" personality endowed with a fictitious name. The client is helped to rehearse and to enact this role experimentally for a period of a week or two. The role is elaborately prepared and carefully introduced. For example, to initiate the role the therapist might say, in part (1955, pp. 384–385):

> For the next two weeks I want you to do something unusual. I want you to act as if you were (Kenneth Norton). We will work it out together. For two weeks try to forget that you are (Ronald Barrett) or that you ever were. You are (Kenneth Norton)! You act like him! You think like him! You talk to your friends the way you think he would talk! You do the things you think he would do! You even have his interests and you enjoy the things he would enjoy!
>
> Now I know this is going to seem very artificial. We expect that. You will have to keep thinking about the way (Kenneth) would do things rather than the way (Ronald) might want to do them.

In the rehearsal phases the client gets special help with his role behavior, especially for meeting difficult situations involving work and close interpersonal situations. Kelly supplies the therapist with detailed techniques to help the client cope effectively with the feelings of artificiality and insincerity that almost inevitably arise in the early stages of role practice, before the client himself discovers that he also "is what he does." The following comments illustrate some typical changes as the person tries and progressively modifies the role, and begins to encounter new satisfactions from it (p. 448):

May 30: Tried the role with friends. Tried to make my comments not quite so preposterous and with evidence of more thought behind them. Seemed to work much better. My comments accepted as interesting additions to conversation.

May 31: The role playing seems easier and more a part of me. I find myself contributing more to conversations—rather than passively listening. It's fun. Keeps me on my toes, though.

Gradually the successfully rehearsed new behaviors begin to seem more comfortable and natural. They become part of the person's spontaneous repertoire and no longer require special or artificial efforts.

A similar technique of behavior rehearsal also has been developed by Wolpe and Lazarus (1966), especially aimed at helping persons to behave more competently and assertively in specific interpersonal situations. For example, one client dreaded interviews with prospective employers. Part of the behavior rehearsal therefore dwelt on this topic (Wolpe & Lazarus, 1966, pp. 49–50). In one role-play situation the therapist portrayed a prominent business executive seeking an experienced accountant to take charge of one of his companies. In the behavior rehearsal the client, Mr. P. R., had applied for the position and was now coming for an interview. In reply to the therapist's deliberately resonant "Come in!," Mr. P. R. entered the consulting room and hesitantly approached the desk with downcast eyes and obvious trepidation. To provide him with feedback they soon shifted roles so that the client could see himself as the prospective employer would probably view him. For this purpose, P. R. was now seated at the desk in the role of the business executive while the therapist portrayed the client's original timid entry into the office. P. R. was asked to evaluate the therapist's performance from the employer's viewpoint. In the light of this critique, the therapist modeled the entry of a more assertive individual. The effects of variations in posture and gait and the importance of eye contact were noted, and new ways of introducing himself more self-confidently were rehearsed several times by Mr. P. R. until his approach was totally devoid of any signs of timidity or tension. Therapist and client then proceeded to discuss and rehearse a variety of potentially threatening initial contacts with employers so that problems could be anticipated, and overcome, in the safety of the role situation, and so that adaptive behavior could be rehearsed until it was proficient and spontaneous.

Behavior rehearsals (like all other techniques for strengthening coping patterns and social skills) can be applied to develop satisfying constructive new alternatives for the person; such techniques need not be limited to remedying gross deficiencies or social "pathology." Traditional approaches to personality assessment often focus on the individual's handicaps and the historical etiology of his troubles, neglecting the development of positive resources. It is important, however, to help the individual to devise creative alternative behaviors—so that he can find, as Kurt Goldstein (1939) put it, things that he *can* do and that enable him to discover new competences and satisfactions, rather than dwelling on the hypothetical etiology of his weaknesses.

SUMMARY

Social behavior theory leads to a radically different approach to both personality assessment and change. Since the emphasis is on observable specific stimulus conditions, rather than on broad intrapsychic dynamics or dispositions, assessment requires measurement of the critical conditions and contingencies that evoke and support an individual's behavior, rather than inferences about his attributes. If future behavior depends on the consequences that similar behavior produced before in related situations, and on the emotion-arousing properties of stimuli, then treatment programs must deal with the modification of the consequences of behavior and with alterations in the valence of stimuli.

The conditioned emotional meaning or valence of a stimulus can be altered by systematically associating it with a new stimulus that elicits an incompatible emotional reaction. The pairing between the conditioned stimulus and the one that generates an incompatible response may be achieved in a number of ways. The individual may be confronted by samples of the conditioned stimulus that range from the highly symbolic to the completely direct and realistic. For example, a person who fears snakes may be asked to imagine snakes, may be supplied with pictures of them or toy snakes, may see them on realistic movie films, or may actually encounter live snakes directly. Similarly, the incompatible emotional reactions may be generated symbolically, as in instructions to relax and "think calm"; physiologically, with drugs that produce relaxation; by observation of the fearless emotional reactions of other persons (models); or by engaging directly in behavior under conditions arranged to assure the occurrence of the incompatible emotional response (such as eating while hungry in the presence of mildly arousing snake stimuli).

Maladaptive response patterns also can be changed by altering the consequences to which they lead. These changes can be accomplished by directly modifying response-reinforcement relations, as well as through more symbolic and cognitive processes that depend on observation, on instructions, and on cognitive and live rehearsals of the desired behavior patterns.

As we have seen, social behavior theory deals chiefly with the effects of changes in stimulus conditions upon changes in behavior. In assessments, therefore, the primary concern is to identify the stimulus conditions that require modification in order for the individual to more optimally achieve his goals. After the situations provoking problematic behavior are established, their effects can be altered by applying principles of behavior change to them, as this chapter has illustrated. The results have value not only for their therapeutic benefits; they also help to clarify the conditions controlling complex behavior, and consequently facilitate the modification, progressive revision, and further development of basic theory about social behavior. For each individual person the appropriate change procedures hinge, of course, on a careful assessment of his unique case, as discussed in the next chapter.

It is evident that in the present approach the same principles that have been developed as a result of experimental research into the causes of normal behavior are also invoked to understand deviance. The principles illustrated in the therapeutic examples cited in this chapter are the same ones invoked to understand the determinants of the less unusual patterns—such as children's aggression or dependency—discussed in the previous chapter. Thus the schisms between laboratory and clinic, between theory and application, and between research and practice begin to close.

/8
ASSESSMENT FOR BEHAVIOR CHANGE

We have stressed the fundamental unity between the experimenter's activities and those of the assessor and therapist, but there is a critical difference between them. In experiments it is the experimenter who thinks about what he wants to study; he selects and defines his independent variable and the dependent measures for assessing the effects of his treatment manipulations. He may begin with more interest in the dependent variable—for example, self-control or aggression—and inquire into the effects of various manipulations on it. Or he can start by focusing on the independent variable, say the effects of exposure to particular influence procedures. The experimenter must select for measurement and manipulation events that represent those in which he is interested and with which he claims to be concerned. The operations for specifying the exact content and measurement of the variables in the experiment are assessments and they entail many of the same steps and problems involved in the clinical assessment of the individual case.

In most clinical situations, in contrast, it is the "subject" or client who must define the problematic behaviors and the objectives he seeks. In that sense he assumes something of the role of the scientist who must delineate his problems. The most urgent goal in assessment is to design the treatments required by the client's problems. The person usually presents a global description of general malaise or perhaps numerous complaints in a variety of areas; consequently the first assessment task is to develop a priority list of specific problems and to delineate the appropriate treatment for each. This presupposes that different problems require different treatment and that specific treatments can be designed to fit them—an assumption that is basic to social behavior theory.

THE MEASUREMENT OF BEHAVIOR

Assessments to change social behavior have several phases. The problem behaviors and the desired objectives have to be defined with clear behavioral referents. Next it is necessary to describe the exact circumstances provoking the problem behaviors and to identify the conditions maintaining them. In light of this information the particular behavior-change operations most likely to produce the desired objectives must be selected. Finally, the efficacy of the treatments themselves has to be evaluated.

Clients usually are not behaviorists and they do not describe themselves and their difficulties with operational definitions. Some proponents of operant conditioning and reinforcement theory have assumed erroneously that verbal reports from the subject about stimulus meanings do not constitute proper data. Yet it is perfectly appropriate, and usually essential, for the assessor to verbally explore with the subject his reactions to symbolically presented, hypothetical stimulus conditions. The assessor's eschewal of trait-state theories does not imply that he should not use reports from the person, either about his history or about the meaning that stimulus conditions have acquired for him. There is no hazard here as long as these reports are not taken as automatic revelations of nonverbal, nontest behavior, and as long as relations between the individual's reports about his reactions to various events and his other behaviors are treated as an empirical issue (Chapter 4). Most assessors, guided by trait and psychodynamic theories, have dwelt on verbalizations as signs of personality, rather than as descriptions of reactions to stimulus conditions. On the other hand, in social behavior assessment, reports from the subject are intended to help define the problematic stimuli and the disadvantageous responses that they have come to evoke, and to specify the covariations between them.

The Subject Is a Trait Theorist

Human interactions usually are not described by a metric of movements in space, but rather by verbal statements about psychological attributes, as in trait ratings (Chapter 3). Thus a person might construe an event as aggressive, nice, inadequate, French, anxiety provoking, or theory confirming. The subject or client, whether in the laboratory or the clinic, behaves like a trait theorist who assigns global trait labels; he describes his diverse behaviors as if they were consistent entities.

Persons may present themselves and their objectives initially in terms of very diffuse, oversimplified, global trait-state labels. For example, a man may want to "feel more fulfilled," "be less neurotic," "get along better," or "be happier." He may want to "be less anxious," "get out of this depression," "be less of an introvert," "stop churning myself into knots," or "become less self-defeating." He may call himself "too aggressive," "too shy," "too weak," or "too sharp." Categorizing behavior is equally evident when one tries to describe a private problem, oneself or another person, or a scientific theory; all of these activities are efforts to categorize experiences. Constructions, and not objective behavior descriptions on clear dimensions, are presented by individuals when they seek help as clients, just as scientists offer constructs when they discuss phenomena such as anxiety, or ego strength, or achievement needs.

The main information from a client usually consists of verbal reports and descriptions. The sounds that the client emits are "verbal behavior," but these verbalizations have meanings whose content must be analyzed. Some behaviorists have intentionally chosen to exclude from study such critical domains of human functioning as language. Ironically, psychologists occasionally have even used their own words to declare the illegitimacy of studying the meaning of what other people say. Thus Pascal and Jenkins (1961, p. 23) declare that the "basic attributes of verbal behavior" are such dimensions as loudness:

> *The content of a verbal response such as "I hate you" is not the subject matter of the present approach. For such a response, the measures applied are presence or absence, loudness, pitch, etc.*

Or (p. 24):

> *Thinking and cerebration are usually considered synonymous. Cerebration is not grossly observable and, therefore, is not an object of study for us.*

An adequate assessment of utterances usually cannot be restricted to tape-recording them or to analyzing their tonal properties and sound waves, but instead entails an analysis of their meaning. If it is absurdly limiting to treat verbal behavior merely as discriminable sound patterns, the question becomes what meanings and referents to attribute to what another person says.

The difficulties of accurately identifying the referents for a speaker's utterances are being recognized even in the analysis of simple speech under carefully controlled laboratory conditions (e.g., Rosenberg & Cohen, 1966). Recent research on language suggests, for example, that the accuracy with which a stimulus event (such as a color) is labeled in communication influences the ease with which listeners can subsequently decode and remember the labeled event (Lantz & Stefflre, 1964). Although these investigations into the labeling process and the consequences of various kinds of names on subsequent behavior are not directly relevant to personality assessment, they do highlight the complex relations between words and the events that the words represent.

Psychodynamically oriented clinicians rely chiefly on their intuitive inferences about the symbolic and dynamic meanings of the client's verbal behavior. Trait-oriented psychometric assessments investigate either the accuracy of the client's statements as indices of his nontest behavior, or treat his verbalizations as signs of his relative position on a personality dimension or on a criterion variable. A social behavior analysis of language, on the other hand, proceeds in a completely different manner. The primary aim of such an analysis is to decipher the content of what is being conveyed and to discover its behavioral referents and consequences, and not to decode the significance of language as signs of underlying psychodynamics, of unconscious processes, or of personality dimensions. In this sense, a social behavior analysis of the meaning of a client's constructs has some of the same goals as the analysis of a scientist's constructs; both seek useful operational definitions for constructions.

Many utterances about private experiences, including thoughts and feelings, are ambiguous because it is difficult to find appropriate words for such subjective states. Ambiguity about meanings becomes evident when one is faced with statements of the kind commonly presented in clinical contexts. Here are two real examples:

> *I'd be in better shape if I were a mustard cutter.*
> *I can never really give myself.*

A literal interpretation of these complaints would be entirely misleading. In the first instance, for example, the person who talked about being in "better shape" had no discernible weight problems and his reference to "mustard cutting" had little to do with food. Rather, these descriptions, like most human statements, are abstractions about behavior that cannot be grasped intelligently without pinning them to relevant referents. Instead of inquiring into *why* the person feels he "can never really give himself," social behavior assessments try to discover referents for just *what* he would like to do or become and the specific steps necessary to achieve these goals. Usually the probable consequences and costs of alternative action plans also must be examined.

In these instances the assessor's initial task is not dissimilar to the one faced whenever behavioral referents and operational definitions are sought for unclear theoretical constructs. Just as the psychologist interested in identity, or ego strength, or anxiety must find public referents to help specify what he means, so must the client find public referents for his personal problems and objectives.

Public Referents for Private Experiences

The behavioral referents for statements are fairly apparent when both the observer and the subject clearly know the environmental contingencies that are being construed. In verbal conditioning studies, for example, the subject's statement, "He says 'mhm' whenever I say a personal pronoun," has external behavioral referents whose accuracy may be easily assessed. Meaning is less clear, however, when the behavioral referents are not known to the observer, as in the preceding clinical illustrations, and as was found so often with all inferences about traits and states (Chapter 3).

Just as there are differences among scientists in the concrete referents to which they anchor such abstractions as "anxiety" or "aggression," so are their divergences among all men in the particular meanings they attribute to any event that they experience. Hypotheses about another person's behavior need to be based on direct evidence from him. The observer is often mistaken if he believes that the constructions based on the theory which he brings into the situation necessarily fit or describe the subject whom he finds there. As George Kelly put it:

> *It is presumptuous to construe John Doe's agitated behavior patently as "anxiety," just because it is agitated. . . . It may, in his particular case, be far more adequate to understand his personal construct of "kick" or "guts" or "lift" and construe it within the public domain as a form of "aggression" or "reality testing."* (Kelly, 1955, p. 40.)

239

When objectives and problems are presented globally the assessor must help the client to specify them with public behavioral referents and to delineate as precisely as possible the circumstances associated with changes in the occurrence or magnitude of the described states. This may be done verbally in direct discussion, or by asking the person to perform in specially structured situations in which the stimulus conditions are deliberately and systematically varied as in an experiment. It should not be assumed, however, that personal constructs (any more than scientific constructs) mirror the nonverbal behavior to which they refer, or that verbal constructs necessarily cause or even influence the person's nonverbal behavior. In spite of these reservations, since people usually present their problems verbally, the analysis of what they mean is generally a necessary first step.

Examples of appropriate questions for the verbal portions of the first phase of such assessments come from Kelly's "psychology of personal constructs" (1955). Kelly urged a specific and elaborate inquiry into the verbally presented problems, with detailed exploration of the exact content of the client's abstractions or constructs by obtaining numerous behavioral examples as referents for them. Kelly has described in detail useful techniques to assess verbally, and in role-play situations, the conditions under which the individual's particular constructions about his emotional reactions increase, decrease, and change. The focus of such assessments is not to categorize people, but to help them discriminate the events that agitate or diminish their acquired disturbing emotional reactions and disadvantageous behavior.

If a client describes himself as, for example, "anxious," the assessor can explore with him just when he feels this way and when he does not. To specify the operations or behavioral referents for anxiousness, the assessor inquires into just what happens when the client feels more anxious and less anxious and the changes that occur in himself and in his behavior when he experiences the problematic anxiety. For example, the assessor might ask, "How do you know when you are anxious?" The purpose of these probes is to obtain public referents for subjective experiences, and not to validate or invalidate the truth or falseness of the client's phenomenology. The issue here is not whether the person is "really" anxious, but rather the discovery of referents for his perceptions regardless of their accuracy.

After the client has tentatively formulated some response referents for his subjective problem, the assessor tries to discover the exact conditions under which the referent behaviors change. To discover the situational or stimulus changes that covary with alterations in the magnitude and nature of the problematic responses, he may inquire into the conditions under which the problem seems "a little better" as contrasted to those in which it seems "a little worse." Similarly, the assessor can question the client about the kinds of things that he has done to deal with the problem and about the specific consequences produced by these attempts. The recognition that behavior depends on specific stimulus conditions suggests that such inquiries must be highly situation-specific since it is hazardous to generalize from any one instance to responses in different unsampled situations. The subject's anxiousness, for example, changes as a function of where he is and what is happening; it is not a constant state oblivious to conditions.

In the elaboration of the client's objectives the emphasis is also on behavioral referents for the states that the client wants to achieve. Thus if a person wants to "feel more secure" the questions become just what would he have to *do,* how would he have to change, in order to experience that state. Interest here is in necessary actions to achieve specified objectives. The focus throughout is on the behavioral response referents for the individual's subjective reactions and on the stimulus conditions in which they occur and change. Inquiries of this kind can be made more systematically with the help of a structured interview schedule.

Kanfer and Saslow (1965) have devised an interview guide for the functional analysis of individual behavior. Their detailed outline helps the interviewer to explore behavioral excesses, deficits, and assets in the client's current life situation. The consequences of these behaviors, and the conditions maintaining and controlling them, are explored verbally and directly. The discussion includes the key incentives in the client's life and their relative importance for him. Major aversive stimuli, fears, future concerns and risks, as the client sees them, are also elaborated. The interview examines the client's views of the main response-reinforcement contingencies that are relevant to his problems. The focus is on the specific treatments that the client will probably require and on the resources that he and his environment have that could help to facilitate these changes effectively.

Such initial verbal explorations narrow the range of potentially problematic situations and help to specify appropriate objectives. Thereafter the client, guided by the assessor, can expose himself to symbolic—and ultimately to real—examples of the conditions which he described verbally as problem producing. These efforts are accompanied by assessment of the procedures necessary to achieve the selected objectives.

The client's own verbal descriptions may be facilitated by presenting samples of the relevant situations in symbolic form, by rehearsing illustrative situations in role play and in other life contexts, and by introducing stimulus conditions directly into the assessment. The purpose of these inquiries is to isolate the conditions in which the maladaptive behaviors occur. For example, if the client says, "I fall apart when I talk to my boss—I just can't describe it," the assessor might structure a short role situation, as was illustrated in the last chapter. On the basis of the client's verbal descriptions the assessor can briefly role play the boss while the client behaves as he naturally would toward his boss in a predefined situation. These more lifelike experiences can provide both client and assessor the opportunity to evaluate more accurately the nature of the verbalized problem and its controlling conditions. Likewise, they are the bases and first steps of treatment itself. Role play provides a useful interim phase between purely verbal discussions and actual presentations of vivid stimuli in lifelike contexts (e.g., Janis & Mann, 1965; Kelly, 1955).

Assessments of the evoking stimulus conditions frequently have to rely on the individual's own self-report as discussed earlier, because it is usually difficult to observe the person in almost infinite situations and to sample these situations either directly or in vivid role enactments. As we have seen, in social behavior assessments (again in contrast to the trait and state position) these self-reports are not obtained to infer the overall situation-free magnitude of the problem, nor to divine its original causes, but to establish the particular stimulus conditions that currently appear to control its occurrence and intensity.

Interview techniques to obtain self-reports have already been described in the preceding pages, but a variety of self-report techniques besides interviews have been used to identify the conditions that covary with changes in problematic behaviors. Metcalfe (1956), for example, reported an analysis of stimulus conditions controlling bronchial asthmatic seizures in a young female patient. The patient kept a detailed diary during an eighty-five-day period in which she was hospitalized but free to visit outside. She was asked to record all symptoms related to respiration, particularly "real asthmatic attacks" such as tightness, wheezing, and severe respiration distress; all other physical symptoms not related to respiration; and all her activities such as games, dancing, occupational therapy, shopping, meetings, visits, as well as moods, dreams, and so on.

Asthmatic attacks occurred on fifteen days in this time period. Inspection of the temporal relations between her self-reported activities and asthmatic attacks revealed that contacts with her mother appeared to be a main eliciting condition. Inspection of contingency data for other events (such as stressful interviews, violent exercise) indicated

TABLE 8. RELATIONSHIP BETWEEN CONTACT WITH MOTHER
AND ASTHMATIC ATTACKS

Contact with Mother[a]	Days with Asthma (15)	Days without Asthma (70)
Yes	9 (60%)	14 (20%)
No	6 (40%)	56 (80%)

(Adapted from Metcalfe, 1956, p. 65.)
[a]Within the preceding 24 hours.

no strong relations between them and the occurrence of attacks. Table 8 shows the frequency of attacks that followed within twenty-four hours of a contact with her mother as opposed to those that occurred more than twenty-four hours after a contact with her. Nine of her fifteen attacks followed recent contact with her mother; these were in turn analyzed for setting as shown in Table 9, revealing that contact with her mother in the home appeared to be the main stimulus for asthmatic episodes.

During the twenty months following her discharge from the hospital she had nine additional attacks, eight of which occurred when she was in contact with her mother in her mother's home. The percentage of time she spent near her mother as opposed to away from her during this period was not reported. In spite of the fairly gross way in which stimulus conditions were analyzed, this study indicates a valuable direction for assessment. It is also of interest that this woman was able to collect and supply the necessary data although her tested intelligence was well below average, suggesting that useful reports of stimu-

TABLE 9. RELATIONSHIP BETWEEN PLACE OF CONTACT WITH
MOTHER AND ASTHMATIC ATTACKS

Place of Contact	Followed by Asthma	Not Followed by Asthma
At home	7	5
Not at home	2	9

(Adapted from Metcalfe, 1956, p. 65.)

243

lus-response covariations do not necessarily require highly verbal, articulate self-reporters.

Metcalfe also exposed his client to words associated with the mother, and to mother-relevant pictorial stimuli on TAT and Rorschach cards. These stimuli, as well as interview discussion about the mother, did not provoke any asthmatic attacks; asthma occurred when the client was with her mother but not when she was faced with symbols about mothers. These findings again underline the fact that assessment of responses to verbal or symbolic presentations of stimuli does not necessarily serve as an adequate substitute for assessment of direct reactions to the events that the symbolic stimuli supposedly represent.

A daily record like the diary employed by Metcalfe's patient provides one preliminary step in the identification of problems. Wolpe and his colleagues routinely ask their clients to keep very specific daily records listing the exact conditions under which their anxieties seem to increase or decrease markedly (Wolpe & Lazarus, 1966). Usually the person is asked to prepare his own lists of all the stimulus conditions or events that engender discomfort, distress, or other painful emotional reactions in him. These self-reports also can be supplemented by questionnaires, inventories, and checklists completed both by the client and by those who know him.

Many available inventories obtain reports of the magnitude of anxiety and avoidance reactions to common potentially stressful situations like examinations and interpersonal relations. Usually such rating scales have served observers, such as attendants or researchers, to assign subjects into trait categories, as was discussed in Chapter 3. Scales like this, however, also could be valuable preliminary steps in assessments to devise individual treatments. An item like "refuses to eat," for example, would not merely be left as a recorded symptom or simply quantified for its relative frequency. Rather, the individual himself can be asked to estimate the relative magnitude of particular problems for him and can compare them to the urgency of his other troubles. These self-ratings would provide one step in designing a priority of behavior modification goals. Equally important, the details of the conditions that affect the occurrence and magnitude of particular self-described problems can be explored. In addition to having the client describe his own behaviors, observers could rate his behaviors on the same scales. The purpose of both types of rating would not be to classify the subject with trait adjectives, but to identify the problematic behaviors. To accomplish this goal a detailed inquiry could be conducted into the intensity and variations of particular problems as a function of changes in stimulus conditions. The subject's behavior ratings and those of observers then can be discussed directly, the aim being to delineate conditions rather than to infer personal attributes. For example, the individual's "refusal to eat" would not be interpreted as a sign of his possible negativism, or stubbornness, or passive oral dependency needs. Rather, the analysis would focus candidly on just when he is more likely, less likely, and least likely to "refuse to eat"; its functional relationship to other conditions, such as the reactions of particular people to him, would also be considered. In this manner ratings can serve as a step in the development of treatment goals and tactics, rather than as signs to infer durable dispositions.

In this approach, behavior ratings need not be secret or concealed; attendants and other personnel can record time-sampled instances of the client's behavior and the client himself can record his own behavior. Discrepancies between the rater's and the client's reports can be discussed frankly in assessment interviews. This procedure would not be designed to "peg" the person on individual difference variables, or to see if he lies or shows other inconsistencies between his version of himself and the reports of other raters. Rather, the assessment would be aimed at delineating the subjective acquired meanings of stimuli for him so that their aversive and pain-producing consequences could be modified.

An interesting behavior-rating scale (Endler, Hunt, & Rosenstein, 1962) provides self-reports of anxiety and avoidance behavior to specific persons and objects in clearly delineated situations. Scales of this kind can help the client as well as the therapist to discriminate more clearly the contexts in which the presented anxieties and problems increase or decrease. Such ratings help to specify the exact stimulus conditions that covary with changes in subjective distress, as well as the particular type of response evoked.

Recently some fear survey schedules have been developed for behavior therapy (Geer, 1965; Lang & Lazovik, 1963; Wolpe & Lang, 1964). These schedules list many items that were found to elicit anxiety frequently in patients. The respondent indicates on scales the degree of disturbance provoked by such items as strangers, bats, ugly people, mice, making mistakes, and looking foolish.

Inventories like the fear survey schedule provide a useful screening and sampling of anxiety-eliciting stimuli. Geer (1965), for example, administered a fear survey schedule to undergraduates to select two fear groups for spider phobia. In the high-fear group, students rated their fear of spiders as either "very much" or "terror" but rated their fear of snakes as "none." The low-fear group consisted of subjects who rated their fear of both spiders and snakes as "none." An equal number of high- and low-fear subjects then were assigned into an experimental and control condition. In the experimental condition subjects were shown pictures of a spider; in the control condition they saw pictures of a snake. In both conditions measures of autonomic arousal were taken physiologically in the form of GSR responses through finger electrodes. When presented with pictures of spiders, people who had reported high spider fear on the inventory showed significantly greater GSR's than did subjects in all other groups. Equally interesting, increased autonomic arousal was found only in response to directly relevant fear stimuli. When subjects with high fear of spiders were shown pictures of snakes there was no increase in GSR.

Similar results come from a recent study by Bandura and Menlove (1968). Parents were interviewed about any traumatic fears shown by their preschool children. In addition, they reported their own fears of common objects and situations, regardless of whether or not their child displayed them. Subsequently the children were placed in a controlled situation in which their actual approach behavior to a dog was scored. Some children were remarkably brave with the dog, entered the playpen in which he sat, fed him, and obviously were fearless. With only two exceptions the parents of these youngsters had reported no previous direct or vicarious traumatic episodes with dogs in the family. In contrast, significantly more of the children who were fearful of the dog also had parents who themselves were afraid of dogs and hence modeled the fearful behavior. Again it is notable that reported fears were only very specifically related to fearful behavior toward dogs. Children who were afraid of dogs had twice as many animal fears as children who behaved fearlessly with dogs; however, reported differences in irrelevant fear areas (for example, social and interpersonal relations) were entirely unrelated to fearful behavior with dogs. Once more, stimulus specificity rather than broad response predispositions seems to be the rule.

The preceding studies indicate that specific verbal reports have some validity as indicators of autonomic and avoidance responses. As repeatedly noted (Chapter 4), however, self-reports of anxiety and autonomic arousal measures usually are poorly correlated. Consequently, some researchers (e.g., Clark, 1963a) prefer to use both self-reports and direct autonomic measures both during assessment of emotion-arousing stimuli and during treatment itself. In clinical situations, if the ultimate concern is the client's subjective state and not prediction to other situations, his self-reports may be as useful as, if not more useful than, his autonomic measurements.

Direct Sampling

Describing problems with words, or enacting them in roles, are not fully adequate substitutes for directly sampling them in either controlled or lifelike situations. Many clients, especially children, or adults with severe speech deficiencies or highly disorganized behavior, cannot supply verbal descriptions or engage in imaginative role enactments. Not only do the client's detailed verbal reports not necessarily correspond accurately to the behaviors they supposedly describe, but also he may be unable to anticipate abstractly the consequences that different conditions and patterns of behavior would actually produce. Behavior sampling gives both client and assessor a more realistic opportunity to assess problems and to select further treatment objectives. Direct behavior sampling is also important in systematic assessment of the efficacy of the treatment procedure itself.

The magnitude of a variety of avoidance behaviors has been assessed fairly precisely in clinical situations by exposing subjects to series of live or symbolic stimuli. For example, fear of heights was measured by tabulating the distance that the phobic individual could climb on a metal fire escape (Lazarus, 1961). To assess the effects of treatments, subjects were required to ascend eight stories by elevator to a roof garden above street level and to count the passing cars below for two minutes. To measure claustrophobia each person sat in a cubicle containing large French windows opening onto a balcony. The assessor closed the windows and slowly moved a large screen closer and closer to the subject, thus constricting his space. The subject was free, of course, to open the windows and to terminate the procedure whenever he wished, but was instructed to persevere as long as possible, the measure consisting of the closest distance at which he could tolerate the screen.

Avoidance responses to snakes were measured directly by exposing fearful volunteers to them in a laboratory (Lang & Lazovik, 1963; Lang, Lazovik, & Reynolds, 1965). Each person was asked to look down into a topless glass case containing a nonpoisonous five-foot black snake located fifteen feet from the entrance to the room. The subject was assured that the snake was harmless and was asked to come as close as he could as this distance was recorded. If the fearful volunteer was able to come all the way to the case the experimenter touched the snake and invited the subject to do so also. If the latter succeeded, the assessor picked up the snake and asked the subject to hold the snake barehanded. Each of these progressive approach steps was scored. In some studies people were also asked to rate their subjective reactions after attempting the actual approach behavior. For example, subjects rated the intensity of their fears on a ten-point scale immediately after they had tried to approach and handle a live snake (Lang, Lazovik, & Reynolds, 1965). Other investigations have included physiological measures of anxiety as well as direct behavior indices of public-speaking anxiety (Paul, 1966).

Bandura, Grusec, and Menlove (1967) assessed nursery school children's intense fear of dogs. As one part of their measurement the child was escorted into a room containing, in the far corner, a playpen in which a dog was enclosed. The children's approach behavior was scaled objectively in terms of how near they ventured toward the animal. The highest scores required climbing into the playpen and sitting in it while playing with the cavorting dog. None of the children could accomplish this before treatment, but the majority were able to do so happily afterward.

Direct behavior sampling has been used extensively in the analysis of psychotic behavior by Ayllon and his associates, discussed in the last chapter. In one study, for instance, a time-sampling technique was employed in which the nurses sought out and observed each patient at regular thirty-minute intervals for periods of one to three minutes, without directly interacting with him (Ayllon & Haughton, 1964). The events observed in each sample were not scored for content but were classified for the occurrence of the previously defined undesirable behavior (like psychotic talk); for incompatible but more desirable alternatives that could replace it; and for "neutral" activities such as sleeping, eating, and dressing. Time-check recordings were used to compute the relative frequency of the undesirable behavior. For example, with one patient psychotic talk was the defined behavior requiring change. On the first day psychotic talk was observed on nine occasions and "sensible" talk on eight, yielding .53 as the relative frequency of psychotic talk. This time-sampling technique was supplemented by direct recording of all interactions between the patients and nurses (such as entering the nursing office).

Because current behavior sampling tends to be costly, especially of time, it should be used with discretion, usually after tentative decisions have been made about treatment objectives and problematic stimuli. Symbolic explorations and role play are especially helpful since it is inconvenient and costly for the practicing clinician to stock his office with a supply of snakes, insects, movable screens, cribs, or infinite assortments of potentially aversive or attractive conditioned stimuli. In the future, however, economical diagnostic laboratories, analogous to those in pathology, may become a reality (e.g., Lindsley, 1962).

Once the problematic response patterns, and the stimulus conditions under which they seem to occur, have been grossly identified, it becomes important to assess the more precise covariations between alterations in stimulus conditions and changes in the problematic response syndrome. Such functional analyses are the core of all social behavior assessments, as the last chapter implied.

One form of functional analysis is illustrated clearly in the case of a mother who had problems with her six-year-old son, whom she described as extremely overdemanding (Bijou, 1965). After she was oriented to the procedures and data-collection techniques of the researchers she and her son were asked to play in a playroom as they normally would at home. With the family's consent, two observers monitored the interactions from an observation room and recorded all the mother's verbal and nonverbal immediate reactions to each of her child's behaviors. On the basis of preliminary observations in the first two sessions, and in accord with the mother's presenting complaint, overdemanding or commanding behaviors were defined as verbal instructions by the child to the mother such as, "Now, let's play this!"; "You go there and I'll stay here!"; "No, that's wrong! Do it this way!" Cooperative responses were defined as any verbal or nonverbal behaviors directed to the mother that were not aggressive or imperative in content. Examples of cooperative behavior were, "Will you help me?," or "This is fun," or placing a toy in his mother's lap. The mother's responses following the child's commanding or cooperative behaviors also were recorded and classified, and these provided some clues about the social reinforcers she used in interactions with her son.

In the next two sessions the child's and the mother's behaviors were classified and tabulated on a checklist during every five-second period. The resulting data for each session were plotted as two separate cumulative curves. The first showed the frequency of the child's commanding behaviors and the mother's complying reactions to them—for example, "OK, let's do it," or "OK, if that's what you think." The second curve depicted the frequency of cooperative behaviors and the mother's reactions to them, such as looking, smiling, and saying, "Aren't you good," or "That's fun." These data indicated, as expected, a much greater rate of occurrence and reinforcement for commanding behaviors than for cooperative behaviors. The reliability of observations, in the form of interscorer agreement, was not given in this report. These reliabilities, however, tend to be acceptably high in similar projects. For example, interscorer agreement from 81 to 91 percent was reported for interaction scoring (Allen et al., 1964).

The subsequent assessment phases tested how the mother's reactions actually maintained the child's undue demandingness. During the next two sessions, each of twenty minute's duration, the mother was requested to ignore her child completely except when a red light, visible only to her, was flashed by the experimenter from the adjacent room. The red light signaled the mother to do whatever seemed natural to the situation but to restrict herself to one action or statement. The signals were used to assure that the child's cooperative behavior was reinforced each time by a response from the mother while commanding behavior was ignored consistently. As anticipated, the effect was a dramatic reduction in his rate of commanding behavior and an increase in cooperative behavior over baseline rates.

Treatment effects are strikingly evident when it can be demonstrated that removal of treatment variables, in the form of the new response-reinforcement contingencies, produces a strong recurrence of problematic behavior comparable to its baseline rate, and that reinstatement of the therapeutic contingencies again reduces the problematic behavior to low levels. In this case evidence for the functional relations between the behaviors of the boy and his mother's reactions now was obtained by instructing the mother to relate again to her son as she had during the baseline sessions. The resulting cumulative curves in the next two twenty-minute periods under this condition revealed marked increases in his rate of commanding behavior and decreases in his cooperative behavior. Now that these functional relations were clearly established, the treatment phases began. The mother reverted to ignoring commanding behavior and again reinforced her son's cooperativeness. Simultaneously the mother was taught to make increasingly accurate distinctions between these two classes of behavior. For this purpose she was given numerous descriptions and examples of commanding and cooperative behavior and helped to make more skillful discriminations between them. In addition to learning how to identify commanding and cooperative behavior rapidly, the mother was advised on how to react positively to the desired behavior and how to effectively ignore, and hence extinguish, the problematic behavior. In the final stages, the generality of her new responses and discriminatory skills was assessed by similar observation techniques in new situations and in her own home.

Once again this study illustrates the genuine integration that can be achieved between assessment and treatment procedures in a social behavior approach. The same principles have been extended to assess and modify difficulties within the home itself. At the parents' request, the problematic parent-child relationship is observed directly in the home and the parent is helped to change his own behavior toward the child in everyday home situations in ways that lead to a more satisfying relationship (e.g., Hawkins et al., 1966; Wahler et al., 1965).

Behavior sampling can permit extremely precise analyses of functional relations. A series of studies assessed the exact conditions controlling the occurrence of self-destructive behavior in a young schizophrenic girl (Lovaas et al., 1965a). This nine-year-old child was extensively and severely self-destructive. She banged her head and arms and pinched and slapped herself repeatedly. Among many other self-tortures she had stuck her head into an electric wall heater thereby setting her hair on fire. These intensely maladaptive behaviors seemed to have begun in her third year of life, and her current prosocial activities were minimal. Her play and interactions were restricted and stereotyped, her speech was largely echolalic, and she did much repetitive and stereotyped physical self-stimulation. The investigators studied the effects of several variables on changes in the child's objectively measured self-destructive behavior over a period of many sessions. Most important, the study investigated systematically any changes in self-destructive behavior resulting from withdrawal of reinforcement (attention) for behavior which had been rewarded previously.

Changes in the frequency of her self-destructive behaviors were studied systematically under various experimental conditions. The results revealed that stable increases in her self-destructive behavior consistently occurred only when reinforcement was removed from a response which had been rewarded before. The authors interpreted this to mean that, in the child's past, whenever previously reinforced responses began to be extinguished, she could consistently reinstate the reinforcement, but only provided that she hurt herself.

The authors also showed how highly discriminating this child was in the very specific times and particular circumstances during which she became self-destructive. For example, a physically gross operation, such as the experimenter's withdrawal of smiles and attention from entire sessions, did not alter her self-destructive behavior. Yet the removal of attention and smiles only for previously reinforced responses did generate dramatic changes in her behavior. Moreover, the day when her self-destruction in one setting (the music room) reached a peak was her "best" day in another setting (the preschool room). Her acceptable social behaviors in the preschool room were completely independent of her self-destructive behavior in the music room.

Assessment of Reinforcing Stimuli

Treatments based on the programming of response-reinforcement relations can succeed only if they employ effective reinforcers. Reinforcement values can be investigated by measuring the individual's actual choices in lifelike situations, as well as his verbal preferences or ratings. For example, subjects are confronted with real choices between rewards, or between punishments, and must choose among outcomes that vary in magnitude, type, or in the contingency required for their attainment (e.g., Mischel, 1966b; Mischel & Grusec, 1967). Alternatively, subjects may be asked to rank-order actual or hypothetical rewards (Rotter, 1954).

In some laboratory studies the reinforcement value of particular stimuli is assessed by observing their effects on the subject's performance. One popular procedure in personality research requires a child to drop marbles into one of two holes and measures his baseline preferences over many trials (Gewirtz & Baer, 1958a, b). Susceptibility to social reinforcement is assessed by measuring preference changes as a function of social reinforcement to the subject for dropping his marble into the initially less preferred hole. The effects of the particular reinforcing agents such as parents, peers, or experimenter (e.g., Patterson & Anderson, 1964; Patterson, Littman, & Hinsey, 1964), or of reinforcement schedules (e. g., Weir, 1964b, 1965) , and many other parameters (e.g., Weir, 1964a) have been investigated systematically using such paradigms. Designs of this kind have been applied with some interesting innovations to assess the effects of various reinforcers on response rate. For example, lever-pressing response rates of psychotic patients have been compared when the reinforcing stimuli were candy, money, female nude pictures or male nude pictures projected on a wall with colored slides, or the sight of a hungry kitten being fed milk (Lindsley, 1956, 1962).

Understandably, however, most clinicians would be unimpressed by data that deal with the effects of various reinforcers on such impersonal, nonsocial responses as lever pressing, plunger pulling, or marble dropping. Considering the specificity of behavior and its precise control by particular stimulus conditions, one cannot be sure that the particular reinforcers which may effectively control an individual's lever pressing in a laboratory are necessarily the same ones that could effectively modify his social behaviors when introduced into naturalistic settings.

In some clinical situations effective reinforcers are discovered more or less accidentally. For example, in the case of an anorexic young woman who had nearly starved herself to death, pleasant social conversation with the investigators during meals, contingent on eating, proved effective. Subsequently, walks, visits with other patients, and television viewing were also used successfully as contingent reinforcing stimuli (Bachrach, Erwin, & Mohr, 1965).

Although primary reinforcers like food, and generalized conditioned reinforcers such as praise, social approval, and money usually are effective for most persons, sometimes it is difficult to discover reinforcers that are both potent and feasible. Experimental studies of discrimination and symbolic learning attest to the difficulty of discovering adequate incentives for many pupils in learning situations (e.g., Brackbill & Jack, 1958; Walters & Kosowski, 1963) and for "chronic" behavior problems. The need to assess systematically the reinforcers that will produce and maintain behavior change seems evident but sometimes is overlooked. In one programmed instruction project, for example, the investigators initially used social approval and knowledge of results as reinforcers for their pupils (Birnbrauer et al., 1965). They soon discovered, however, that incorrect and correct answers seemed to be one and the same to the children; often the youngsters did not even look at the answers supplied by the teaching programs. As the authors pointed out, learning academic subjects had little value to these children, and more effective reinforcers had to be discovered.

Similarly, many social rewards may have little value for schizophrenic or delinquent patients (e.g., Atkinson, 1957; Cairns, 1959), and smiles and praise from the clinician may even engender anxiety, hostility, or indifference rather than the intended effects. It is possible, of course, to alter a person's responsiveness to incentives by changing his level of emotional arousal or his state of deprivation. For example, people who have been deprived of social reinforcers, or who are emotionally aroused, tend to become more susceptible to social reinforcement (e.g., Gewirtz & Baer, 1958a; Walters & Ray, 1960). Physiologically produced emotional arousal and cognitive changes also may increase susceptibility to social influence (e.g., Schachter & Wheeler, 1962) and presumably alter the valence of stimuli. Sometimes motivational states can be produced by drugs designed to enhance the effectiveness of particular classes of reinforcers. For example, schizophrenic patients have received insulin injections to increase the effectiveness of fudge which served as a reinforcer in their rehabilitation program (Peters & Jenkins, 1954).

The problem of ineffective reinforcers often can be circumvented more readily, however, by using tokens or other symbols that the person can later trade for whatever outcomes he wants from a large array of alternatives. Tokens also help to avoid satiation effects, and their advantages have been demonstrated repeatedly (Birnbrauer & Lawler,

1964; Heid, 1964; Staats et al., 1964; Staats et al., 1962). The value and the effectiveness of token reinforcers hinges, of course, on the available reinforcers for which they can be exchanged.

It generally has been assumed that chronic schizophrenics develop severe motivational deficits, especially after they have spent many years on the back wards of a mental hospital. Recent research by Ayllon and Azrin (1965) shows how effective reinforcers can be discovered for these psychotic patients and can help to motivate them to engage in more adaptive behavior. The authors were guided by the principle that any behavior that has a high natural frequency of occurrence can serve as a reinforcer for other less likely behaviors (Premack, 1965). As a first step the patients' free behavior was observed directly on the ward to discover their frequent behaviors that could later be used as reinforcers. Throughout the day observers carefully recorded the things that the patients did, or tried to do, without any outside staff pressures. It was noted, for example, that many of them lingered near the exits, tried to leave the ward, or hoarded items under their mattresses.

On the basis of extensive observation six categories of reinforcers were established: privacy, leave from the ward, social interactions with the staff, devotional opportunities, recreational opportunities, and commissary items. Included under "privacy," for example, were such freedoms as choice of bedroom or of eating group, as well as other ways of preserving autonomy and privacy by getting a personal cabinet or a room divider screen. Recreational opportunities included the chance to have exclusive use of a radio or television set, as well as attendance at movies and dances. Each of the reinforcers could be obtained with a specified number of tokens; in turn, patients could earn these tokens contingent on engaging in rehabilitative functions (self-care, job training) as discussed in the last chapter. The outcomes for which the patients later chose to exchange their tokens gives an excellent index of the subjective reinforcement value of the available activities. In one experiment with eight patients over 42 days the mean tokens exchanged was as follows: 1352 for privacy, 970 for commissary items, and 616 for leave from the ward. In contrast, the average tokens in the same period exchanged for social interactions with the staff was only 3.75, for recreational opportunities 2.37, and for devotional opportunities 0.62. Considering these data on reinforcement value, it is understandable that programs that rely on social motivations with chronic hospitalized patients generally do not fare well.

Graded Learning Sequences

After effective reinforcers have been identified, their receipt can be made contingent upon the person's appropriate behavior. When the desired criterion behaviors already are easily available to the subject (have been learned previously or can be learned readily), no special problems of sequencing arise. In these instances, as long as the attainment of reinforcers is made contingent on the subject's specified behavior, the change program can proceed readily and often in very large steps, as it did, for example, in the case of Ann (Chapter 6). When complex behavioral sequences and new skills must be learned, however, as in severe behavior deficits, the steps in the learning program have to be arranged with special care.

Learning programs must be arranged into small substeps either when the learner is greatly handicapped by deficits or when the material to be learned is complex or intensely emotion arousing. The first task is to clearly specify the treatment objectives and to obtain baseline assessments of each individual. These initial assessments find the subjects' current level of behavior so that appropriate changes can be planned and evaluated. For example, increments in class time and productive work time were selected as goals for programmed learning in a class of severely retarded but educable children. In this study the youngsters ranged in chronological age from nine to thirteen years and in mental age from five years and five months to seven years and three months (Birnbrauer et al., 1965). Specific subgoals were selected, such as increments in minutes of reading, arithmetic, cursive writing, and in independent "desk work" and homework. The goals were to increase the time the youngsters devoted to these tasks and to steadily improve the rate and adequacy of their work. Increments in these productive activities necessarily involved decrements in task-irrelevant or disruptive activities, such as tantrums, which most of the children had displayed frequently at the start of the program.

In addition to assessing the children's progress at each step of the program, the instruction techniques themselves were evaluated continuously and modified to develop optimal programs for each child and the most effective organization for the total classroom. This aspect of assessment involved decisions about the presentation, content, and sequencing of instruction, appropriate reinforcement systems, and ways of coping with disruptive behavior. Specific programs for teaching different topics required various formats and equipment, but they all shared the following characteristics.

Each child began at a simple level so that he never experienced massive failure and its disruptive consequences. All items were questions or problems whose answers could be recorded rapidly and objectively. Every response unit was followed by immediate feedback of results to the child, and the children received token reinforcers and praise for correct answers. Items were arranged in a sequence to assure that new material was presented only when the child was adequately prepared and ready for it. Daily analyses of errors helped to determine the proper sequencing for each individual. All programs (whether or not they were aided by automatic equipment) were designed to help the pupils teach themselves by increasing their own autonomy over the learning process.

The program for teaching retardates to write illustrates the typical major stages. Writing was taught in a sequence from tracing, to tracing and copying, to copying alone. Subjects first traced on an illuminated tracing box which provided a clear model. In the early phases this model was almost constantly illuminated to provide continuous information about the lines to be traced. At first tracing was confined to simple strokes. The margin of error permitted was progressively decreased and the complexity of the model was slowly increased to include larger units such as letters and letter groups. Gradually the proportion of light-on time was decreased so that the students became less dependent on the model. Competence at each stage was assessed before the next stage of the program (tracing combined with copying) commenced.

The basic approach in these programs could be extended quite readily to diagnose and analyze the components of almost any learning deficit. Such analysis would focus on the organization and reorganization of stimulus materials and incentive conditions needed to improve or restore the particular skills. Diagnostic tests developed from this viewpoint might use samples from each of the graded phases in the training program in a sequence of increasing difficulty, much as graded series of performance samples are used in the traditional measurement of intelligence. The results would not merely index the degree of deficiency, but also help to assign the person to the appropriate phase in the treatment program. Everything that has been said about intellectual and vocational deficits applies equally to teaching social and interpersonal skills. For example, when persons try to learn new complex social skills, as in assertiveness training or fixed-role therapy, it is also important to carefully arrange the sequence and the conditions so that the client can gradually progress to master increasingly difficult behaviors.

In the studies of behavior deficits that have been discussed, the individual's performance is assessed at each step in a progressively more difficult series of tasks. The results at each criterion test determine the next step that the subject can take. These tests thus compare the person's performance against an explicit criterion in the learning sequence rather than against the performance of other people. In an instructional program for automobile driver training, for example, it is useful to assess whether or not the candidate knows the location of the brakes before he begins his road test. This assessment is valuable irrespective of any norms that compare the speed with which different candidates learn to locate the brakes. A much needed distinction between criterion-referenced and norm-referenced performance measures makes it apparent that assessment does not necessarily require comparisons between individuals (Glaser, 1963; Hammock, 1960). Criterion-referenced assessments compare the person's performance against a performance standard; norm-referenced assessments compare people against each other, usually on trait or attribute dimensions. Norm-referenced assessments indicate the individual's *relative* standing on a continuum in relation to others, and they have been the principal measures of trait and state assessors. These norms for other people, however, give little or no information about how the individual's behavior compares with a performance standard, and this latter information is often the most important to have.

Carefully arranged, graded stimulus sequences are also important when the stimuli are likely to arouse strong emotional reactions because extreme arousal levels tend to disrupt attention and learning (Kausler & Trapp, 1960). Thus procedures to alter the valence of problematic, emotionally disturbing stimuli also have to scale the stimuli into a graded series. As was evident in counterconditioning, for example, aversive stimuli have to be graded into sufficiently mild samples so that reactions to them can be modified in small steps without overwhelming the individual and without generating defensive escape and avoidance reactions.

In clinical situations the anxiety hierarchy for counterconditioning is usually based on life history data from interviews, on impressions from questionnaire responses, and on special verbal probing into the situations in which the patient feels especially anxious (Wolpe, 1958). On the basis of frankly clinical and intuitive procedures, anxiety-arousing events are ranked for severity. The assessor groups the items into thematic categories, but the client ranks them (Wolpe, 1961). Sometimes this procedure involves a gross type of informal scaling. Within a particular thematic group, for example, the client is asked to think of the most disturbing situation he can imagine. This item is placed at the top of the hierarchy. Next, the low point of the hierarchy is established by isolating a situation in which subjective anxiety would be entirely absent. After the extreme points have been identified, the client can scale roughly the relative severity of other situational examples by placing them in the intermediate range on the fear continuum.

The scaling of items within a thematic category is relatively straightforward when the person reports a problem on a clear dimension. For example, if a person fears enclosed spaces the problematic stimuli usually can be ranked for severity in a fashion roughly correlated with physical distance. Likewise, if examinations or illness are selected as problematic situations, they can be ranked for severity on relatively simple dimensions such as temporal delay or magnitude. The thought of a mild illness twenty years hence is likely to be less disturbing than contemplating an imminent major disease. Recall, in this context, the many previously cited techniques for scaling objectively the magnitude of fear and avoidance responses to aversive stimuli. In these instances the aversive stimuli can be graded readily on such dimensions as physical and temporal distance, or on the extent to which they are presented symbolically (e.g., a toy snake) or realistically (an active, unrestricted, live snake).

As Wolpe (1961) acknowledged, there are many cases in which the main sources of anxiety are not immediately clarified by the person's reports of what he avoids, and in such cases hierarchy construction may become more difficult. Often the array of circumstances that elicit aversive emotional reactions from a person is heterogeneous, idiosyncratic, and not confined to any simple dimension of physical stimulus similarity. Apparently heterogeneous items may be included even within a seemingly simple theme. A claustrophobic client, for example, had a twelve-item hierarchy that contained "having polish on her fingernails and no access to remover" (Wolpe, 1961, p. 197) imbedded among more typical items like "being stuck in an elevator." This common finding reflects the fact that through generalization a multitude of stimuli may come to elicit autonomic reactions. Consequently the same person often reacts with inappropriate emotional arousal to highly diverse stimuli. These heterogeneous stimuli cannot be grouped readily on any one single dimension; rather, several more or less discrete dimensions seem to be involved. In many cases at least two different categories of emotion-provoking stimuli may be present.

Wolpe and his colleagues emphasize the importance of identifying clear "themes" and claim that ". . . unless different hierarchies have unmistakable common features desensitization to one hierarchy does not in the least diminish the reactivity to another (untreated) hierarchy" (Wolpe, 1961, p. 201). Often conditioning may occur among adventitiously associated events, and accidental vicissitudes can govern the particular neutral stimuli that happen to occur contiguously with aversive stimulation or with higher-order conditioned stimuli. Therefore the dimensions of stimulus generalization involved may be especially hard to identify.

Intuitive attempts by the clinician to identify definite, discrete themes or generalization gradients may entail all the hazards of clinical inference discussed in relation to psychodynamic assessment. Certainly a minimal requirement would be to demonstrate that clinicians can reliably establish discrete themes and reach agreement about particular themes independently. The data on the unreliability of clinical judgments in similar undertakings (Chapter 5) should make one skeptical of reliability among judges in this context also.

As stated before, Wolpe and his coworkers usually construct the themes themselves, the therapist classifying the themes into groups if there is more than one theme (Wolpe, 1961). Since desensitization procedures have to rely heavily on the client's own self-report and cooperation, it would be more consistent, and perhaps more efficacious, to have the client rather than the clinician group his own themes. If subjective theme clusters are to be sought, it might be more reasonable to base them on dimensions that seem subjectively pertinent to the client rather than intuitively relevant for the therapist.

Usually the categories within each hierarchy also vary greatly in breadth. Some deal with a seemingly narrow range of situations, as in "elevators" or "fear of falling"; other categories appear to be extremely broad, as in "guilt" or "disapproval." Here, for example, are the items from a "guilt series" for a 41-year-old gynecologist (Wolpe, 1961, p. 197):

(1) *"Jackson (Dean of the Medical School) wants to see you."*
(2) *Thinks "I only did ten minutes' work today."*
(3) *Thinks "I only did an hour's work today."*
(4) *Thinks "I only did six hours' work today."*
(5) *Sitting at the movies.*
(6) *Reading an enjoyable novel.*
(7) *Going on a casual stroll.*
(8) *Staying in bed during the day (even though ill).*

At present little is known about how the breadth of the stimulus category at each step affects the ease of desensitization and facilitates generalization effects to other related stimuli. In the foregoing hierarchy, for example, would one broader category like "having fun" or "enjoying pleasurable amusements" serve as an effective substitute for the more specific situations that were used (sitting at the movies, reading an enjoyable novel, going on a casual stroll)? To focus "in imagination" on a situation may require dwelling on a concrete instance of it. Even when a category is broad, the person may specify it privately with concrete instances on which he can focus vividly in imagination. The details of this process are not understood and merit study; indeed the cognitive desensitization paradigm seems an excellent situation for research on cognitive processes, thought, and imagery.

Further research aimed at clarifying how the "imagining" of problematic stimuli works and how this process can be enhanced is sorely needed (Rachman, 1967). One possibility is to provide the subject vivid external cues about the aversive stimuli in the form of pictures, slides, or films. The presentation and speed of these cues then could be controlled by the client himself. Considerable autonomy could be given so that each client could control his own desensitization procedure at the pace most appropriate for him. A large step in this direction has been taken by Bandura (1968), who is developing film-mediated modeling procedures for counterconditioning.

In counterconditioning, after the hierarchy has been established tentatively, the lowest hierarchy item can be paired with a preestablished incompatible response, and then treatment itself begins. Just as in programs to correct behavior deficits, the person's reactions at each step in the progressively more complex anxiety hierarchy are assessed and his readiness for the next item is evaluated. As soon as he can master and sustain his desired emotional reaction to one stimulus configuration, the next most difficult item in the hierarchy is presented.

The parallels between the grading and sequencing procedures in both direct and vicarious emotional counterconditioning and extinction on the one hand, and teaching programs to correct deficits on the other hand, seem self-evident. In all of these programs the person proceeds at his own pace through a progressively more difficult graded hierarchy of problems, and his progress is evaluated against specified performance criteria rather than against the norms set by other people. These learning programs also share the basic goal of freeing the person from dependence on the constraints of the program itself as quickly as possible. Just like all good treatments, relearning programs try to help the subject to become independent of the therapy as rapidly as he can.

Graded learning sequences are designed so that the person attains increasingly high levels of competence and can perform more and more adequately and independently at progressively higher levels of difficulty and of quality. Coinciding with these increments in performance are deliberate reductions in the external rewards, cues, and controls that were initially helpful to prompt and regulate the person's early learning efforts. Simultaneously the individual learns to regulate and control his own emotional reactions in daily life situations independent of the therapy, providing himself with his own cues and self-instructions to cope adaptively with previously traumatic events (Wolpe & Lazarus, 1966). Just as rapidly as his own progress permits, the person thus advances to more complicated, challenging tasks, while external cues and rewards become more delayed (e.g., Staats & Butterfield, 1965). Gradually the individual becomes more autonomous and self-directed; his behavior comes to be supported by intrinsic reinforcement from the new behavior itself and more and more independent of the specific external controls required by the treatment in its initial phases.

Clinical versus Actuarial Hierarchies

It may often be possible to avoid the time-consuming procedure of designing a unique set of stimulus materials and a completely idiosyncratic program for every client. Obviously teaching programs for common academic topics like fundamental mathematics can be designed actuarially, and the same basic program can be appropriate for whole classes of people, although each learner proceeds through the common program at his own speed. Some of the components of a larger program also can be individually tailored, especially in computer-assisted teaching arrangements (Atkinson & Hansen, 1966). Actuarial learning programs also can be designed to alter common maladaptive emotional responses or to strengthen essential social skills.

Numerous common sexual, achievement-related, and affiliative situations repeatedly evoke emotional problems for many people in the culture. It should be possible to construct essentially actuarial hierarchies for these frequently encountered problem areas. Especially for common emotion-arousing situations, a large pool of items can be printed on cards (as in the MMPI), each card describing a specific situation, thus minimizing the amount of time needed for individual interviews to construct hierarchies. Davison (1967a), for example, wrote brief snake scenes of varying severity, such as "picking up and handling a toy snake" or "barehanded, picking up the snake and it is moving around" on each of twenty-six cards. Each subject simply ranked the cards in order of increasing aversiveness to establish his own hierarchy. Similarly, a twelve-item temporal hierarchy was developed for public-speaking fears in anxious college students (Paul, 1966). Items ranged from thinking about the speech privately a week or two before it was due to actually walking up before the audience and presenting the speech. This actuarially designed common hierarchy was then modified, if necessary, to fit each individual.

Preprogrammed stimulus arrays for actuarially common problems could include filmed modeling sequences to prevent or desensitize common anxieties and to model necessary social skills. Bandura (1968) has been using appropriately constructed film sequences to extinguish debilitating anxiety to such common traumatic objects as snakes and dogs. In this technique the client views a motion picture film that shows the anxiety-provoking scenes in graded sequence. He then desensitizes himself with the film by practicing relaxation to the scenes which he projects to himself on a screen at his own pace. The client can control the film automatically, so that he can review each scene as often as necessary before showing the next one. This procedure continues until he achieves complete relaxation.

Special film sequences also could help to prevent the development of prevalent maladjustments in the culture. In this manner deviant reactions to sexual stimuli, to work and social failures, and to other widespread sources of threat might be prevented or treated with considerable efficacy. Information about base rates and highly frequent problems in the culture thus could serve to design treatments actuarially rather than to describe people with Barnum labels (Chapter 5). Although there is little utility in calling an adolescent boy "sexually insecure," it is valuable to have predesigned treatment programs widely available for such common problems.

THE ANALYSIS OF CAUSES

Treatments based on learning principles have been available since the 1920's and have been applied to a variety of problems ranging from enuresis to all kinds of phobias (Metzner, 1961). For many years direct behavior modification remained fairly rare because therapists feared that "symptom substitution" would occur, as psychodynamic theory suggests. According to psychodynamic theory, unless the treatment removes the "basic causes" of disturbance, by making the unconscious conscious, the removal of symptoms is followed by other symptoms that may be even more severely debilitating than the original ones. As was noted previously, this reasoning follows from the assumption that underlying core personality forces are the roots of disturbed behavior; problematic behaviors are seen as merely the superficial symptoms of these internal forces.

The results of both experimental and clinical studies of behavior change, however, make it plain that enduring removal of "symptoms" (phobic and in other forms) have been regularly achieved on the basis of learning principles without analyzing the unconscious meanings or the supposed psychodynamic etiology of the behavior. In fact, empirical studies consistently reveal that behavior-change programs of the kind discussed in this and the previous chapter tend to be effective and that the changed behaviors are not automatically replaced by other problems (e.g., Bergin, 1966; Davison, 1967a; Eysenck & Rachman, 1965; Grossberg, 1964; Lang & Lazovik, 1963; Lazarus, 1961; Paul, 1966, 1967; Rachman, 1967; Wolpe, 1958). On the contrary, and not surprisingly, when clients are freed from debilitating emotional reactions and constricting crippling avoidance patterns, they may become more free to behave in new adaptive ways that in turn lead to more positive consequences for them. After reviewing the relevant literature on behavior therapy, Grossberg (1964, p. 83) says about symptom substitution:

> The overwhelming evidence of the present review is that therapy directed at elimination of maladaptive behavior ("symptoms") is successful and long-lasting. . . . Unfortunately, psychotherapists seem to have stressed the hypothetical dangers of only curing the symptoms, while ignoring the very real dangers of the harm that is done by not curing them.

In light of the generally encouraging results, behavior therapy procedures are now being applied much more widely and to a far broader range of problems. The basic techniques are being adapted to problems ranging from specific fears to diffuse anxieties, from fetishes to long-established homosexuality and alcoholism, from mild school phobias in children to intense delusions and psychotic ideation in adults (e.g., Davison, 1967b).

The search for "underlying" or "basic" causes and for original traumatic etiologies has not been confined to psychodynamic therapies. In counterconditioning therapies, for example, there also has been much concern with identifying the "primary" or original conditioned stimuli which first became associated with maladaptive emotional reactions in the individual's past. Presumably many of the stimuli that currently evoke problematic emotional responses acquired their powers through processes of generalization from the original conditioned events. Even if the original conditioned stimulus could ever be correctly identified, however, it is unlikely that its neutralization would produce more beneficial effects on current behavior than would desensitization of the current emotion-provoking stimuli themselves. Consider, for example, a woman presently experiencing sexual frigidity in relation to her husband. Assume that one of the early origins of her sexual fearfulness toward men involved a traumatically upsetting sexual episode when she was a five-year-old child. According to social behavior theory, improvement in her current behavior should be accomplished better by desensitization of the fears that she now has than of their remote historical origins. Lazarus (1963), for instance, reported the successful treatment of chronically frigid women through systematic relaxation. Examples of increasingly aversive sexual situations were obtained from each woman. With one woman, for example, the series ranged from dancing with her husband and embracing him while fully clothed to highly erotic descriptions of sexual acts. Although none of the stimuli involved events from early history, dramatic improvement was obtained in her sexual life. The bulk of the behavior therapy literature consists of successful treatments for emotional problems whose historical origins remain both unknown and untreated.

The few laboratory studies relevant to this topic suggest that the extinction of emotional reactions to a stimulus generalizes most strongly to those stimuli that are closest to the one on which extinction is induced; when the generalization stimuli are farther away on the gradient from the stimulus that is being neutralized, the generalization effect to them is less substantial (e.g., Hoffeld, 1962; Hovland, 1937). Extrapolating to life situations, neutralization of the original conditioned stimuli should alleviate reactions to the original conditioned stimuli and those most similar to them. To the extent, however, that these events are no longer relevant (e.g., a childhood sweetheart for a now sixty-year-old man), it would be more efficacious to change the valence of currently problematic stimuli than to search for their remote roots.

The symptom substitution issue has led to an erroneous dichotomy between symptomatic behaviors (with which behavior therapies are supposedly preoccupied) and basic or underlying causes (which dynamic therapies preempt as their domain). In fact, all analyses of behavior seek causes; the difference between social behavior and trait-state analyses is in whether current controlling causes or historically distant antecedents are invoked. Behavioral analyses seek the current variables and conditions controlling the behavior of interest, as was demonstrated in the functional analyses illustrated in earlier sections. Traditional personality theories have looked, instead, for historical roots and developmental etiology.

A Key Illustration: Pearson Brack Reanalyzed

Some of the main differences between the psychodynamic assessment of causes and the approach of social behavior theory are best illustrated by comparing their analyses of a clinical problem. The well-known case of "Pearson Brack," an American airman in the Second World War, serves as a clear example (Grinker & Spiegel, 1945, pp. 197–207).

Pearson Brack was a B-25 bombardier in the Tunisian theater of operations when his problems began. On his tenth and eleventh bombing missions he had fainted when his airplane reached an altitude of 10,000 feet. Afterward, trying to recall what had happened, Brack remembered only that he had felt cold and sleepy and then had awakened, finding himself leaning on his bomb sight. Just before the two missions on which Brack had fainted he had experienced a narrow escape from death; during his ninth mission his airplane was almost destroyed and he was injured seriously. While nearing an important bombing target, and under very heavy flak and fighter resistance, Brack's plane had suddently jolted and rolled over, and then began to fall in a seemingly endless dive. The pilot did regain control, barely in time to avoid crashing to the ground, and successfully brought the plane back into the flight formation to complete the mission. During the plane's fall, however, Brack was hurled violently against the bomb sight. He sustained a heavy blow on the left side of his chest and his injuries were so severe that he immediately began to cough up blood. Nevertheless, he managed to release his bombs on the target. Upon his return, Brack was hospitalized for four weeks, and then seemed to be healed and was returned to full duty. It was on the next two missions, the tenth and eleventh, that he fainted. The two fainting episodes again brought Brack to the attention of the flight surgeon. As a first step, the medical board that reviewed his case considered and ruled out any residual organic damage as the possible cause of his fainting at high altitudes. After excluding an organic etiology the case was interpreted from a psychodynamic viewpoint. The psychiatrist hypothesized that the fainting was symptomatic of deep underlying anxiety, related to Brack's brittle personality structure. He viewed Brack's fainting as a surface manifestation of basic fear and anxiety, and of dynamics that could be understood and treated only in the light of the analysis of childhood traumas and identifications. He therefore proceeded, in accord with psychodynamic theory, to search for signs of latent or repressed pervasive anxiety and for their hypothetical distant historical sources.

When interviewed Brack clearly recognized that he could not fly above about 9000 feet. But he rejected the idea that his troubles resulted from basic underlying, long-standing anxieties, and he asked for specific help that might make it possible for him to rejoin his crew in combat flying. The psychiatrist, however, interpreted Brack's overt behavior as a defensive facade (Grinker & Spiegel, 1945, p. 198):

> *Although he did not directly show hostility when told that his troubles might be due to fear, he constantly rejected this idea,*

laughing and joking at such a possibility. He stated that he had never been afraid of anything. He described himself as one of the best bombardiers in his outfit, and talked about his activities in combat with a great deal of pride and jocularity. He attempted to produce the impression of the typical carefree, aggressive combat crew member. There was something about his attitude, however, which was not wholly convincing. The effect was theatrical and overplayed.

Brack's refusal to accept the psychiatrist's interpretation about the "underlying anxieties" supposedly responsible for his problem led to further assessments apparently designed to convince him (p. 198):

Because it was impossible to establish any insight into his underlying anxieties in psychotherapeutic interviews, a pentothal interview was undertaken overseas. He was told that he was in his plane with his crew going to the target.

The pentothal interview, however, produced no direct evidence of anxiety. He talked about the ninth mission in great detail, speaking with various crew members as if he were actually in the plane again, but he remained entirely calm and unemotional and "showed no anxiety whatsoever" (p. 198). Because "no anxiety could be realized either in interviews or under pentothal" (p. 199), the psychiatrist next took the rare (and excellent) step of accompanying Brack on a practice flight so that he could watch his reactions while in the air. Brack's behavior en route to the field, and during the early stages of the flight, was described as showing "more than his usual amount of jocularity and aggressive humor" (p. 199). He seemed to be "in good humor and cheerful." A few times Brack teased the psychiatrist (who presumably had spent little time in combat) about the possibility that distant unidentified planes might really turn out to be German fighter planes. The psychiatrist, however, grimly noted that "the joke was unrealistic since German aircraft had never penetrated to this area" (p. 199). Indeed, he interpreted Brack's total behavior as a sign of "a frightened individual whistling past the graveyard" (p. 199).

When the plane reached an altitude of about 10,000 feet, Brack began to pale, tremble, and breathe rapidly; fainting was barely avoided by having him breathe slowly and deeply. As soon as the pilot brought the plane down to an altitude of 8500 feet, Brack recovered and again became fully alert and calm.

It should be noted that, from the viewpoint of social behavior theory, a fairly clear causal relationship now seemed to be established. When Brack's plane ascended to an altitude of 10,000 feet he became ill; when he remained below that altitude he felt well. This relationship occurred not only on the practice flight but also on the tenth and eleventh mission when his fainting problem had first begun. Although post hoc speculations about etiology are never satisfying, it is plausible that Brack's severe injury on the ninth mission may have occurred when his plane was at the cruising altitude of about 10,000 feet. The contiguity between altitude cues at that height and Brack's painful, nearly fatal, traumatic experience may have made the former conditioned stimuli capable of eliciting an intense arousal reaction that led to fainting. Although the etiology cannot be certain the treatment implications seem clear for social behavior theory: render the traumatic cues neutral by desensitizing Brack to them through slow, graded exposure under conditions that prevent arousal and that, instead, insure incompatible responses such as relaxation.

Thus, from the perspective of social behavior theory, the relevant causes of Brack's problem are the current conditions that actually control its occurrence, in this case altitude cues previously associated with a trauma. From the perspective of psychodynamic theory, however, the causes are his underlying, inferred characterological anxiety and its supposed childhood antecedents. Consequently the psychiatrist ignored the evident correlation between the altitude and the problem and instead continued his search for hypothesized "roots" in the form of repressed underlying anxieties.

Brack fully recognized, of course, that he collapsed and could not function in planes at high altitudes. He firmly rejected, however, the belief that unconscious anxieties rooted in his basic character development and early childhood were the causes responsible for this problem. He felt, instead, that his trouble was somehow related to his painful injury and traumatic experiences on the ninth mission. The psychiatrist, however, kept pressing for Brack to admit his underlying fears, and the two men became embroiled in a prolonged semantic dispute. This controversy seemed to center on such words as "afraid" and "nervous" which the psychiatrist wanted Brack to call himself. In this phase the psychiatrist reported repeatedly that the patient still completely resisted any interpretation about his underlying deep fears; Brack insisted that the after-effects of his painful injury and trauma in the plane made him faint on planes. In subsequent interviews, the psychiatrist, for example, "pointed out to the patient that the tremor he exhibited in the air was very similar to the tremor of nervousness" (p. 200). Brack, however, "took the attitude that the therapist, if the latter wanted to, had a right to think that he was scared but that he, the patient, could never be convinced that this was the source of his trouble."

The semantic dispute between the bombardier and his psychiatrist about Brack's true subjective internal state continued and had serious consequences (p. 200):

> *Since it was manifestly impossible to establish any insight in a patient with such strong resistance and so much organic fixation, it was felt that the best method of procedure would be to have the patient return to combat and to ask his Flight Surgeon to observe him carefully for signs of anxiety and to work out the anxiety with him on the spot.*

On his next mission Brack efficiently executed his duties over a very rough target and, although he did not faint when the altitude exceeded 9000 feet, he returned exhausted and soaked with perspiration. The flight surgeon feared that Brack might still be suffering from the effects of his pulmonary injury and so referred him to the hospital. The chief medical officer interpreted his cardiogram as possibly showing recent posterior wall damage. He informed Brack that he had a contusion of the heart, ordering six months of rest from the date of the injury. When Brack next saw his therapist he told him that (p. 200):

> *. . . he guessed there was something wrong with him after all, because the doctor in the hospital had found it. He was more cheerful than ever, although somewhat more calm and less talkative than when first seen. Because there was now so much organic fixation, psychotherapy did not appear likely to be successful and it was determined to return the patient to the United States for further observation and treatment.*

After his return to the United States Brack felt increasingly nervous and depressed. He complained of anxiety dreams of falling in an airplane. He was admitted to a convalescent hospital where, remarkably, he found himself facing the same psychiatrist who also had been transferred to the United States. Brack interpreted his own nervous and depressed feelings as due to not having completed his job overseas. He had left his friends behind in combat while he was returned to his family and safety in the midst of war. The psychiatrist, however, in accord with his theoretical convictions, pressed for analogies between Brack's current problems and his childhood, exploring in pentothal interviews his early life memories and his feelings about his alcoholic father. For example, Brack was asked why he felt depressed (p. 203):

> He answered that he felt it was probably because he had failed to complete his job overseas. He was then asked if possibly he did not also feel bad because his behavior had been evasive and he had escaped facing his responsibilities in the same way as his father escaped similar responsibilities. He said, "No, I don't drink." He was told that his way of escaping was not through drinking but through failing to face his real feelings. He was then reminded that overseas he had failed to face up to his own anxiety and fear of flying. He answered that he did not know at that time he was afraid. He was asked if he knew it now, and he said he was not sure.

While the persistence and directness with which the psychiatrist seemed to seek validating evidence for his own theoretical hypotheses may seem extreme, it is not necessarily atypical. Indeed the case of Brack has been used in a major neodynamic text on abnormal behavior (White, 1964) as one of the main illustrations. It is not surprising therefore that after reviewing literature on psychodynamic therapy Bandura (1967) concludes that clients' "insights" after traditional psychotherapy can be predicted better from knowledge of their therapists' belief systems than from information about the clients' actual past history. He takes the view that insight into the supposedly "basic" intrapsychic causes of behavior "may primarily represent a conversion to the therapist's point of view rather than a process of self-discovery" (Bandura, 1967, p. 78). Considering the data on the constraining effects of trait hypotheses upon observation (Chapter 3), this interpretation seems especially plausible.

The struggle between patient and psychiatrist continued. Brack sought direct help, suggesting, for example, that he might "get over his uneasiness in planes by repeatedly exposing himself to flights" (p. 204). Predictably, his intuitively sound suggestion for extinction treatment was interpreted as "markedly evasive," and "because of his continued difficulty in clearly recognizing the source of his anxiety, it was determined to give him another pentothal interview" (p. 204).

Gradually, over the course of many sessions, Brack's "resistance" was indeed slowly worn down, and at last he began to offer the expected self-revelations. For example:

> *"I guess I have been trying to fool myself about a lot of things. I am really worried about a lot of things and I don't like to admit it."* (p. 205)

These confessions were promptly reinforced by the therapist (p. 205):

> *He was then told that his confidence and general feeling of security had been shattered by his flying experiences when he had the fall and injury, and that this was only natural, but that he would get over it. He was told that he could never really get better as long as he would not recognize how he really felt, but that, now that he knew what was the matter with him, he would start on the road to recovery.*

At this point Brack again asked for direct help to overcome his flying problems, possibly by returning to flying itself. According to the therapist's dynamic interpretations, the "basic" cause of Brack's fainting in the plane, and of his nervousness and depression when removed from his duties, was the result of an inadequate identification with his father. Until that was handled he could not fly (p. 205):

> *The patient's maturity, achieved through identification with his grandfather and based on a rejection of his own father, was at best tenuous. It did not appear to represent an actual maturity but rather an imitation of maturity. The attempt to achieve an ego-ideal by imitation, rather than through a real identification, was characteristic of this man. It was the essence of his behavior as a combat crew member, which was characterized by evasive aggressiveness, jocularity and sangfroid. These reactions, actually felt by some combat crew members, were only imitated by the patient while in combat to cover up his actual fright—the whistling in the dark technique.*

Although throughout the many months of arguing Brack had kept asking for a chance to be helped to overcome his flying problem (p. 206):

> *In view of his fragile maturity, his long-standing insecurity and the actual psychological trauma incurred during his fall,*

270

it was considered that a return to a flying assignment at this time would not be wise.

At this point the case description ended.

The Client's Role

The case of Brack highlights some of the chief differences between the current social behavior approach and traditional psychodynamic assessments. Social behavior theory searches for causes in the conditions that demonstrably control the defined behaviors of interest; traditional dynamic theories infer hypothetical causes, such as deficient "ego ideals," from behavioral "signs" and tie these to post hoc historical reconstructions on the basis of the clinician's theory. It is generally impossible, of course, to accurately reconstruct unique historical circumstances many years after they occurred even if one hunts for them diligently. Indeed, it is notoriously difficult to obtain even a partially accurate reconstruction of personal events long after they have taken place, since even such close eyewitnesses as parents simply forget the bulk of what happened (Mednick & Shaffer, 1963; Pyles, Stolz, & MacFarlane, 1935; Robbins, 1963; Wenar, 1961; Wenar & Coulter, 1962).

The research on clinical inferences discussed in earlier chapters makes it untenable to prefer the clinician's judgments about the hypothetical causes of behavior to the client's own constructions and interpretations about himself. Psychodynamic assessments further assume that persons are victims of enduring unconscious and irrational forces that prevent them from properly evaluating themselves. In fact, there in no convincing evidence that unconscious processes play an important role in learning, discrimination, and performance (e.g., Eriksen, 1960, 1966). As we have seen (Chapter 6), awareness appears to be a critical ingredient in most learning situations. In the context of prediction, we have also seen that the person's predictions about his own behavior, and his self-reports, generally are more accurate than the clinician's predictions about him (Chapter 5). In light of these considerations it seems unjustified to retain the psychodynamic belief that persons with problems cannot reach appropriate decisions about their desired goals without the benefit of interpretations about their unconscious processes from clinical "experts."

Social behavior assessments look for the client's definition of his own problems and then offer courses of action to help him achieve his own goals, leaving the choices to him whenever possible and as soon as possible. In Brack's case, for example, social behavior theory probably would have led to a treatment program of counterconditioning and gradual extinction not dissimilar to the one he requested spontaneously. Brack's goals—to be helped to fly again and to overcome the aftermath of his injury—would be accepted as reasonable, rather than as the defensive facade of a brittle and immature individual from whom "unconscious anxieties" had to be extracted, in spite of himself. Social behavior assessments and treatments are intended to remove problems and to help people develop more constructive behavior—but not to remake the people in a new mold. Elimination of a problem—such as fainting at high altitudes—is not intended to reconstruct the whole person but only to help him with specified goals. If professionals in other fields substituted their own omnibus goals for the client's particular self-described problems as freely as psychodynamicists routinely do, they surely would be brought to court as defendants rather than as expert witnesses. In social behavior assessments the client is viewed as an active collaborator, who may require specific guidance and information about action alternatives and contingencies—just as clients expect from all other professionals. However, it is the client who, as long as he is legally responsible for himself, has ultimate responsibility for his own choices. In the behavior-change programs described by Bijou (1965) and his colleagues, for example, parents are taught principles about the conditions that affect their relations to their children, and are shown concretely how to implement them. Whether or not they choose to use them is, at every step, entirely up to them.

Finally, social behavior therapies, like other forms of planned change, do not and should not intend to achieve highly generalized, total personality reorganizations except in the unlikely event that this is the client's explicit goal. The aim of behavior assessments is to design treatments for specified objectives rather than to produce overall conversions. The behavioral changes that are in fact achieved are discussed in the following section.

THE SPECIFICITY OF BEHAVIOR CHANGE

Our review of the specificity of behavior and its dependence on the details of the particular stimulus variables operating in each situation leads us as well to expect considerable specificity in therapeutically induced behavioral changes. In the light of the findings on specificity from earlier chapters, we should expect relationship therapy primarily to affect relationships, insight therapy mainly to supply insight, relaxation treatments to increase relaxation, and approach training to especially enhance approach responses. Moreover, we should even expect each of these effects to be far more specific than usually has been assumed. Relationship therapy, for example, should affect the relationship between client and therapist, with no necessary massive transfer to extratherapeutic relations unless the latter are treated explicitly. "Insight" likewise should depend on the types of interpretation and theory practiced and discussed within the therapy sessions. The nature of the insight achieved may depend mainly on the theoretical orientation of the particular therapist that the client happened to choose (Heine, 1953), Freudian therapy yielding Freudian insights, Jungian therapy providing Jungian insights, and so on.

These "insights," however, are not necessarily trivial and may influence the client's expectations and his self-descriptions. In Paul's (1966) study to reduce public-speaking anxiety, recall that the insight-oriented, brief psychotherapy condition and the "attention-placebo" treatment both produced a significant reduction in cognitive and behavioral measures of anxiety. Indeed, subjects in the "attention-placebo" condition, which had been especially designed to generate expectations of anxiety relief, reduced their self-reported "expected anxiety" for public speeches as much as those who had received systematic desensitization. Interestingly, the only one outstanding improvement after insight treatment over the other conditions was more frequent eye contact when speaking. This finding again highlights the specificity of behavior; obviously the insight subjects had engaged in far more eye contact with their therapists than those in any other groups.

In the six-week follow-up inquiry conducted in Paul's study, subjects were also asked to indicate any other situations or areas that they thought had been affected. Students who had received desensitization, as well as those in the attention-placebo condition, tended to mention specific situations, such as talking at house meetings, taking exams, and dealing with people. On the other hand, insight subjects tended to cite more global examples congruent with the values and expectations espoused by the insight therapists to whom they had been exposed. These subjects mentioned such improvements as "understanding their emotional problem, understanding themselves better, gaining more self-control, forming new attitudes toward goals, acquiring new attitudes toward their personal life" (Paul, 1966, p. 52). As Paul noted, and in accord with earlier findings (Heine, 1953; Rosenthal, 1955), changes in the verbalizations of the insight subjects seemed to be:

> . . . *more in the direction of general attitudes and values held*
> *by the therapists, than in the direction of attitudes and ex-*

pectancies related to interpersonal-performance situations. (Paul, 1966, p. 72.)

In light of these considerations it is especially noteworthy that the insight-oriented therapists themselves rated the desensitization subjects after treatment as significantly lower in performance anxiety, as having better prognoses, and therefore as requiring less further treatment than those who had received insight therapy.

Although the attention-placebo and insight treatment changed attitudes and expectancies about anxiety, they did not reduce anxiety in physiological reactions to stress. Moreover, on measures of reactions under actual stress both the insight-oriented group and the attention-placebo subjects were consistently inferior to those who had been systematically desensitized to stress stimuli. Thus, although insight and attention altered expectancies and even produced some behavioral improvements, they were clearly less effective in generating more adaptive behavior under stress than was the desensitization treatment which, after all, is designed for that purpose. It is also noteworthy that at the follow-up assessments the desensitization and attention-placebo groups tended to maintain their gains, whereas the insight group no longer differed from the no-treatment controls even on the self-report measures of anxiety.

The clinical literature, regardless of the theoretical orientation of the particular author, usually leads one to expect highly generalized "cures." On the one hand, behavior therapists have criticized the omnibus treatments and all-purpose cures claimed by monolithic verbal relationship psychotherapies. On the other hand, some behavior therapists themselves have suggested an automatic and perfect transfer from events in the consulting room during relaxation to actual life behaviors in the real world. Thus Wolpe (1961, p. 191) claims:

> *It has consistently been found that at every stage a stimulus that evokes no anxiety when imagined in a state of relaxation will also evoke no anxiety when encountered in reality.*

In spite of these contentions, however, the effects of behavior change procedures should be most evident for the particular stimuli that were directly treated and should generalize most to similar situations. Unless deliberate steps are taken to assure transfer effects it is theoretically unreasonable to expect broad transfer and, indeed, it does not inevitably occur. In fact, most of the carefully controlled studies on the effects of counterconditioning report a failure to find complete fearlessness in the actual approach behavior of subjects who have been successfully desensitized to the cognitive representations of aversive conditioned stimuli (Davison, 1967a; Lang & Lazovik, 1963; Lang, Lazovik, & Reynolds, 1965; Paul, 1966). For example, subjects who had been successfully desensitized to thinking about handling snakes still showed considerable anxiety when actually required to perform approach responses high in the graduated series of tasks during the post-treatment tests (Davison, 1967a). While these persons showed bold approach behavior they still reported a mean anxiety self-rating of 7.75 on a 10-point fear scale. These results are congruent with data from several other studies (Lang & Lazovik, 1963; Lang, Lazovik, & Reynolds, 1965; Paul, 1966).

There is no theoretical basis to expect complete generalization in treatment effects from symbolic representations to real-life confrontations. Words and other symbols serve as signs for events, but they often are exceedingly ambiguous signs because the same symbol can represent highly diverse events. Words and symbols only partially or fractionally represent the events they designate. As the discussion of mediating states and response-mediated generalization has indicated (Chapter 6), any word or other symbol that becomes associated with another stimulus event evokes only a partial component of the mediating response produced by the stimulus with which it was associated. The verbal sign or symbol, and the events that it represents, thus are not completely equivalent and not entirely interchangeable. The meanings evoked by the referent stimulus and by the symbols associated with it may overlap but they are not identical. Thus it is understandable that desensitization to the symbolic stimulus does not inevitably and automatically transfer to the live event.

Davison (1967a), drawing on stimulus sampling theory, has noted that a complex stimulus (like a snake) contains many stimulus elements. The hierarchy constructed during desensitization does not exhaustively sample the total population of elements feared by the person. Moreover, not all the stimulus elements at each point of the hierarchy are likely to be visualized and hence desensitized.

Research on vicarious extinction also supports the importance of broad stimulus sampling in treatment. Fear reduction may be most effective if the observer watches the fearless behavior of several models who display diversified modes of positive approach to many samples from the class of feared stimuli. Children who strongly feared dogs watched filmed models display progressively more bold behavior to the animal (Bandura & Menlove, 1968). Youngsters who watched films depicting the graduated approach behavior of several models with several different dogs were compared with those who watched films of a single model with a single dog. Exposure to the more diverse modeling cues resulted in greater mastery of potentially threatening live interactions with dogs and in far more enduring maintenance of the therapeutic benefits over time.

Because of imperfect transfer, direct and vicarious techniques for strengthening appropriate instrumental approach and avoidance reactions to lifelike stimulus situations are important supplements to cognitively induced change. Indeed, in clinical practice systematic cognitive desensitization generally is augmented with direct and symbolic behavior practice, either in miniature role situations or under completely realistic conditions.

Considering the imperfect transfer of treatment-induced changes, imperfect correlations among different criteria of change also are not surprising. Changes in an individual's diverse behaviors are not necessarily highly correlated, even when the behaviors seem to be fairly similar. Forsyth and Fairweather (1961), for example, found that among post-hospital adjustment criteria different measures were often unrelated. For example, post-hospital full-time employment correlated only .12 with the number of friends the ex-patient had. Similar specificity in criteria was found in most investigations of psychotherapeutically produced changes (e.g., Cartwright, Kirtner, & Fiske, 1963; Fairweather, 1964; Kelman & Parloff, 1957), and is equally evident in virtually every piece of personality research that employs multiple criterion data. Although these results might not seem surprising they again illustrate the inappropriateness of viewing diffuse domains such as "adjustment" as if they were unitary entities.

For example, Kelman and Parloff (1957) studied changes on seven measures administered to a small sample of neurotic adults before and after twenty weeks of analytically oriented group therapy. "Comfort" was measured by a self-satisfaction Q sort, a symptom-disability checklist, and a discomfort evaluation scale; "effectiveness" ratings were based on sociometrics and a behavior evaluation scale; and "self-awareness" was measured by a Q sort and predictions of sociometric ratings. Scores were computed for changes from before treatment to after treatment for each of the seven measures. Significant changes were reported on three measures but the absence of a control group makes it impossible to evaluate them as evidence for treatment-produced changes. That, however, is not the point; of interest here is the fact that twenty-one intercorrelations *between* change scores yielded only one significant at the .05 level. These data suggest that within-person changes in adjustment over time were not very consistent or generalized across measures.

Diverse behaviors tend to be relatively specific to the particular stimulus conditions; they also do not necessarily change in a highly correlated way over time or as a function of intervening events.

Paul (1966) did find statistically significant correlations among his diverse indices of changes in public-speaking fears. The only exceptions were the physiological data; these were significantly associated only with an overt behavior change measure and not with self-reports. However, the intercorrelations among various improvement measures, although significant, generally averaged only .40. Lang and Lazovik (1963) also found an association of .40 between actual avoidance behavior toward the snake and the subject's self-ratings of snake fear right after the behavior test. As the authors noted, since precisely the same event was being evaluated, this correlation is low.

Successful cognitive desensitization to a symbolic stimulus does not necessarily guarantee that the person will be completely fearless when he tries to actually approach the object, but it does greatly facilitate motoric approach behavior. In Davison's (1967a) study, four of the five subjects who were fully desensitized cognitively were also able to perform the terminal post-treatment behavior successfully (holding the snake barehanded for thirty seconds); no other subjects in his desensitization groups or in his other two groups were able to perform the terminal task.

Similarly, Lang, Lazovik, and Reynolds (1965) found that all measures of fear reduction, including actual approach, were in fact correlated with the number of hierarchy items completed cognitively during the desensitization program. The correlations between number of anxiety hierarchy items successfully completed during desensitization and fear reduction measures ranged from .40 to .60. Indeed, only those subjects who moved far along the hierarchy during cognitive desensitization (completing at least fifteen items) also showed significantly greater approach behavior than did people in the control groups. Thus there does seem to be a clear relation between progress through the cognitive desensitization hierarchy and subsequent approach toward the real aversive stimulus. Cognitive change appears to be a valuable prelude to overt behavior change, even if it is not an automatic substitute for in vivo practice of the actual approach behavior itself. Consistent with the facilitating effect of cognitive change is the finding that verbal discussions in group therapy enhanced the subsequent speed of counterconditioning (Lazarus, 1961). Lazarus reported that fifteen severely phobic clients achieved no apparent reduction in their avoidance behaviors after a series of verbal, traditional, group therapy sessions. When these people later received desensitization treatments, however, they progressed twice as rapidly as comparable subjects who had undergone desensitization without the prelude of verbal group therapy.

The implications of the relative specificity of treatments are similar to those found for the specificity of predictors and of criteria. Predictions tend to be best when the predictor behavior is sampled in situations that approximate the criterion situation as much as possible. Likewise, behavior change in a given situation generalizes most to the most closely similar situations. Consequently, therapists should structure situations that approximate and sample as much as possible the criterion situations in which behavioral improvements are intended. The ultimate goal of most behavior therapies is to help the client to function well in naturalistic life contexts outside the clinic or hospital rather than to remain subject to external contingencies in artificial or special environments. To achieve this aim the critical conditions in the treatment environment should evoke and develop behaviors similar to those desired in the life environment, thus minimizing the transition from the therapy program to the settings in which the client functions naturally.

In light of the foregoing considerations the choice of treatment also has to be more specific than is usually assumed, depending of course on the client's particular goals and needs. For example, if a client can think calmly about examinations but becomes debilitated when he takes them, treatment might be directed at training exam-taking skills rather than relaxation alone. If a person is able to cope effectively with a class of situations but devalues and derogates his own behavior, the appropriate treatment might involve helping him to reconstrue and to reevaluate his goals and standards, rather than to alter his coping skills.

Behavior therapists would be in a curious position if they rejected the idea of psychological "diseases" while simultaneously clinging to the notion of broad "cures" that transcend stimulus conditions. Fortunately the recognition that behavior is controlled by highly specific variables has led increasingly to analyses and treatments conducted in the actual settings in which the problematic behaviors occur. Daily life situations, often within the person's own school or home rather than in consulting rooms, then become the settings for behavior change. In these settings teachers and parents and relatives, rather than therapists or other professional psychology staffs, have a critical part both in the assessment and in the treatment process. This trend toward engaging in the treatment process the people with whom the client has important daily role relations, rather than relying on repeated contacts with clinics, hospitals, special agencies, and professional personnel, was illustrated in the work of Bijou (1965) and his colleagues in school situations and, more recently, in the home itself (Hawkins et al., 1966). Similarly, group situations often may have advantages over treating the individual in isolation. Paul and Shannon (1966) in their group desensitization found that the group provided a setting of anxious students in which the members could spontaneously and naturally extinguish many of their social fears through their own mutually supportive interactions, while simultaneously practicing new social skills in vivo. The same trend is seen most clearly in Fairweather's community lodge programs in which the treatment situation and the community merge completely (1967).

Although we have emphasized the specificity of treatment effects, often fairly generalized gains do develop, as the literature on behavior change reviewed in the preceding chapters suggests. Likewise, the altered patterns of behavior may be maintained for considerable periods of time, as Paul's (1967) two-year follow-up study revealed. In spite of highly encouraging results, however, the quest for global personality changes, for massive highly generalized "cures," or for overall total "personality reorganizations" as a result of specific change programs seems as oversimplified and theoretically unjustified as the search for global personality traits and states. The amount and type of generalization achieved, and the durability of behavior change, depends on the environment in which the new behaviors can be practiced and enacted, as discussed in the next chapter, as well as on the nature of the treatment program that helped to generate the new behaviors in the first place, and on the person's prior history.

SUMMARY

Most traditional clinical assessments have ignored the individual's actual behavior in real-life situations. The behaviors that are sampled usually consist of verbal responses to artificial test stimuli such as inkblots, blurred pictorial scenes, barely audible sounds, sentences, sentence stems, or single words. The closest approximations of directly relevant life behavior elicited by traditional tests probably come from questions sampling knowledge of elementary school academic content. For example, intelligence and achievement tests sample arithmetic, vocabulary, information, and so forth. Conventional performance tests do provide samples of nonverbal behavior but usually require the subject only to assemble puzzles or blocks, identify missing parts, string beads, sort colors, or draw pictures. Many intensive clinical assessments also include interviews designed to reconstruct portions of the life history including current behavior. This life information, however, is obtained typically from unstructured, open-ended questions presented unsystematically and with few prescribed coding techniques. Therefore the data tend to be fragmented, nonspecific reconstructions of past events from which the clinician rapidly proceeds to interpret the person's hypothesized personality structure.

In contrast, as this chapter has illustrated, social behavior assessments seek behavioral referents for the client's complaints; thereafter they identify the precise conditions that seem to be maintaining and influencing these problems so that appropriate rearrangements can be designed to achieve more advantageous outcomes. This process is especially complex because clients, like most other people, tend to characterize themselves and their problems with global trait terms, rather than with carefully operationalized behavioral descriptions. Behavior assessments therefore often have to begin by establishing clear referents for highly subjective problems and goals. Through verbal, symbolic, and direct sampling techniques behavior assessments then examine systematically the changes in stimulus conditions that would be required to achieve the specified therapeutic objectives. These procedures were illustrated and contrasted with a traditional psychodynamic assessment. Then the implications of these differences for the role of the client were analyzed.

Unlike most traditional approaches to measurement, in social behavior assessment the critical issue is not how a given individual will respond to a particular fixed treatment; it is what specialized treatment must be designed to change the particular problems. Rather than estimating individual differences in response to particular predetermined treatments, social behavior assessments try to design the best possible treatment for each individual problem. The focus of prediction research then becomes experimentation into how given treatment variables alter behavior and their relative effectiveness for specific purposes. Just as predictive efficacy is greatest when the predictor measure and the criterion are most similar, so therapeutic transfer is best when the treatment situation most closely overlaps with the life situation in which change is desired. The manner in which conditions interact to determine the durability and generalization of behavior change is discussed further in the next chapter.

/9
PERSONALITY AND PREDICTION

The three preceding chapters showed how behaviors (even seemingly "deeply ingrained" and extremely deviant patterns) can be altered by appropriate rearrangements of conditions in accord with principles of social learning. These findings are consistent with the specific dependence of behavior on the environment, as documented throughout the previous chapters. However, although behavior may be highly contingent on specific conditions, it is not haphazard. Therapeutically induced behavior changes often endure over considerable periods of time; likewise, behaviors generated under more naturalistic conditions outside therapeutic contexts also are often stable. The same basic variables that determine the maintenance or modification over time of new, therapeutically produced changes also govern the future course of social behaviors arising from other, less planned sources. This final chapter examines further some of the conditions that determine the durability of behavior patterns. It also explores the maintenance and dynamics of personality from the perspective of social behavior theory and, in the light of the principles and data presented throughout this book, again considers issues of prediction.

STABILITIES IN BEHAVIOR

While abstractly acknowledging the "interaction of person and situation," most trait and state theories assume internalized behavioral dispositions relatively independent of stimulus conditions. It is the existence of such stimulus-free, highly generalized behavioral sets—not the occurrence of long-term individual differences in response to stimuli— that is unsupported by the data reviewed in earlier chapters. Most conceptions of personality have focused on those broadly generalized patterns of the individual's behavior that endure over time (e.g., Byrne, 1966). Although behavior patterns often may be stable, they usually are not highly generalized across situations (Chapters 2 and 4). On the other hand, the trait categories and abstractions with which people label themselves, and each other, are often global and generalized as well as lasting over time, as we have seen. The findings on consistency over time, reviewed in Chapter 2, like the data on the cross-situational specificity of social behaviors, fit the view that behaviors depend on highly specific events but remain stable when the consequences to which they lead, and the evoking conditions, remain similar (Chapter 6). When response-reinforcement relations and discriminative and eliciting stimuli endure over time, then behavior remains stable; when the maintaining conditions for behavior change, the behavior itself changes. It is not hard to imagine, for example, how therapeutically encouraged efforts in the hospital to express feelings more freely extinguish rapidly when the discharged patient takes up again his clerical office job, or how therapeutic attempts to combat alcoholism in the hospital fail when the client returns to his unchanged stressful environment.

The analysis of behavior requires attention not only to the modification of behavior but also to its maintenance. Behaviors differ considerably not only in the ease with which they can be produced but also in the ease with which they can be maintained. Newly established patterns, particularly when they are associated with less optimal reinforcement conditions, as in self-imposed denial of readily available rewarding resources, require especially strong environmental supports. For example, voluntary delay of reward tends to be both harder to establish, and more difficult to maintain, than immediate self-reward patterns (Bandura & Mischel, 1965).

Since behavior depends on stimulus conditions, regularities in them lead to predictable behavior. Under many naturalistic circumstances stimulus conditions do remain similar over time, producing temporally stable behavior. This process of behavior maintenance, and its implications for prediction, are discussed in the following pages.

Environmental Stabilities

Many environments provide the individual with stable outcomes for similar behaviors at different times. Temporally stable maintaining conditions are especially evident in the formal and informal routines and institutions of society (Secord & Backman, 1965). The outcomes an individual obtains for particular behavior patterns tend to be relatively permanent when he remains in a social environment that reacts to his behaviors consistently. Since people typically live within the same culture for considerable periods of time, they remain exposed to fairly constant contingencies within their own home, school, social, and vocational settings. Societal rules and sanctions usually are deliberately constant, and even codified formally, thus facilitating temporal consistencies in social behavior. Social institutions, like schools, the military service, mental hospitals, or prisons tend to have fixed-rule systems according to which fairly constant outcomes are dispensed at different times for similar behaviors.

Consistent with the foregoing, and in accord with the principle of stimulus control, a response pattern is most likely to occur at the usual or anticipated time and place of reinforcement of that behavior (Ferster & Skinner, 1957). Often it is not too difficult to predict well beyond chance whether a person will or will not work, eat, sleep, play, love, and even dream, by simply knowing the time and the place in which he happens to be at the moment. As Barker (1963) has said, in church people "behave church" and in school they "behave school." Knowledge of the particular culture and of its stable routines and environments should provide reasonable predictions even about the specific content and style of many of the activities of its members—for example, common preferences, values, and aversions. These predictions, crude as they may be, based on information about environmental regularities and conditions, often compare favorably with those from inferences about the individual's idiosyncratic trait and dynamic predispositions, as is evident from the relative utility of demographic variables (Chapter 5).

The dependence of personality consistencies upon stable environmental supports is well illustrated by the effects of massive alterations in routine living conditions. Disruption in habitual role behaviors and environmental relations can alter even long-standing personality patterns. For example, British soldiers who were war prisoners during the Second World War found after a few years in prison that their new existence in the prisoner-of-war camps had more reality than their previous patterns of life (Curle, 1947). As a result, on their return home they faced major readjustments and new learning experiences that proved exceedingly difficult when attempted too abruptly. Living in a special "transitional community" for a while helped to make the shift, and those who had this interim experience adapted much better than those who were sent home directly (Curle & Trist, 1947). Similarly, the total environmental control applied by the Chinese Communists produced some major "brainwashing" changes in American war prisoners (Schein, 1957).

These findings also are congruent with the fact that after patients have been labeled psychotic and confined in mental hospitals for several years they tend to become so dependent on their roles in the hospital community that rehabilitation and a return to the outside world becomes very difficult (Fairweather, 1964). If the chronic manages to overcome his years of reliance on the supports of the hospital and to be discharged, he usually enters an environment that makes it almost impossible for him to sustain himself. In the outside world the former "mental patient" usually cannot find and hold employment and may spend much of his time isolated and companionless in his room watching television. On the other hand, if the ex-patient can live in a special "half-way house" community that provides him with a viable role, then he can function more adaptively (Fairweather et al., 1967).

Constructed Stabilities

Temporal stability is also enhanced when individuals categorize themselves with relatively permanent trait labels (smart, dumb, attractive, excessively dependent), as Chapter 3 suggests they often do. Constructions about others and about the self tend to endure, as we have seen. Recall also that these concepts, once formed, tend to be retained, often tenaciously and in the face of contradictory evidence (Chapter 3). The results found for trait raters, therapists, and scientists hold for other people as well: their constructs may constrain observation and tend to be retained over time, with a selective search for confirming evidence and a tendency to disregard discrepant facts. Global semantically ambiguous categories, such as trait labels, tend to be especially difficult to disconfirm because almost any evidence seems to fit them (Chapters 3 and 5).

To the extent that the reactions people receive from others (and themselves) are affected by these labels they may encounter considerable constancies in the reinforcing outcomes they obtain at different times. For example, when persons are endowed with labels like "mental patient," "alcoholic," "retarded," "psychopathic," or "ex-convict," the bearer of the label is likely to encounter fairly consistent social reactions from others who know the category to which he has been assigned.

The labels and categories that people attribute to themselves also may exert stabilizing effects on their own subsequent behavior and on their reactions to themselves (e.g., Mischel & Liebert, 1966). It has often been said that the probability of predicting a behavior—for example, resistance to temptation—from one situation to another also might be enhanced if we knew the particular situations that have come to be categorized as equivalent by the individual (Burton, 1963). Idiosyncratic equivalences between situations may be estimated by assessing the situations that the subject defines as similar (e.g., Wallach, 1958). Inquiries into subjectively defined or semantic equivalence among events, through the elaboration of personal constructs and the individual's own rule systems, have long been advocated (e.g., Kelly, 1955). The assessment of constructs is a valuable phase in assessment, but, as previous chapters have shown, it is hazardous to assume that verbally defined equivalences necessarily mirror, or are even consistent with, nonverbal behavior. Unfortunately, few empirical personality researches have actually addressed themselves to the assessment of subjective equivalences. One of the rare attempts to measure subjectively perceived equivalences among stimuli failed to increase predictive accuracy (Heath, 1959).

Sociologists have noted repeatedly that societal roles and role labels convey stable expectations and contingencies that serve to stabilize the behavior of the individual who holds that role (Secord & Backman, 1965). Thus, for example, judges on the bench are supposed to be deliberate and sober, pilots are expected to be cool in the cockpit, and bookkeepers are supposed to be accurate and neat in their work (Goffman, 1961). The role labels assigned to the individual prescribe many of the behaviors that are expected from him and that are most likely to be reinforced (Sarbin, 1965). The effects are especially strong when the role labels are permanent. This is seen, for example, in the development of relatively stable sex roles and of fairly enduring self-concepts about one's masculine or feminine attributes (e.g., Kohlberg, 1966).

A few studies have demonstrated some relations between the manner in which a person categorizes or construes other people and how he behaves toward them (Farina & Ring, 1965; Farina, Holland, & Ring, 1966; Kelley, 1950). In one study, college students were led to believe that their coworkers on a laboratory motor task were either "normal" or had been "mentally ill" (Farina & Ring, 1965). These different categorizations of their partners significantly influenced the student's behavior with them. For example, students who believed their coworkers were mentally ill performed the task better. More important, these students also preferred to work alone, thus further isolating the ostensibly mentally ill person.

In another study, Taylor and Epstein (1967) exposed male and female college students in a competitive situation to fictitious opponents described as either male or female. Specifically, each student was told that his (or her) reaction time was being compared to that of either a male or a female seated in an adjoining room. On trials when the subject responded faster than the opponent he set a dial that supposedly determined the amount of electric shock that the opponent would receive. On trials when the opponent was faster the subject received a shock. In fact, all feedbacks to the subject, including shocks, were actually manipulated by the experimenter from an adjoining room, and there was no opponent. The design permitted assessment of the relative aggressiveness of each sex, when provoked increasingly by an allegedly male or female opponent, by measuring the amount of shock the subject tried to administer in each condition. In addition, the fictitious opponent's provocativeness was manipulated by giving subjects increasing amounts of shock as the trials progressed.

The fictitious opponent's sex role had a strong effect on behavior toward him. Both sexes were much less aggressive toward opponents whom they believed were females than toward those they thought were males. Even when the female opponent became increasingly provocative both sexes remained reluctant to use strong electric shock against her. These results seem consistent with the widespread role sanctions restricting physical aggression against women. Even when subjects became infuriated against their increasingly sadistic female opponent, and lashed out verbally, they continued to inhibit their physical aggression. One male, for example, after being severely shocked, yelled a curse and threatened, "I'll kill her"—although he actually continued to use the lowest shock level against his opponent. Asked why he never tried to hurt his opponent, another male simply said, "Because she was a girl." The sex-role taboos against hurting females physically are obviously familiar to the females themselves: as one young lady noted, "I hope he knows I'm a girl."

The reactions of females were especially interesting when they were receiving electric shock from opponents described as males. As Taylor and Epstein noted, it is broadly assumed that females are expected to be generally unaggressive physically. This assumption has been held widely, and usually implies a generalized inhibition of physical aggression by women in their relations to both sexes. In fact, when girls were faced by ostensible male opponents who shocked them increasingly, then they themselves became extraordinarily aggressive. Indeed, in this condition it was the females who ultimately became most aggressive, and who finally used electric shocks averaging more than twice their initial intensity against their male opponents. Thus roles and role labels, like other concepts and categories, can have considerable effects on behavior. At the same time, however, one is reminded that these effects usually are moderated by numerous other variables—in this case the sex of the subject as well as the sex and aggressiveness of the opponent—and hence do not exert broadly generalized situation-free influences.

Trait and role labels are likely to have particularly strong stabilizing effects on behavior when they lead the labeled person into special consistent environments in which he regularly encounters people who model the labeled behavior or who reinforce behaviors congruent with the label. Consider, for instance, some of the role consequences of being judged psychotic and institutionalized. Institutions such as the mental hospital provide their inmates with standardized expectations about psychotic behavior and often inadvertently reinforce psychotic behavior and psychotic ideation in the course of their therapies (Ayllon & Michael, 1959; Ayllon, 1965). The mental hospital, for example, supplies role models in the form of other patients who repeatedly display the very psychotic and bizarre patterns that the institution supposedly was designed to reduce. Under such paradoxical conditions it becomes understandable that patients may learn to become more enduringly psychotic within the hospital than outside it, and that the more contacts a mental patient has had with a mental hospital in the past the more likely he is to continue to be hospitalized (Chapter 5). The same phenomenon is found when children who were institutionally defined as retarded and assigned to a special class subsequently became more self-derogatory than equally retarded children who were not given this special status (Meyerowitz, 1962).

The Patterning of Response Consequences

Often persons continue to expect reinforcement for particular behaviors although they experienced reinforcing outcomes in similar past situations only occasionally and irregularly. The patterning or scheduling of the reinforcing consequences produced by behavior critically determines its future occurrence and persistence (Chapter 6). Behaviors tend to be maintained with especially great resilience when they have been learned under conditions of intermittent reinforcement (Ferster & Skinner, 1957).

In the course of human socialization most behaviors are intermittently reinforced under combined schedules. Under these circumstances both the number of unreinforced responses and the temporal intervals between reinforcements vary freely. These schedules, so common during socialization, tend to make many patterns (both the adaptive and the deviant) highly durable and resistant to extinction. For example, noxious behaviors, like persistent high-magnitude attention-seeking and aggressive responses, may be generated and maintained when parents or other social agents unwittingly reinforce them on combined schedules (Bandura & Walters, 1963). It is particularly difficult to extinguish such syndromes under noncontrolled life conditions because they are likely to encounter some reinforcing consequences at least occasionally from some sources. In one study, for example, the psychotic talk of a hospitalized patient was being successfully extinguished by having the nurses and ward staff withhold all attention from her for psychotic talk while reinforcing rational speech (Ayllon & Michael, 1959). After a few weeks, however, these efforts were undermined when the patient was unwittingly reinforced for psychotic talk by a social worker and by visiting nonward staff and volunteers. As the patient herself told one of the nurses:

> *Well you're not listening to me. I'll have to go and see Miss ————— (the Social Worker) again, 'cause she told me that if she would listen to my past she could help me. (p. 328.)*

Intermittent direct and vicarious reinforcement is readily available from some sources in the culture for almost all patterns of behavior, including deviant, antisocial sexual and aggressive syndromes. For example, through films and television, youngsters are exposed abundantly to many heroes whose violent, antisocial behavior is rewarded by control over people as well as by obtaining cars, planes, yachts, and mansions. Generally the consequences and scheduling of outcomes produced when an individual recombines and practices the behaviors he has learned are highly variable; under these conditions behavior patterns may be retained with considerable tenacity.

BASES FOR PREDICTION

Increments from the Measurement of Environments

The focus on internal traits and states as the key determinants of behavior has led to a tremendous concern with individual characteristics, as the earlier chapters showed. Attention to internalized traits and states has been accompanied by an equally massive neglect of environmental considerations in assessment. This fact is reflected in the existence of literally thousands of measures designed to tap individual differences in traits and states while measures of the environment generally have been limited to a handful of fairly gross estimates of socioeconomic status.

288

Of course there also have been many efforts to relate a host of child-rearing variables to the individual's subsequent behavior (e.g., Sears, Maccoby, & Levin, 1957). These studies, however, usually have dealt with relatively global and historical aspects of the child-rearing process and with subtle relationship variables like the mother's "warmth" or other interpersonal attitudes. The associations between these broad parental child-rearing conditions and the child's later behavior generally have been very low (e.g., Sears, Rau, & Alpert, 1965). On the other hand, efforts to assess how specific social learning variables and environmental conditions serve to maintain and mold current behavior have yielded striking results.

Wolf (1966) measured a number of variables in the home which were likely to facilitate intellectual development and academic accomplishments in children. His assessments of environmental opportunities for verbal development included such social learning variables as the quality of language models available to the child; opportunities for enlarging vocabulary; feedback about appropriate language usage; and opportunities for language practice in a variety of situations. Measures of this kind provided an extensive battery for rating the intellectual environment for the child's current development. The results yielded some of the highest correlations found in personality research.

The correlations between total ratings for the intellectual environment and tested general intelligence was .69. As Wolf (1966) pointed out, this association provides a substantial increment over the correlations of .20 to .40 usually found between IQ and more global indices of social status. The correlation between Wolf's overall ratings for the environment conducive to academic achievement and actual total achievement-battery test score was .80. This impressive level of association is high enough to permit considerable predictive power. Moreover, Wolf evaluated the effects of combining his measures of the intellectual environment with individual IQ test data. The multiple correlation between IQ and overall rating of the achievement-enhancing environment with the childrens' total achievement-test battery scores provided an association of .87. Thus the combined measure of environmental achievement supports and IQ test accounted for 76 percent of the variance in academic achievement scores. This outcome compares favorably to the correlation of .76, accounting for 58 percent of the variance, obtained between IQ alone and academic achievement scores.

Data from a very different context also support the view that some of the best predictions can come from analyses of environmental variables. Fairweather's (1964) data strikingly revealed that mental patients who could remain out of the hospital the longest were those who had relatively more supportive living and employment situations available in the community. The most reliable and profound result of this extensive study was the fact that post-hospital adjustment correlated with no significant hospital behavior but it was highly related to the post-hospital environment to which the patient returned. A sophisticated cluster analysis showed that the degree to which the living situation was socially supportive had a loading of .71 on the total post-hospital adjustment cluster. Consistently it has been found that the situation in which the ex-patient has to live critically affects his ability to remain outside the hospital, whereas the usual indices of rated job and ward behavior during neuropsychiatric hospitalization are relatively unrelated to his post-hospital adjustment (Fairweather, 1964; Forsyth & Fairweather, 1961; Fairweather et al., 1967; Sanders, 1966). Fairweather's (1964) original predictors and treatments worked well within the hospital community itself but did not extend beyond it; when the environment changed, the new environment seemed to determine the individual's behavior most critically. The other strong predictors of post-hospital adjustment were the sheer total duration of previous hospitalization and the amount of time the patient required to complete his treatment program before discharge. Patients with less total hospital experience, and those who were discharged most rapidly, made the more adequate post-hospital adjustment (Fairweather, 1964).

Increments from Past Behavior

As discussed before, direct measures of a person's past behavior often have value as predictors of his future behavior in closely similar situations (Chapter 5). Efforts to predict reactions to behavior change from direct indices of past behavior are representative. For example, highly fearful individuals are also likely to progress less rapidly in treatment than those who are less fearful and less emotionally aroused from the outset. A negative correlation ($r = -.58$) was found between self-reported fears at pretesting and number of anxiety hierarchy items ultimately completed by individuals undergoing cognitive desensitization (Lang & Lazovik, 1963). It may be that individuals with pervasive or intense fears find it more difficult to visualize and relax to anxiety stimuli cognitively and hence progress less rapidly. Similarly, at least under some conditions children who are less pervasively fearful tend to benefit most readily from vicarious procedures designed to extinguish their fear of dogs (Bandura & Menlove, 1968).

As the foregoing studies imply, knowledge of the person's fear intensity may help the assessor to select the therapeutic condition most suitable for him. For example, persons with more intense fears benefit from counterconditioning under conditions of deep relaxation, whereas those who are less fearful gain as much from counterconditioning in the waking state (Schubot, 1966). The consistent finding that more intense or enduring behaviors require more intense and longer treatments was also apparent in the relationship between premorbid history and prognosis, those with poorer initial adjustments tending to fare worse in the future (Chapter 5).

While information about an individual's past reactions often may be helpful predictors of his behavior in closely relevant new situations, it can become hazardous to extrapolate broadly from less directly relevant past behaviors or personality measures to new situations, as has been stressed repeatedly. This caution, elaborated in earlier chapters in the context of trait-state assessment, holds equally when trying to predict reactions to behavior change programs. For example, the specificity of behavior is again illustrated in studies that tried to predict reactions to cognitive desensitization therapy from measures of suggestibility. Suggestibility tends to predict suggestible behavior best—but little beyond that. In one study, suggestibility, measured by the Stanford Hypnotic Susceptibility Scales, was related moderately but significantly to initial self-ratings of anxiety after confrontations with snakes, and also to changes in self-reported fears in the *untreated* control group (Lang, Lazovik, & Reynolds, 1965). Suggestibility was unrelated, however, to actual improvement and fear reduction from desensitization therapy.

Another study did find significant correlations between hypnotic susceptibility and improvement in approach behavior to snakes (Schubot, 1966). This finding, however, held only for subjects in a group receiving desensitization under deep hypnotic relaxation and was based on a very small sample. In the same study subjects who said they were able to visualize the aversive stimuli more vividly in imagination during desensitization also tended to improve more in their actual approach behavior. This correlation also held only for subjects who were desensitized under hypnotic relaxation and not for those who received counterconditioning during the normal waking state (Schubot, 1966).

Many personality psychologists have sought to establish general relations between global trait and state dimensions and various indices of learning. As the earlier chapters in this book have suggested, and for reasons discussed in those earlier pages, correlations between such broad individual difference measures and other diverse behaviors tend to be low and to have limited utility. Some of the most notable work includes efforts to relate individual differences on such dimensions as extraversion-introversion, anxiety, and emotionality to indices of conditionability (e.g., Eysenck, 1961; Eysenck & Rachman, 1965; Franks, 1961; Lovibond, 1964; Spence & Spence, 1964). Reviewing the specific correlations between personality variables and conditionability, however, Franks (1961, p. 481) correctly noted their generally "diminutive magnitude." In the present view there is no reason to expect broad trait measures to predict responses to learning situations any better than they can predict other behavior. Paul (1966), for example, correlated scores on several personality tests intending to measure extraversion-introversion, general emotionality, and anxiety with numerous indices of improvement after counterconditioning treatment for public-speaking anxiety. His results were totally nonsignificant; of the thirty-six coefficients computed only one reached the 5 percent level of significance.

In the present view, while correlational studies that seek links between personality dimensions and responsivity to particular learning situations have research interest, they provide a precarious basis for designing individual treatments. The individual's problematic behavior itself generally can directly dictate the nature of the required treatment. If, for example, the person's behavior is antisocial or criminal, inferences about his presumed underlying personality traits may be redundant. The type of learning program he requires should depend on his specific deficits, problems, and goals. Likewise, if a person's complaints are phobias and anxieties then these behaviors seem the most relevant considerations for making specific treatment decisions.

Reasonable and Unreasonable Predictions

Unless the environmental maintaining conditions change markedly, past behavior tends to be the best predictor of future behavior in similar situations, even when the samples of past behavior are very fragmentary, as in gross indices of previous marital history, occupation, or hospitalization (Chapter 5). Although these predictions from past behavior may be as good as, or better than, those from indirect inferences about states and traits, it is not reasonable to expect them to be impressively high. Social behavior theory does not divorce an individual's behaviors from the conditions in which they occur. If future behavior is determined by social learning conditions, rather than by highly generalized internal traits, behavior change can come about readily with environmental modification. To the extent that the exact learning conditions in the environment are not taken into account, accurate forecasts are unrealistic hopes. Moreover, in the uncontrolled settings in which life events unfold, many of the determinants are accidental and unpredictable by any science. A highway accident, a war, an explosion, a chance meeting with another person, may significantly alter the entire course of an individual's life, although neither the person nor the scientist can either forecast or control the critical event.

The implausibility of accurately forecasting events over which the scientist has virtually no control, and when he cannot even guess the interventions that might occur, was pointed out clearly by Murray in 1948:

> *It is easy to predict precisely the outcome of the meeting of one known chemical with another known chemical in an immaculate test tube. But where is the chemist who can predict what will happen to a known chemical if it meets an unknown chemical in an unknown vessel? And even if all the properties of all the chemicals resident in a given laboratory are exactly defined, is there a chemist who can predict every chemical engagement that will take place if Chance, the blind technician, is in charge of the proceedings?* (O.S.S. Assessment of Men, 1948, p. 8.)

Most prediction studies of personality have been guided by trait and state theory with the assumptions that behavioral signs can reveal enduring generalized personality structures that serve as broad behavioral predispositions, and that future behavior is chiefly determined by these predispositions. These two basic assumptions focus on stable individual difference or personality variables as the key determinants of behavior; they largely ignore the role of environmental conditions or stimulus situations in the regulation of behavior. As has been stressed repeatedly, however, individuals discriminate sharply among even seemingly close stimulus situations and consequently the widespread response consistencies assumed by trait theories usually do not exist. Changes in stimulus conditions, ranging from trivial changes in the details of the assessment procedure (such as the sex of the experimenter or the method of data collection) to alterations in the individual's life conditions, all modify the behavior that occurs. People simply are not inanimate objects like tables (as the assumptions of early psychometricians had implied): what a person does cannot be isolated meaningfully from the conditions in which he does it.

When stimulus conditions and treatment manipulations are either weak or ambiguous then individual differences arising from past history in similar situations are most noticeable. The effects of prior history on behavior are especially apparent in the absence of situationally supplied information about the probable consequences for behavior in the particular evoking situation. This phenomenon is illustrated in a study that investigated voluntary delay of reward and that showed the inter-action of some of the historical and situational determinants of such choices (Mischel & Staub, 1965). Specifically, this study investigated the effects of situational outcomes and past expectancies for success on choices of immediate, less valuable, noncontingent rewards as opposed to more valuable but contingent rewards. Measures of expectancy for success were administered to eighth-grade boys. These measures required the youngsters to estimate their probable standing, in relation to their peers, on various tasks. In a later session the children worked on a series of problems and, depending on the condition to which they had been assigned, obtained either success, failure, or no information for per-formance. Thereafter, each child chose between less valuable, non-contingent rewards and more valuable rewards. The children were led to believe that they could attain the more valuable rewards only con-tingent upon "successfully solving" problems. Some of the problems were described with labels similar to the problems for which they had received manipulated success, failure, or no information.

Under these circumstances children who had gotten no information about their own situational performance now based their choices sig-nificantly on their relevant past expectancies. In this condition children with high expectancies for success chose far more contingent larger re-wards than those whose relevant past expectancies were low. In the other conditions, manipulated situational success or failure feedback tended to minimize the effects of prior expectancies. Contingent rewards were chosen more by children who had received situational success than by youngsters who were assigned to the failure condition, overshadowing the effects of expectancies from related past experiences. Moreover, all children discriminated sharply among the various choice contingencies; the most powerful effects were due to these specific contingencies for each choice. Likewise, Bandura and Whalen (1966) found that the effects of prior success and failure histories in related earlier situations were virtually eliminated by strong situationally induced success or failure manipulations.

When stimulus conditions are potent, predictions based on their probable effects often are better than those from knowledge of the in-dividual's past behavior, as has been documented in the last three chapters. In Paul's (1966) study, for example, essentially every person assigned to the counterconditioning treatment showed reduced anxiety on the measures of improvement while only a small percent of those in the control group decreased substantially in anxiety. Simply knowing the condition to which the subject is assigned thus could permit excel-lent prediction of his prognosis. Similarly, when response-reinforcement relations are controlled systematically, knowledge of the existing contingencies permits virtually perfect predictions of the subject's behavior (Chapter 7). On the other hand, efforts to predict to unknown stimulus conditions in which unknown contingencies operate do indeed invite "Chance, the blind technician" to take charge of the proceedings.

THE DYNAMICS OF BEHAVIOR

In a recent argument to try to show that traits are the basic unit of personality study, Allport (1966) recognized the enormous evidence that the behavior of the same person is variable and may change in accord with situations. Nevertheless, he rightly insists that this variability should not lead us to mistake persons for "empty organisms." Allport used trait as a general term referring to the structural counterparts of all enduring predispositional tendencies, covering all the "permanent possibilities for action," including such functional concepts as "expectancy" and "goal-directedness." "Traits are cortical, sub-cortical or postural dispositions having the capacity to gate or guide specific phasic reactions" (Allport, 1966, p. 3). While not denying the evidence for the intraindividual variability of behavior across situations, Allport argued that behavior is determined by the "integrated structure within the skin" (p. 2).

> Whatever tendencies exist reside in a person, for a person is the sole possessor of the energy that leads to action. Admittedly different situations elicit differing tendencies from my repertoire. I do not perspire except in the heat, nor shiver except in the cold; but the outside temperature is not the mechanism of perspiring or shivering. My capacities and my tendencies lie within. (p. 2.)

It is of course self-evident that there would be no human behavior without persons, and while stimuli or situations come to evoke and maintain behavior patterns they do not respond by themselves. No one challenges the fact that response potentiality resides in persons; situations may evoke behavior but they do not perform it. Living organisms are not empty and their repertoires of potential behavior exist nowhere outside their own skins; it is a person who perspires or shivers, not a situation. After agreeing on this point, however, it also seems that it is not the critical issue. The key question, rather, is how to study, understand, predict, and modify these human responses. The trait position leads one to infer enduring generalized attributes in persons and to predict from the inferred trait to behavior in various situations. This would be an appropriate procedure if it could be done reliably and provided predictive power. The problem is that the heuristic yield from the trait approach over the last five or more decades has been, even in the view of many sympathetic critics, remarkably slim (e.g., Vernon, 1964).

In Allport's example, the behaviors of interest are perspiring and shivering, and the question is how they can be predicted and controlled most efficaciously. Will the occurrence and degree of perspiring and shivering be understood best by constructing scales to infer individual differences in a stable underlying thermal trait, or by measuring and manipulating, in the criterion situation, the conditions that control these responses—for example, the room temperature?

If behavior depends on specific situational stimuli, as trait proponents have come to acknowledge, and if the same person behaves differently in different situations, it becomes important to understand the covariations between situations and behavior; this task, as we have seen, is the focus of social behavior theory and assessment. Although it is evident that persons are the source from which human responses are evoked, it is situational stimuli that evoke them, and it is changes in conditions that alter them. Since the assumption of massive behavioral similarity across diverse situations no longer is tenable, it becomes essential to study the differences in the behaviors of a given person as a function of the conditions in which they occur. It should then also be possible to identify the commonalities among stimulus conditions that evoke similar behaviors. The notion of "typical" behavior, which is fundamental to trait conceptualizations, has led psychometricians and trait theorists to view situational variability as a form of "error." The social behavior position, however, construes what the psychometrician considers error to actually be critical determinants of behavior.

The focus on stimulus conditions in no way ignores the fact that the individual's history in prior related situations modifies how new stimuli affect him, as has been demonstrated over and over again (Chapter 6). Past experiences with related stimuli change the current meaning and value of evoking stimuli and thereby affect performance in new situations. Prior reinforcement history alters the response strength or probability of particular response patterns in relation to discriminative stimuli. The individual's social learning history thus increases the probability of future behaviors similar to those previously reinforced, thereby producing temporal stability. For example, if church-going is reinforced directly or vicariously the probability of future church-going, and of other closely church-related behaviors, also increases. The person's new behavior further changes where he is, what he does, and the reactions and consequences he gets from others. Of course his own reactions to his own behavior also become stimuli in this chain (e.g., Valins, 1966). For example, the labels and meanings that the subject attributes to his own emotional reaction may in turn affect his subsequent behavior (Schachter & Wheeler, 1962). Thus every major change in his behavior and emotional arousal can affect what he attends to, what he learns observationally, the new skills he acquires, the incentive conditions that affect him, and so on.

The conditions under which self-selection of stimulus conditions serves to further maintain previously acquired behaviors, and even prevents new learning, may be understood most clearly in avoidance reactions. If an event was previously associated with fear-producing experiences, similar events may come to elicit fear reactions. To the extent that the person now avoids these events and selects situations in which they are not likely to be present, his emotional reactions to them cannot be unlearned or extinguished and his avoidance behavior will continue. For example, in the case of a woman who acquired a fear of cats when she saw her father deliberately drown one of her favorite kittens, extinction was prevented by her persistent turning and running whenever subsequently confronted by a cat. Her avoidance behaviors were highly reinforced (by successfully eliminating fear-provoking cats from her vision), thus preventing extinction of the conditioned fear reaction (Eysenck & Rachman, 1965).

In the same way, the inhibited adolescent who avoids contacts with girls, and selects situations in which he does not have to deal with them closely, prevents the occurrence of new consequences which could modify his reactions to women. He may even select and create situations which further confirm his negative anticipations (Aronson, 1961) and may take objectively neutral or even positive feedbacks as additional confirmation for his reactions. When persons are confronted with stimuli which have become aversive for them but which cannot be avoided by complete motoric escape from the situation, they also tend to avoid exposing themselves to the painful stimulus by generating their own interfering stimuli. They may do this, for example, by thinking about other distracting things, or attending to less aversive aspects of the stimulus situation (Bandura & Rosenthal, 1966).

On the other hand, if the individual is freed of constraints such as phobias and anxieties, he often can engage in a variety of new activities that were previously unavailable for him. Although treatment-produced changes may themselves be fairly specific, they may free the individual for many new alternatives and thus indirectly lead to many diverse changes in his life. A person who overcomes public-speaking anxieties, for example, may as a result gain considerable social, interpersonal, and professional freedom of movement (Paul & Shannon, 1966). After debilitating problems have been eliminated, gains also may occur in other more or less directly connected areas. Thus people who were successfully desensitized cognitively to fear of snakes also reported some reduction in other fears (Lang, Lazovik, & Reynolds, 1965). In another study to reduce social-evaluative anxiety in college students by cognitive counterconditioning, the improvements were fairly widespread (Paul & Shannon, 1966). The treatment not only reduced emotionality and anxiety and simultaneously improved public speaking; it also produced significant gains in effectiveness in other areas. Students treated by group counterconditioning gained almost half a point in grade-point average while their matched controls showed a mean loss of almost a full point when overall grades for the semester before and after the treatment period were computed.

An adequate approach to the dynamics of behavior must also deal with the manner in which persons acquire standards and rules for regulating their own behavior (e.g., Bandura & Kupers, 1964; Bandura & Perloff, 1967; Kanfer & Marston, 1963a, b; Mischel & Liebert, 1966, 1967; Mischel, Coates, & Raskoff, 1967). The resulting self-evaluations determine, in part, just how the person reacts to his own actions, feelings, and accomplishments, as well as how he compares himself with other people (Festinger, 1954), and the standards he transmits to others (Mischel & Liebert, 1966). The stream of behavior thus involves constant reaction to one's own behavior, as well as to environmental events, and interactions between the person and the environment as they change each other.

A social behavior view of dynamics, rather than being exclusively intrapsychic, focuses on the relations between behavior and the conditions in which the behavior occurs, and on how an individual's behavior in any one condition is functionally related to what he does on another occasion. What a person does, both in his overt behavior and in his private thoughts and affective reactions, changes the stimulus conditions that he subsequently encounters. Every motoric, autonomic, and cognitive response from the person produces further consequences for him, both from his own reactions to his new behavior, and from the environmental changes that his behavior engenders. The consequences that occur in turn alter his subsequent behavior, in long and complex chains.

In this perspective, consider a question like the relations between changes in verbal and nonverbal behavior. If one studies the effects of what a person says upon what he does, and how alterations in what he says influence other aspects of his behavior, it becomes apparent that changes in what the person says may modify what he does in many different and complicated ways. If, for example, one comes to describe himself differently—say in regard to political views or personal beliefs—the new things he says alter his environment and in turn lead to new responses from himself and from others. If a person says within earshot of his boss that he now detests the boss, his environment is likely to be altered more, and to facilitate greater behavior change, than if he grumbles quietly and momentarily to himself. Even his quiet transitory mumblings, however, produce further consequences for him by altering other things he says and does—including the things he says and does to himself.

Individuals are constantly confronted with choices and each choice, in turn, places the chooser under new contingencies and produces new consequences. Consider, for example, a person's choice when faced with an immediately available but smaller reward as opposed to a larger, more desirable outcome whose attainment is contingent on waiting. The chosen outcome presumably is the one which on the basis of prior experience is most likely to lead to the most valued outcome available. The choice itself, however, sets up a new series of consequences for the person. If he chooses to get the immediate reward, for example, he cannot experience the consequences that would have occurred if he had elected to wait. A person who has had little prior reward for self-control behavior, like waiting for larger goals, therefore may never make the response choices necessary to obtain reward for waiting behavior. Consequently he may become involved in a virtually endless chain of immediate reward behaviors, in which delay choices rarely are made, and hence cannot be reinforced even if the environmental consequences would be favorable (Bandura & Mischel, 1965).

It is often mistakenly assumed that social behavior and learning theories deny the existence of mediating cognitive processes. Humans do think, experience wishes, fears, hopes, dreams—and much more. The present social behavior view, rather than denying such intrapsychic activities, seeks public referents for them so that they can be studied. However, although the person's subjective experiences are a critical part of the chain of behavior, they do not necessarily have singular unidirectional causal powers. Instead, it is recognized that behavior change can lead to cognitive reorganization, just as cognitive changes can lead to behavior modification.

Indeed there is much evidence that cognitive and value changes may often *follow* after new behaviors have been performed, rather than being the prerequisites for these new performances (e.g., Brehm &

Cohen, 1962; Festinger, 1957). That is, values and cognitions are re-aligned to make them consistent with behavior changes and may be used to justify the altered behavior. On the other hand, cognitive changes and affective internal modifications can also generate and enhance overt behavior, as seen, for example, in the facilitating effects of cognitive desensitization upon actual approach behavior toward the feared object (Chapter 8). In the present view, cognitions, affects, and other mediating events are construed as internal responses that also serve as stimuli, linking external stimulus inputs with the ultimate overt terminal outputs in complex stimulus-response chains (Berlyne, 1965). The links among these components often are moderated by many variables that may jointly determine the extent of consistency—or of inconsistency—found among affect, cognition, and action (e.g., Insko & Schopler, 1967).

As has been stressed (Chapters 3 and 8), it is important to include the subject's own phenomenology and constructs as data sources since he construes, abstracts, and experiences behavior, as well as performing overtly, just as much as the psychologist who tries to study him. In the present view, the assessor's concern is with the particular meanings that stimuli have acquired and their power to evoke particular responses from the organism. The acquired meanings of a stimulus, however, can only be known by determining what the organism does with it in sampled situations. The search, then, is not for generalized response predispositions and response consistencies, but rather for unique stimulus meanings manifested by the cognitive, emotional, and behavioral reactions that the stimuli evoke from the person in particular contexts.

We have also stressed, however, that the individual's constructions and phenomenology (irrespective of whether or not he is a "scientist") do not necessarily parallel his other behaviors, nor do they necessarily determine them. The person is neither "empty," nor "passive," nor is he an automaton filled with psychological glue that mechanically attaches responses to stimuli. His social behaviors, however, like those of other organisms in nature, are viewed as regulated by internal and external conditions. The individual's personal constructs, for example, presumably also depend on stimulus events and are integrally related to many other conditions that affect their future course (Chapter 6).

The focus of assessment therefore is on the behavioral referents for problems and on the isolation of the stimulus conditions that covary with their presence or magnitude. In this view, the dynamics of behavior involve the intricate relations between what the individual does and the conditions that evoke, support, undermine, or otherwise modify his behavior patterns. Experimental research will undoubtedly provide increasing understanding of the mechanisms and processes through which stimulus changes exert their effects on behavior. In particular, research on cognition and information-processing should help to clarify the mental activities through which stimulus events become transformed into behavioral products. It should be apparent that theory and hypothesis testing are not restricted to trait validation strategies and to the search for predispositions inferred from personality signs. The constructs hypothesized in behavior assessment, however, involve the effects of stimulus conditions on response patterns, whereas those in trait and state validation deal chiefly with hypothesized relations between response patterns.

Sometimes it is argued that analyses of behavior which focus on the role of stimulus events imply a "mechanistically determined" view of man. A scientific analysis of behavior is equally deterministic, however, whether the focus is on hypothesized intraorganismic conditions, such as ego strength or Oedipal complexes, as determining states or on stimulus conditions in the form of social learning variables. The term "mechanistic" introduces an irrelevant value judgment that should not be allowed to interfere with our understanding of human behavior.

Global traits and states are excessively crude, gross units to encompass adequately the extraordinary complexity and subtlety of the discriminations that people constantly make. Traditional trait-state conceptions of man have depicted him as victimized by his infantile history, as possessed by unchanging rigid trait attributes, and as driven inexorably by unconscious irrational forces. This conceptualization of man, besides being philosophically unappetizing, is contradicted by massive experimental data. The traditional trait-state conceptualizations of personality, while often paying lip service to man's complexity and to the uniqueness of each person, in fact lead to a grossly oversimplified view that misses both the richness and the uniqueness of individual lives. A more adequate conceptualization must take full account of man's extraordinary adaptiveness and capacities for discrimination, awareness, and self-regulation; it must also recognize that men can and do reconceptualize themselves and change, and that an understanding of how humans can constructively modify their behavior in systematic ways is the core of a truly dynamic personality psychology.

REFERENCES

Abelson, R. P., & Rosenberg, M. J. Symbolic psycho-logic: A model of attitudinal cognition. *Behav. Sci.*, 1958, **3**, 1–13.

Adorno, I. W., Frenkel-Brunswik, Else, Levinson, D. J., & Sanford, R. N. *The authoritarian personality*. New York: Harper, 1950.

Allen, Eileen K., Hart, Betty M., Buell, Joan S., Harris, Florence R., & Wolf, M. M. Effects of social reinforcement on isolate behavior of a nursery school child. *Child Develpm.*, 1964, **35**, 511–518.

Allinsmith, W. The learning of moral standards. In D. R. Miller & G. E. Swanson (Eds.), *Inner conflict and defense*. New York: Holt, 1960. Pp. 141–176.

Allport, G.W. *Personality: A psychological interpretation*. New York: Holt, 1937.

Allport, G. W. Traits revisited. *Am. Psychol.*, 1966, **21**, 1–10.

Allport, G. W., & Odbert, H. S. Trait-names: A psycho-lexical study. *Psychol. Monogr.*, 1936, **47** (Whole No. 211) .

American Psychiatric Association. *Diagnostic and statistical manual for mental disorders*. Washington, D. C.: Mental Hospital Service, 1952.

Anastasi, Anne. *Psychological testing*. (Rev. ed.) New York: Macmillan, 1961.

Anastasi, Anne. *Individual differences*. New York: Wiley, 1965.

Anastasi, Anne. Psychology, psychologists, and psychological testing. *Am. Psychol.*, 1967, **22**, 297–306.

Anderson, N. H. Primacy effects in personality impression formation using a generalized order effect paradigm. *J. Pers. Soc. Psychol.*, 1965, **2**, 1–9.

Applezweig, Dee G. Some determinants of behavioral rigidity. *J. Abnorm. Soc. Psychol.*, 1954, **49**, 224–228.

Aronfreed, J. The nature, variety, and social patterning of moral responses to transgression. *J. Abnorm. Soc. Psychol.*, 1961, **63**, 223–240.

Aronfreed, J.   The origin of self-criticism. *Psychol. Rev.*, 1964, **71**, 193–218.

Aronfreed, J.   The internalization of social control through punishment: Experimental studies of the role of conditioning and the second signal system in the development of conscience. *Proc. XVIIIth Intern. Congr. Psychol.* (Moscow, U.S.S.R., August 1966), **35**, 219–230.

Aronfreed, J., & Reber, A.   Internalized behavioral suppression and the timing of social punishment. *J. Pers. Soc. Psychol.*, 1965, **1**, 3–16.

Aronson, E., & Carlsmith, J. M.   Performance expectancy as a determinant of actual performance. *J. Abnorm. Soc. Psychol.*, 1962, **65**, 178–182.

Asch, S. E.   Forming impressions of personality. *J. Abnorm. Soc. Psychol.*, 1946, **41**, 258–290.

Ash, P.   The reliability of psychiatric diagnoses. *J. Abnorm. Soc. Psychol.*, 1949, **44**, 272–276.

Atkinson, J. W., & Feather, N. T. (Eds.)   *A theory of achievement motivation.* New York: Wiley, 1966.

Atkinson, R. C., & Hansen, D. N.   Computer-assisted instruction in initial reading: The Stanford project. *Reading Res. Quart.*, 1966, **2**, 5–25.

Atkinson, R. C., & Suppes, P.   Project for an automated primary-grade reading and arithmetic curriculum for culturally-deprived children. Progress Report No. 5, Institute for Mathematical Studies in the Social Sciences, Stanford University, 1967.

Atkinson, Rita L.   Paired-associate learning by schizophrenic and normal subjects under conditions of verbal reward and verbal punishment. Unpublished doctoral dissertation, Indiana University, 1957.

Atthowe, J. M., Jr., & Krasner, L.   A preliminary report on the application of contingent reinforcement procedures (token economy) on a "chronic" psychiatric ward. *J. Abnorm. Psychol.*, 1967, in press.

Ayllon, T.   Some behavioral problems associated with eating in chronic schizophrenic patients. In L. P. Ullmann & L. Krasner (Eds.), *Case studies in behavior modification.* New York: Holt, Rinehart & Winston, 1965. Pp. 73–77.

Ayllon, T., & Azrin, N. H.   The measurement and reinforcement of behavior of psychotics. *J. Exp. Anal. Behav.*, 1965, **8**, 357–383.

Ayllon, T., & Haughton, E.   Modification of symptomatic verbal behaviour of mental patients. *Behav. Res. Ther.*, 1964, **2**, 87–97.

Ayllon, T., & Haughton, E.   Control of the behavior of schizophrenic patients by food. *J. Exp. Anal. Behav.*, 1962, **5**, 343–352.

Ayllon, T., & Michael, J.   The psychiatric nurse as a behavioral engineer. *J. Exp. Anal. Behav.*, 1959, **2**, 323–334.

Bachrach, A. J., Erwin, W. J., & Mohr, J. P.   The control of eating behavior in an anorexic by operant conditioning techniques. In L. P. Ullmann & L. Krasner (Eds.), *Case studies in behavior modification.* New York: Holt, Rinehart & Winston, 1965. Pp. 153–163.

REFERENCES

Bandura, A. Relationship of family patterns to child behavior disorders. Progress Report, U.S.P.H. Research Grant M-1734, Stanford University, 1960.

Bandura, A. Behavioral modification through modeling procedures. In L. Krasner and L. P. Ullmann (Eds.), *Research in behavior modification.* New York: Holt, Rinehart & Winston, 1965. Pp. 310–340. (a)

Bandura, A. Vicarious processes: A case of no-trial learning. In L. Berkowitz (Ed.), *Advances in experimental social psychology.* Vol. 2. New York: Academic Press, 1965. Pp. 1–55. (b)

Bandura, A. Behavioral psychotherapy. *Scientific Amer.,* 1967, **216**, 78–86.

Bandura, A. *Principles of behavior modification.* New York: Holt, Rinehart & Winston, 1968, in press.

Bandura, A., Blanchard, E. B., & Ritter, Brunhilde J. The relative efficacy of modeling therapeutic approaches for producing behavioral, attitudinal and affective changes. Unpublished manuscript, Stanford University, 1968.

Bandura, A., Grusec, Joan E., & Menlove, Frances L. Observational learning as a function of symbolization and incentive set. *Child Develpm.,* 1966, **37**, 499–506.

Bandura, A., Grusec, Joan E., & Menlove, Frances L. Vicarious extinction of avoidance behavior. *J. Pers. Soc. Psychol.,* 1967, **5**, 16–23.

Bandura, A., & Harris, Mary Bierman. Modification of syntactic style. *J. Exptl. Child Psychol.,* 1966, **4**, 341–352.

Bandura, A., & Huston, Aletha C. Identification as a process of incidental learning. *J. Abnorm. Soc. Psychol.,* 1961, **63**, 311–318.

Bandura, A., & Kupers, Carol J. Transmission of patterns of self-reinforcement through modeling. *J. Abnorm. Soc. Psychol.,* 1964, **69**, 1–9.

Bandura, A., & McDonald, F. J. Influence of social reinforcement and the behavior of models in shaping children's moral judgments. *J. Abnorm. Soc. Psychol.,* 1963, **67**, 274–281.

Bandura, A., & Menlove, Frances L. Factors determining vicarious extinction of avoidance behavior through symbolic modeling. *J. Pers. Soc. Psychol.,* 1968, in press.

Bandura, A., & Mischel, W. Modification of self-imposed delay of reward through exposure to live and symbolic models. *J. Pers. Soc. Psychol.,* 1965, **2**, 698–705.

Bandura, A., & Perloff, B. Relative efficacy of self-monitored and externally imposed reinforcement systems. *J. Pers. Soc. Psychol.,* 1967, **7**, 111–116.

Bandura, A., & Rosenthal, T. L. Vicarious classical conditioning as a function of arousal level. *J. Pers. Soc. Psychol.,* 1966, **3**, 54–62.

Bandura, A., Ross, Dorothea, & Ross, Sheila A. Transmission of aggression through imitation of aggressive models. *J. Abnorm. Soc. Psychol.,* 1961, **63**, 575–582.

Bandura, A., Ross, Dorothea, & Ross, Sheila A.   Imitation of film-mediated aggressive models. *J. Abnorm. Soc. Psychol.*, 1963, **66**, 3–11.

Bandura, A., & Walters, R.   *Social learning and personality development.* New York: Holt, Rinehart & Winston, 1963.

Bandura, A., & Whalen, Carol K.   The influence of antecedent reinforcement and divergent modeling cues on patterns of self-reward. *J. Pers. Soc. Psychol.*, 1966, **3**, 373–382.

Bannister, D., Salmon, Phillida, & Leiberman, D. M.   Diagnosis-treatment relationships in psychiatry: A statistical analysis. *Brit. J. Psychiat.*, 1964, **110**, 726–732.

Barker, R.   On the nature of the environment. *J. Soc. Issues*, 1963, **19**, 17–38.

Barlow, J. A., & Burt, C. L.   The identification of factors from different experiments. *Brit. J. Statist. Psychol.*, 1954, **7**, 52–53.

Barr, Harriet Linton.   Dependence on external influence: Correlates in perception, attitude, and judgment. *J. Abnorm. Soc. Psychol.*, 1955, **51**, 502–507.

Bass, B. M.   Authoritarianism or acquiescence? *J. Abnorm. Soc. Psychol.*, 1955, **51**, 616–623.

Bass, B., & Berg, I. (Eds.)   *Objective approaches to personality assessment.* Princeton, N. J.: Van Nostrand, 1959.

Bechtoldt, H.   Construct validity: A critique. *Am. Psychol.*, 1959, **14**, 619–629.

Becker, W. C.   A genetic approach to the interpretation and evaluation of the process-reactive distinction in schizophrenia. *J. Abnorm. Soc. Psychol.*, 1956, **53**, 229–236.

Becker, W. C.   The process-reactive distinction: A key to the problem of schizophrenia? *J. Nerv. Ment. Dis.*, 1959, **129**, 442–449.

Becker, W. C.   The matching of behavior rating and questionnaire personality factors. *Psychol. Bull.*, 1960, **57**, 201–212.

Becker, W. C.   Consequences of different kinds of parental discipline. In M. L. Hoffman & Lois W. Hoffman (Eds.), *Review of child development research.* Vol. 1. New York: Russell Sage Foundation, 1964. Pp. 169–208.

Beller, E. K.   Dependency and independence in young children. *J. Genet. Psychol.*, 1955, **87**, 25–35.

Berger, S. M.   Conditioning through vicarious instigation. *Psychol. Rev.*, 1962, **69**, 450–466.

Bergin, A. E.   Some implications of psychotherapy research for therapeutic practice. *J. Abnorm. Psychol.*, 1966, **71**, 235–246.

Berlyne, D. E.   *Structure and direction in thinking.* New York: Wiley, 1965.

Bernstein, L.   The examiner as an inhibiting factor in clinical testing. *J. Consult. Psychol.*, 1956, **20**, 287–290.

Bieri, J.   Cognitive complexity-simplicity and predictive behavior. *J. Abnorm. Soc. Psychol.*, 1955, **51**, 263–268.

REFERENCES

Bieri, J., Atkins, A. L., Briar, S., Leaman, Robin L., Miller, H., & Tripodi, T. *Clinical and social judgment.* New York: Wiley, 1966.

Bijou, S. W. Experimental studies of child behavior, normal and deviant. In L. Krasner & L. P. Ullmann (Eds.), *Research in behavior modification.* New York: Holt, Rinehart & Winston, 1965, Pp. 56–81.

Bijou, S. W., & Orlando, R. Rapid development of multiple-schedule performances with retarded children. *J. Exp. Anal. Behav.,* 1961, **4**, 7–16.

Birch, D. Verbal control of nonverbal behavior. *J. Exptl. Child Psychol.,* 1966, **4**, 266–275.

Birnbrauer, J. S., Bijou, S. W., Wolf, M. M., & Kidder, J. D. Programed instruction in the classroom. In L. P. Ullmann & L. Krasner (Eds.), *Case studies in behavior modification.* New York: Holt, Rinehart & Winston, 1965. Pp. 358–363.

Birnbrauer, J. S., & Lawler, Julia. Token reinforcement for learning. *Ment. Retard.,* 1964, **2**, 275–279.

Birnbrauer, J. S., Wolf, M. M., Kidder, J. D., & Tague, Cecilia E. Classroom behavior of retarded pupils with token reinforcement. *J. Exptl. Child Psychol.,* 1965, **2**, 219–235.

Birney, R. C. The reliability of the achievement motive. *J. Abnorm. Soc. Psychol.,* 1959, **58**, 266–267.

Black, A. H. Heart rate changes during avoidance learning in dogs. *Canad. J. Psychol.,* 1959, **13**, 229–242.

Blake, R. R., Helson, H., & Mouton, Jane S. The generality of conformity behavior as a function of factual anchorage, difficulty of task, and amount of situational pressure. *J. Pers.,* 1957, **25**, 294–305.

Blake, R. R., & Vanderplas, J. M. The effect of pre-recognition hypotheses on veridical recognition thresholds in auditory perception. *J. Pers.,* 1950, **19**, 95–115.

Block, J. *The challenge of response sets.* New York: Appleton-Century-Crofts, 1965.

Bloom, B. S. *Stability and change in human characteristics.* New York: Wiley, 1964.

Boisen, A. T. Types of dementia praecox—A study in psychiatric classification. *Psychiatry,* 1938, **2**, 233–236.

Bonarius, J. C. J. Research in the personal construct theory of George A. Kelly: Role Construct Repertory Test and basic theory. In B. A. Maher (Ed.), *Progress in experimental personality research.* Vol. 2. New York: Academic Press, 1965. Pp. 1–46.

Brackbill, Yvonne, & Jack, D. Discrimination learning in children as a function of reinforcement value. *Child Develpm.,* 1958, **29**, 185–190.

Bradway, Katherine P., Thompson, Clare W., & Cravens, R. B. Preschool IQ's after twenty-five years. *J. Educ. Psychol.,* 1958, **49**, 278–281.

Braine, M. D. S. On learning the grammatical order of words. *Psychol. Rev.*, 1963, **70**, 323–348.

Brehm, J. W., & Cohen, A. R. *Explorations in cognitive dissonance.* New York: Wiley, 1962.

Bridges, J. W. An experimental study of decision types and their mental correlates. *Psychol. Monogr.*, 1914, **17** (Whole No. 72).

Brill, A. A. *Basic principles of psychoanalysis.* Garden City, N. Y.: Doubleday, 1949.

Brim, O. G., Jr. Personality development as role-learning. In I. Iscoe & H. W. Stevenson (Eds.), *Personality development in children.* Austin: University of Texas Press, 1960. Pp. 127–159.

Brody, Grace F. Relationship between maternal attitudes and behavior. *J. Pers. Soc. Psychol.*, 1965, **2**, 317–323.

Broverman, D. M. Dimensions of cognitive style. *J. Pers.*, 1960, **28**, 167–185. (a)

Broverman, D. M. Cognitive style and intra-individual variation in abilities. *J. Pers.*, 1960, **28**, 240–256. (b)

Broverman, D. M. Generality and behavioral correlates of cognitive styles. *J. Consult. Psychol.*, 1964, **28**, 487–500.

Brown, R. *Social psychology.* New York: Free Press of Glencoe, 1965.

Bruner, J. S. Social psychology and perception. In Eleanor E. Maccoby, T. M. Newcomb, & E. L. Hartley (Eds.), *Readings in social psychology.* (3rd ed.) New York: Holt, 1958. Pp. 85–94.

Bruner, J. S., Olver, Rose R., & Greenfield, Patricia M. *Studies in cognitive growth.* New York: Wiley, 1966.

Bruner, J. S., & Tagiuri, R. The perception of people. In G. Lindzey (Ed.), *Handbook of social psychology.* Vol. 2. Cambridge, Mass.: Addison-Wesley, 1954. Pp. 634–654.

Buchwald, A. M. Experimental alterations in the effectiveness of verbal reinforcement combinations. *J. Exptl. Psychol.*, 1959, **57**, 351–361.

Buchwald, A. M. Variations in the apparent effects of "right" and "wrong" on subsequent behavior. *J. Verb. Learn. Verb. Behav.*, 1962, **1**, 71–78.

Bunt, A. van de, & Barendregt, J. T. Inter-correlations of three measures of conditioning. In J. T. Barendregt (Ed.), *Research in psychodiagnostics.* The Hague: Mouton, 1961.

Burton, R. V. Generality of honesty reconsidered. *Psychol. Rev.*, 1963, **70**, 481–499.

Burwen, L. S., & Campbell, D. T. The generality of attitudes toward authority and nonauthority figures. *J. Abnorm. Soc. Psychol.*, 1957, **54**, 24–31.

Byrne, D. Repression-sensitization as a dimension of personality. In B. A. Maher (Ed.), *Progress in experimental personality research.* Vol. 1. New York: Academic Press, 1964.

Byrne, D. *An introduction to personality*. Englewood Cliffs, N. J.: Prentice-Hall, 1966.

Byrne, D., & Holcomb, Joan. The reliability of a response measure: Differential recognition-threshold scores. *Psychol. Bull.*, 1962, **59**, 70–73.

Cairns, R. B. The influence of dependency-anxiety on the effectiveness of social reinforcers. Unpublished doctoral dissertation, Stanford University, 1959.

Cairns, R. B. Informational properties of verbal and nonverbal events. *J. Pers. Soc. Psychol.*, 1967, **5**, 353–357.

Campbell, A. A. The interrelations of two measures of conditioning in man. *J. Exptl. Psychol.*, 1938, **22**, 225–243.

Campbell, D. T. Recommendations for APA test standards regarding construct, trait, or discriminant validity. *Am. Psychol.*, 1960, **15**, 546–553.

Campbell, D. T. Conformity in psychology's theories of acquired behavioral dispositions. In I. A. Berg & B. M. Bass (Eds.), *Conformity and deviation*. New York: Harper, 1961. Pp. 101–142.

Campbell, D., & Fiske, D. Convergent and discriminant validation by the multitrait-multimethod matrix. *Psychol. Bull.*, 1959, **56**, 81–105.

Carlin, M. T. The effects of modeled behavior during imposed delay on the observer's subsequent willingness to delay rewards. Unpublished doctoral dissertation, Stanford University, 1965.

Carrigan, Patricia M. Extraversion-introversion as a dimension of personality: A reappraisal. *Psychol. Bull.*, 1960, **57**, 329–360.

Cartwright, D. S., Kirtner, W. L., & Fiske, D. W. Method factors in changes associated with psychotherapy. *J. Abnorm. Soc. Psychol.*, 1963, **66**, 164–175.

Cattell, R. B. Confirmation and clarification of primary personality factors. *Psychometrika*, 1947, **12**, 197–220.

Cattell, R. B. *Personality: A systematic theoretical and factual study*. New York: McGraw-Hill, 1950.

Cattell, R. B. *Personality and motivation: Structure and measurement*. Yonkers-on-Hudson: World Book, 1957.

Cattell, R. B. Extracting the correct number of factors in factor analysis. *Educ. Psychol. Meas.*, 1958, **18**, 791–838.

Cattell, R. B., & Beloff, H. La structure factorielle de la personalité des enfants de onze ans a travers trois types d'epreuves. *Rev. Psychol. Appl.*, 1956, **6**, 65–89.

Cattell, R. B., & Dickman, K. A dynamic model of physical influences demonstrating the necessity of oblique simple structure. *Psychol. Bull.*, 1962, **59**, 389–400 .

Cattell, R. B., & Saunders, D. R. Interrelation and matching of personality factors from behavior rating, questionnaire, and objective test data. *J. Soc. Psychol.*, 1950, **31**, 243–260.

Cattell, R. B., & Saunders, D. R.   Beitrage zur faktoren-analyse der personlich-keit. *Zeitschrift fur Experimentelle und Angewandte Psychologie*, 1955, **2**, 325–357.

Cattell, R. B., & Sullivan, W.   The scientific nature of factors: A demonstration by cups of coffee. *Behav. Sci.*, 1962, **7**, 184–193.

Chance, June E.   Generalization of expectancies as a function of need relatedness. Unpublished doctoral dissertation, Ohio State University, 1952.

Chatterjee, B. B., & Eriksen, C. W.   Conditioning and generalization of GSR as a function of awareness. *J. Abnorm. Soc. Psychol.*, 1960, **60**, 397–403.

Chatterjee, B. B., & Eriksen, C. W.   Cognitive factors in heart rate conditioning. *J. Exptl. Psychol.*, 1962, **64**, 272–279.

Chittenden, Gertrude E.   An experimental study in measuring and modifying assertive behavior in young children. *Monogr. Soc. Res. Child Develpm.*, 1942, **7**, No. 1 (Serial No. 31).

Chown, Sheila M.   Rigidity—A flexible concept. *Psychol. Bull.*, 1959, **56**, 195–223.

Christie, R.   Authoritarianism re-examined. In R. Christie & Marie Jahoda (Eds.), *Studies in the scope and method of "The Authoritarian Personality."* Glencoe, Ill.: Free Press, 1954. Pp. 123–196.

Christie, R., Havel, Joan, & Seidenberg, B.   Is the *F* scale irreversible? *J. Abnorm. Soc. Psychol.*, 1958, **56**, 143–159.

Clark, D. F.   Fetishism treated by negative conditioning. *Brit. J. Psychiat.*, 1963, **109**, 404–407. (a)

Clark, D. F.   The treatment of monosymptomatic phobia by systematic desensitization. *Behav. Res. Ther.*, 1963, **1**, 63–68. (b)

Cline, V. B.   Interpersonal perception. In B. A. Maher (Ed.), *Progress in experimental personality research.* Vol. 1. New York: Academic Press, 1964. Pp. 221–284.

Cohen, A. R.   Cognitive tuning as a factor affecting impression formation. *J. Pers.*, 1961, **29**, 235–245.

Couch, A. S., & Keniston, K.   Yea-sayers and nay-sayers: Agreeing response set as personality variable. *J. Abnorm. Soc. Psychol.*, 1960, **60**, 151–174.

Crandall, V. J., Preston, Anne, & Rabson, Alice.   Maternal reactions and the development of independence and achievement behavior in young children. *Child Develpm.*, 1960, **31**, 243–251.

Crandall, V. J., & Sinkeldam, Carol.   Children's dependent and achievement behaviors in social situations and their perceptual field dependence. *J. Pers.*, 1964, **32**, 1–22.

Crandall, Virginia C., Good, Suzanne, & Crandall, V. J.   Reinforcement effects of adult reactions and nonreactions on children's achievement expectations: A replication study. *Child Develpm.*, 1964, **35**, 485–497.

Crockett, W. H.   Cognitive complexity and impression formation. In B. A.

Maher (Ed.), *Progress in experimental personality research.* Vol. 2. New York: Academic Press, 1965. Pp. 47–90.

Cronbach, L. J. Statistical methods applied to Rorschach scores: A review. *Psychol. Bull.,* 1949, **46**, 393–429.

Cronbach, L. J. Processes affecting scores on "understanding of others" and "assumed similarity." *Psychol. Bull.,* 1955, **52**, 177–193.

Cronbach, L. J. Assessment of individual differences. *Ann. Rev. Psychol.,* 1956, **7**, 173–196.

Cronbach, L. J. *Essentials of psychological testing.* (2nd ed.) New York: Harper, 1960.

Cronbach, L. J., & Gleser, Goldine C. *Psychological tests and personnel decisions.* (Rev. ed.) Urbana: University of Illinois Press, 1965.

Cronbach, L. J., & Meehl, P. E. Construct validity in psychological tests. *Psychol. Bull.,* 1955, **52**, 281–302.

Crow, W. J. The effect of training upon accuracy and variability in interpersonal perception. *J. Abnorm. Soc. Psychol.,* 1957, **55**, 355–359.

Crow, W. J., & Hammond, K. R. The generality of accuracy and response sets in interpersonal perception. *J. Abnorm. Soc. Psychol.,* 1957, **54**, 384–390.

Curle, A. Transitional communities and social reconnection. Part I. *Human Relat.,* 1947, **1**, 45–68.

Curle, A., & Trist, E. L. Transitional communities and social reconnection. Part II. *Human Relat.,* 1947, **1**, 240–288.

Dailey, C. A. The practical utility of the clinical report. *J. Consult. Psychol.,* 1953, **17**, 297–302.

D'Andrade, R. G. Trait psychology and componential analysis. *Am. Anthropol.,* 1965, **67**, 215–228.

Danet, B. N. Prediction of mental illness in college students on the basis of "nonpsychiatric" MMPI profiles. *J. Consult. Psychol.,* 1965, **29**, 577–580.

Davidson, P. O., Payne, R. W., & Sloane, R. B. Introversion, neuroticism, and conditioning. *J. Abnorm. Soc. Psychol.,* 1964, **68**, 136–143.

Davison, G. C. The negative effects of early exposure to suboptimal visual stimuli. *J. Pers.,* 1964, **32**, 278–295.

Davison, G. C. Differential relaxation and cognitive restructuring in therapy with a "paranoid schizophrenic" or "paranoid state." *Proc. 74th Ann. Conv. Am. Psychol. Assoc.* Washington, D. C.: APA, 1966.

Davison, G. C. Systematic desensitization as a counterconditioning process. *J. Abnorm. Psychol.,* 1967, in press. (a)

Davison, G. C. The elimination of a sadistic fantasy by a client-controlled counterconditioning technique: A case study. *J. Abnorm. Psychol.,* 1967, in press. (b)

Davitz, J. R. The effects of previous training on postfrustration behavior. *J. Abnorm. Soc. Psychol.,* 1952, **47**, 309–315.

Deutsch, J. A., & Deutsch, Diana. *Physiological psychology.* Homewood, Ill.: Dorsey Press, 1966.

Diven, K. Certain determinants in the conditioning of anxiety reactions. *J. Psychol.,* 1937, **3**, 291–308.

Dornbusch, S. M., Hastorf, A. H., Richardson, S. A., Muzzy, R. E., & Vreeland, Rebecca S. The perceiver and the perceived: Their relative influence on the categories of interpersonal cognition. *J. Pers. Soc. Psychol.,* 1965, **1**, 434–440.

DuBois, P. H., & Watson, R. I. The selection of patrolmen. *J. Appl. Psychol.,* 1950, **34**, 90–95.

Duncker, K. Experimental modification of children's food preferences through social suggestion. *J. Abnorm. Psychol.,* 1938, **33**, 489–507.

Edwards, A. L. *The social desirability variable in personality assessment and research.* New York: Dryden, 1957.

Edwards, A. L. Social desirability and the description of others. *J. Abnorm. Soc. Psychol.,* 1959, **59**, 434–436.

Edwards, A. L. Social desirability or acquiescence in the MMPI? A case study with the *SD* scale. *J. Abnorm. Soc. Psychol.,* 1961, **63**, 351–359.

Edwards, A. L. The social desirability hypothesis: Theoretical implications for personality measurement. In S. Messick & J. Ross (Eds.), *Measurement in personality and cognition.* New York: Wiley, 1962. Pp. 91–108.

Egger, M. D., & Miller, N. E. Secondary reinforcement in rats as a function of information value and reliability of the stimulus. *J. Exptl. Psychol.,* 1962, **64**, 97–104.

Elliott, R. Interrelationships among measures of field dependence, ability, and personality traits. *J. Abnorm. Soc. Psychol.,* 1961, **63**, 27–36.

Endler, N. S., Hunt, J. McV., & Rosenstein, A. J. An S-R inventory of anxiousness. *Psychol. Monogr.,* 1962, **76** (Whole No. 536).

Eriksen, C. W. Individual differences in defensive forgetting. *J. Exptl. Psychol.,* 1952, **44**, 442–446.

Eriksen, C. W. Discrimination and learning without awareness: A methodological survey and evaluation. *Psychol. Rev.,* 1960, **67**, 279–300.

Eriksen, C. W. Perception and personality dynamics. In J. M. Wepman & R. W. Heine (Eds.), *Concepts of personality.* Chicago: Aldine, 1963. Pp. 31–62.

Eriksen, C. W. Cognitive responses to internally cued anxiety. In C. D. Spielberger (Ed.), *Anxiety and behavior.* New York: Academic Press, 1966. Pp. 327–360.

Eriksen, C. W., & Kuethe, J. L. Avoidance conditioning of verbal behavior without awareness: A paradigm of repression. *J. Abnorm. Soc. Psychol.,* 1956, **53**, 203–209.

Eriksen, C. W., & Lazarus, R. S. Perceptual defense and projective tests. *J. Abnorm. Soc. Psychol.,* 1952, **47**, 302–308.

REFERENCES

Eschenbach, A. E., & Borgatta, E. F.   Testing behavior hypotheses with the Rorschach: An exploration in validation. *J. Consult. Psychol.*, 1955, **19**, 267–273.

Eysenck, H. J.   The effects of psychotherapy: An evaluation. *J. Consult. Psychol.*, 1952, **16**, 319–324.

Eysenck, H. J.   The questionnaire measurement of neuroticism and extraversion. *Riv. Psicol.*, 1956, **50**, 113–140.

Eysenck, H. J.   *The dynamics of anxiety and hysteria*. New York: Praeger, 1957.

Eysenck, H. J. (Ed.)   *Behaviour therapy and the neuroses*. New York: Pergamon, 1960.

Eysenck, H. J.   The effects of psychotherapy. In H. J. Eysenck (Ed.), *Handbook of abnormal psychology: An experimental approach*. New York: Basic Books, 1961, Pp. 697–725.

Eysenck, H. J.   Extraversion and the acquisition of eyeblink and GSR conditioned responses. *Psychol. Bull.*, 1965, **63**, 258–270.

Eysenck, H. J., & Rachman, S.   *The causes and cures of neurosis: An introduction to modern behaviour therapy based on learning theory and the principles of conditioning*. San Diego: Knapp, 1965.

Fairweather, G. W. (Ed.)   *Social psychology in treating mental illness: An experimental approach*. New York: Wiley, 1964.

Fairweather, G. W.   *Methods in experimental social innovation*. New York: Wiley, 1967.

Fairweather, G. W., Sanders, D. H., Maynard, H., & Cressler, D. L.   *Treating mental illness in the community: An experiment in social innovation*. In preparation, 1967.

Fairweather, G. W., Simon, R., Gebhard, M. E., Weingarten, E., Holland, J. L., Sanders, R., Stone, G. B., & Reahl, J. E.   Relative effectiveness of psychotherapeutic programs: A multicriteria comparison of four programs for three different patient groups. *Psychol. Monogr.*, 1960, **74** (Whole No. 492).

Farber, I. E.   The things people say to themselves. *Am. Psychol.*, 1963, **18**, 185–197.

Farber, I. E.   A framework for the study of personality as a behavioral science. In P. Worchel & D. Byrne (Eds.), *Personality change*. New York: Wiley, 1964. Pp. 3–37.

Farberow, N. L., & McEvoy, T. L.   Suicide among patients with diagnoses of anxiety reaction or depressive reaction in general medical and surgical hospitals. *J. Abnorm. Psychol.*, 1966, **71**, 287–299.

Farina, A., Garmezy, N., & Barry, H. III.   Relationship of marital status to incidence and prognosis of schizophrenia. *J. Abnorm. Soc. Psychol.*, 1963, **67**, 624–630.

Farina, A., Holland, C. H., & Ring, K.   Role of stigma and set in interpersonal interaction. *J. Abnorm. Psychol.*, 1966, **71**, 421–428.

313

Farina, A., & Ring, K.   The influence of perceived mental illness on interpersonal relations. *J. Abnorm. Psychol.*, 1965, **70**, 47–51.

Farnham-Diggory, S.   Self-evaluation and subjective life expectancy among suicidal and nonsuicidal psychotic males. *J. Abnorm. Soc. Psychol.*, 1964, **69**, 628–634.

Feather, B. W.   Semantic generalization of classically conditioned responses: A review. *Psychol. Bull.*, 1965, **63**, 425–441.

Feldt, L. S.   The use of extreme groups to test for the presence of a relationship. *Psychometrika*, 1961, **26**, 307–316.

Ferster, C. B., & DeMyer, Marian K.   The development of performance in autistic children in an automatically controlled environment. *J. Chron. Dis.*, 1961, **13**, 312–345.

Ferster, C. B., & Skinner, B. F.   *Schedules of reinforcement.* New York: Appleton-Century-Crofts, 1957.

Festinger, L.   *A theory of cognitive dissonance.* Stanford: Stanford University Press, 1957.

Festinger, L.   A theory of social comparison processes. *Human Relat.*, 1954, **7**, 117–140.

Fiske, D. W.   The inherent variability of behavior. In D. W. Fiske & S. R. Maddi (Eds.), *Functions of varied experience.* Homewood, Ill.: Dorsey Press, 1961. Pp. 326–354.

Flescher, I.   Anxiety and achievement of intellectually gifted and creatively gifted children. *J. Psychol.*, 1963, **56**, 251–268.

Forsyth, R. P., & Fairweather, G. W.   Psychotherapeutic and other hospital treatment criteria: The dilemma. *J. Abnorm. Soc. Psychol.*, 1961, **62**, 598–604.

Franks, C. M.   Conditioning and personality: A study of normal and neurotic subjects. *J. Abnorm. Soc. Psychol.*, 1956, **52**, 143–150.

Franks, C. M.   Conditioning and abnormal behaviour. In H. J. Eysenck (Ed.), *Handbook of abnormal psychology.* New York: Basic Books, 1961. Pp. 457–487.

Freeman, H. L., & Kendrick, D. C.   A case of cat phobia: Treatment by a method derived from experimental psychology. *Brit. Med. J.*, 1960, **2**, 497–502.

French, J. W.   Comparative prediction of college major-field grades by pure-factor aptitude, interest, and personality measures. *Educ. Psychol. Meas.*, 1963, **23**, 767–774.

Freud, S.   Analysis of a phobia in a five-year-old boy. In *Collected papers.* Vol. III. London: Hogarth Press, 1953.

Freud, S.   *Collected papers.* Vols. I & II. New York: Basic Books, 1959.

Freudenberg, R. K., & Robertson, J. P. S.   Symptoms in relation to psychiatric diagnosis and treatment. *Arch. Neurol. Psychiat.*, 1956, **76**, 14–22.

From, F.   Perception of human action. In H. P. David and J. C. Brengelmann (Eds.), *Perspectives in personality research*. New York: Springer, 1960. Pp. 161–174.

Fuhrer, M. J., & Baer, P. E.   Differential classical conditioning: Verbalization of stimulus contingencies. *Science*, 1965, **150**, 1479–1481.

Fulkerson, S. C., & Barry, J. R.   Methodology and research on the prognostic use of psychological tests. *Psychol. Bull.*, 1961, **58**, 177–204.

Gage, N. L.   Judging interests from expressive behavior. *Psychol. Monogr.*, 1952, **66** (Whole No. 350).

Gage, N. L., & Cronbach, L. J.   Conceptual and methodological problems in interpersonal perception. *Psychol. Rev.*, 1955, **62**, 411–422.

Gardner, R. W., & Long, R. I.   The stability of cognitive controls. *J. Abnorm. Soc. Psychol.*, 1960, **61**, 485–487.

Garfield, S. L., & Affleck, D. C.   Therapists' judgments concerning patients considered for psychotherapy. *J. Consult. Psychol.*, 1961, **25**, 505–509.

Garmezy, N., & Rodnick, E. H.   Premorbid adjustment and performance in schizophrenia: Implications for interpreting heterogeneity in schizophrenia. *J. Nerv. Ment. Dis.*, 1959, **129**, 450–466.

Geer, J. H.   The development of a scale to measure fear. *Behav. Res. Ther.*, 1965, **3**, 45–53.

Gendlin, E. T.   Client-centered developments and work with schizophrenics. *J. Counsel. Psychol.*, 1962, **9**, 205–211.

Getzels, J. W., & Jackson, P. W.   *Creativity and intelligence*. New York: Wiley, 1962.

Gewirtz, J. L.   A factor analysis of some attention-seeking behaviors of young children. *Child Develpm.*, 1956, **27**, 17–36.

Gewirtz, J. L. & Baer, D. M.   The effect of brief social deprivation on behaviors for a social reinforcer. *J. Abnorm. Soc. Psychol.*, 1958, **56**, 49–56. (a)

Gewirtz, J. L., & Baer, D. M.   Deprivation and satiation of social reinforcers as drive conditions. *J. Abnorm. Soc. Psychol.*, 1958, **57**, 165–172. (b)

Gilberstadt, H., & Duker, J.   *A handbook for clinical and actuarial MMPI interpretations*. Philadelphia: Saunders, 1965.

Glaser, R.   Instructional technology and the measurement of learning outcomes: some questions. *Am. Psychol.*, 1963, **18**, 519–521.

Glass, D. C.   Theories of consistency and the study of personality. In E. F. Borgatta & W. W. Lambert (Eds.), *Handbook of personality theory and research*. Chicago: Rand McNally, 1968, in press.

Glixman, A. F.   Categorizing behavior as a function of meaning domain. *J. Pers. Soc. Psychol.*, 1965, **2**, 370–377.

Goffman, E.   *Encounters: Two studies in the sociology of interaction*. Indianapolis: Bobbs-Merrill, 1961.

Goldberg, L. R. The effectiveness of clinicians' judgments: The diagnosis of organic brain damage from the Bender-Gestalt Test. *J. Consult. Psychol.*, 1959, **23**, 25–33.

Goldberg, L. R. Diagnosticians vs. diagnostic signs: The diagnosis of psychosis vs. neurosis from the MMPI. *Psychol. Monogr.*, 1965, **79** (Whole No. 602).

Goldberg, L. R., & Werts, C. E. The reliability of clinicians' judgments: A multitrait-multimethod approach. *J. Consult. Psychol.*, 1966, **30**, 199–206.

Goldberg, S. C. Three situational determinants of conformity to social norms. *J. Abnorm. Soc. Psychol.*, 1954, **49**, 325–329.

Golden, M. Some effects of combining psychological tests on clinical inferences. *J. Consult. Psychol.*, 1964, **28**, 440–446.

Goldstein, K. *The organism.* New York: American Book, 1939.

Gough, H. G. *Manual for the California Psychological Inventory.* Palo Alto, Calif: Consulting Psychologists Press, 1957.

Gough, H. G. Clinical versus statistical prediction in psychology. In L. J. Postman (Ed.), *Psychology in the making.* New York: Knopf, 1962. Pp. 526–584.

Gough, H. G., Hall, W. B., & Harris, R. E. Admissions procedures as forecasters of performance in medical education. *J. Med. Educ.*, 1963, **38**, 983–998.

Gough, H. G., Wenk, E. A., & Rozynko, V. V. Parole outcome as predicted from the CPI, the MMPI, and a base expectancy table. *J. Abnorm. Psychol.*, 1965, **70**, 432–441.

Grant, D. A., & Schiller, J. J. Generalization of the conditioned galvanic skin response to visual stimuli. *J. Exptl. Psychol.*, 1953, **46**, 309–313.

Grinder, R. E. Parental childrearing practices, conscience, and resistance to temptation of sixth-grade children. *Child Develpm.*, 1962, **33**, 803–820.

Grings, W. W. Verbal-perceptual factors in the conditioning of autonomic responses. In W. F. Prokasy (Ed.), *Classical conditioning: A symposium.* New York: Appleton-Century-Crofts, 1965. Pp. 71–89.

Grinker, R. R., & Spiegel, J. P. *Men under stress.* Philadelphia: Blakiston, 1945.

Grossberg, J. M. Behavior therapy: A review. *Psychol. Bull.*, 1964, **62**, 73–88.

Grossberg, J. M. Successful behavior therapy in a case of speech phobia ("stage fright"). *J. Speech Hear. Disord.*, 1965, **30**, 285–288.

Grosz, H. J., & Grossmann, K. G. The sources of observer variation and bias in clinical judgments: I. The item of psychiatric history. *J. Nerv. Ment. Dis.*, 1964, **138**, 105–113.

Grusec, Joan, & Mischel, W. Model's characteristics as determinants of social learning. *J. Pers. Soc. Psychol.*, 1966, **4**, 211–215.

Guilford, J. P. *Personality.* New York: McGraw-Hill, 1959.

Guilford, J. P. Zero correlations among tests of intellectual abilities. *Psychol. Bull.*, 1964, **61**, 401–404.

Guion, R. M. *Personnel testing.* New York: McGraw-Hill, 1965.

Guthrie, E. R. *The psychology of learning.* New York: Harper, 1935.

Haber, R. N., & Alpert, R. The role of situation and picture cues in projective measurement of the achievement motive. In J. W. Atkinson (Ed.), *Motives in fantasy, action, and society.* Princeton: Van Nostrand, 1958. Pp. 644–663.

Hammock, J. Criterion measures: Instruction vs. selection research. *Am. Psychol.*, 1960, **15**, 435. (Abstract)

Harding, J., Kutner, B., Proshansky, H., & Chein, I. Prejudice and ethnic relations. In G. Lindzey (Ed.), *Handbook of social psychology.* Vol. 2. Reading, Mass.: Addison-Wesley, 1954. Pp. 1021–1061.

Harris, Florence R., Johnston, Margaret K., Kelley, Susan C., & Wolf, M. M. Effects of positive social reinforcement on regressed crawling of a nursery school child. *J. Educ. Psychol.*, 1964, **55**, 35–41.

Hart, Betty M., Allen, Eileen K., Buell, Joan S., Harris, Florence R., & Wolf, M. M. Effects of social reinforcement on operant crying. *J. Exptl. Child Psychol.*, 1964, **1**, 145–153.

Hartshorne, H., & May, M. A. *Studies in the nature of character.* Vol. I. *Studies in deceit.* New York: Macmillan, 1928.

Hartshorne, H., May, M. A., & Shuttleworth, F. K. *Studies in the nature of character.* Vol. 3. *Studies in the organization of character.* New York: Macmillan, 1930.

Hartup, W. W. Dependence and independence. In H. W. Stevenson et al. (Eds.), *Child psychology.* 62nd Yearbook of the National Society for the Study of Education. Part 1. Chicago: University of Chicago Press, 1963. Pp. 333–363.

Hase, H. D., & Goldberg, L. R. Comparative validity of different strategies of constructing personality inventory scales. *Psychol. Bull.*, 1967, **67**, 231–248.

Hawkins, R. P., Peterson, R. F., Schweid, Edda, & Bijou, S. W. Behavior therapy in the home: Amelioration of problem parent-child relations with the parent in a therapeutic role. *J. Exptl. Child Psychol.*, 1966, **4**, 99–107.

Heath, D. Stimulus similarity and task familiarity as determinants of expectancy generalization. *J. Exptl. Psychol.*, 1959, **58**, 289–294.

Heathers, G. Emotional dependence and independence in a physical threat situation. *Child Develpm.*, 1953, **24**, 169–179.

Hebb, D. O. *Psychology.* Philadelphia: Saunders, 1966.

Heid, W. H. Nonverbal conceptual behavior of young children with programmed material. Unpublished doctoral thesis, University of Washington, 1964.

Heider, F.   *The psychology of interpersonal relations*. New York: Wiley, 1958.

Heider, F., & Simmel, Marianne.   An experimental study of apparent behavior. *Am. J. Psychol.*, 1944, **57**, 243–259.

Heine, R. W.   A comparison of patients' reports on psychotherapeutic experience with psychoanalytic, nondirective and Adlerian therapists. *Am. J. Psychother.*, 1953, **7**, 16–23.

Helson, H.   *Adaptation-level theory*. New York: Harper & Row, 1964.

Henry, Edith M., & Rotter, J. B.   Situational influences on Rorschach responses. *J. Consult. Psychol.*, 1956, **20**, 457–462.

Herzberg, A.   Short treatment of neuroses by graduated tasks. *Brit. J. Med. Psychol.*, 1941, **19**, 19–36.

Hobbs, N.   Helping disturbed children: Psychological and ecological strategies. *Am. Psychol.*, 1966, **21**, 1105–1115.

Hoffeld, D. R.   Primary stimulus generalization and secondary extinction as a function of strength of conditioning. *J. Comp. Physiol. Psychol.*, 1962, **55**, 27–31.

Hoffman, M. L.   Child rearing practices and moral development: Generalizations from empirical research. *Child Develpm.*, 1963, **34**, 295–318.

Holland, J. L., & Nichols, R. C.   Prediction of academic and extra-curricular achievement in college. *J. Educ. Psychol.*, 1964, **55**, 55–65.

Holland, J. L., & Richards, J. M., Jr.   Academic and nonacademic accomplishment: Correlated or uncorrelated? *J. Educ. Psychol.*, 1965, **56**, 165–174.

Hollingshead, A. B., & Redlich, F. C.   *Social class and mental illness*. New York: Wiley, 1958.

Holt, R. R.   Clinical *and* statistical prediction: A reformulation and some new data. *J. Abnorm. Soc. Psychol.*, 1958, **56**, 1–12.

Holtzman, W. H., & Sells, S. B.   Prediction of flying success by clinical analysis of test protocols. *J. Abnorm. Soc. Psychol.*, 1954, **49**, 485–490.

Horowitz, Miriam J.   A study of clinicians' judgments from projective test protocols. *J. Consult. Psychol.*, 1962, **26**, 251–256.

Hovland, C. I.   The generalization of conditioned responses: I. The sensory generalization of conditioned responses with varying frequencies of tone. *J. Gen. Psychol.*, 1937, **17**, 125–148.

Hovland, C. I., & Janis, I. L. (Eds.)   *Personality and persuasability*. New Haven: Yale University Press, 1959.

Hovland, C. I., Janis, I. L., & Kelley, H. H.   *Communication and persuasion*. New Haven: Yale University Press, 1953.

Howard, K. I.   The convergent and discriminant validation of ipsative ratings from three projective instruments. *J. Clin. Psychol.*, 1962, **18**, 183–188.

Howard, K. I.   Ratings of projective test protocols as a function of degree of inference. *Educ. Psychol. Meas.*, 1963, **23**, 267–275.

Hunt, J. McV.   Traditional personality theory in the light of recent evidence. *Am. Scient.*, 1965, **53**, 80–96.

Hunt, W. A., Wittson, C. L., & Hunt, Edna B. A theoretical and practical analysis of the diagnostic process. In P. H. Hoch & J. Zubin (Eds.), *Current problems in psychiatric diagnosis.* New York: Grune & Stratton, 1953. Pp. 53–65.

Hyman, H. H., & Sheatsley, T. B. The authoritarian personality: A methodological critique. In R. Christie & Marie Jahoda (Eds.), *Studies in the scope and method of "The Authoritarian Personality."* Glencoe, Ill.: Free Press, 1954. Pp. 50–122.

Insko, C. A., & Oakes, W. F. Awareness and the "conditioning" of attitudes. *J. Pers. Soc. Psychol.*, 1966, **4**, 487–496.

Insko, C. A., & Schopler, J. Triadic consistency: A statement of affective-cognitive-conative consistency. *Psychol. Rev.*, 1967, **74**, 361–376.

Jackson, D. N., & Messick, S. Content and style in personality assessment. *Psychol. Bull.*, 1958, **55**, 243–252.

Jacobson, E. *Progressive relaxation.* Chicago: University of Chicago Press, 1929.

Janis, I. L., & Mann, L. Effectiveness of emotional role-playing in modifying smoking habits and attitudes. *J. Exptl. Res. Pers.*, 1965, **1**, 84–90.

Jessor, R. The generalization of expectancies. *J. Abnorm. Soc. Psychol.*, 1954, **49**, 196–200.

Johnson, D. M. Confidence and speed in the two-category judgment. *Arch. Psychol.*, 1939, **34** (No. 241).

Johnson, L. C. An investigation of speed and confidence of judgment as psychological variables. Unpublished doctoral dissertation, Stanford University, 1954.

Johnson, L. C. Generality of speed and confidence of judgment. *J. Abnorm. Soc. Psychol.*, 1957, **54**, 264–266.

Johnson, R. C. A study of children's moral judgments. *Child Develpm.*, 1962, **33**, 327–354.

Jones, A. Information deprivation in humans. In B. A. Maher (Ed.), *Progress in experimental personality research.* Vol. 3. New York: Academic Press, 1966. Pp. 241–307.

Jones, Mary C. A laboratory study of fear: The case of Peter. *Pedagog. Sem. & J. Genet. Psychol.*, 1924, **31**, 308–315.

Kagan, J. The evaluation of hypotheses: An inquiry into individual differences in decision time. Unpublished paper presented at American Psychological Association, 1965.

Kagan, J. Reflection-impulsivity: The generality and dynamics of conceptual tempo. *J. Abnorm. Psychol.*, 1966, **71**, 17–24.

Kagan, J., & Moss, H. A. Stability and validity of achievement fantasy. *J. Abnorm. Soc. Psychol.*, 1959, **58**, 357–364.

Kagan, J., & Moss, H. A. *Birth to maturity: A study in psychological development.* New York: Wiley, 1962.

Kagan, J., Moss, H. A., & Siegel, J. E.   Conceptual style and the use of affect labels. *Merrill-Palmer Quart. Behav. Develpm.*, 1960, 261–278.

Kagan, J., Moss, H. A., & Siegel, J. E.   Psychological significance of styles of conceptualization. *Monogr. Soc. Res. Child Develpm.*, 1963, **28** (Whole No. 2), 73–112.

Kagan, J., Rosman, Bernice L., Day, Deborah, Albert, J., & Phillips, W.   Information processing in the child. Significance of analytic and reflective attitudes. *Psychol. Monogr.*, 1964, **78** (Whole No. 578).

Kanfer, F. H., & Marston, A. R.   Determinants of self-reinforcement in human learning. *J. Exptl. Psychol.*, 1963, **66**, 245–254 (a)

Kanfer, F. H., & Marston, A. R.   Conditioning of self-reinforcing responses: An analogue to self-confidence training. *Psychol. Rep.*, 1963, **13**, 63–70. (b)

Kanfer, F. H., & Saslow, G.   Behavioral analysis: An alternative to diagnostic classification. *Arch. Gen. Psychiat.*, 1965, **12**, 529–538.

Kantor, R. E., & Winder, C. L.   The process-reactive continuum: A theoretical proposal. *J. Nerv. Ment. Dis.*, 1959, **129**, 429–434.

Katkin, E. S.   Relationship between manifest anxiety and two indices of autonomic response to stress. *J. Pers. Soc. Psychol.*, 1965, **2**, 324–333.

Kausler, D. H., & Trapp, E. P.   Motivation and cue utilization in intentional and incidental learning. *Psychol. Rev.*, 1960, **67**, 373–379.

Kelley, H. H.   The warm-cold variable in first impressions of persons. *J. Pers.*, 1950, **18**, 431–439.

Kelly, E. L.   Consistency of the adult personality. *Am. Psychol.*, 1955, **10**, 659–681.

Kelly, E. L.   Clinical psychology—1960; a report of survey findings. *Newsletter, Div. of Clin. Psychol. of APA*, 1961, **14** (Winter isue), 1–11.

Kelly, E. L.   Alternate criteria in medical education and their correlates. In Anne Anastasi (Ed.), *Testing problems in perspective.* Washington, D. C.: American Council on Education, 1966. Pp. 176–194.

Kelly, E. L., & Fiske, D. W.   *The prediction of performance in clinical psychology.* Ann Arbor: University of Michigan Press, 1951.

Kelly, E. L., & Goldberg, L. R.   Correlates of later performance and specialization in psychology; a follow-up study of the trainees assessed in the VA Selection Research Project. *Psychol. Monogr.*, 1959, **73** (Whole No. 482).

Kelly, G. A.   *The psychology of personal constructs.* Vols. 1 & 2. New York: Norton, 1955.

Kelly, G. A.   Man's construction of his alternatives. In G. Lindzey (Ed.), *Assessment of human motives.* New York: Rinehart, 1958. Pp. 33–64.

Kelly, G. A.   Training for professional obsolescence. Unpublished manuscript, Brandeis University, 1965.

Kelman, H. C., & Parloff, M. B. Interrelations among three criteria of improvement in group therapy: Comfort, effectiveness, and self-awareness. *J. Abnorm. Soc. Psychol.*, 1957, **54**, 281–288.

Kenny, D. T., & Ginsberg, Rose. The specificity of intolerance of ambiguity measures. *J. Abnorm. Soc. Psychol.*, 1958, **56**, 300–304.

Kerr, Nancy, Meyerson, L., & Michael, J. A procedure for shaping vocalizations in a mute child. In L. P. Ullmann & L. Krasner (Eds.), *Case studies in behavior modification.* New York: Holt, Rinehart & Winston, 1965. Pp. 366–370.

Kiesler, D. J. Some myths of psychotherapy research and the search for a paradigm. *Psychol. Bull.*, 1966, **65**, 110–136.

Kleinmuntz, B. Personality test interpretation by digital computer. *Science,* 1963, **139**, 416–418.

Kleinmuntz, B. *Personality measurement: An introduction.* Homewood, Ill.: Dorsey Press, 1967.

Kogan, N., & Wallach, M. A. *Risk taking: A study in cognition and personality.* New York: Holt, Rinehart & Winston, 1964.

Kohlberg, L. The development of children's orientations toward a moral order: I. Sequence in the development of moral thought. *Vita Humana,* 1963, **6**, 11–33.

Kohlberg, L. A cognitive-developmental analysis of children's sex-role concepts and attitudes. In Eleanor E. Maccoby (Ed.), *The development of sex differences.* Stanford: Stanford University Press, 1966. Pp. 25–55.

Kostlan, A. A method for the empirical study of psychodiagnosis. *J. Consult. Psychol.*, 1954, **18**, 83–88.

Krasner. L. Verbal conditioning and psychotherapy. In L. Krasner & L. P. Ullmann (Eds.), *Research in behavior modification.* New York: Holt, Rinehart & Winston, 1965. Pp. 211–228.

Krasner, L., Knowles, J. B., & Ullmann, L. P. Effect of verbal conditioning of attitudes on subsequent motor performance. *J. Pers. Soc. Psychol.*, 1965, **1**, 407–412.

Krech, D., Crutchfield, R. S., & Ballachey, E. L. *Individual in society.* New York: McGraw-Hill, 1962.

Kremers, J. *Scientific psychology and naive psychology.* (Trans. by L. Grooten.) Groningen, Netherlands: Nordhoff, 1960.

Krumboltz, J. D., & Farquhar, W. W. Reliability and validity of the *n*-Achievement test. *J. Consult. Psychol.*, 1957, **21**, 226–228.

Kurland, S. H. The lack of generality in defense mechanisms as indicated in auditory perception. *J. Abnorm. Soc. Psychol.*, 1954, **49**, 173–177.

Lacey, J. I., & Smith, R. L. Conditioning and generalization of unconscious anxiety. *Science,* 1954, **120**, 1045–1052.

Landfield, A. W., Stern, M., & Fjeld, S. Social conceptual processes and change in students undergoing psychotherapy. *Psychol. Rep.*, 1961, **8**, 63–68.

Lang, P. J., Geer, J., & Hnatiow, M. Semantic generalization of conditioned autonomic responses. *J. Exptl. Psychol.*, 1963, **65**, 552-558.

Lang, P. J., & Lazovik, A. D. Experimental desensitization of a phobia. *J. Abnorm. Soc. Psychol.*, 1963, **66**, 519–525.

Lang, P. J., Lazovik, A. D., & Reynolds, D. J. Desensitization, suggestibility, and pseudotherapy. *J. Abnorm. Psychol.*, 1965, **70**, 395–402.

Lansky, L. M., Crandall, V. J., Kagan, J., & Baker, C. T. Sex differences in aggression and its correlates in middle-class adolescents. *Child Develpm.*, 1961, **32**, 45–58.

Lantz, DeLee, & Stefflre, Volney. Language and cognition revisited. *J. Abnorm. Soc. Psychol.*, 1964, **69**, 472–481.

LaPiere, R. T. Attitudes vs. actions. *Soc. Forces*, 1934, **13**, 230–237.

Lasky, J. J., Hover, G. L., Smith, P. A., Bostian, D. W., Duffendack, S. C., & Nord, C. L. Post-hospital adjustment as predicted by psychiatric patients and by their staff. *J. Consult. Psychol.*, 1959, **23**, 213–218.

Lazarus, A. A. Group therapy of phobic disorders by systematic desensitization. *J. Abnorm. Soc. Psychol.*, 1961, **63**, 504–510.

Lazarus, A. A. The treatment of chronic frigidity by systematic desensitization. *J. Nerv. Ment. Dis.*, 1963, **136**, 272–278.

Lazarus, A. A., & Abramovitz, A. The use of "emotive imagery" in the treatment of children's phobias. *J. Ment. Sci.*, 1962, **108**, 191–195.

Lazarus, R. S., Eriksen, C. W., & Fonda, C. P. Personality dynamics and auditory perceptual recognition. *J. Pers.*, 1951, **19**, 471–482.

Lazarus, R. S., & Longo, N. The consistency of psychological defenses against threat. *J. Abnorm. Soc. Psychol.*, 1953, **48**, 495–499.

Leary, T. F. *Interpersonal diagnosis of personality*. New York: Ronald Press, 1957.

Leib, J. W., Cusack, Julia, Hughes, Deanna, Pilette, S., Werther, Jacqueline, & Kintz, B. L. Teaching machines and programmed instruction: Areas of application. *Psychol. Bull.*, 1967, **67**, 12–26.

Leventhal, H., Jacobs, R. L., & Kudirka, Nijole Z. Authoritarianism, ideology, and political candidate choice. *J. Abnorm. Soc. Psychol.*, 1964, **69**, 539–549.

Leventhal, H., Jones, Susan, & Trembly, Grevilda. Sex differences in attitude and behavior change under conditions of fear and specific instructions. *J. Exptl. Soc. Psychol.*, 1966, **2**, 387–399.

Leventhal, H., & Singer, D. L. Cognitive complexity, impression formation and impression change. *J. Pers.*, 1964, **32**, 210–226.

Leventhal, H., Singer, R., & Jones, Susan. Effects of fear and specificity of recommendation upon attitudes and behavior. *J. Pers. Soc. Psychol.*, 1965, **2**, 20–29.

Levitt, E. E. *The psychology of anxiety*. Indianapolis: Bobbs-Merrill, 1967.

Levy, L. H. *Psychological interpretation*. New York: Holt, Rinehart & Winston, 1963.

Lewinsohn, P. M., Nichols, R. C., Pulos, L., Lomont, J. F., Nickel, H. J., & Siskind, G. The reliability and validity of quantified judgments from psychological tests. *J. Clin. Psychol.*, 1963, **19**, 64–73.

Liebert, R. M., & Allen, Mary Kathleen. The effects of rule structure and reward magnitude on the acquisition and adoption of self-reward criteria. *Psychol. Rep.*, 1967, **21**, 445–452.

Lindemann, J. E., Fairweather, G. W., Stone, G. B., & Smith, R. S. The use of demographic characteristics in predicting length of neuropsychiatric hospital stay. *J. Consult. Psychol.*, 1959, **23**, 85–89.

Lindsley, O. R. Operant conditioning methods applied to research in chronic schizophrenia. *Psychiat. Res. Rep.*, 1956, **5**, 118–139.

Lindsley, O. R. Operant conditioning methods in diagnosis. In J. H. Nodine & J. H. Moyer (Eds.), *First Hahnemann symposium: Psychosomatic medicine*. Philadelphia: Lea & Febiger, 1962. Pp. 41–54.

Lindzey, G. Seer versus sign. *J. Exptl. Res. Pers.*, 1965, **1**, 17–26.

Lindzey, G., & Tejessy, Charlotte. Thematic Apperception Test: Indices of aggression in relation to measures of overt and covert behavior. *Am. J. Orthopsychiat.*, 1956, **26**, 567–576.

Linton, Harriet B. Dependence on external influence: Correlates in perception, attitudes, and judgment. *J. Abnorm. Soc. Psychol.*, 1955, **51**, 502–507.

Little, K. B., & Shneidman, E. S. Congruencies among interpretations of psychological test and anamnestic data. *Psychol. Monogr.*, 1959, **73** (Whole No. 476).

Loehlin, J. C. Word meanings and self-descriptions. *J. Abnorm. Soc. Psychol.*, 1961, **62**, 28–34.

Loehlin, J. C. Word meanings and self-descriptions: A replication and extension. *J. Pers. Soc. Psychol.*, 1967, **5**, 107–110.

Loevinger, Jane. Objective tests as instruments of psychological theory. *Psychol. Rep. Monogr.*, 1957, No. 9.

Lorei, T. W. Prediction of length of stay out of the hospital for released psychiatric patients. *J. Consult. Psychol.*, 1964, **28**, 358–363.

Lorei, T. W. Prediction of community stay and employment for released psychiatric patients. *J. Consult. Psychol.*, 1967, **31**, 349–357.

Lorr, M., Bishop, Patricia F., & McNair, D. M. Interpersonal types among psychiatric patients. *J. Abnorm. Psychol.*, 1965, **70**, 468–472.

Lorr, M., & McNair, D. M. An interpersonal behavior circle. *J. Abnorm. Soc. Psychol.*, 1963, **67**, 68–75.

Lorr, M., & McNair, D. M. Expansion of the interpersonal behavior circle. *J. Pers. Soc. Psychol.*, 1965, **2**, 823–830.

Lovaas, O. I. Interaction between verbal and nonverbal behavior. *Child Develpm.*, 1961, **32**, 329–336.

Lovaas, O. I. Control of food intake in children by reinforcement of relevant verbal behavior. *J. Abnorm. Soc. Psychol.*, 1964, **68**, 672–678. (a)

Lovaas, O. I. Cue properties of words: The control of operant responding by rate and content of verbal operants. *Child Develpm.*, 1964, **35**, 245–256. (b)

Lovaas, O. I., Berberich, J. P., Perloff, B. F., & Schaeffer, B. Acquisition of imitative speech by schizophrenic children. *Science*, 1966, **151**, 705–707.

Lovaas, O. I., Freitag, G., Gold, Vivian J., & Kassorla, Irene C. Experimental studies in childhood schizophrenia: I. Analysis of self-destructive behavior. *J. Exptl. Child Psychol.*, 1965, **2**, 67–84. (a)

Lovaas, O. I., Freitag, G., Gold, Vivian J., & Kassorla, Irene C. Recording apparatus for observation of behaviors of children in free play settings. *J. Exptl. Child Psychol.*, 1965, **2**, 108–120. (b)

Lovibond, S. H. Personality and conditioning. In B. A. Maher (Ed.), *Progress in experimental personality research.* Vol. 1. New York: Academic Press, 1964. Pp. 115–168.

Luft, J. Differences in prediction based on hearing versus reading verbatim clinical interviews. *J. Consult. Psychol.*, 1951, **15**, 115–119.

Luria, A. R. *The role of speech in the regulation of normal and abnormal behavior.* (Ed. by J. Tizard.) New York: Pergamon Press, 1961.

MacFarlane, Jean W., & Tuddenham, R. D. Problems in the validation of projective techniques. In H. H. Anderson & Gladys L. Anderson (Eds.), *Projective techniques.* Englewood Cliffs, N. J.: Prentice-Hall, 1951. Pp. 26–54.

MacKinnon, D. W. Violation of prohibitions. In H. A. Murray, *Explorations in personality.* New York: Oxford University Press, 1938. Pp. 491–501.

MacKinnon, D. W. What do we mean by talent and how do we test for it? In *The search for talent.* New York: College Entrance Examination Board, 1960. Pp. 20–29.

MacLeod, R. B. The phenomenological approach to social psychology. In R. Tagiuri & L. Petrullo (Eds.), *Person perception and interpersonal behavior.* Stanford: Stanford University Press, 1958. Pp. 33–53.

Maher, B. A. Personality, problem solving, and the Einstellung effect. *J. Abnorm. Soc. Psychol.*, 1957, **54**, 70–74.

Mandler, G. Comments on Professor Russell's paper. In C. N. Cofer (Ed.), *Verbal learning and verbal behavior.* New York: McGraw-Hill, 1961. Pp. 123–128.

Mandler, G. Organization and memory. In K. W. Spence & Janet T. Spence (Eds.), *The psychology of learning and motivation: Advances in research and theory.* New York: Academic Press, 1968, in press.

Mann, R. D. A review of the relationships between personality and performance in small groups. *Psychol. Bull.*, 1959, **56**, 241–270.

REFERENCES

Marks, J., Stauffacher, J. C., & Lyle, C.   Predicting outcome in schizophrenia. *J. Abnorm. Soc. Psychol.*, 1963, **66**, 117–127.

Marks, P. A.   An assessment of the diagnostic process in a child guidance setting. *Psychol. Monogr.*, 1961, **75** (Whole No. 507).

Marks, P. A., & Seeman, W.   *Actuarial description of abnormal personality.* Baltimore: Williams & Wilkins, 1963.

Marlowe, D., & Crowne, D. P.   Social desirability and response to perceived situational demands. *J. Consult. Psychol.*, 1961, **25**, 109–115.

Marston, A. R.   Imitation, self-reinforcement and reinforcement of another person. *J. Pers. Soc. Psychol.*, 1965, **2**, 255–261.

Martin, B.   The assessment of anxiety by physiological behavioral measures. *Psychol. Bull.*, 1961, **58**, 234–255.

Masling, J.   The influence of situational and interpersonal variables in projective testing. *Psychol. Bull.*, 1960, **57**, 65–85.

Masserman, J. H., & Carmichael, H. T.   Diagnosis and prognosis in psychiatry: With a follow-up study of the results of short-term general hospital therapy of psychiatric cases. *J. Ment. Sci.*, 1938, **84**, 893–946.

Matarazzo, J. D.   The interview. In B. B. Wolman (Ed.), *Handbook of clinical psychology.* New York: McGraw-Hill, 1965. Pp. 403–450.

Mayo, Clara W., & Crockett, W. H.   Cognitive complexity and primacy-recency effects in impression formation. *J. Abnorm. Soc. Psychol.*, 1964, **69**, 98–101.

McArthur, C., & Stevens, Lucia Beth.   The validation of expressed interests as compared with inventoried interests: A fourteen-year follow-up. *J. Appl. Psychol.*, 1955, **39**, 184–189.

McClelland, D. C.   Longitudinal trends in the relation of thought to action. *J. Consult. Psychol.*, 1966, **30**, 479–483.

McClelland, D. C., Atkinson, J. W., Clark, R. A., & Lowell, E. L.   *The achievement motive.* New York: Appleton-Century-Crofts, 1953.

McGee, R. K.   Response style as a personality variable: By what criterion? *Psychol. Bull.*, 1962, **59**, 284–295.

McGuire, W. J.   Cognitive consistency and attitude change. *J. Abnorm. Soc. Psychol.*, 1960, **60**, 345–353.

McGuire, W. J.   Personality and susceptibility to social influence. In E. F. Borgatta & W. W. Lambert (Eds.), *Handbook of personality theory and research.* Chicago: Rand McNally, 1968, in press.

McNair, D. M., & Lorr, M.   Differential typing of psychiatric outpatients. *Psychol. Rec.*, 1965, **15**, 33–41.

McNemar, Q.   Lost: Our intelligence. Why? *Am. Psychol.*, 1964, **19**, 871–882.

Mednick, S. A., & Shaffer, J. B.   Mothers' retrospective reports in child-rearing research. *Am. J. Orthopsychiat.*, 1963, **33**, 457–461.

Meehl, P. E.   *Clinical versus statistical prediction.* Minneapolis: University of Minnesota Press, 1954.

Meehl, P. E., Wanted—A good cookbook. *Am. Psychol.*, 1956, 11, 263–272.

Meehl, P. E. The cognitive activity of the clinician. *Am. Psychol.*, 1960, 15, 19–27.

Meehl, P. E. Seer over sign: The first good example. *J. Exptl. Res. Pers.*, 1965, 1, 27–32.

Meehl, P. E., & Rosen, A. Antecedent probability and the efficiency of psychometric signs, patterns, or cutting scores. *Psychol. Bull.*, 1955, 52, 194–216.

Meeland, T. An investigation of hypotheses for distinguishing personality factors A, F, and H. Unpublished doctoral dissertation, University of Illinois, 1952.

Melei, Janet P., & Hilgard, E. R. Attitudes toward hypnosis, self-predictions, and hypnotic susceptibility. *Int. J. Clin. Exp. Hyp.*, 1964, 12, 99–108.

Messick, S., & Jackson, D. N. Acquiescence and the factorial interpretation of the MMPI. *Psychol. Bull.*, 1961, 58, 299–304.

Metcalfe, M. Demonstration of a psychosomatic relationship. *Brit. J. Med. Psychol.*, 1956, 29, 63–66.

Metzner, R. Learning theory and the therapy of neurosis. *Brit. J. Psychol. Monogr. Suppl.*, 1961 (No. 33).

Meyerowitz, J. H. Self-derogations in young retardates and special class placement. *Child Develpm.*, 1962, 33, 443-451.

Michotte, A. *La perception de la causalite.* (2nd ed.) Louvain: Publications universitaires de Louvain, 1954.

Miller, G. A. The magical number seven, plus or minus two: Some limits on our capacity for processing information. *Psychol. Rev.*, 1956, 63, 81–97.

Miller, G. A. Some preliminaries to psycholinguistics. *Am. Psychol.*, 1965, 20, 15–20.

Miller, J. G. Future impact of psychological theory on personality assessments. In B. M. Bass & I. A. Berg (Eds.), *Objective approaches to personality assessment.* Princeton, N. J.: Van Nostrand, 1958. Pp. 204–216.

Mischel, T. Personal constructs, rules, and the logic of clinical activity. *Psychol. Rev.*, 1964, 71, 180–192.

Mischel, W. The effect of the commitment situation on the generalization of expectancies. *J. Pers.*, 1958, 26, 508–516. (a)

Mischel, W. Preference for delayed reinforcement: An experimental study of a cultural observation. *J. Abnorm. Soc. Psychol.*, 1958, 56, 57–61. (b)

Mischel, W. Preference for delayed reinforcement and social responsibility. *J. Abnorm. Soc. Psychol.*, 1961, 62, 1–7. (a)

Mischel, W. Delay of gratification, need for achievement, and acquiescence in another culture. *J. Abnorm. Soc. Psychol.*, 1961, 62, 543–552. (b)

Mischel, W. Father absence and delay of gratification: Cross-cultural comparisons. *J. Abnorm. Soc. Psychol.*, 1961, 63, 116–124. (c)

REFERENCES

Mischel, W. Delay of gratification in choice situations. NIMH Progress Report, Stanford University, 1962.

Mischel, W. Predicting the success of Peace Corps Volunteers in Nigeria. *J. Pers. Soc. Psychol.*, 1965, **1**, 510–517.

Mischel, W. A social learning view of sex differences in behavior. In Eleanor E. Maccoby (Ed.), *The development of sex differences.* Stanford: Stanford University Press, 1966. Pp. 56–81. (a)

Mischel, W. Theory and research on the antecedents of self-imposed delay of reward. In B. A. Maher (Ed.), *Progress in experimental personality research.* Vol. 3. New York: Academic Press, 1966. Pp. 85–132. (b)

Mischel, W., & Bentler, P. The ability of persons to predict their own behavior. Unpublished manuscript, Stanford University, 1965.

Mischel, W., Coates, B., & Raskoff, Antonette. Effects of success and failure on noncontingent self-indulgence. Unpublished manuscript, Stanford University, 1967.

Mischel, W., & Gilligan, Carol. Delay of gratification, motivation for the prohibited gratification, and responses to temptation. *J. Abnorm. Soc. Psychol.*, 1964, **69**, 411–417.

Mischel, W., & Grusec, Joan. Determinants of the rehearsal and transmission of neutral and aversive behaviors. *J. Pers. Soc. Psychol.*, 1966, **3**, 197–205.

Mischel, W., & Grusec, Joan. Waiting for rewards and punishments: Effects of time and probability on choice. *J. Pers. Soc. Psychol.*, 1967, **5**, 24–31.

Mischel, W., & Liebert, R. M. Effects of discrepancies between observed and imposed reward criteria on their acquisition and transmission. *J. Pers. Soc. Psychol.*, 1966, **3**, 45–53.

Mischel, W., & Liebert, R. M. The role of power in the adoption of self-reward patterns. *Child Develpm.*, 1967, **38**, 673–683.

Mischel, W., & Masters, J. C. Effects of probability of reward attainment on responses to frustration. *J. Pers. Soc. Psychol.*, 1966, **3**, 390–396.

Mischel, W., & Metzner, R. Preference for delayed reward as a function of age, intelligence, and length of delay interval. *J. Abnorm. Soc. Psychol.*, 1962, **64**, 425–431.

Mischel, W., & Mischel, Frances. Psychological aspects of spirit possession. *Am. Anthropol.*, 1958, **60**, 249–260.

Mischel, W., & Schopler, J. Authoritarianism and reactions to "sputniks." *J. Abnorm. Soc. Psychol.*, 1959, **59**, 142–145.

Mischel, W., & Staub, E. Effects of expectancy on working and waiting for larger rewards. *J. Pers. Soc. Psychol.*, 1965, **2**, 625–633.

Moore, A. U., & Marcuse, F. L. Salivary, cardiac and motor indices of conditioning in two sows. *J. Comp. Psychol.*, 1945, **38**, 1–16.

Morgan, H. H. Measuring achievement motivation with "picture interpretations." *J. Consult. Psychol.*, 1953, **17**, 289–292.

Morse, W. H., & Kelleher, R. T.   Schedules using noxious stimuli. I. Multiple fixed-ratio and fixed-interval termination of schedule complexes. *J. Exp. Anal. Behav.*, 1966, **9**, 267–290.

Moss, H. A., & Kagan, J.   Stability of achievement and recognition seeking behaviors from early childhood through adulthood. *J. Abnorm. Soc. Psychol.*, 1961, **62**, 504–518.

Mowrer, O. H.   *Learning theory and behavior.* New York: Wiley, 1960.

Mulaik, S. A.   Are personality factors raters' conceptual factors? *J. Consult. Psychol.*, 1964, **28**, 506–511.

Murstein, B. I.   *Theory and research in projective techniques.* New York: Wiley, 1963.

Mussen, P.   Some antecedents and consequents of masculine sex-typing in adolescent boys. *Psychol. Monogr.*, 1961, **75** (Whole No. 506).

Mussen, P. H., & Scodel, A.   The effects of sexual stimulation under varying conditions on TAT sexual responsiveness. *J. Consult. Psychol.*, 1955, **19**, 90.

Norman, W. T.   Development of self-report tests to measure personality factors identified from peer nominations. *USAF ASK Tech. Note*, 1961, No. 61-44.

Norman, W. T.   Toward an adequate taxonomy of personality attributes: Replicated factor structures in peer nomination personality ratings. *J. Abnorm. Soc. Psychol.*, 1963, **66**, 574–583.

Norman, W. T.   Convergent and discriminant validation of personality factor measurement. Unpublished manuscript, University of Michigan, 1966.

Norman, W. T.   On estimating psychological relationships: Social desirability and self-report. *Psychol. Bull.*, 1967, **67**, 273–293.

Odom, C. L.   A study of the time required to do a Rorschach examination. *J. Proj. Tech.*, 1950, **14**, 464–468.

Office of Strategic Services Staff.   *Assessment of men.* New York: Rinehart, 1948.

Osgood, C. E.   *Method and theory in experimental psychology.* New York: Oxford University Press, 1953.

Osgood, C. E., Suci, G. J., & Tannenbaum, P. H.   *The measurement of meaning.* Urbana: University of Illinois Press, 1957.

Oskamp, S.   The relationship of clinical experience and training methods to several criteria of clinical prediction. *Psychol. Monogr.*, 1962, **76** (Whole No. 547).

Oskamp, S.   Overconfidence in case-study judgments. *J. Consult. Psychol.*, 1965, **29**, 261–265.

Overall, J. E.   Note on the scientific status of factors. *Psychol. Bull.*, 1964, **61**, 270–276.

Parker, C. A.   As a clinician thinks. . . . *J. Counsel. Psychol.*, 1958, **5**, 253–261.

REFERENCES

Pascal, G. R., & Jenkins, W. O. *Systematic observation of gross human behavior.* New York: Grune & Stratton, 1961.

Passini, F. T., & Norman, W. T. A universal conception of personality structure? *J. Pers. Soc. Psychol.*, 1966, **4**, 44–49.

Patterson, C. H. Is psychotherapy dependent upon diagnosis? *Am. Psychol.*, 1948, **3**, 155–159.

Patterson, G. R., & Anderson, D. Peers as social reinforcers. *Child Develpm.*, 1964, **35**, 951–960.

Patterson, G. R., & Hinsey, W. C. Investigations of some assumptions and characteristics of a procedure for instrumental conditioning in children. *J. Exptl. Child Psychol.*, 1964, **1**, 111–122.

Patterson, G. R., Littman, R. E., & Hinsey, W. C. Parental effectiveness as reinforcers in the laboratory and its relation to child rearing practices and child adjustment in the classroom. *J. Pers.*, 1964, **32**, 180–199.

Paul, G. L. *Insight vs. desensitization in psychotherapy.* Stanford: Stanford University Press, 1966.

Paul, G. L. Insight versus desensitization in psychotherapy two years after termination. *J. Consult. Psychol.*, 1967, **31**, 333–348.

Paul, G. L., & Shannon, D. T. Treatment of anxiety through systematic desensitization in therapy groups. *J. Abnorm. Psychol.*, 1966, **71**, 124–135.

Pedersen, F. A. Consistency data on the role construct repertory test. Unpublished manuscript, Ohio State University, 1958.

Pervin, L. A. Rigidity in neurosis and general personality functioning. *J. Abnorm. Soc. Psychol.*, 1960, **61**, 389–395.

Peters, H. N., & Jenkins, R. L. Improvement of chronic schizophrenic patients with guided problem-solving, motivated by hunger. *Psychiat. Quart. Suppl.*, 1954, **28**, 84–101.

Peterson, D. R. Scope and generality of verbally defined personality factors. *Psychol. Rev.*, 1965, **72**, 48–59.

Phillips, L., & Rabinovitch, M. S. Social role and patterns of symptomatic behaviors. *J. Abnorm. Soc. Psychol.*, 1958, **57**, 181–186.

Piaget, J. *Play, dreams, and imitation in childhood.* New York: Norton, 1951.

Postman, L., & Sassenrath, J. The automatic action of verbal rewards and punishments. *J. Gen. Psychol.*, 1961, **65**, 109–136.

Premack, D. Reinforcement theory. In D. Levine (Ed.), *Nebraska symposium on motivation.* Lincoln: University of Nebraska Press, 1965. Pp. 123–180.

Pyles, M. K., Stolz, H. R., & MacFarlane, Jean W. The accuracy of mothers' reports on birth and developmental data. *Child Develpm.*, 1935, **6**, 165–176.

Rachman, S. Systematic desensitization. *Psychol. Bull.*, 1967, **67**, 93–103.

Raphelson, A. C. The relationships among imaginative, direct verbal, and physiological measures of anxiety in an achievement situation. *J. Abnorm. Soc. Psychol.*, 1957, **54**, 13–18.

329

Raymond, M. J. Case of fetishism treated by aversion therapy. *Brit. Med. J.*, 1956, **2**, 854–857.

Razran, G. H. S. Conditioned response changes in rating and appraising sociopolitical slogans. *Psychol. Bull.*, 1940, **37**, 481.

Robbins, Lillian C. The accuracy of parental recall of aspects of child development and of child rearing practices. *J. Abnorm. Soc. Psychol.*, 1963, **66**, 261–270.

Rogers, L. S. An adult neurotic. In A. Burton & R. E. Harris (Eds.), *Clinical studies of personality*. Vol. 2. New York: Harper, 1955.

Rorer, L. G. The great response-style myth. *Psychol. Bull.*, 1965, **63**, 129–156.

Rosenberg, S., & Cohen, B. D. Referential processes of speakers and listeners. *Psychol. Rev.*, 1966, **73**, 208–231.

Rosenkrantz, P. S., & Crockett, W. H. Some factors influencing the assimilation of disparate information in impression formation. *J. Pers. Soc. Psychol.*, 1965, **2**, 397–402.

Rosenstein, A. J. Psychometric versus physiological anxiety and serial learning. *J. Pers.*, 1960, **28**, 279–292.

Rosenthal, D. Changes in some moral values following psychotherapy. *J. Consult. Psychol.*, 1955, **19**, 431–436.

Rosenthal, R. On the social psychology of the psychological experiment: The experimenter's hypothesis as unintended determinant of experimental results. *Am. Scient.*, 1963, **51**, 268–283.

Rosenzweig, S. A transvaluation of psychotherapy: A reply to Hans Eysenck. *J. Abnorm. Soc. Psychol.*, 1954, **49**, 298–304.

Rotter, J. B. *Social learning and clinical psychology*. Englewood Cliffs, N. J.: Prentice-Hall, 1954.

Rotter, J. B. Some implications of a social learning theory for the prediction of goal directed behavior from testing procedures. *Psychol. Rev.*, 1960, **67**, 301–316.

Rubin, M., & Shontz, F. C. Diagnostic prototypes and diagnostic processes of clinical psychologists. *J. Consult. Psychol.*, 1960, **24**, 234–239.

Ruebush, B. K. Anxiety. In H. W. Stevenson et al. (Eds.), *Child psychology*. 62nd Yearbook of the National Society for the Study of Education. Part 1. Chicago: University of Chicago Press, 1963. Pp. 460–516.

Sanders, D. H. Social psychology in the treatment of mental illness: A model approach for treatment of addiction—The effect of group membership on community adjustment. Unpublished paper presented at the Institute on Rehabilitation of the Narcotic Addict, Fort Worth, Texas, 1966.

Sanford, N. Personality: Its place in psychology. In S. Koch (Ed.), *Psychology: A study of a science*. Vol. 5. New York: McGraw-Hill, 1963. Pp. 488–592.

Sarason, I. G. *Personality: An objective approach*. New York: Wiley, 1966.

Sarason, S. B., Davidson, K. S., Lighthall, F. F., Waite, R. R., & Ruebush, B. K. *Anxiety in elementary school children*. New York: Wiley, 1960.

Sarbin, T. R.   Hypnosis as a behavior modification technique. In L. Krasner & L. P. Ullmann (Eds.), *Research in behavior modification*. New York: Holt, Rinehart & Winston, 1966. Pp. 341–357.

Sarbin, T. R., Taft, R., & Bailey, D. E.   *Clinical inference and cognitive theory*. New York: Holt, Rinehart & Winston, 1960.

Saslow, G., Matarazzo, J. D., Phillips, Jeanne S., & Matarazzo, Ruth G.   Test-retest stability of interaction patterns during interviews conducted one week apart. *J. Abnorm. Soc. Psychol.*, 1957, **54**, 295–302.

Schachter, S.   The interaction of cognitive and physiological determinants of emotional state. In L. Berkowitz (Ed.), *Advances in experimental social psychology*. Vol. 1. New York: Academic Press, 1964. Pp. 49–80.

Schachter, S., & Singer, J. E.   Cognitive, social, and physiological determinants of emotional state. *Psychol. Rev.*, 1962, **69**, 379–399.

Schachter, S., & Wheeler, L.   Epinephrine, chlorpromazine, and amusement. *J. Abnorm. Soc. Psychol.*, 1962, **65**, 121–128.

Scheier, I. H., & Cattell, R. B.   Confirmation of objective test factors and assessment of their relation to questionnaire factors: A factor analysis of 113 rating, questionnaire and objective test measurements of personality. *J. Ment. Sci.*, 1958, **104**, 608–624.

Schein, E.   Reaction patterns to severe, chronic stress in American prisoners of war of the Chinese. *J. Soc. Issues*, 1957, **13**, 21–30.

Schmidt, H. O., & Fonda, C. P.   The reliability of psychiatric diagnosis: A new look. *J. Abnorm. Soc. Psychol.*, 1956, **52**, 262–267.

Schubot, E. D.   The influence of hypnotic and muscular relaxation in systematic desensitization of phobias. Unpublished doctoral dissertation, Stanford University, 1966.

Scott, W. A.   Attitude change through reward of verbal behavior.   *J. Abnorm. Soc. Psychol.*, 1957, **55**, 72–75.

Scott, W. A.   Research definitions of mental health and mental illness. *Psychol. Bull.*, 1958, **55**, 29–45. (a)

Scott, W. A.   Social psychological correlates of mental illness and mental health. *Psychol. Bull.*, 1958, **55**, 65–87. (b)

Sears, R. R.   Relation of early socialization experiences to aggression in middle childhood. *J. Abnorm. Soc. Psychol.*, 1961, **63**, 466–492.

Sears, R. R.   Dependency motivation. In M. R. Jones (Ed.), *Nebraska symposium on motivation*. Lincoln: University of Nebraska Press, 1963. Pp. 25–64.

Sears, R. R., Maccoby, Eleanor E., & Levin, H.   *Patterns of child rearing*. Evanston, Ill.: Row, Peterson, 1957.

Sears, R. R., Rau, Lucy, & Alpert, R.   *Identification and child rearing*. Stanford, Calif.: Stanford University Press, 1965.

Sechrest, L., Gallimore, R., & Hersch, P. D.   Feedback and accuracy of clinical predictions. *J. Consult. Psychol.*, 1967, **31**, 1–11.

Sechrest, L. B., & Jackson, D. N.   Social intelligence and accuracy of interpersonal predictions. *J. Pers.*, 1961, **29**, 167–182.

Secord, P. F., & Backman, C. W.   An interpersonal approach to personality. In B. A. Maher (Ed.), *Progress in experimental personality research.* Vol. 2. New York: Academic Press, 1965. Pp. 91–125.

Secord, P. F., & Muthard, J.E.   Personalities in faces: IV. A descriptive analysis of the perception of women's faces and the identification of some physiognomic determinants. *J. Psychol.*, 1955, **39**, 269–278.

Sherwood, J. J.   Self-report and projective measures of achievement and affiliation. *J. Consult. Psychol.*, 1966, **30**, 329–337.

Shippee-Blum, Eva-Marie.   The young rebel: Self-regard and ego-ideal. *J. Consult. Psychol.*, 1959, **23**, 44–50.

Shure, G. H., & Rogers, M. S.   Note of caution on the factor analysis of the MMPI. *Psychol. Bull.*, 1965, **63**, 14–18.

Simpson, R. H.   The specific meanings of certain terms indicating differing degrees of frequency. *Quart. J. Speech*, 1944, **30**, 328–330.

Sines, L. K.   The relative contribution of four kinds of data to accuracy in personality assessment. *J. Consult. Psychol.*, 1959, **23**, 483–492.

Singer, J. L.   Delayed gratification and ego development: Implications for clinical and experimental research. *J. Consult. Psychol.*, 1955, **19**, 259–266.

Skinner, B. F.   *Science and human behavior.* New York: Macmillan, 1953.

Skinner, B. F.   What is psychotic behavior? In *Theory and treatment of the psychoses: Some newer aspects.* St. Louis: Washington University Studies, 1956. Pp. 77–99.

Skinner, B. F.   Pigeons in a pelican. *Am. Psychol.*, 1960, **15**, 28–37.

Skinner, B. F.   Behaviorism at fifty. In T. W. Wann (Ed.), *Behaviorism and phenomenolgy.* Chicago: University of Chicago Press, 1964. Pp. 79–108.

Skinner, B. F.   Operant behavior. In W. K. Honig (Ed.), *Operant behavior: Areas of research and application.* New York: Appleton-Century-Crofts, 1966. Pp. 12–32.

Skolnick, Arlene.   Motivational imagery and behavior over twenty years. *J. Consult. Psychol.*, 1966, **30**, 463–478. (a)

Skolnick, Arlene.   Stability and interrelations of thematic test imagery over 20 years. *Child Develpm.*, 1966, **37**, 389–396. (b)

Soskin, W. F.   Bias in postdiction from projective tests. *J. Abnorm. Soc. Psychol.*, 1954, **49**, 69–74.

Soskin, W. F.   Influence of four types of data on diagnostic conceptualization in psychological testing. *J. Abnorm. Soc. Psychol.*, 1959, **58**, 69–78.

Spence, Janet T.   Effects of verbal reinforcement combinations and instructional condition on performance of a problem-solving task. *J. Pers. Soc. Psychol.*, 1966, **3**, 163–170.

REFERENCES

Spence, K. W., & Spence, Janet T. Relation of eyelid conditioning to manifest anxiety, extraversion, and rigidity. *J. Abnorm. Soc. Psychol.*, 1964, **68**, 144–149.

Spielberger, C. D., & DeNike, L. D. Descriptive behaviorism versus cognitive theory in verbal operant conditioning. *Psychol. Rev.*, 1966, **73**, 306–326.

Staats, A. W. A case in and a strategy for the extension of learning principles to problems of human behavior. In L. Krasner & L. P. Ullmann (Eds.), *Research in behavior modification.* New York: Holt, Rinehart & Winston, 1965. Pp. 27–55.

Staats, A. W., & Butterfield, W. H. Treatment of nonreading in a culturally deprived juvenile delinquent: An application of reinforcement principles. *Child Develpm.*, 1965, **36**, 925–942.

Staats, A. W., Finley, J. R., Minke, K. A., & Wolf, M. M. Reinforcement variables in the control of unit reading responses. *J. Exp. Anal. Behav.*, 1964, **7**, 139–149.

Staats, A. W., Minke, K. A., Finley, J. R., Wolf, M. M., & Brooks, L. O. A reinforcer system and experimental procedure for the laboratory study of reading acquisition. *Child Develpm.*, 1964, **35**, 209–231.

Staats, A. W., & Staats, Carolyn, K. Attitudes established by classical conditioning. *J. Abnorm. Soc. Psychol.*, 1958, **57**, 37–40.

Staats, A. W., & Staats, Carolyn K. *Complex human behavior.* New York: Holt, Rinehart & Winston, 1963.

Staats, A. W., Staats, Carolyn K., Schutz, R. E., & Wolf, M. M. The conditioning of textual responses using "extrinsic" reinforcers. *J. Exp. Anal. Behav.*, 1962, **5**, 33–40.

Staats, Carolyn K., & Staats, A. W. Meaning established by classical conditioning. *J. Exptl. Psychol.*, 1957, **54**, 74–80.

Staub, E. The effects of persuasion, modeling, and related influence procedures on delay of reward choices and attitudes. Unpublished doctoral dissertation, Stanford University, 1965.

Stelmachers, Z. T., & McHugh, R. B. Contribution of stereotyped and individualized information to predictive accuracy. *J. Consult. Psychol.*, 1964, **28**, 234–242.

Sundberg, N. D., & Tyler, Leona E. *Clinical psychology.* New York: Appleton-Century-Crofts, 1962.

Szasz, T. S. The myth of mental illness. *Am. Psychol.*, 1960, **15**, 113–118.

Szasz, T. S. *The myth of mental illness.* New York: Hoeber-Harper, 1961.

Taft, R. The ability to judge people. *Psychol. Bull.*, 1955, **52**, 1–23.

Tagiuri, R. Introduction. In R. Tagiuri & L. Petrullo (Eds.), *Person perception and interpersonal behavior.* Stanford: Stanford University Press, 1958. Pp. ix–xvii.

Tagiuri, R., & Petrullo, L. (Eds.). *Person perception and interpersonal behavior.* Stanford: Stanford University Press, 1958.

Taylor, S. P., & Epstein, S. Aggression as a function of the interaction of the sex of the aggressor and the sex of the victim. *J. Pers.*, 1967, **35**, 474–486.

Technical recommendations for psychological tests and diagnostic techniques. *Psychol. Bull. Suppl.*, 1954, **51**, Part 2, 1–38.

Thorndike, R. L., & Hagen, Elizabeth. *10,000 careers.* New York: Wiley, 1959.

Thornton, G. R. The effect of wearing glasses upon judgments of personality traits of persons seen briefly. *J. Appl. Psychol.*, 1944, **28**, 203–207.

Titus, H. E., & Hollander, E. P. The California *F* scale in psychological research: 1950–1955. *Psychol. Bull.*, 1957, **54**, 47–64.

Truax, C. B., & Carkhuff, R. R. Experimental manipulation of therapeutic conditions. *J. Consult. Psychol.*, 1965, **29**, 119–124. (a)

Truax, C. B., & Carkhuff, R. R. Client and therapist transparency in the psychotherapeutic encounter. *J. Counsel. Psychol.*, 1965, **12**, 3–9. (b)

Tupes, E. C., & Christal, R. E. Stability of personality trait rating factors obtained under diverse conditions. *USAF WADC Tech. Note*, 1958, No. 58-61.

Tupes, E. C., & Christal, R. E. Recurrent personality factors based on trait ratings. *USAF ASD Tech. Rep.*, 1961, No. 61–97.

Ullmann, L. P., Krasner, L., & Collins, Beverly J. Modification of behavior through verbal conditioning: Effects in group therapy. *J. Abnorm. Soc. Psychol.*, 1961, **62**, 128–132.

Ulrich, R. E., Stachnick, T. J., & Stainton, S. R. Student acceptance of generalized personality interpretations. *Psychol. Rep.*, 1963, **13**, 831–834.

Valins, S. Cognitive effects of false heart-rate feedback. *J. Pers. Soc. Psychol.*, 1966, **4**, 400–408.

Vannoy, J. S. Generality of cognitive complexity-simplicity as a personality construct. *J. Pers. Soc. Psychol.*, 1965, **2**, 385–396.

Vaughan, G. M. The trans-situational aspect of conforming behavior. *J. Pers.*, 1964, **32**, 335–354.

Vernon, P. E. *Personality assessment: A critical survey.* New York: Wiley, 1964.

Vernon, P. E. Ability factors and environmental influences. *Am. Psychol.*, 1965, **20**, 723–733.

Wahler, R. G., Winkel, G. H., Peterson, R. F., & Morrison, D. C. Mothers as behavior therapists for their own children. *Behav. Res. Ther.*, 1965, **3**, 113–124.

Wallace, J., & Sechrest, L. Frequency hypothesis and content analysis of projective techniques. *J. Consult. Psychol.*, 1963, **27**, 387–393.

Wallach, M. A. On psychological similarity. *Psychol. Rev.*, 1958, **65**, 103–116.

Wallach, M. A. Commentary: Active-analytical vs. passive-global cognitive functioning. In S. Messick & J. Ross (Eds.), *Measurement in personality and cognition.* New York: Wiley, 1962. Pp. 199–215.

Wallach, M. A., & Kogan, N. *Modes of thinking in young children.* New York: Holt, Rinehart & Winston, 1965.

Wallen, R. W. *Clinical psychology: The study of persons.* New York: Mc-Graw-Hill, 1956.

Walters, R. H., & Kosowski, Irene. Symbolic learning and reading retardation. *J. Consult. Psychol.,* 1963, **27,** 75–82.

Walters, R. H., & Ray, E. Anxiety, socialization, and reinforcer effectiveness. *J. Pers.,* 1960, **28,** 358–367.

Walton, D., & Mather, M. D. The relevance of generalization techniques to the treatment of stammering and phobic symptoms. *Behav. Res. Ther.,* 1963, **1,** 121–125.

Watley, D. J., & Vance, F. L. Clinical versus actuarial prediction of college achievement and leadership activity. *U. S. Off. of Educ. Coop. Res. Proj. No. 2202.* Minneapolis: University of Minnesota, 1964.

Watson, J. B., & Rayner, Rosalie. Conditioned emotional reactions. *J. Exptl. Psychol.,* 1920, **3,** 1–14.

Watson, R. I. Historical review of objective personality testing: The search for objectivity. In B. M. Bass & I. A. Berg (Eds.), *Objective approaches to personality assessment.* Princeton, N. J.: Van Nostrand, 1959. Pp. 1–23.

Webb, E. J., Campbell, D. T., Schwartz, R. D., & Sechrest, L. *Unobtrusive measures: Non-reactive research in the social sciences.* Chicago: Rand McNally, 1966.

Weir, M. W. Development changes in problem-solving strategies. *Psychol. Rev.,* 1964, **71,** 473–490. (a)

Weir, M. W. Effect of patterned partial reinforcement on children's performance in a two-choice task. *Child Develpm.,* 1964, **35,** 257–264 (b)

Weir, M. W. Children's behavior in a two-choice task as a function of patterned reinforcement following forced-choice trials. *J. Exptl. Child Psychol.,* 1965, **2,** 85–91.

Wenar, C. The reliability of mothers' histories. *Child Develpm.,* 1961, **32,** 491–500.

Wenar, C., & Coulter, Jane B. A reliability study of developmental histories. *Child Develpm.,* 1962, **33,** 453–462.

White, R. W. *The abnormal personality.* New York: Ronald Press, 1964.

Whiting, J. W. M. Sorcery, sin, and the superego. A cross-cultural study of some mechanisms of social control. In M. R. Jones (Ed.), *Nebraska symposium on motivation.* Lincoln: University of Nebraska Press, 1959. Pp. 174–195.

Wickes, T. A., Jr. Examiner influence in a testing situation. *J. Consult. Psychol.,* 1956, **20,** 23–26.

Wiener, M., Carpenter, Janeth T., & Carpenter, B. External validation of a measure of conformity behavior. *J. Abnorm. Soc. Psychol.*, 1956, **52**, 421–422.

Wiener, M., Carpenter, Janeth T., & Carpenter, B. Some determinants of conformity behavior. *J. Soc. Psychol.*, 1957, **45**, 289–297.

Wiggins, J. S. Strategic, method, and stylistic variance in the MMPI. *Psychol. Bull.*, 1962, **59**, 224–242.

Wiggins, J. S. Substantive dimensions of self-report in the MMPI item pool. *Psychol. Monogr.*, 1966, **80** (Whole No. 22).

Winder, C. L., & Wiggins, J. S. Social reputation and social behavior: A further validation of the peer nomination inventory. *J. Abnorm. Soc. Psychol.*, 1964, **68**, 681–684.

Wishner, J. Reanalysis of "impressions of personality." *Psychol. Rev.*, 1960, **67**, 96–112.

Witkin, H. A. Psychological differentiation and forms of pathology. *J. Abnorm. Psychol.*, 1965, **70**, 317–336.

Witkin, H. A., Dyk, Ruth B., Faterson, Hanna F., Goodenough, D. R., & Karp, S. A. *Psychological differentiation.* New York: Wiley, 1962.

Witkin, H. A., Goodenough, D. R., & Karp, S. A. Stability of cognitive style from childhood to young adulthood. *J. Pers. Soc. Psychol.*, 1967, **7**, 291–300.

Witkin, H. A., Lewis, Helen B., Hertzman, M., Machover, Karen, Meissner, Pearl B., & Wapner, S. *Personality through perception, an experimental and clinical study.* New York: Harper, 1954.

Wittenborn, J. R. The dimensions of psychosis. *J. Nerv. Ment. Dis.*, 1962, **134**, 117–128.

Wittenborn, J., Holzberg, J., & Simon, B. Symptom correlates for descriptive diagnosis. *Genet. Psychol. Monogr.*, 1953, **47**, 237–301.

Wolf, R. The measurement of environments. In Anne Anastasi (Ed.), *Testing problems in perspective.* Washington, D. C.: American Council on Education, 1966. Pp. 491–503.

Wolpe, J. *Psychotherapy by reciprocal inhibition.* Stanford: Stanford University Press, 1958.

Wolpe, J. The systematic desensitization treatment of neuroses. *J. Nerv. Ment. Dis.*, 1961, **132**, 189–203.

Wolpe, J. Psychotherapy: The nonscientific heritage and the new science. *Behav. Res. Ther.*, 1963, **1**, 23–28.

Wolpe, J., & Lang, P. J. A fear survey schedule for use in behaviour therapy. *Behav. Res. Ther.*, 1964, **2**, 27–30.

Wolpe, J., & Lazarus, A. A. *Behavior therapy techniques: A guide to the treatment of neuroses.* Oxford: Pergamon Press, 1966.

REFERENCES

Wrightsman, L. S., Jr., & Baumeister, A. A. A comparison of actual and paper-and-pencil versions of the Water Jar Test of Rigidity. *J. Abnorm. Soc. Psychol.*, 1961, **63**, 191–193.

Wyatt, D. F., & Campbell, D. T. On the liability of stereotype or hypothesis. *J. Abnorm. Soc. Psychol.*, 1951, **46**, 496–500.

Wynne, L. C., & Solomon, R. L. Traumatic avoidance learning: Acquisition and extinction in dogs deprived of normal peripheral autonomic function. *Genet. Psychol. Monogr.*, 1955, **52**, 241–284.

Zajonc, R. B. The process of cognitive tuning in communication. *J. Abnorm. Soc. Psychol.*, 1960, **61**, 159–167.

Zigler, E., & Phillips, L. Social effectiveness and symptomatic behaviors. *J. Abnorm. Soc. Psychol.*, 1960, **61**, 231–238.

Zigler, E., & Phillips, L. Case history data and psychiatric diagnosis. *J. Consult. Psychol.*, 1961, **25**, 458. (a)

Zigler, E., & Phillips, L. Psychiatric diagnosis: A critique. *J. Abnorm. Soc. Psychol.*, 1961, **63**, 607–618. (b)

Zigler, E., & Phillips, L. Psychiatric diagnosis and symptomatology. *J. Abnorm. Soc. Psychol.*, 1961, **63**, 69–75. (c)

Zigler, E., & Phillips, L. Social competence and outcome in psychiatric disorder. *J. Abnorm. Soc. Psychol.*, 1961, **63**, 264–271. (d)

Zigler, E., & Phillips, L. Social competence and the process-reactive distinction in psychopathology. *J. Abnorm. Soc. Psychol.*, 1962, **65**, 215–222.

Zubin, J., Eron, L. D., & Schumer, Florence. *An experimental approach to projective techniques.* New York: Wiley, 1965.

AUTHOR INDEX

SUBJECT INDEX

Ability:
  academic, 15—16
    specificity of predictions from, 16
  and achievement, 14—16
  see also Intelligence
Abnormal behavior:
  acquisition of, 200—201
  client's definition of, 199, 235
  as deficits in behavior, 200, 223, 255
  definition of, 194, 198, 217, 235
  determinants of, 188
  discrimination learning in, 202
  disease approach to, 194—197
  self-evaluations of, 229—230
  as symptoms, 262
  see also Assessment, Social behavior
    therapy, Treatment
Achievement behavior:
  consistency of, 14—16
  stability of, 33—34
  see also Intelligence
Achievement motivation, 100
Acquisition (of behavior) :
  of abnormal behavior, 200—201
  and awareness, 271
  of constructs, 227—229
  without direct reinforcement, 150—161,
    225
  and generalization or discrimination,
    172—173
  in graded learning sequences, 254—261
  without overt response, 150

Acquisition (*cont.*)
  and performance, 159—161
  of self-control, 227—229
  of stereotypes, 151
  of trait labels, 151
Actuarial hierarchies, 261—262
Actuarial learning programs, 261
Actuarial methods:
  clinical dispute over, 133—134
  code types, 132
  example of, 131—132
  incremental utility of, 129—135
  obtaining data for, 135
  and personality description, 129—135
  prediction from, 129—135
  and use of data, 134
    past behavior measures, 135
    self-reports, 135
Adjustment:
  criteria of post-hospital, 276
  predicted from past behavior, 135—139
  prediction of post-hospital, 289—290
  social judgments of, 198—199
Aggression:
  acquisition versus performance of, 160
  assessment of, 286
  consistency of, 26-28
  effect of sex roles on, 286
  modeling of, 154
  observation of response consequences
    for, 167—168
  reinforcement of, 165

347

Attitude *(cont.)*
    effects of observation of, 168
    self-reports of, 35
    toward authority, 21—23, 47
        determinants of, 188
    toward peers, 22
    see also Cognition
Authoritarianism, correlations with
        intelligence, 88
Authoritarian personality, 28—29
Authority, attitudes toward, 21, 47
Autistic children, treatment of, 223—224
Autonomic responses:
    and awareness of contingencies,
        171—172
    and classical conditioning, 157
    and GSR changes, 211
    relation to self-reports, 246
    see also Physiological measures
Avoidance:
    assessment of, 210, 245—248
    as central nervous system process,
        202—203
    as classically conditioned autonomic
        response, 202—203
    counterconditioning of, 205—214
    development and maintenance of, 202
        through self-selection of stimuli, 297
    and emotional responses, 203—204
    generalization of, 173
    and incompatible responses, 210
    objective scaling of, 248
    operant conditioning therapy for, 214
    self-reports of, 244
        snake fear, 277
    vicarious extinction of, 225
    see also Anxiety, Phobia
Awareness:
    and behavior acquisition, 271
    and classical conditioning, 171—172
    of contingencies, 171

Barnum effect, 128—129
Baseline measures, in assessment,
        162—163, 217
Base rates:
    and clinical judgment, 115—116
    definition of, 106
    expectancy table for parole outcomes,
        135
    and predictive increments, 106

Behavior (s) :
    acquisition of, 150—164, 188—190
    acquisition versus performance of,
        159—161
    in ambiguous situations, 293—294
    and attitudes, 79
    and categories about behavior, 63—68
    and choice among alternatives, 176
    complex chains of, 154, 298
    constructed consistency in, 41—53
    correlations among, 73, 76—83, 95
    defined, 4
    description versus interpretation,
        62—63
        and psychometric tests, 60
        strategies for, 66—67
    dimensions of interpersonal, 46
    direct sampling of, 247—251
    dynamics of, 295—301
    effects of social role on, 285
    generating novel patterns of, 154
    of high frequency as reinforcer, 254
    as idiographic result, 188—190
    incompatible with anxiety, 210
    as instrumental response patterns, 161
    measurement of, 66—67, 236—262
    mental states as explanations of, 95
    modeling of appropriate, 223
    modification of, 214—233
        symbolically, 225—233
        vicariously, 225—233
    multiple contingencies influencing,
        229
    predictions from relevant past,
        135—142, 290—292
    recording device for, 66—67
    referents for, 189
    repertoire of potential, 176, 295
    self-regulations of, 226—229
    and self-reports, 79
    as signs, 5
        and surplus meaning, 42
        symbolic interpretation of, 7—8
    specificity of, 176—188
    stabilities in, 281—288
    and stimulus situations, 177, 296
    transmitted by modeling, 156—157
    and verbal events, 170, 240—246
Behavior change, *see* Modification,
        Social behavior therapy,
        Treatment

Treatment *(cont.)*
of inappropriate positive emotional
reactions, 213—214
integration with research and
assessment, 201
and life environment, 250—251, 278
measuring effects of, 247—248
of mental retardation, 224, 255—256
plans in traditional assessment,
142—145
prediction of effects from past
behavior, 290
of problematic response patterns,
214—233
reinforcers in, 218—220, 251
and response-reinforcement relations,
216
role rehearsals in, 231—232
specificity of changes from, 272—279
and stimulus sampling, 275—276
transfer of effects from, 208, 273—298
vicariously and symbolically, 225—233
see also Modification, Programmed
instruction, Social behavior
treatment

Unconscious, 7—8, 262, 271
see also Awareness
Utility:
of actuarial methods, 129—135, 262
assessment of, 137, 220
of base-rate predictions, 106
of behavior therapy, 206, 218—223
of biographical data, 120, 283
of clinical diagnosis, 123—126
of clinical judgment, 113—116
of combined tests, 120
and construct validity, 93—94
and costs of alternatives, 239
of counterconditioning, 206
of fear intensity measures, 290—291
and incremental validity, 103
of increments from personality tests,
118—123
of insights, 196—197
of intelligence tests, 17
of past behavior, 135—142, 283
of personality constructs, 4
of projective data, 110—113
of psychiatric categories, 124—125
of self-ratings, 107

Utility *(cont.)*
and statistical significance, 103
of therapeutic community lodge,
221—223
of trait-state assessments, 142—145, 193,
196
of trait-state theory, 178
see also Construct validity, Prediction,
Reliability, Validity

Validity:
of actuarial data, 131
of code types, 132
concurrent, 77
construct, 91—94, 96—100
definition of, 13—14, 65, 76—77, 87—88
examples of, 74—83
incremental, 106—145
interpreting correlations of, 83—101
and method variance, 87
predictive, 77
of projective techniques, 111—112
and reliability, 13—14, 74
research with California *F* scale,
77—80
of tests and construct validity, 104
see also Reliability, Utility
Verbal behavior:
of client, 237
effects of context on, 169—170
generalization to nonverbal behavior,
175—176, 298—299
stability of, 35
and trait labels, 68—69
see also Language, Self-reports, Verbal
reports
Verbal conditioning, 171, 239
Verbal psychotherapies, 230
Verbal reports:
ambiguity of, 238
client's, 236—237
identifying referents for, 238
maintaining conditions for, 183
about moral attitudes and nonverbal
moral behavior, 80
of reinforcement value, 252
relations to behavior, 240—246
see also Language, Self-reports,
Verbal behavior
Vicarious classical conditioning,
158—159